The Moral Psychology of Love

Moral Psychology of the Emotions

Series Editor: Mark Alfano, Associate Professor
of Philosophy, Macquarie University

How do our emotions influence our other mental states (perceptions, beliefs, motivations, intentions) and our behavior? How are they influenced by our other mental states, our environments, and our cultures? What is the moral value of a particular emotion in a particular context? This series explores the causes, consequences, and value of the emotions from an interdisciplinary perspective. Emotions are diverse, with components at various levels (biological, neural, psychological, social), so each book in this series is devoted to a distinct emotion. This focus allows the author and reader to delve into a specific mental state, rather than trying to sum up emotions en masse. Authors approach a particular emotion from their own disciplinary angle (e.g., conceptual analysis, feminist philosophy, critical race theory, phenomenology, social psychology, personality psychology, neuroscience) while connecting with other fields. In so doing, they build a mosaic for each emotion, evaluating both its nature and its moral properties.

Other Titles in This Series

The Moral Psychology of Love

Edited by
Arina Pismenny and Berit Brogaard

ROWMAN & LITTLEFIELD
Lanham • Boulder • New York • London

Published by Rowman & Littlefield
An imprint of The Rowman & Littlefield Publishing Group, Inc.
4501 Forbes Boulevard, Suite 200, Lanham, Maryland 20706
www.rowman.com

British Library Cataloguing in Publication Information Available

Library of Congress Cataloging-in-Publication Data

Names: Brogaard, Berit, editor. | Pismenny, Arina, 1985- editor.
Title: The moral psychology of love / edited by Berit Brogaard and Arina Pismenny.
Description: Lanham : Rowman & Littlefield, [2022] | Series: Moral psychology of the emotions | Includes bibliographical references and index. | Summary: "This book will explore the moral dimensions of love from the standpoint of political philosophy, psychology, and neuroscience"—Provided by publisher.
Identifiers: LCCN 2021062438 (print) | LCCN 2021062439 (ebook) | ISBN 9781538151006 (cloth) | ISBN 9781538151020 (pbk.) | ISBN 9781538151013 (ebook)
Subjects: LCSH: Love—Moral and ethical aspects. | Love—Philosophy.
Classification: LCC BF575.L8 M67 2022 (print) | LCC BF575.L8 (ebook) | DDC 152.4/1—dc23/eng/20220111
LC record available at https://lccn.loc.gov/2021062438
LC ebook record available at https://lccn.loc.gov/2021062439

"For our lovers and teachers"

Contents

Acknowledgments

We are very grateful to our contributors and our editors at Rowman and Littlefield for their patience and hard work during the Covid-19 pandemic.

A very special thanks to our bright and diligent research assistant, Marriah Alcanatara, who has been a tremendous help in putting this volume together.

We are also grateful to Mark Alfano, Rebecca Britney Brogaard, Noël Carroll, Ronald de Sousa, Deepak Devjani, John Doris, Konstantinos Fotiou, Christopher Grau, John Greenwood, Aleks Hernandez, Sarah Levinson, Hichem Naar, Olga Pismenny, Jesse Prinz, Mark Sisti, Eric Slosberg, Aaron Smuts, Ardit Xholi, and our students for insightful discussions on this topic, and for their unwavering support.

The Moral Psychology of Love (or How to Think About Love)

Introduction

Arina Pismenny and Berit Brogaard

Love is a misunderstanding between two fools.

—Oscar Wilde

Love has nothing to do with what you are expecting to get—only with what you are expecting to give—which is everything.

—Katherine Hepburn

True love comes quietly, without banners or flashing lights. If you hear bells, get your ears checked.

—Erich Segal

The cliché "if you haven't loved, you haven't lived" conjures up about 512 million Google search results. The cliché's popularity attests to the importance and diversity of roles that love plays in our lives. Love is thought to be a fulfilling experience not only because it is often pleasant (when it isn't excruciatingly painful) but also because it aims to forge connections with others, brings meaning to our lives, and often feels like an indispensable ingredient of happiness. At the same time, love is hemmed with imperatives and taboos that imbue it with numerous often-contradictory social meanings: "love is blind" versus "love is seeing clearly," "all is fair in love and war" versus "love is kindness," "if you love them, never let them go" versus "if you love them, set them free." These different love-narratives create a complex set of normative constraints reflected in cultural attitudes toward love. These attitudes are embedded in the minds of individuals and guide their experiences and practices of love. These love-narratives specify the appropriate circumstances, objects, ways of feeling, expressing, and acting in love. Due to their widely accepted status and normative force, the resulting attitudes and expectations are often felt as commands. And these commands are often rendered as moral imperatives.

This suggests several questions: To what extent are moral concerns a part of love itself? What makes love good or bad? What makes love morally praiseworthy—if or when it is? What role can and should moral considerations play in love? We might ask similar questions about practical or prudential concerns: When is love good or bad for us, our life goals, people and things we care about, the society at large? The answers to prudential questions might conflict with the answers to moral ones.[1]

To find our way in the maze of love and norms, we cannot avoid confronting the question of the relative importance of rules and conventions and biological constraints, as these seem reflected in the diversity as well as in whatever seems to be universal in human love. But we intend to avoid the old nature-nurture debate. This dichotomy rests on the false dilemma that one or the other must be the primary determinant of love. The rise of epigenetics has exposed the extent to which development and genetics are interdependent, making it impossible to single out phenomena whose origin is dominated by one or the other (Powledge 2011). That fact and the sheer complexity of the phenomena of love call for interdisciplinary cooperation.

Moral psychology approaches the questions we have raised in just such a spirit. It is a multidisciplinary field of study concerned with human reasoning, motivation, and behavior in moral contexts. Despite the tendency toward armchair speculation often imputed to analytic philosophers, historically moral philosophers have not shied away from making empirical claims the truth of which directly bears on their theories. Drawing on the empirical sciences for evidence helps warrant the premises of philosophical arguments and the factual import of philosophical theories. Empirical scientists, in turn, have been drawing on philosophy in constructing rigorous theoretical frameworks (Tiberius 2015; Alfano 2016). As Mark Alfano aptly puts it, "[M]oral philosophy without psychological content is empty, whereas psychological investigation without philosophical insight is blind" (2016, 1). Thus, the field of moral psychology has emerged as a collaborative effort between philosophers and empirical scientists (mainly psychologists and neuroscientists) to investigate the psychological aspects of moral agents.

This volume is dedicated to the moral psychology of love. It investigates the ways in which the various normative dimensions of love interact with moral and other norms. Insofar as love is or gives rise to one or more affective states, it has intrinsic normativity since affective states are necessarily evaluative. What sort of state is it? The series to which this volume belongs suggests that it is an emotion. Indeed, Berit Brogaard defends an account of love as an emotion (2015). Other views characterize love as a sentiment, or what psychologists call an "emotion trait" (Frijda 1994; Bartels and Zeki

2000; Revelle and Scherer 2009; Deonna and Teroni 2012), as a syndrome (de Sousa 2015; Pismenny and Prinz 2017; Pismenny 2018), as a drive (Fisher 2006), and as a desire (Plato 1989) to name a few. Describing love as one of these kinds of state highlights some of its core aspects. For instance, on all these accounts (with the possible exception of Fisher's), love is an intentional state as it is always directed at someone or something. It is a kind of assessment of the object at which it is directed. In particular, it is a positive evaluation of its object. While the term "love" is used loosely in everyday parlance to indicate a strong preference or liking for seemingly any kind of object ("Salem loves raspberries," "Darra loves to travel," "Jelani loves their new guitar"), in this volume we are primarily concerned with love as it exists in intimate relationships, love that takes as its objects individuals in such relationships, such as family members, romantic partners, and friends.

Philosophers have been debating whether love, like paradigmatic emotions such as fear and anger, has correctness conditions, that is, whether love is the kind of phenomenon that can correctly or incorrectly identify its target as lovable. If it is, that raises the question of what makes someone or something lovable. Is someone lovable because they possess some properties that ground the value of lovability or simply because they are loved? The former suggests that love can fail to correctly identify the lovable, whereas the latter suggests that love can neither fail nor succeed at any such task. The former view entails that love can be justified and hence that there are reasons for love, whereas the latter entails that we can only ever get at its cause, never its reason, as love has no reason.[2]

If love is a response to properties, one can ask further what it is about these properties that makes their possessor lovable. Is someone lovable because they have positive character traits? If so, must these character traits necessarily be moral traits? Or is a person lovable because their character traits and perhaps some other characteristics are compatible in some relevant way with the lover's? One aim of the moral psychology of love is to address the question of what kind of valuing love entails.

This evaluative aspect of the intrinsic normativity of love is complemented by love's motivational component. Indeed, Harry Frankfurt construes love as a volitional state (1998, 2004).[3] What does love move us to think and do? If the heart has its reasons, what sort of reasons might they be? Frankfurt argues that they are *sui generis*, whereas others have tried to show that they are moral reasons (Sadler 2006; Schaubroeck 2019). If reasons of love are *sui generis*, we might further ask whether they are morally justifiable. Whether or not reasons of love are necessarily moral in nature depends in part on the definition of "love." If love is defined as promoting only moral reasons, then whenever a reason fails to be a moral one, it must be rejected as a reason of love. But why should we accept this as a conceptual constraint on love? Claims of the kind "if you loved me, you would (not) do X" sometimes amount to a demand that the beloved commit an immoral action. Such a demand is intelligible on the common view of love as unconditional and selfless. Similarly, "I did it because I love you" is often offered as an excuse for some morally condemnable action against the beloved (Ben-Ze'ev and Goussinsky 2008; Pismenny 2021). Another aim of the moral psychology of love is to elucidate the kinds of motivation love elicits.

Love and loving relationships are involved in or presupposed by numerous social structures, such as family units, nuclear or extended, romantic partnerships, and friendships. These social structures in turn steer love relationships in socially acceptable directions. In the West, dominant social institutions such as monogamous marriages and nuclear families promote sexual and emotional exclusivity among romantic partners. Most people consider monogamy the only morally acceptable relationship style. The prominence of this norm is what provides it with its normative weight (Brake 2017). Furthermore, many have advocated the view that romantic love, but not familial love or love of friends, must be emotionally exclusive to qualify as "true" love (e.g., Nozick 1990). We must ask, however, whether the "true" qualifier is meant to dismiss all nonexclusive cases as cases of something other than love, or it is meant to characterize nonexclusive cases as defective, yet instances of love, nonetheless. Here, once again, we are faced with the question of how to define "love." Since numerous individuals engage in extradyadic romantic affairs in their lifetime despite their explicit monogamous commitments, and since polyamorous individuals attest to the possibility of loving multiple partners at once (Jenkins 2017), it appears that defining "true" love as necessarily exclusive is an inept piece of conceptual engineering.

If romantic love can be nonexclusive, the "true" qualifier might be understood as marking the moral superiority of exclusive monogamous love. Indeed, moral reasons are often cited in support both of monogamy and of heteronormativity. Discussing such reasons with care is beyond the scope of this Introduction (but see Brake 2017; de Sousa 2017; Brunning 2016, 2020). Clearly, however, the facts mentioned set a clear agenda for the moral psychology of love: to explain the origin of widely held (though far from universal) beliefs in the superiority—moral or practical—of certain forms of love. To do so, we must unpack the complex biological, social, and psychological factors that underlie culture- and time-specific attitudes toward romantic love, driving people to convictions that are as resistant to change as they are hard to justify.

The contributors to the present volume do not pretend to answer all the questions raised by the moral psychology of love. But their essays jointly illustrate the variety of those questions and the diversity of perspectives that can be adopted to address them.

The volume is divided into three sections. The chapters in section I showcase the diversity of approaches to the study of love, key findings in the psychology and neuroscience of love, and meta questions about how love and valuing should be conceptualized. Chapters in section II raise questions about the social norms grounding mono-normativity, polyamory, and sexual and gender identities in romantic relationships. The chapters in section III explore connections between love, morality, and some of the conflicts to which they give rise.

In his chapter, "Don't Ask If Love Is Moral," Ronald de Sousa argues that the question of whether love is a moral emotion should not even be asked. He begins by calling attention to the lack of consensus among philosophers about the nature of love, its moral status, and the very notion of a moral emotion. On that basis, he aims to show that attempts to decide whether love is a moral emotion are bound to degenerate into question-begging disputes about the definitions of the terms involved and that these terms in any case are devoid of any practical import beyond the promotion of harmful prejudices. He concludes that difficulties presented by the question of whether love is a moral emotion stem in part from the fact that any debate about morality will lure us into fruitless and insoluble disagreements about foundational issues, and in part from the fact that moral discourse does little but encourage moralistic guilt and blame.

In their chapter "The Neurobiology of Love," Donatella Marazziti and Alessandra Della Vecchia provide an account of the neural underpinnings of the early stages of romantic love—a state of being *in* love, sometimes called infatuation. They adopt the dominant theory in evolutionary psychology, according to which romantic love has evolved to serve as a link between lust and attachment—two other systems that help facilitate human reproduction. The brain chemistry as well as the psychological symptoms of a person in love are strikingly similar to those experienced by individuals with obsessive-compulsive disorder (OCD) or addiction. They hypothesize that the obsessive intrusive thoughts, cravings, and feelings of euphoria experienced by people in love might help one to focus their sexual and romantic energies on one other person, thereby facilitating the attachment and pair-bonding between two individuals required for them to jointly raise offspring.

In "The Good and Bad of Love and Hate," Katherine Aumer and Michael A. Erickson present their research on the values of love and hate. They use signal detection theory to explain the difficulty of gauging the costs and benefits of engaging in a love relationship or of adopting the attitude of hate. They point out that although it is often assumed that love is unequivocally good and hate is unequivocally bad, there can be advantages to hate and disadvantages to love. While love can contribute to our happiness, comfort, and well-being, it can also be painful when it is unrequited or it compels us to stay in an abusive relationship. Hatred directed at individuals or groups can be destructive and harmful. Yet it can play a positive role as a motivational factor to eliminate or otherwise curtail the odious object. It can also help unite people against the hated target, reinforcing social bonds. Aumer and Erickson attribute the dearth of research on hatred to the prevalence of a negative moralistic attitude toward it, which they urge us to drop so we can get to the core of both the good and the bad of this emotion.

Robert Sternberg's "The Role of Ideals in Intimate Relationships" discusses the clash between our love ideals—our conception of what a perfect romantic partner is—and our actual romantic partners. Using his triangular theory, which posits three dimensions of love—intimacy, passion, and commitment—Sternberg examines two sets of ideal love triangles. The first represents how one wants to feel about one's partner, the second, how one wishes to be regarded by them. Sternberg has found that relationship satisfaction is high when the discrepancy between ideal and actual relationships is low. Flexibility and openness to modify one's romantic ideals is also likely to increase relationship satisfaction.

The second section of this volume is concerned with romantic relationships and the social norms that guide them. The chapters address questions about the social norms underpinning prevalent relationship structures such as monogamous relationships as they stem from mono- and heteronormativity. The advantages and disadvantages of polyamorous relationship structures are discussed, as are the effects of transitioning on the gender and sexual identities of romantic partners and their relationships.

In her "Romantic Love and Altruism in Pair-bonds," Bianca Acevedo investigates the moral aspects of pair-bonds in connection with monogamy and fairness. She points out that although monogamy is the most common relationship style in many cultures, where its rule of exclusivity is enforced with uneven strictness, monogamy is extremely rare in nature. Many species practice "social monogamy," that is, the rearing of offspring, regardless of whether one has contributed one's genetic material to the offspring. Studies of different species suggest that a genetic factor may be driving the widespread preference for sexual exclusivity. Acevedo concludes that the potential genetic underpinning of sexual exclusivity or non-exclusivity, together with the finding that the altruistic behavior involved in romantic relationships may take different forms in different cultures, may explain why monogamy works for some while others opt for consensual nonmonogamy (CNM).

In his chapter, "'I Am Glad That My Partner Is Happy with Her Lover': On Jealousy, and Compersion," Aaron Ben-Ze'ev analyzes the roles that jealousy and compersion play in monogamous and polyamorous love relationships. Compersion is a joyful emotion in response to the pleasure a romantic partner experiences with another lover. Compersion is most likely to be experienced in polyamorous relationships since polyamory typically is committed to emotional and sexual non-exclusivity. Monogamy, on the other hand, is committed to sexual and emotional exclusivity. Hence, a lover's extradyadic involvement typically arouses jealousy. Jealousy construes non-exclusivity as a threat, and the external lover as a rival. Ben-Ze'ev argues that polyamorous relationships are more difficult to sustain because of their practical limitations such as spreading love too thinly among partners, difficulties managing time and other resources, and bouts of jealousy despite the polyamorous commitment to non-exclusivity.

In his "Multiple Loves and Shaped Selves," by contrast, Luke Brunning concentrates on the virtues of polyamory. He explores the ways in which romantic partners can influence one another—a phenomenon he calls *fashioning*. This concept aims to capture the variety of ways in which partners can shape each other, for example, by developing their character or enhancing their self-perception, while avoiding a complete merger of their identities or selves. Brunning argues that within the context of polyamory, such fashioning can be particularly unique and beneficial because of the kinds of challenges polyamory presents.

Gen Eickers's "Being Trans, Being Loved: Clashing Identities and the Limits of Love" catalogs a variety of obstacles faced by trans people in their pursuit of romantic love. They analyze the ways in which culturally dominant romantic love-narratives tend to exclude trans identities. Trans persons are thus rendered undesirable, thereby significantly narrowing the dating pool available to them. They furthermore discuss how transitioning impacts the sexual identities of those transitioning as well as their partners. The centrality of one's sexual identity to one's self may prevent one from amending it in such a way as to accommodate the trans partner's gender identity. Transitioning within the context of a romantic relationship can thus result in heartbreak and the dissolution of the relationship.

The chapters in section III highlight some of the specific tensions that arise from attempts to assess love relationships in moral terms.

In "The Possibility of a Duty to Love," Lotte Spreeuwenberg outlines the ways in which a moral duty to love could be construed. It is typically objected that there cannot be a duty to love because love is not under our control, because love is particularly valuable when it is freely given, because love is not reason-responsive, and because motivation stemming from love is incompatible with acting from duty. Spreeuwenberg aims to show that each of these objections can be addressed by modifying our understanding of "moral duty."

Raja Halwani's "Love and Integrity" presents a puzzle of the conflict between love and integrity: this can occur when one's deeply held values clash with the values of one's romantic partner. Halwani examines cases in which such a conflict poses a threat to love because one lover cannot endorse or adopt their beloved's values. When such conflicts arise, one might turn a blind eye, revise one's values, or terminate the relationship. Each option can incur a high cost, either to the lover's integrity, or to the love relation's viability. Such cases invite us to reexamine the ways in which the endorsement and adaptation of the beloved's values should be understood as a requirements of love.

In "Vices of Friendship," Pismenny and Brogaard argue that the neo-Aristotelian conception of friendships of character misrepresents true friendship. They question the view that friendship entails disinterested love of the beloved for their own sake, and they reject the requirement that friends should strive to enhance one another's moral virtues. They proceed by proposing a more modest alternative conception of friendship as involving closeness, intimacy, identity, and trust. However, they argue, even on this minimal construal, friendship can turn vicious when one of its characteristics becomes overpowering and thereby undermines the very goods for which the friendship was originally sought.

Caroline Lundquist's "Internal Bleeding: How Covert Misogyny within Loving Relationships Tears Us Apart" describes zozobra, that is, the feeling that something isn't right that so often is experienced by women in heterosexual romantic relationships, owing to the covert misogyny that is built into the conflicting narratives of gender and romantic love. Covert misogyny is manifested in behaviors that stem from beliefs about the inferiority of women, which are not explicitly endorsed but hidden deeply in the psyches of men and women. These love and gender narratives normalize and excuse covert misogyny and thereby encourage women to rationalize their choice to stay in abusive relationships. Lundquist argues that while covert misogyny need not make the love that obtains between the partners any less real, addressing the misogyny is not only to everyone's benefit, it is also everyone's responsibility.

In their "Interrogating the Immorality of Infidelity," Jennifer Piemonte, Staci Gusakova, Jennifer Rubin, and Terri Conley argue that distinguishing between opportunistic and planned infidelity can help us assess the moral status of unfaithfulness. Their studies have shown that infidelity occurs far more often when it results from an unexpected proposition than when it is deliberately planned. This suggests that infidelity is often opportunistic. Given the prevalence of cases in which opportunity plays a role in infidelity, Piemonte, Gusakova, Rubin, and Conley suggest that an opportunity to cheat is a more likely determinant of infidelity than a flawed moral character. For this reason, they argue, opportunistic cheating does not deserve the same moral condemnation as planned cheating.

Taken together, this volume's chapters explore questions in the moral psychology of love from a variety of research perspectives. We hope that the diversity of perspectives represented here will spur further collaborative work between neuroscientists, psychologists, and philosophers on the descriptive and normative questions about love and intimate relationships.

NOTES

1. One might also ask a set of aesthetic questions: When is love beautiful or ugly? And one might want to distinguish between asking what love is good for, and asking what makes love good *qua* love.

2. For discussion, see Keller 2000; Abramson and Leite 2011; Zangwill 2013; Smuts 2014; Brogaard, 2015, 2019, 2020; Pismenny and Prinz 2017; Pismenny 2018; Pismenny 2021.

3. However, Frankfurt dismisses romantic love as a genuine form of love (e.g., Frankfurt, 1998, 2004).

REFERENCES

Abramson, Kate, and Adam Leite. 2011. "Love as a Reactive Emotion." *The Philosophical Quarterly* 61 (245): 673–99.

Alfano, Mark. 2016. *Moral Psychology: An Introduction*. Cambridge: Polity.

Ben-Ze'ev, Aaron, and Ruhama Goussinsky. 2008. *In the Name of Love: Romantic Ideology and Its Victims*. New York: Oxford University Press, USA.

Brake, Elizabeth. 2017. "Is 'Loving More' Better?: The Values of Polyamory." In *The Philosophy of Sex: Contemporary Readings*, edited by Raja Halwani, Alan Soble, Sarah Hoffman, and Jacob M. Held, 7th ed., 201–19. New York: Rowman & Littlefield.

Brogaard, Berit. 2015. *On Romantic Love: Simple Truths about a Complex Emotion*. New York: Oxford University Press.

———. 2019. "Love in Contemporary Psychology and Neuroscience." In *The Routledge Handbook of Love in Philosophy*, edited by A. Martin, 465–78. New York: Routledge.

———. 2020. "Romantic Love for a Reason." In *The Oxford Handbook of Philosophy of Love*, edited by Christopher Grau and Aaron Smuts. New York: Oxford University Press.

Brunning, Luke. 2016. "The Distinctiveness of Polyamory." *Journal of Applied Philosophy* 35 (3): 1–19.

———. 2020. Compersion: An Alternative to Jealousy?" *Journal of the American Philosophical Association*, 6 (2): 1–21.

de Sousa, Ronald. 2015. *Love: A Very Short Introduction*. New York: Oxford University Press, USA.

———. 2017. "Love, Jealousy, and Compersion." In *Oxford Handbook of Philosophy of Love*, edited by Christopher Grau and Aaron Smuts. New York, NY: Oxford University Press. 10.1093/oxfordhb/9780199395729.013.30.

Deonna, Julien, and Fabrice Teroni. 2012. *The Emotions: A Philosophical Introduction.* New York: Routledge.

Fisher, Helen E. 2006. "The Drive to Love: The Neural Mechanism for Mate Selection." In *The New Psychology of Love*, edited by Robert J. Sternberg and Karin Weis, 87–115. New Haven: Yale University Press.

Frankfurt, Harry G. 1998. *Necessity, Volition, and Love.* Cambridge: Cambridge University Press.

———. 2004. *The Reasons of Love.* Princeton: Princeton University Press.

Jenkins, C. S. 2017. What Love Is: And What It Could Be. New York: Basic Books.

Keller, Simon. 2000. "How Do I Love Thee? Let Me Count the Properties." *American Philosophical Quarterly* 37 (2): 163–73.

Nozick, Robert. 1990. *Examined Life: Philosophical Meditations.* New York: Simon and Schuster.

Pismenny, Arina. 2018. "The Syndrome of Romantic Love." Doctoral dissertation, New York: City University of New York, The Graduate Center. CUNY Academic Works. https://academicworks-cuny-edu.ezproxy.gc.cuny.edu/gc_etds/2827.

———. 2021. "The Amorality of Romantic Love." In *Love, Justice, and Autonomy: Philosophical Perspectives*, edited by Rachel Fedock, Michael Kühler, and Raja Rosenhagen, 23–42. New York: Routledge.

Pismenny, Arina, and Jesse Prinz. 2017. "Is Love an Emotion?" In *The Oxford Handbook of Philosophy of Love*, edited by Christopher Grau and Aaron Smuts. New York: Oxford University Press.

Plato. 1989. *Symposium.* Translated by Alexander Nehamas and Paul Woodruff. Indianapolis: Hackett Publishing.

Powledge, Tabitha M. 2011. "Behavioral Epigenetics: How Nurture Shapes Nature." *BioScience* 61 (8): 588–92. https://doi.org/10.1525/bio.2011.61.8.4.

Revelle, W. & Scherer, K.R. (2009). "Personality and Emotion." In *The Oxford Companion to Emotion and the Affective Sciences*, edited by David Sander & Klaus R. Scherer, 304–06. New York: Oxford University Press.

Sadler, Brook J. 2006. "Love, Friendship, Morality." *The Philosophical Forum* 37 (3): 243–63. https://doi.org/10.1111/j.1467-9191.2006.00241.x.

Schaubroeck, Katrien. 2019. "Reasons of Love." In *The Routledge Handbook of Love in Philosophy*, edited by Adrienne M. Martin, 288–99. New York: Routledge.

Smuts, Aaron. 2014. "Is It Better to Love Better Things?" In *Love and Its Objects: What Can We Care For?*, edited by Christian Maurer, Tony Milligan, and Kamila Pacovská, 91–107. London: Palgrave Macmillan.

Tiberius, Valerie. 2015. *Moral Psychology: A Contemporary Introduction.* New York: Routledge.

Zangwill, Nick. 2013. "Love: Gloriously Amoral and Arational." *An International Journal for the Philosophy of Mind and Action* 16 (3): 298–314.

Section I

LOVE

APPROACHES AND META-QUESTIONS

Chapter 1

Don't Ask If Love Is Moral

Ronald de Sousa

That useless dreamer be forever cursed
Who while obsessed, in his stupidity,
With insoluble puzzles, was the first
To try and mix love and morality

– Charles Baudelaire

As philosophers, we sometimes take pride in the diversity of views our profession affords. Few topics can better illustrate that diversity than the question of love's morality. Some have maintained that "love is a central concept in morals" (Murdoch 1970, p. 2). Others have seen love as violating a principle of impartiality that is widely regarded as central to morality (Wolf 1992). In the same vein, some have held that for consequentialism, "it seems that we always act immorally when we are led by reasons of love" (Schaubroeck 2019, p. 289). For still others, love is just the culminating form of Kantian respect (Smith 2007). For Kant himself, love is "pathological" when it is "seated . . . in the propensities of feeling" and therefore "cannot be commanded" (Kant 2005 [1785], p. 60 [399]). In contrast, it has also been claimed that "the demands and motives of love and friendship—often thought to lie outside the moral domain, even to oppose it—are instead deeply constituted by moral considerations and motives" (Sadler 2006, p. 243). Yet another suggestion is that love is a process of "receptivity to direction and interpretation" of the beloved by the lover, resulting in the adoption of the ends of another agent as one' s own (Cocking & Kennett 2000, p. 286). On this last view, love's moral worth would be determined by the moral worth of the beloved's ends. Love, like empathy, would then not be an emotion at all, but rather a capacity to experience another's emotion whatever it may be. Such a capacity might well be useful and provide practically relevant information, but its value would be epistemic rather than intrinsically moral. Indeed, it would present a "moral danger," in moving the lover to adopt, as their own, ends that might be bad or even criminal, since it "is even possible for a person to come to love something despite recognizing that its inherent nature is actually and utterly bad" (Frankfurt 2004, p. 38).

This brief sampling suggests that the diversity of philosophical views on the morality of love illustrates a lack of consensus about the meanings of the terms involved. In response, one might join the fray, try to sort it all out, regiment the concepts involved, and arrive at an answer. More irenically, one might try to construct a "hybrid view" that concedes that love can be moral and also immoral depending on the circumstances. Or one might just give it up as a futile exercise.

I propose to argue for the third option. I begin by addressing the apparent absurdity of the suggestion that some things are better not discussed at all. I will then illustrate the futility of the debate on love's morality by sketching some of the difficulties encountered in trying to characterize the basic terms of the debate. How should we understand "love," "moral emotion," and the word "moral" itself? Proposed answers to these questions of definition, I will try to show, are necessarily question-begging. Things are not improved by framing the argument in terms of the reasons that might be adduced *for* loving, and the reasons that love provides for other acts and emotions, or reasons *of* love. Furthermore, given the stalemate that attends debates about foundations of morality, attempts to ground the debate in meta-ethical considerations can only make things worse. Finally, I shall sketch a more general argument for rejecting moral discourse altogether, as necessarily involving a fallacious double counting of reasons, and as grounded in a bankrupt meta-ethical quest for foundations.

IS ANYTHING BETTER NOT DISCUSSED?

It may seem peculiar for a philosopher to think anything should not be discussed. On the face of it, only the sacred and the absolutely uninteresting could qualify. But the sacred is a religious, not a philosophical category: indeed, a worthy motto for philosophy might be *Nothing is sacred*. And as for interest, the volume of ink spent on the question bodes ill for my case. What grounds might there be, then, for declaring that something is better not discussed?

Such a claim has sometimes been grounded in arguments constraining what propositions are meaningful. A well-known formulation is Hume's: "Does a book, [or, we might amend, an assertion] contain any abstract reasoning concerning quantity or number? No. Does it contain any experimental reasoning concerning matter of fact and existence? No. Commit it then to the flames: for it can contain nothing but sophistry and illusion" (Hume 1975, Pt. III). Hume's test, however, cannot give us a good reason to reject sophistry and illusion, let alone not discuss them. For the premise on which it rests, confining meaningful discourse to matters of existing fact and "relations of ideas," itself fails the test. That makes it a paradox, and many paradoxes are undoubtedly interesting: they challenge us to diagnose some mistake, or derive some useful lesson from their insolubility.

Still, a stricture related to Hume's was defended by the logical positivists in the early twentieth century, and argued, perhaps with tongue in cheek, by Frank Ramsey in a talk to the Cambridge Apostles in 1903. In that talk, entitled "On There Being Nothing to Discuss," Ramsey began by conceding that there once were legitimate topics of discussion, but "no longer," because "we have really settled everything, by realizing that there is nothing to know except science" (Ramsey 1990, p. 245). And science, he continued, is not worth discussing by anyone but experts. The rest of us will be unable to say anything worth hearing about what we do not know or understand.

Ramsey further notes that "Theology and Absolute Ethics are two famous subjects which we have realized to have no real objects" (Ramsey 1990, p. 247). The nonexistence of a particular object, one might protest, is not sufficient to preclude useful discussion. Theoretical debate about hypothetical situations can at least clarify our thinking, if not illuminate reality. Thought experiments clearly do the former, whether or not they involve entities that actually exist; and some philosophers have argued that they can even do the latter (Brown 1991). Atheists are sometimes fond of invoking God to make a logical point. A familiar example is provided by the *Euthyphro* problem of whether God's commands create goodness or merely reflect it. Regardless of God's existence, that puzzle draws our attention to the important question of the origin and objectivity of values.

Nevertheless, I persist in thinking some topics in theology should never have been discussed at all. Consider two examples from the history of Christianity: the Trinity and the doctrine of transubstantiation. It is difficult to think of any fact or value in the real world that would be affected by the objective truth or falsity of either doctrine. People's *beliefs* about them, of course, have had all too real effects on history. But those effects have been horrific. The debates to which they gave rise wasted innumerable hours in the lives of able minds. Worse, both disputes resulted in the torture and murder of thousands—for the good of their souls.

Is it an exaggeration to say that opening the question of the morality of love can be equally nefarious? I think not. Those who have been persecuted or murdered, and still are today, because their love is thought "immoral" are probably more numerous than the victims of the Spanish Inquisition's autos-da-fé.[1] Such consequences are admittedly rare in modern democracies. Nevertheless, the theological and the moral debates are similar, both in the potentially tragic character of their practical consequences, and in the futility of their substance. As Ramsey wrote,

> we realize too little how often our arguments are of the form A.: "I went to Grantchester this afternoon" B.: "No I didn't." . . . E.g. when we discuss constancy of affection it consists in A saying he would feel guilty if he weren't constant, B saying he wouldn't feel guilty in the least. But that, although a pleasant way of passing the time, is not discussing anything whatever, but simply comparing notes. (Ramsey 1990, p. 247)

In the case of the morality of love, "comparing notes" mimics the form of debate, but consists in question-begging assertions that illuminate nothing and cause actual harm. Or so I shall argue.

DEFINING THE TOPIC TO NOT DISCUSS

At the end of this chapter, I will be enlarging the scope of my complaint. I will suggest that the futility of debates about love's morality is merely illustrative of a more general truth: that moral discourse serves no good purpose and would be best avoided altogether. For now, however, I will write as if my reader understood what it is for something to be moral or immoral.

Given this understanding, we should first distinguish between moral judgments directed at some individual lover's behavior (either toward their beloved, or toward others insofar as it is motivated by their love of the beloved), and judgments about love as such. I am concerned only with the latter. Criticism of the first sort is common; its grounds can range from accusations of betrayal, through exploitation to manipulation and emotional abuse. Normative evaluations of individual behavior can invoke a variety of reasons, only some of which are commonly labeled "moral." But since it is true of almost any emotion that it can be good or bad depending on the situation, such particular cases cannot determine the morality of love as such. Furthermore, normative judgments about love frequently involve social conventions of caste or class, or gender, or religious taboos, all of which at least some moralists would regard as outside their sphere. Normative judgments of love's place in a human life also frequently presuppose nonmoral, practical, or social functions for romantic attachments. These functions may vary at different stages of life: sow your wild oats in youth, perhaps, then settle down for life in monogamous marriage. Sorting the resulting heterogeneous list of norms into moral and nonmoral can give rise to much intrepid casuistry. But the considerations adduced in those debates are doomed to remain inconclusive, and their point remains obscure. So-called "moral" norms concerning love undoubtedly deserve scrutiny from sociologists or anthropologists: why have religious leaders been so intensely concerned with condemning the transgressions of particular lovers—especially women? (Berkowitz 2012). Why have writers and artists been so often preoccupied with the bliss and the torment of particular loves? (Illouz 2012). These are not philosophical questions. As my sampling of philosophical opinions about the moral status of love illustrated, however, it seems to be about the inherent morality of love itself, as a kind of emotion, that philosophers have been eager to pronounce. And it is to those pronouncements that I mean to object.

What exactly they are about, however, is far from clear. Some clarification is needed. How are we to understand "love," "moral emotion," and most tricky of all, "moral"?

WHAT IS LOVE?

Let me at the outset dissociate myself from the common practice of relying on a persuasive definition.[2] As Charles Stevenson noted, "Persuasive definitions are often recognisable from the words 'real' or 'true', employed in a metaphorical sense . . . [for example,] true love is the communion between minds alone" (Stevenson 1938, p. 334). I mean by love pretty much whatever is referred to by speakers of English using the word in its standard senses. If that excludes anything, it is only those colloquial uses in which people talk about loving chocolate or ice cream or sunning yourself on the beach. It does not exclude objectophilia, erotic love of inanimate objects, as illustrated by Erika LaBrie, the champion archer who first fell in love with her bow, then "married" the Eiffel Tower (Anon 2021). If we are to discuss values and norms governing any human activity or emotion, it is important to start with a purely descriptive identification of our subject matter.

For my purposes, then, I do not exclude either the love of children or the love of God, each of which has sometimes been taken as the paradigm case of the "best" kind of love. It is worth noting, however, that almost *any* emotion whatever, given the right story, can be a manifestation of love. That is attested by the fact that most fictional stories, designed to depict and arouse many emotions, are "love stories": in any good love story, we can expect the protagonists to endure multifarious emotions. This protean character of the emotional aspects of love obviously complicates the question of its alleged morality or immorality. It is too easy to insist that love is immoral when it is manifested as murderous jealousy, or to regard it as the very paradigm of moral goodness when it takes the form of tender, self-effacing care.

Indeed, this last observation might be sufficient to dismiss the debate about love's morality outright: if any emotion can figure as an avatar of love, then love can hardly be expected to have any firm moral character.[3] But that would also be too easy. So let me approach the question by considering first what could be (and has been) meant by a moral emotion, and then ask whether an emotion that most speakers of English would recognize as love could be fitted into the category of moral emotion.

WHAT IS A MORAL EMOTION?

Defining what counts as "moral" is best postponed as long as possible—or at least to a later part of this chapter. But let me take the word for granted long enough to consider how it might apply to an emotion. One way to start is to construe "moral emotion" on the model of "moral action." Uncontroversially, though not very helpfully, a moral action is one that deserves moral approval.[4] But what marks approval as moral? Kantians, Utilitarians and Virtue theorists—among others—provide different answers. They hold, respectively, that the right sort of approval must be based on an assessment of the action's motive (does it manifest a "good will"?), on the basis of its likely consequences, or on its role in a life worth living overall.

All three of these characterizations are typically intended to apply to moral actions, but they raise problems enough even in those cases to keep many employed. For example: The Kantian criterion for the evaluation of an action faces a difficulty that is nicely illustrated by Scholastic contortions about the principle of double effect. That principle holds that a harmful consequence of your act is permissible, even if you are able to *foresee* it, providing you did not *intend* it, either as an end or as a means (McIntyre 2019). "In fact, it is absolutely impossible to make out by experience with complete certainty a single case in which the maxim of an action, however right in itself, rested simply on moral grounds" (Kant 2005 [1785], p. 67 [477]). Only God, they say, can know for certain if your heart is pure. So for us mortals the test is not easy to apply. For the Utilitarian, the problem is that ultimate consequences are unfathomable (Marks 2016, pp. 70–71). In practice, moralists of both schools rarely avoid appealing to one another's intuitions, boosted by what passes for common sense. So it is not easy to characterize an action unequivocally as moral or immoral. As for Aristotelian virtue theory, it is typically concerned less with the moral worth of a particular act than whether it manifests a virtue, that is, whether it fits into a general structure of character conducive to a thriving life as a whole. But not all virtues are moral virtues, so the Aristotelian criterion does not really address the issue.

Emotions are even harder than actions to assess from the moral point of view. One reason is that they are not obviously subject to the will. For emotions, there is no analog to the principle of double effect. Whether a given emotion either springs from or results in a goodwill is no easier to determine than the long-term results consequentialists are concerned with. As for Aristotle, his conception of virtue implies that most emotions would be moral at least at some times, namely "at the right times, with reference to the right objects, towards the right people, with the right aim, and in the right way" (Aristotle 1984, p. 25 [1106b]). On the face of it, then, the prospects for a verdict on the moral worth of any specific emotion type are dim.

To assess the inherent morality of an emotion, we can suppose that its moral character springs either from the nature of its eliciting conditions or from the action tendencies it motivates. One promising approach, focusing on the former, requires that a moral emotion be such that its appropriateness is tied directly to moral features of its target. That approach has been given currency by Alan Gibbard. His suggestion is that a moral emotion is one that takes a moral property as its formal object. Guilt, "perhaps the quintessential moral emotion" (Prinz & Nichols 2010, p. 132), and anger, or at least "moral anger," indignation or outrage, are moral emotions, in virtue of the fact that their formal objects are violations of a moral norm, either by oneself or by another (Gibbard 1990; see also D'Arms and Jacobson 2000). Such violations can obviously elicit other emotions as well: disgust, despair, sadness, or other negative feelings. But only guilt and indignation are apt specifically when elicited by the moral character of their target: My guilt is apt, strictly speaking, if and only if I have transgressed a moral rule; and my indignation is likewise apt if and only if you have done so. To be sure, I might also respond to such a violation with sympathy, shame, or disgust; but unlike guilt and indignation, those emotions can be apt where no moral transgression has occurred. Curiously, we have no positive words to refer to emotions elicited exclusively by morally good actions. Positive responses to morally good acts might be admiration, gratitude, and perhaps pride; but none of these positive emotions is exclusively reserved, like guilt and anger, for moral properties.

The range of strictly moral emotions identified by Gibbard, then, is narrow. But the grounds for moral appraisal can be made more specific. To this end, Jesse Prinz and Shaun Nichols have proposed to identify "one class of moral emotions as the emotions that promote moral behaviors, and another class as the ones that are either constitutively or causally related to moral judgments." They note further that three features have been held to characterize moral emotions and the associated moral judgments. They are (1) "regarded as more serious," (2) "less dependent on authority," and (3) "more likely to be justified with reference to empathy and the suffering of others" (Prinz & Nichols 2010, p. 120).

As Prinz and Nichols concede, however, these markers all fail. Taking them in turn:

(1) How is "seriousness" measured? If it is more than a matter of an agent's subjective estimate, seriousness might be assessed in terms of the degree to which agents conform strictly to the rules. But that clearly varies between individuals. The seriousness of a moral conviction varies no less than that of the religious belief in the threat of hell fire. While there is evidence that the prospect of Hell (though not the promise of heaven) has some deterrent effect (Henrich 2020, pp. 146 ff), that deterrent can hardly be said to be taken equally "seriously" by all those who profess to believe it. The same is surely true of moral convictions, the strength of which varies not only among cultural groups but within single individuals at different times, depending on, among other things, the current state of their brain chemistry (Crockett et al. 2010).

(2) The general validity of the second criterion is doubtful, if only because so many people insist that morality is grounded in the authority of the Bible, the Koran, or other religious text. And a moral conviction way well have been *caused* by the influence of an authority even when an agent makes no attempt to justify the rule by explicit reference to that authority.

(3) The relevance to morality of "empathy and the suffering of others" cannot be doubted. But it can hardly be viewed as sufficient to explain all moral intuitions. For as Richard Shweder, Jonathan Haidt, and others have stressed, concern for fairness or others' suffering forms only a subset of the class of intuitions that most people, particularly in conservative cultures or subcultures, regard as moral (Shweder et al. 2000; Haidt 2012). And since those intuitions are far from uniform, their guidance is uncertain.

Given the failure of (1)–(3), Prinz and Nichols then propose defining moral rules "negatively, as rules that are not believed to depend on any specific social conventions" (Prinz & Nichols 2010, p. 120). But whether a convention is actually causally responsible for someone's conviction can't be reliably intuited. So, in the end, they fall back on suggesting that "moral norms are defined in terms of moral emotions, and moral emotions are simply stipulated" (p. 121). Moral properties elicit moral emotions, and moral emotions are fitting in response to moral properties. The circle is closed, and we are still in the dark.

Enough has been said to suggest that, taken as a whole, philosophy's verdict on love's morality is ambivalent. It ranges from the claim that love is the very core of morality to the opposite extreme of claiming that love is inherently immoral. Those that insist that "true love" is moral are careful to contrast it with ersatz or counterfeit relatives such as lust, or possessiveness, or dependency. But what if the global ambivalence of philosophy were actually a reflection of ambivalence in love itself?

AMBIVALENCE

Ambivalence is widely regarded as a moral failure. Surely, we can't be half-hearted about right and wrong! As Berit Brogaard has noted, "[a] whole-hearted ranking of alternatives is an ethical ideal" (Brogaard 2015, p. 179). Discussions of ambivalence tend to regard it as involving rapid alternations of "opposite" feelings, taking it for granted that "opposites" cannot rationally coexist. But that confuses different kinds of "opposition." From the standpoint of agency, it makes sense to regard ambivalence as inefficient at best, since in the face of any particular decision, there is never any option beyond *doing* and *refraining*. Vacillation, being of two minds, desiring while wanting not to desire something—all these have been regarded as forms of ambivalence; and they are all hindrances to decisive action. You won't act unless you *make up your mind*.

But ambivalence need not be about what to do. Rather than an obstacle to action or decision, it can be a feature of an attitude. An emotion, particularly one that, like love, can exist without being occurrently felt, can be usefully thought of as an attitude (Deonna & Teroni 2015). It can be viewed as a response to a value, analogous to perception, even if it includes an element of projection (Rossi & Tappolet 2018). Unlike deciding, valuing does not require that we commit the will. We cannot *do* two incompatible things at once, but we can *value* two "incompatible" qualities. "Incompatibility," when applied to emotions, is three-ways ambiguous: first, it could refer to the psychological impossibility of experiencing both at once: rage and quiet contentment might be incompatible in that sense. Second, it could mean that the action tendencies entailed by each emotion cannot both be simultaneously realized: I can't both approach and retreat at the same time. But the third sort of "incompatibility" is merely apparent. It arises when emotional ambivalence consists in holding simultaneously two attitudes of opposite valence—favorable and unfavorable—to the same thing or person. Where attitudes, desires, or emotions are concerned, it is quite wrong to say that ambivalence is "a disease of the mind" (Frankfurt 2004, p. 95). On the contrary: as Justin Coates (2017) points out, it can manifest a correct appraisal of a situation. In such cases, decisiveness can be a bad thing even for the purposes of rational deliberation about what to do. Citing Martha Nussbaum's (2001) analysis of the tragic dilemma faced by Agamemnon, Coates points out that when Agamemnon *decides* to sacrifice his daughter for the sake of his army's greater good, he may be *justified*, whether or not he is *blameworthy*; but "it nevertheless seems that it would be appropriate (maybe even necessary) for him to feel remorse, frustration, guilt, and perhaps even disgust at his role in her death" (Coates 2017, p. 437). If he were wholehearted when making his decision, his attitude would not do justice to the values involved.

In short, without prejudice to the practical advantages of wholeheartedness for an agent aspiring to decisiveness, there is nothing wrong with ambivalence in attitudes. Indeed, where love is concerned, the contrary is true. There is reason aplenty to think an ambivalent love far more likely to track the real world. The proper objects of love are individuals—typically persons—not specific properties. But a person has many properties. Some of them may not contribute to the beloved's lovability. The lover may then focus on the lovable ones and ignore the others; or, alternatively, may find the negative ones momentarily transfigured. In responding thus, however, the beloved may fail of love's aspiration to see the beloved's full reality. That aspiration has been viewed as essential to love: Iris Murdoch and others have argued that love can be regarded as an intense and realistic mode of *vision*, "a just and loving gaze directed upon an individual reality" (Murdoch 1970, p. 34; Jollimore 2011, p. 73). If that is right, then love's target is the beloved as an individual, not just their laudable or attractive parts, and a love that incorporates ambivalence might be the only "true" love. For if love apprehends the beloved as a whole, its "just and loving gaze" must match both the positive and the negative reality.

The idea that an ambivalence of this sort is at the heart of love is familiar to some exponents of psychoanalysis. An infant experiences both the Good Breast and the Bad Breast, the Good nurturing Mother and the Bad frustrating Mother (Klein 1975). This gives rise to an ambivalent attitude to the mother as a person who embodies both. More generally, Jerome Neu has noted two reasons for thinking that love can scarcely escape ambivalence. First, love "brings with it dependence and vulnerability. And these are fertile grounds for hatred. The more dependent an individual is on another, whether for freely given love or for other things, the more opportunities there will be for disappointment." Second, love can appear to enact the Hegelian Master-Slave paradox: "Aiming at the full possession of a free being, our desire must fail as possession insofar as the other is free, and it must fail in terms of freedom insofar as the other is possessed" (Neu 2000b, p. 83).

If ambivalence is seen as a psychological defect, it will remain tempting to think, as do many philosophers, that only wholehearted love is "true love": when it fails to meet that high-minded standard, it is spurious. This might further incline one to think that if any love is morally good it must be the wholehearted kind. Yet if ambivalence is inseparable from love itself, then the moral status of love will depend on one's assessment of the place of ambivalence in morality. Those who require wholeheartedness of any morally good person (if perhaps only of a moral saint) will have to conclude that love is inherently immoral.

But perhaps, on the contrary, wholeheartedness should be rejected as the germ of fanaticism: a defense against the very possibility of questioning commitment. It represents a failure to realize the multiplicity of potentially incompatible values—such as the demands that faced Agamemnon, of a father's love and military duty. Even love should be tempered with irony (Rorty 1979).

An objector might grant that we can scarcely hope to escape ambivalence about the particular object of our love. For as Yeats warned, "only God, my dear, can love you for yourself alone, and not your yellow hair." Perhaps we must give up on the hope that any person's actual love—their vision of the beloved as a whole—could be wholehearted. Still, our objector might suggest, perhaps we should look further into the specific *qualities* that constitute or detract from lovability. If they are the source of ambivalence, we might sort them into the positive and the negative and regard them, taken one by one, as moral or immoral accordingly. Insofar as lovability is constituted by altruistic concern, love might be morally good as such; insofar as loving might amount to willingness to commit any crime, it would be immoral. To pursue this suggestion, we can draw inspiration from Prinz and Nichols's twofold division of moral emotions mentioned above. These roughly correspond to reasons *for* love, and reasons *of* love. We could then ask whether typical reasons in each of those two classes might unequivocally be classified as morally good or bad. One could then render a pure verdict on each of those types of reasons, while acknowledging the inevitable ambivalence that is bound to be elicited by any actual beloved whose nature provides reasons to love, or by any actual lover who is moved to respond to that nature.

REASONS FOR AND REASONS OF LOVE

Such a focus on reasons will afford two sets of criteria for judging love's morality. First, love would be moral or immoral if and only if its aptness depends on its *object or target*'s positive or negative moral value. Just as guilt or indignation are responses to moral disvalue, so a sort of narrow analog of love, directed at specific reasons, might be the missing positive emotion that responds to positive moral value. That kind of love, or component of love, would be moral in virtue of being, by definition, a response to a morally good property. Its value would derive either from the morally good character of the quality to which it is a response, or from the goodness of some reasons *of* love, that is, from the moral worth of the actions or other states supported by that specific reason.

It seems undeniable that people offer reasons of both kinds. *Why do I love thee?* prompts some lovers eagerly to count the ways, even while third parties find themselves bemused. On the output side, we might say, love also generates reasons to act, or justifies other emotions. Because love is a powerful motivator, it invites us to demand that its power be used for good. From there, it is a short leap to the view that nothing qualifies as "true love" unless that demand is met.[5]

Instructive examples are provided by Plato's *Symposium*, toward which a nod is required of any philosopher writing on love. At least two of the speeches at that drinking party insist on a moral dimension of love. Both are no less instructive for being unconvincing.

Phaedrus, the dialogue's first speaker, praises love's power to improve character. The reason given is that a beloved behaving badly will be more embarrassed to be seen by their lover than by anyone else. And so, Phaedrus muses, "If only there were a way to start a city or an army made up of lovers and the boys they love! Theirs would be the best possible system of society, for they would hold back from all that is shameful, and seek honor in each other's eyes" (Plato 1997, 178e). It is a nice point that should have carried more weight than it did against "Don't ask, don't tell." On Phaedrus's view, however, love's role is indirect. It is really shame that motivates the good behavior; love just makes one more susceptible to shame. My beloved is the person before whom I am most likely to feel shame if I fail to live up to the standards we share.

Nothing warrants, however, that the values we share are morally good. Besides, even if love does motivate virtuous behavior, a stern moralist might regard it as providing the wrong sort of reason: evincing not so much the moral power of love as its affinity with vanity.

The second speech that idealizes love's moral force is the *Symposium*'s most famous one, which Socrates claims to borrow from Diotima, a priestess and seer. That speech achieves sublime absurdity in concluding that no mere human being is actually worthy of love. Love's true object, according to Diotima, is not a person but the Form of Beauty itself—which may or may not be identical to the Form of the Good (Plato 1997, 211e–212a).

Among our contemporaries, no philosopher is disposed to go quite so far. In many philosophers of love, however, the moralizing tone remains. Here are two examples.

When considering proper reasons *for* love, David Velleman argues that the true object of love is a person's moral core, understood much in the same way as Kant's rational will: "This rational will, in Kant's view, is also the intelligible essence of a person: Kant calls it a person's true or proper self. Respect for this law is thus the same attitude as respect for the person; and so it can perhaps be compared with love, after all" (Velleman 1999, p. 344). Although he finesses the question of how we can love a specific person and not just anyone (assuming everyone is equipped with a rational core), Velleman clearly regards as morally inferior any love motivated by less elevated considerations. That makes love moral by definition, in the specific sense that it is a response to a person's essential moral nature. And definition, as Russell once noted, has all the advantages of theft over honest toil.

What of reasons *of* love? These are the focus of Katrien Schaubroek (2019), who defines them as "normative reasons for action that a person has in virtue of loving someone or something." She prudently refrains from hazarding a definition of "moral reason." But let us continue to pretend we understand roughly what is meant. Schaubroek frames her treatment in terms of the potential for conflict or consonance between reasons of love and reasons of morality. That leads her to distinguish two possible camps. A "separatist" camp regards love as potentially trumping moral reasons in at least some of the cases where they conflict. On the alternative "reductionist" position, reasons of love are simply a subset of moral reasons.

Schaubroek writes that from the reductionist position "it follows that reasons of love can never trump reasons of morality because they are not of a different, competing kind" (p. 288). But this seems confused. Any two reasons can compete, regardless of kind. Admittedly, most philosophers insist that moral reasons trump all others: they are "definitive, final, overriding, or supremely authoritative" (Frankena 1966, p. 688). But that again is a stipulation that can be resisted (Williams 1986; Wolf 2015). Moral reasons, however we define them, can conflict with one another, not just with nonmoral reasons. So Schaubroek's insistence that "whether reasons of love are reducible to moral reasons or not is an important question" (p. 289) launches a large red herring. Any two reasons can support different courses of action, possibly carrying different weights, whether or not they are in the same domain or belong to the same "kind." And they can do so without ceasing to be good reasons.

Consider, for example, the case where I am moved by love to protect my beloved from an unpleasant truth. That pits a reason of love against a reason of morality, namely the presumptive duty not to lie. Which is the stronger will depend on circumstances. Is my beloved on the point of death? And does the unpleasant truth concern a minor domestic mishap, or her child's conviction for a serious crime? A verdict might reasonably favor love's reason or morality's, depending on a fuller description of the case. The categories to which the reason of love and the reason of morality belong are irrelevant.

ANYWAY, WHAT DIFFERENCE WOULD IT MAKE?

Asking whether the reasons for and of love are moral has not yielded much theoretical insight. But one might also ask, on a topic of such importance to life as love, what the point of answering the question would be in practical terms. I have already noted that moral verdicts on different kinds of love get used mainly to control, condemn, and ostracize. Setting aside such measures of triage between good and bad loves, a moment's thought suggests that a global verdict on the morality of love would have bizarre consequences.

I shall assume that if an emotion is a Moral Emotion, it is also thereby a Good Thing. Now for any emotion generally reputed to be a Good Thing, such as gratitude, it seems reasonable to encourage its cultivation. Conversely, emotions regarded as bad, such as envy, are reasonably discouraged. Those who believe that jealousy is a moral emotion, like Kristján Kristjánsson (1996; 2002), like those who believe it to be morally bad, such as Luke Brunning (2020), have little hesitation in recommending that educators respectively foster or resist them. But suppose, *per impossibile*, that we had found a definitive, objective answer to the question of love's morality. What would be the practical implication of such a verdict?

If the answer is positive, we will have a good defense against those who want to ban it. But should we not go further, and encourage people to fall in love? Modern chemistry will doubtless soon make available a reliable and effective love potion. When that happens, must we then favor its widest possible distribution? But suppose that on the contrary the global verdict is negative. This would do more than merely encourage on the wrong kind of love. If the verdict is global, should we not promote love-inhibiting drugs, and behavior likely to elicit love?

If both love-enhancing and love-suppressing drugs are available, only one should be approved, depending on whether the global verdict is positive or negative. We might devise incentives to take the right kind of drug and avoid the wrong kind. In the unlikely event that politicians in power had the wisdom to avoid embarking on another war on drug users, the authorities would need to decide whether to legalize the bad drug, thus requiring that some cases of love—or non-love, as the case might be—be tolerated by the society as a whole. That would secure some state revenue from the practice while minimizing the harm done by love or its absence. Alternatively, the powers that be might decide, in their wisdom, on a harm reduction strategy: they would decriminalize it, in the hope that social disapproval would contain the spread of the undesirable practice.

The absurdity of such speculation is obvious. In any particular situation, the desirability of someone's experiencing loving or being loved would depend on a myriad of factors. Most would have nothing to do with love's inherent morality or immorality. Since advocacy does not seem to be such a problem for other good or bad emotions, love is peculiar in that regard. Neither a positive nor a negative verdict on love would offer us any practical guidance. The verdict would be as useless as the debate was idle.

CUTTING OUT MORALITY

Before concluding, I want to suggest that the uselessness—or worse—of the debate about love's morality is not due merely to the peculiarities of love. Rather, the fault lies with the very discourse of morality. That the morality of love is best left out of any serious discussion is merely an illustration of some serious deficiencies in the idea of morality itself.

This generalization of the argument rests mainly on two claims:[6] first, that the invocation of a moral rule amounts to double counting of reasons. For every moral judgment supervenes on nonmoral reasons, and cannot therefore count as a separate additional reason. Second, whenever a normative judgment is contested, it is defended on the basis of some bankrupt meta-ethical foundations. The original reason is weakened rather than strengthened by what purports to ground it.

Let me explain.

SUPERVENIENCE

My first argument is most conveniently illustrated by looking at some remarks of Frankfurt's, contrasting the force of moral reasons with that of reasons of love. Frankfurt invites us to consider two agents. Both regard a person's need as a reason to help them:

> Both donors give money to the needy person for the same reason: namely, that the money will be helpful to him. The explanation of why this counts as a reason, however, differs in the two cases. It counts as a reason for the person who acts out of duty only because he believes, presumably on the basis of considering the applicability of pertinent moral norms to the specific features of the situation, that he is obligated to help the needy person. It counts as a reason for the person who acts out of love without the mediation of any such inference or belief. (Frankfurt 1998, p. 9)

But why should a reason's origin—its "explanation"—affect its traction as a reason? True, the strength of one agent's motivation might be greater than another's because of the way it was acquired. That might be a psychological fact. But it would be quite irrelevant to the reason's force as justification. A reason's origin might in some cases add a separate reason. It might be, for example, that I owe something to Jane in virtue of the fact that she is my colleague, and also in virtue of the fact that she is my friend. Those are two different reasons, and their weight may be simply additive, or affect one another in more subtle ways. In Frankfurt's example, however, that is not the case. The duty supervenes on the needy person's plight. And the needy person's plight is an intelligible and sufficient reason to help, quite apart from any mention of morality. By contrast, my love for Jane does not supervene on her needs, and so may indeed provide me with an additional reason to help her. But to ask whether that additional reason is itself "moral" just sends us back to the question of love's morality. It does nothing to resolve it.

Several writers have worried that when a situation gives us a reason to act, putting that reason through the filter of a moral principle—utilitarian calculation or Kantian universalizability—constitutes "one thought too many" (Williams 1981, p. 18; Stocker 1976; Driver 2020). What I am suggesting here is that once we have a reason to act, dubbing that reason "moral" is always a thought too many: at best, it adds nothing to the original reason. The reason for this is that moral reasons, as is widely acknowledged, supervene on nonmoral facts. Those underlying facts (that someone might be hurt, or benefited; or that something would be unfair, or kind, or helpful), already exist, and they provide reasons for acting, when they do, regardless of the further label that is applied to them. A reason cannot change unless there is a change in the facts on which it supervenes. If any reason for action or appraisal seems to be strengthened by that label, it is an illusion that results in *double counting*. We must be supposing that a certain transaction is objectionable for two reasons: both because it is unfair and also because it is immoral. And if the unfairness left you unmoved, why would the addition of the "immoral" label change that? To be sure, it is psychologically possible that someone might change their intentions in the light of the application of that term. Just so, a NO PARKING notice might affect your inclination to park in a place that seemed otherwise available. But the threat of a fine is added to the concern not to block traffic. In Frankfurt's case, on the contrary, the addition of a label reading "IMMORAL" does not add a second reason to the original reason. On the contrary: the labels of "moral" or "immoral" that ground the double counting are both less reliable and more open to doubt than the original reasons.

In fact, if anything, the original reason might well be weakened. This is the second problem raised by the intrusion of moral discourse into our practical deliberation.

THE BANKRUPTCY OF META-ETHICAL FOUNDATIONS

Moral reasons, most philosophers insist, are "definitive, final, overriding, or supremely authoritative" (Frankena 1966, p. 688); they are "inescapable" (Williams 1986, p. 177). But just what does that mean and why should we believe it?

When there is disagreement about a specific normative rule, moral philosophers appeal to foundational principles. Thus, for an Aristotelian, the supremacy of the moral reason derives from the fact that it somehow conforms to what is both unique and universal in human nature. For a Kantian deontologist, it is inferred from one or another formulation of the Categorical Imperative, derivable from pure practical reason. A Utilitarian will justify the rule by reference to the calculus that takes account of the ultimate value of pleasure and disvalue of pain. And so on. Different foundations don't generate the same rules, even though they might agree in certain obvious cases.

So how do we decide between them? A standard way is to confront intuitions about specific cases with intuitions about general principles. If they appear to conflict, we adjust one in the light of the other, depending on which it seems less plausible to deny. Using tests of coherence and any relevant factual and logical considerations, we arrive at a "reflective equilibrium" among our intuitions, just as we do in any other sort of inquiry. As Nelson Goodman put it in discussing rules of deductive inference, "A rule is amended if it yields an inference we are unwilling to accept. An inference is rejected if it violates a rule we are unwilling to amend" (Goodman 1983, p. 64).

There are three problems with the application of this to morality. Despite the fact that the concept of reflective equilibrium originated in the context of the theory of justice (Rawls 1977), it doesn't work well when we are trying to decide between foundational principles. Intuitions about singular cases often seem far more obvious than do the abstract general principles adduced to support them. We already have reasons. Why not evaluate on their own terms the reasons we have for or against any particular judgment or course of action? If we really think our reasons are overriding and supremely authoritative, it seems counterproductive to adduce in their support further reasons that are widely contested. The existence of moral dilemmas shows that segregating a class of reasons privileged by the label "moral" does not mitigate the difficulty of weighing and comparing reasons. We need first to delineate a domain of moral reasons, and then make two lists—one of moral, one of nonmoral reasons—before weighing them again. That simply adds a long detour. In view of the question-begging nature of meta-ethical and foundational disputes, that detour can only weaken the force of the original reasons, by purporting to justify them in terms of a meta-ethical system less plausible than the original reasons.

Debates between meta-ethical systems offer no hope of resolution. Rival foundational principles are incommensurable. For they are themselves the very measures employed to compare rules appealing to them for adjudication. In defense of rock-bottom fundamental principles, advocates can only resort to question-begging assertion. To weigh intuitions against one another in search of an equilibrium, we would have to feed them into some sort of algorithm. Both the identity of the parameters involved and the nature of that algorithm, however, depend on the foundational principles to which one is committed. But those foundational principles are precisely what the disagreement is about. Any attempt to find common ground will drag us into another cycle in our question-begging meta-ethical detour, where prospects for agreement are nonexistent.

Eliminating that detour will free us to devote our intellectual energy entirely to evaluating the force of the reasons we already have. There is no need to decide first whether these reasons deserve the label *moral*.

CONCLUSION

Put simplistically, the argument about love's inherent morality has three ways to go: positive, negative, and neutral. The extreme positive view is that "true" love is not only morally good but divine. By implication, all other forms of love will be taking us away from the divine, and thus are bound to be deplored. In the extreme negative view—ignoring those that deprecate some forms of love as deriving from our inferior, beastly nature—the essential partiality of love conflicts directly with an essential principle of morality. By focusing selectively on ideal forms of love, many philosophers have arrived at persuasive definitions that entail that some forms of love are morally good or even central to morality, while others are "pathological" or otherwise disqualified. To assume that love is an emotion is misleading; but even taking it to be so for the purposes of argument, it turns out that no satisfactory account is available of what a moral emotion might be. There are good reasons for regarding love itself as inherently ambivalent, which would partly explain our ambivalent attitude to it. Love's ambivalence, we may allow, stems from its complexity: its targets are particulars, but both the reasons for it and the reasons it motivates are kinds. That suggests that we could address the morality of those specific reasons, rather than the morality of love as a whole. But that path turns out to be equally unpromising, because of the difficulty of understanding how to assess the morality of reasons for and of love. Unlike other emotions, moreover, even a definite verdict about the morality of love would have no useful practical implications.

Finally, I sketched two sorts of reasons for thinking that the discourse of morality itself is best avoided. First, because it involves a kind of fallacious double counting of reasons, which gives moral discourse a delusive rhetorical force. And second, because any singular moral judgment can be justified only by appeal to a meta-ethical doctrine. The question-begging nature of such foundational principles, when it is seen for what it is, only ends up weakening the reasons we had in the first place.

In sum, it would be better not to discuss the question of love's morality at all. By ignoring my own advice, and discussing it anyway, I hope I have provided compelling evidence of the wisdom of my injunction:[7] don't ask if love is moral.

NOTES

1. An auto-da-fé was an execution by burning alive. The term means "act of faith."

2. "[P]ersuasive definitions are often used in philosophy, and . . . the widespread failure to recognise them for what they are—the temptation to consider them as definitions which merely abbreviate, or which analyse, common concepts—has led to important philosophical confusions" (Stevenson 1938, p. 331).

3. For this reason, I have argued that love is not an emotion but more like a syndrome (de Sousa 2015, pp. 4, 89 ff.) For a more searching elaboration of that view, see also (Pismenny and Prinz 2017). For present purposes, however, I shall continue to assume that love can be regarded as an emotion or cluster of emotions.

4. "An obvious way to distinguish specifically moral attitudes would be to do so in terms of moral content—to disapprove of something morally is to disapprove of it because it is morally wrong, as one sees it" (Kauppinen 2010, p. 226). Ah, yes! At least that's clear.

5. For a critical analysis of moralizing reasons for and of love, see Pismenny (2021).

6. Elsewhere, I make a more general case against morality (de Sousa 2019). For more extensive discussions of amoralism, see Garner and Joyce (2019).

7. In case the other essays in the present volume have not convinced you.

REFERENCES

Anon. Erika Eiffel. Retrieved from https://en.wikipedia.org/wiki/Erika_Eiffel#:~ :text=Erika%20%22Aya%22%20Eiffel%20(n%C3%A9e,a%20commitment%20 ceremony%20in%202007.

Aristotle. (1984). Nicomachean ethics. In J. Barnes (ed.), *The complete works: The revised Oxford translation.* Bollingen Series LXXI. Princeton: Princeton University Press.

Berkowitz, E. (2012). *Sex and punishment: Four thousand years of judging desire.* Berkeley: Counterpoint.

Brogaard, B. (2015). *Romantic love: Simple truths about a complex emotion.* New York: Oxford University Press.

Brown, J. R. (1991). *The laboratory of the mind: Thought experiments in the natural sciences.* London: Routledge.

Brunning, L. (2020). Compersion: An alternative to jealousy? *Journal of the American Philosophical Association,* 225–245. doi:10.1017/apa.2019.35.

Coates, D. J. (2017). A wholehearted defense of ambivalence. *Journal of Ethics, 21,* 419–444.

Cocking, D., & Kennett, J. (2000). Friendship and moral danger. *Journal of Philosophy 97*(5), 278–296.

Crockett, M. J., Clark, L., Hauser, M. D., & Robbins, T. W. (2010). Serotonin selectively influences moral judgment and behavior through effects on harm aversion. *Proceedings of the National Academy of Science USA, 107,* 17433–17338. doi:10.1073/pnas.1009396107

D'Arms, J., & Jacobson, D. (2000). The moralistic fallacy: On the 'appropriateness' of emotion. *Philosophy and Phenomenological Research, 61,* 65–90.

de Sousa, R. (1974). The good and the true. *Mind, 83,* 534–551.

de Sousa, R. (2015). *Love: A very short introduction.* Oxford: Oxford University Press.

de Sousa, R. (2019). Pour un amoralisme: Une polémique. *Les Ateliers de l'Éthique-Ethics Forum, 14*(1), 172–189. doi:10.7202/1069956ar

Deonna, J. A., & Teroni, F. (2015). Emotions as attitudes. *Dialectica, 69*(3), 293–311.

Driver, J. (2020). Practical possibilities and the one- thought-too-many objection to moral deliberation. *Proceedings and Addresses of the American Philosophical Association, 94,* 21–40.

Frankena, W. K. (1966). The concept of morality. *Journal of Philosophy, 63*(21), 688–96.

Frankfurt, H. G. (1998). Duty and love. *Philosophical Explorations, 1*(1), 4–9.

Frankfurt, H. G. (2004). *The reasons of love.* Princeton: Princeton University Press.

Garner, R., & Joyce, R. (eds.). (2019). *The end of morality: Taking moral abolitionism seriously.* London; New York: Routledge.

Gibbard, A. (1990). *Wise choices, apt feelings: A theory of normative judgment.* Cambridge, MA: Harvard University Press.

Goodman, N. (1983). *Fact, fiction, and forecast* (4th ed.). Cambridge, MA: Harvard University Press.

Haidt, J. (2012). *The righteous mind: Why good people are divided by politics and religion.* New York: Pantheon.

Henrich, J. (2020). *The WEIRDest people in the world: How the West became psychologically peculiar and particularly prosperous.* New York: Farrar Straus.

Hume, D. (1975). *Enquiry concerning human understanding; A Letter from a gentleman to his friend in Edinburgh* (E. Steoinberg, ed.). Indianapolis: Hackett. (Original work published 1777)

Illouz, E. (2012). *Why love hurts.* Cambridge: Polity.

Jollimore, T. (2011). *Love's vision.* Princeton: Princeton University Press.

Kant, I. (2005 [1785]). *Groundwork for the metaphysics of morals.* (K. Abbot & L. Denis, Trans.). Guelph: Broadview.

Kauppinen, A. (2010). What makes a sentiment moral. *Oxford Studies in Metaethics, 5,* 225–256.

Klein, M. (1975). *Love, guilt and reparation and other works 1921–1945.* In *The complete works of Melanie Klein* (R. E. Money-Kyrle, Introduction). New York: Dell, Delta.

Kristjánsson, K. (1996). Why persons need jealousy. *Personalist Forum, 12*(2), 163–181.

Kristjánsson, K. (2002). *Justifying emotions: Pride and jealousy.* London: Routledge.

Marks, J. (2016) *Hard atheism and the ethics of desire: An alternative to morality.* Cham: Springer.

McIntyre, A. (2019). Doctrine of double effect. In E. A. Zalta (ed.), *The Stanford Encyclopedia of Philosophy (Spring 2019 ed.).* <https://plato.stanford.edu/archives/spr2019/entries/double-effect/>.

Murdoch, I. (1970). *The sovereignty of good.* Cambridge: Cambridge University Press.

Neu, J. (2000a). Odi et amo: On hating the ones we love. In *A tear is an intellectual thing.* Oxford; New York: Oxford University Press.

Neu, J. (2000b). *A tear is an intellectual thing.* Oxford; New York: Oxford University Press.

Nussbaum, M. 2001. *The fragility of goodness: Luck and ethics in Greek tragedy and philosophy* (Revised ed.). Cambridge: Cambridge University Press.

Pismenny, A. (2021). The amorality of romantic love. In R. Fedock, M. Kühler, & Rosenhagen (Eds.), *Love, justice, autonomy.* Routledge.

Pismenny, A., & Prinz, J. (2017). Is love an emotion? In C. Grau & A. Smuts (eds), *The Oxford handbook of philosophy of Love.* New York: Oxford University Press.

Plato. (1997). Symposium (A. Nehamas, & P. Woodruff, Trans.). In J. M. H. Cooper, Douglas (eds.), *Complete works* (pp. 457–505). Indianapolis: Hackett.

Prinz, J. (2011). Is empathy necessary for morality? In P. Goldie & A. Coplan, *Empathy: Philosophical and psychological perspectives* (pp. 211–229). Oxford University Press.

Prinz, J. J., & Nichols, S. (2010). Moral emotions. In J. Doris, F. Cushman & The Moral Psychology Research Group (eds.), *The moral psychology handbook* (pp. 111–146). New York: Oxford University Press.

Ramsey, F. P. (1990). On there being nothing to discuss. In H. Mellor (ed.), *Philosophical papers.* Cambridge: Cambridge University Press.

Rawls, J. (1977). *A theory of justice.* Cambridge, MA: Harvard University Press.

Rorty, R. (1979). *Contingency, irony, and solidarity.* Cambridge: Cambridge University Press.

Rossi, M., & Tappolet, C. (2018). What kind of evaluative states are emotions? The attitudinal theory vs. the perceptual theory of emotions. *Canadian Journal of Philosophy.* doi:10.1080/00455091.2018.1472516

Sadler, B. (2006). Love, friendship, morality. *The Philosophical Forum, 37*(3), 243–263.

Schaubroeck, K. (2019). Reasons of love. In A. M. Martin (ed.), *The Routledge Handbook of Love in Philosophy* (pp. 288–299). New York: Routledge.

Shweder, R. A., Much, N. C., Mahapatra, M., & Park, L. (2000). The 'Big Three' of morality (autonomy, community, divinity) and the 'Big Three' explanations of suffering. In R. A. Shweder, *Why do men barbacue? Recipes for cultural psychology* (pp. 120–169). New York: Routledge.

Smith, M. (2007). The what and why of love's reasons. In E. Engels Kroeker & K. Schaubroeck (eds.), *Love, reason and morality* (pp. 145–162). New York: Routledge.

Stevenson, C. L. (1938). Persuasive definitions. *Mind, 48*(187), 331–350

Stocker, M. (1976). The schizophrenia of modern ethical theories. *Journal of Philosophy, 73*(13), 453–66.

Velleman, D. (1999). Love as a moral emotion. *Ethics, 109,* 338–374.

Williams, B. A. O. (1981). Persons, character and morality. In *Moral luck* (pp. 1–18). Cambridge: Cambridge University Press.

Williams, B. A. O. (1986). *Ethics and the limits of philosophy* (2nd ed.). Cambridge: Harvard University Press.

Wolf, S. (2015). Moral Saints. In *The variety of values: Essays on morality, meaning, and love* (pp. 11–30). New York: Oxford University Press.

Wolf, S. (1992). Morality and partiality. *Philosophical Perspectives, 6,* 243–259.

Chapter 2

The Neurobiology of Love

Donatella Marazziti and Alessandra Della Vecchia

INTRODUCTION

Love is an exquisite human attribute that is embedded in human nature. Love springs and develops because human beings are born with the innate drive toward the rewards intrinsic to loving and being loved. Love is a process, specifically an integrated neurobiobehavioral process promoting proximity, reproduction, and childrearing in the context of a bond that forms between two unrelated individuals. Moreover, in its mature stages, love can reduce feelings of stress and anxiety, while triggering a deep sense of safety, joy, and reward. Love can be understood as a complex process comprising neurobiological processes, physiological changes in the body, a fluctuating phenomenology, and alternating expressions and behaviors. Although some components of this complex process that we call love can also be found in other mammals, what makes love unique to humans is that the formation of pair bonding in our species is related not only to reproduction, but also to the creation of group structures and social institutions. Nature has provided us with this complex process we call love to help our species survive. Love contributes to the continuation of our species by ensuring that our focus is limited to only one or a few partners at the same time, and it contributes to our survival as individuals by enhancing our safety, while rewarding us with the feelings of pleasure and completeness we call love. The sum of emotions + behaviors + subjective awareness of the whole process constitutes, perhaps, the essence of love (Marazziti 2009; Marazziti 2015; de Boer, van Buel, and Ter Horst 2012).

The similarities in the experience of love across different individuals suggest that the experience of love is regulated by shared neurobiological mechanisms. The results of brain imaging and neurobiological techniques

35

have revealed that during the initial stages of love, our physiological state bears a striking similarity to those found in those with psychiatric disorders, such as anxiety disorders, depression, and obsessive compulsive disorders. This finding is unsurprising given that love involves the same systems that modulate anxiety and fear responses and the neurotransmitters and hormones correlated with these responses (Marazziti et al. 1999; Bartels and Zeki 2000; Fisher 1992; Fisher et al. 2016). Attachment, the subsequent state of love, involves activation of dopamine circuits regulating reward processes as well as oxytocin, a nonapeptide produced in the hypothalamus that acts both as a neurotransmitter and as a neurohormone in the central nervous system (CNS) and peripheral organs.

Nature follows its rules in all processes, that is to say, the accomplishment of its goals. Therefore, love is good insofar as it serves natural evolutionary processes, but because it is regulated by the same strong neurobiological systems involved in species' survival, love's intents may collide with human rules. Although love can represent the most extraordinary and joyful experience that nature invented for humans, it can also elicit extreme personal suffering, family destruction, and atrocities like suicides, murders, and ethnic cleansings.

The aim of the present chapter is to provide a careful and updated literature review on the neurobiology of love, together with the authors' personal contributions in this fascinating domain. The first section will focus on attraction, followed by attachment, and the risks of love, including jealousy, stalking, and psychiatric disorders.

THE FIRST STAGE OF LOVE: ATTRACTION

"Attraction" is the biological term that denotes what is commonly called "romantic love" or "falling in love." The fact that the experience of love appears to be common across cultures suggests that love may be underpinned by particular kinds of neurobiological systems (Jankowiak and Fischer 1998). Available data suggest that romantic love generally lasts between six months and two to three years, which is thought to be the time needed to mate, reach the culmination of pregnancy, and take care of the offspring until they are more likely to survive without two parents (Jankowiak and Fischer 1998).

Attraction is something entirely different from pair bonding, sexual activity, and reciprocation. Our hypothesis is that attraction is a basic emotion that shares some of its neurobiological substrates with fear and anxiety (LeDoux 2000; Marazziti 2015). As such, nobody can willfully decide to be attracted to another person. Mutual attraction is driven by strong sensory stimuli occurring more or less at the same time in two unrelated individuals. Indeed, following internal (e.g., hormonal variations) and external changes (e.g., life events), the brain—in particular the amygdala, a group of subcortical nuclei regulating fight/flight responses and emotions—becomes particularly predisposed to otherwise "normal" stimuli coming from another person. These stimuli are first processed by the thalamus, and then projected to the amygdala via two pathways: a direct route and a longer one involving an intermediate step represented by the cortex (figure 2.1). The amygdala modulates the incoming stimuli while detecting its emotional quality (good or bad) and organizes all outputs, such as neurovegetative reactions and hormonal responses, in order to prepare the individual for fight or flight. After an additional six milliseconds, the activated cortex, through the longer pathway, provides the subjective awareness of the bodily changes that everybody in love can relate to. There is evidence to suggest that brain circuits correlated with love overlap with those of fear and anxiety. This aspect of love can be considered "fear without subjective fear," as the anxiety reactions are transformed into a sense of joy by specific biological processes (Marazziti 2015).

Researchers are in broad agreement about the specific features of attraction; they can be summarized as follows: an altered mental state, intrusive thoughts about the partner, and a reduced interest in everyday activities. The altered mental state of infatuation resembles the alternating phases of bipolar disorder (BD): people can experience elevated levels of energy, decreases in

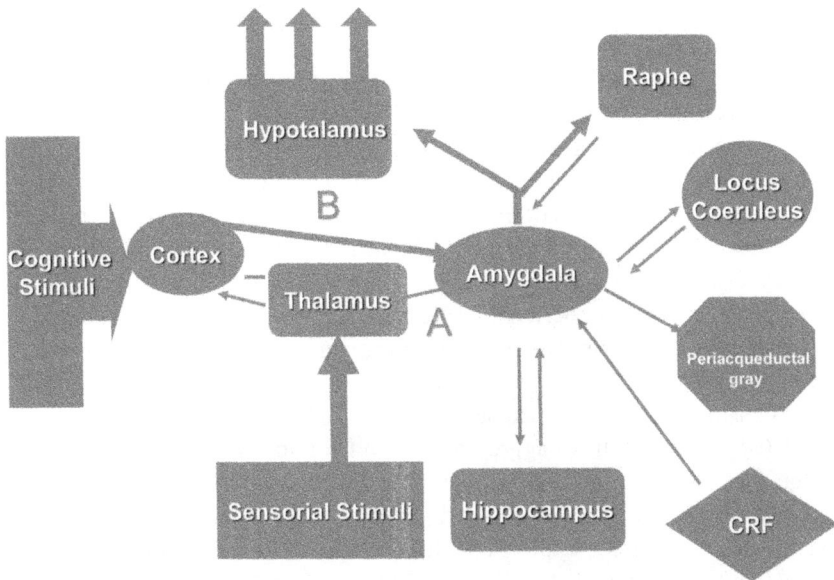

Figure 2.1 The Circuitry of Romantic Love: (a) Shorter Pathway; (b) Longer Pathway.

appetite, a decreased need for sleep, impaired rational judgment, and mood swings. How exactly infatuation is manifested depends in part on whether it is reciprocal. Michael Liebowitz was the first to bring attention to the similarity between infatuation and BD. He proposed that phenylethylamine, a trace neurotransmitter, might be involved in the beginning stages of romantic love, which are often characterized by infatuation (Liebowitz 1983). While intriguing, this theory has never been backed by experimental data. Even so, the altered mental state of love might be due to an increased activation of the norepinephrine and dopamine systems, as well as increased levels of opioid peptides and a decrease in the brain's extracellular levels of serotonin (5-HT). Such putative abnormalities might also explain the significant shift in consciousness occurring in the initial stages of romantic love, that is, the conviction that our partner is the most extraordinary individual in the world, coupled with a focused attention on them that leads to a decreased interest in routine everyday activities. Another component of attraction is represented by intense cravings for the partner, and specific behavioral patterns aimed at evoking reciprocation. As these patterns are similar to grooming behaviors and even to compulsive behaviors, they could also be due to increased levels of dopamine and decreased concentrations of serotonin (Marazziti and Cassano 2003; Marazziti et al. 2015; Marazziti et al. 2017). Again, the decreased activation of the 5-HT system may lead to intrusive thoughts about the partner and repetitive behaviors that serve to gain their attention. This combination of obsession and compulsive behaviors suggests that infatuation may have commonalities with obsessive compulsive disorder (OCD) as well (Marazziti et al. 1999; Marazziti et al. 2015). Interestingly, this "symptomatology" is often considered the most salient feature of romantic love (Fisher et al. 2016). Our hypothesis is that this imaginary activity regarding the object of love is uniquely human, lacking any nonhuman animal parallels. This cognitive feature of love can continue to exist in spite of the fact that no bonding is formed and even in spite of the fact that there may not yet have been any sex involved. This stage of love can sometimes be sublimated through art or religious/mystical experiences. We propose that this component of love, which is typical of the early phases of a romantic relationship, can be understood along a dimensional perspective.

Dimensions can be defined as basic products of the functioning of the mind (or brain), such as aggression, mood, or insight, sometimes related to the functioning of a single or a few neurotransmitters (Changeux 1985). Although speculative, a dimensional perspective has been helpful in providing a research tool for exploring relationships and the continuum between normal and pathological states (Jenike 1990; Hollander 1993; Cassano et al. 1997). Overlapping features between the idealization of the beloved and pathological states, typical in romantic and parental love, have been widely reported (Leckman et al. 1999). Furthermore, romantic and parental love have both been related to a nonpathological obsessive physiological state, one that is necessary to keep two partners together and parents close to their children. In previous work, we have suggested that romantic and parental love are akin to pathological obsession at an ideative level, involving the dimension "certainty/uncertainty" as well as that of "awareness/no awareness." The "certainty/uncertainty" dimension may be predominantly related to the 5-HT serotonin system.

We formulated this hypothesis on the basis of findings from one of our studies (Marazziti et al. 1999). The results showed that the density of the platelet 5-HT transporter, which can be used as a reliable peripheral model of the 5-HT transporter present in presynaptic serotonergic neurons (Lesch and Mössner 1998), was significantly lower in subjects who had recently fallen in love and were still at the romantic phase of the relationship with no sexual intercourse than in "normal" control subjects. Moreover, the levels of the platelet 5-HT transporter were found to be similar to those observed in a group of patients with OCD (Marazziti et al. 1999, table 1). We therefore hypothesize a continuum from OCD (uncertainty/no awareness) through the prevalent ideation typical of romantic love (certainty/awareness) to delusional states (certainty/no awareness). Similar observations have been made on the shifts from normal to pathological state, even in the expression of love that, in some instances, can reach the severity of paranoid states (Forward and Buck 1991; Griffin-Shelley 1991). Thus, we agree with others (Leckman et al. 1999; Kane 1987; O'Dwyer and Marks 2000) that love and pair bonding can be related to the same neurobiological systems as pathological conditions, such as OCD and paranoia.

The risk of becoming fully "obsessive" or "paranoid" about a romantic partner may be the evolutionary cost we pay to increase the likelihood of bonding and commitment to those partners. Nature has probably created this sort of transitory madness in order to render human beings more open toward teaming up with unrelated individuals, helping them overcome the neophobia and separation anxiety associated with leaving the safe "nest" of the original family. Nature may seem mainly interested in perpetuating and strengthening our species, so that it is fundamental that people who are not closely related can meet, fall in love and, possibly, procreate. And, really, humans need to be "crazy" to overcome all their fears and reluctance when they meet "that special person" to abandon all their reluctance and share some of the most intimate aspects of themselves with that person.

The evolutionary perspective to love thus explains why a temporary state of "madness" is so common in the initial phases of romantic love. The primary aim of the "madness" is to render the individual more impulsive in order to overcome fear and neophobia and willingly accept to be close to a stranger that suddenly and promptly becomes the most extraordinary person in the world. Thus, by causing us to experience an emotional storm, infatuation allows us to get out of our comfort zone.

Romantic love is a stressful event, as shown by the hormonal changes it entails. Indeed, both men and women in the early phases of romantic love show increased levels of cortisol, with changes in testosterone going in opposite directions in the two sexes. That is to say, testosterone concentrations decrease in men and increase in women (Marazziti and Canale 2004). This may be useful to the pair formation. If we reflect on the functions of testosterone, men would become less aggressive and women more assertive and more prone to accept the risk of sexual intercourse (Marazziti and Canale 2004).

Human beings cannot escape falling in love: it is embedded in our nature. If we open ourselves up to loving and being loved, we will be rewarded by deep joy and an increased chance of survival, as we are more vulnerable on our own. Not surprisingly, some researchers have reported higher levels of two neurotrophins (NTs), specifically nerve growth factor (NGF) and brain-derived neurotrophic factor (BDNF) in the plasma of romantic lovers (Enzo et al. 2006).

The hormonal and neurobiological activities described do not last forever, however, and the "altered state of mind" returns to a more stable and calm condition over time in order to allow both parties to move toward experiencing the next phase of love, which is romantic attachment. One of our studies showed that the 5-HT abnormalities did not last: twelve to eighteen months into the relationship, the 5-HT levels had returned to their normal values (Marazziti et al. 1999): this is consistent with anthropological studies reporting that infatuation lasts no longer than three years (Jankowiak and Fischer 1998).

Some studies carried out in vivo, by means of fMRI, support our model of infatuation and also suggest a connection to the reward-motivational systems (Bartels and Zeki 2004; Aron et al. 2005; Acevedo et al. 2012).

ROMANTIC ATTACHMENT

If the process of falling in love is successful, which is to say that the partner reciprocates and the two individuals start a relationship that continues, the subjective feelings of love take on a different phenomenology after a while. The mood is more stable, anxiety is reduced, and there are much fewer or no obsessive thoughts about the beloved. Probably, the chemical storm that initially flooded the brain like a deluge has subsided. Were it to continue, it would be quite uneconomical and exhausting, because it would involve a continuous release of neurotransmitters and hyperstimulation of receptors that cannot be tolerated by any organism for too long. However, it is more correct to say that in an ongoing romantic relationship, infatuation is replaced by another process, viz., that of romantic attachment (Jankowiak and Fischer 1998; Marazziti and Cassano 2003). Romantic attachment is fundamental for keeping two individuals together, once the flame of passionate love is extinguished. Romantic attachment could thus be considered the social process of keeping two individuals together for a long period of time, sometimes for the rest of their lives. In this sense, attachment is a sort of "glue" necessary for "tolerating" the partner for a long time and for the continuation of a successful relationship.

For a long time, attachment was merely considered a response to separation, and the research on attachment primarily focused on opiates (Panksepp 1982). However, today, attachment is no longer believed to be a consequence of separation anxiety. It is now clear that attachment can have a positive valence linked to the positive feelings and rewards associated with the formation of social bonds and, as Insel states, "there is no obvious reason for which attachment and separation should be subserved by the same neural system" (Insel 1997).

It is generally believed that attachment is triggered and maintained by the neuropeptide oxytocin (OT), which seems to be involved in the initiation and maintenance of pair bonding, infant attachment, and maternal behavior. OT reduces stress while vasopressin (VP), another nonapeptide, is associated with an increased stress response, reactive aggression, reduced cooperation, and lower parental investment (Carter 1998; Insel and Young 2001). Both OT and VP are produced in the hypothalamus and released by the posterior pituitary (Acher 1996). Oxytocin is produced when infatuation starts, and ordinarily "transforms" the "anxiety/fear" reactions into a sense of well-being, reward, and joy (Kosfeld et al. 2005). This is possible through the deactivation of the stress systems and the activation of the reward-processing systems regulated by the neurotransmitter dopamine (Heinrichs et al. 2003). OT is simultaneously released into the bloodstream, where it conveys information to peripheral organs (Acher 1996). From the peripheral organs, OT returns to the brain as a messenger, linking the brain to the peripheral nervous system. According to the polyvagal theory, the activity of OT on the nucleus vagus, especially on the ventral complex, the so-called smart vagus, explains the different emotions and bodily changes occurring during social bonding processes, such as attachment and love (Porges and Furman 2011).

The relevance of these intriguing findings for humans, and especially for romantic attachment and love, are not yet fully known (Insel and Young 2001; Young and Wang 2004). Oxytocin receptors in the human brain are mainly distributed in the substantia nigra and globus pallidus—areas shown to be activated in adults who are looking at pictures of their partners, and in mothers looking at their children (Bartels and Zeki 2004), along with the anterior cingulate and the medial insula. This pattern of activation overlaps substantially with the pattern observed during a state of cocaine-induced euphoria (Young et al. 2001; Young 2002), which supports the notion that attachment is linked to a reward pathway (Insel 2003).

Recently, OT administration in humans was shown to increase trust, again supporting the involvement of the amygdala, a central component of the neurocircuitry of fear and social cognition, which has been linked to trust and a high expression of OT receptors (Kosfeld et al. 2005).

A double-blind study, using functional magnetic resonance imaging to visualize amygdala activation by fear-inducing visual stimuli showed that human amygdala function is strongly modulated by OT: compared to placebo, OT potently reduced activation of the amygdala and reduced coupling of the amygdala to brainstem regions implicated in autonomic and behavioral manifestations of fear (Kirsch et al. 2005). This effect was located on the level of the midbrain and encompassed both the region of the periaqueductal grey and of the reticular formation, which are prominent among the brainstem areas to which the central nucleus of the amygdala projects (LeDoux 2000) and which mediate fear behavior and arousal (LeDoux et al. 1988). In agreement with these findings, autonomic responses to aversive pictures resulted in reduced OT (Pitman, Orr, and Lasko 1993).

It is of interest to note that OT administration did not affect the scores on self-report scales of participants' psychological state. This is consistent with the observations of Kosfeld et al. (2005), who also did not find an effect of OT on measured calmness and mood but found that at the level of behavior, actual social interaction was necessary to bring out the OT effect. Thus, the neural effect of the neuropeptide on behavior is evident in the social context but not when subjects rate themselves.

Moreover, the reduction in amygdala activation was more significant for socially relevant stimuli (i.e., faces) than for the socially less relevant scenes; the differential impairment of amygdala signaling related to the social relevance of the stimuli is in agreement with emerging primate lesion studies (Prather et al. 2001) and human data indicating that social and nonsocial fear may depend on dissociable neural systems (Meyer-Lindenberg et al. 2005).

Furthermore, OT plays an important role in sexual behavior. It is well documented that levels of circulating OT increase during sexual stimulation and arousal and peak during orgasm in both men and women (Carmichael et al. 1987; Carter 1992). Plasma OT and AVP concentrations were measured in men during sexual arousal and ejaculation, and plasma AVP concentrations were found to be significantly increased during arousal (Murphy and Dwarte 1987). However, at ejaculation, mean plasma OT rose about fivefold and fell back to basal concentrations within 30 minutes, while AVP had already returned to basal levels at the time of ejaculation and remained stable thereafter. Men taking the opioid antagonist naloxone before self-stimulation had reductions of both OT secretion and degree of arousal and orgasm. Peak levels of serum OT were also found to be present in women at or shortly after orgasm (Blaicher et al. 1999). The intensity of muscular contractions during orgasm in both men and women were highly correlated with OT plasma level (Carmichael et al. 1994). This suggests that some of OT's effects may be related to its ability to stimulate the contraction of smooth muscles in the genital-pelvic area. Enhanced sexual arousal and orgasm intensity has been observed in a woman during intranasal administration of OT. One report described the case of a woman who about two hours after the use of a synthetic OT spray noticed copious vaginal transudate and subsequent intense sexual desire. This response was present only while she was taking daily doses of an oral contraceptive (Anderson-Hunt and Dennerstein 1994; 1995). In any case, it seems that there is a significant sexual dimorphism in OT (Marazziti et al. 2019; Carter et al. 2020).

It is worth emphasizing that OT seems to be released during different relaxation techniques in humans and therefore is supposed to be one of the mediators responsible for the decrease in stress responses (Carter 1992). Consequently, it has been proposed that OT may mediate the benefits of positive relationships in promoting health, such as lower incidences of cardiovascular diseases or depression in individuals with stable partners (Uvnäs-Moberg 1998). One of our studies confirmed the relationship between romantic attachment and OT in forty-five healthy subjects (Marazziti et al. 2006). The major finding of this study was the presence of a statistically significant and positive correlation between OT plasma levels and scores on the anxiety scale of the Experience in Close Relationship (ECR), a self-report questionnaire measuring adult romantic attachment: The higher the OT levels, the higher the score on the anxiety scale of the ECR (figure 2.2). It was not possible to determine on the basis of our data whether the OT levels are a consequence or a cause of the anxiety measured by the ECR scale, and further research is needed to clarify this. However, in line with the majority of available findings (Carter 1992; Uvnäs-Moberg 1997; Insel and Young 2001; Heinrichs et al. 2003), we tentatively suggest that the former might be the case, and that OT might serve to help counteract anxiety—or at least the form of anxious stress associated with romantic attachment and deep concern over its continuance (Marazziti et al. 2006; Marazziti et al. 2012).

Although our findings may be considered to be in agreement with previous studies carried out mainly in animals, which have generally suggested a possible role of OT in social bonding, our findings undoubtedly represent the first report of a direct link between OT and the state of anxiety associated with romantic attachment in our species. Previously, only indirect evidence

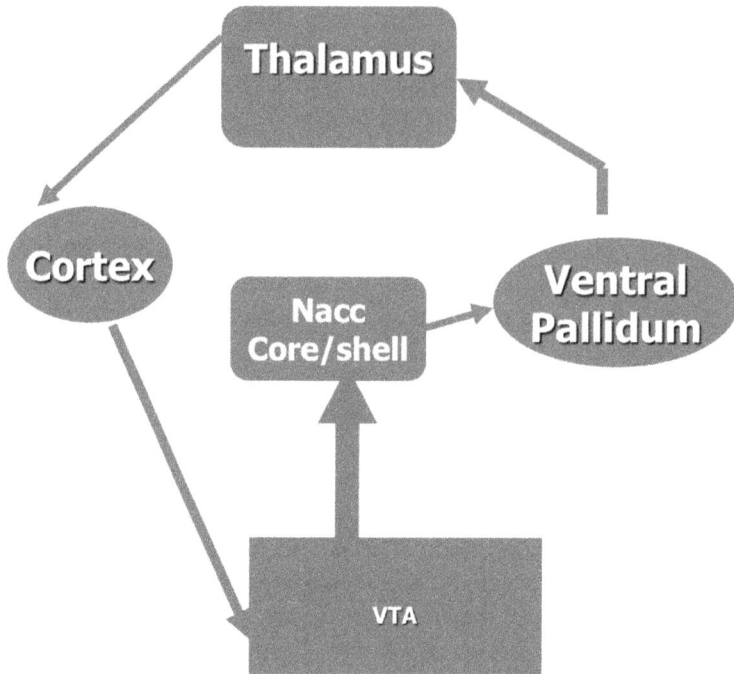

Figure 2.2   The Dopaminergic Circuitry of the Social Brain (VTA: Ventral Tegmental Areas; Nacc: Nucleus Accumbens).

has been found in support of the relationship between OT and anxiety (Uvnäs-Moberg et al. 1991). Furthermore, some studies have reported that low plasma OT levels may be typical in individuals with low anxiety traits (Turner et al. 2002). Pursuing this line of thought, romantic relationships, and perhaps social relationships in general, could be interpreted as kinds of stress conditions, both acute and chronic depending on the phase (Gillath et al. 2005). One role of OT would thus seem to be that of keeping anxiety levels under control to a point where they are no longer harmful. Indeed, low OT concentrations have been linked with pain syndromes, such as fibromyalgia (Anderberg and Uvnäs-Moberg 2000) and abdominal pain (Alfvén 2004). However, they may nevertheless lead to the strategies and behaviors that are best suited for ensuring a partner's continued proximity both during the first stages of the romance and subsequently. Oxytocin can thus be considered an essential element in securing the rewarding effects of a romantic relationship, as a result of its ability to increase a prospective sexual partner's willingness to accept the risk derived from social interaction (Kosfeld et al. 2005), through the modulation of anxiety mechanisms. Of course, with particularly vulnerable individuals, if excessively affected by the relationship itself or by other events, these delicate mechanisms might be maladaptive in the sense that such subjects might become too anxious and thus might cross the line between normal and pathological states, even to the point of developing a full-blown psychiatric disorder.

In addition, the first double-blind studies conducted with functional magnetic resonance imaging (fMRI) confirmed the role of OT in romantic attachment, while showing activation of brain areas rich in OT receptors when individuals look at pictures of the partners (Bartels and Zeki 2000; Fisher et al. 2002). Subsequent studies have confirmed these findings, while highlighting how romantic love can be a strong motivational state that follows the neuronal circuitry of reward and pleasure (Aron et al. 2005) and how long-term love activates the attachment system (Acevedo et al. 2012).

Besides OT and VP, NTs also seem to play a role in this phase, as shown in a study investigating the possible relationship between BDNF plasma levels and romantic attachment in twenty-four healthy adults (twelve men, twelve women), as assessed by the "Experiences in Close Relationships" (ECR) questionnaire (Brennan, Clark, and Shaver 1998). The results highlighted the presence of a strong negative correlation between BDNF levels and the ECR avoidance scale, while suggesting a role of BDNF in promoting social bonding through the decrease of fear and avoidance behaviors in women. This correlation was not present in men. The authors hypothesized that the role of BDNF is gender-related and influenced by the interactions between hormones and genes (Marazziti et al. 2009). Interestingly, estrogens are supposed to induce BDNF synthesis in different brain regions (Sasahara et al. 2007). Therefore, BDNF may be more active in women who are generally more anxious than men (Kessler, Keller, and Wittchen 2001; Afifi 2007). NTs are thus believed to play a role in protecting neurons from stress-induced damage (Bergström et al. 2008).

According to some authors (Insel 2003; Fisher et al. 2016), love resembles an addiction, on the basis of a shared activation of dopamine-rich regions involved in the reward system and drug or behavioral addictions, and overlapping symptoms, such as a sense of euphoria, craving, physical and emotional dependence. Love can be a positive addiction or a negative one when not reciprocated or when it becomes toxic, for example, leading to depression, stalking, suicide, homicide, and other crimes (Fisher et al. 2016).

Using resting state functional magnetic resonance imaging (rsfMRI), Song et al. (2015) aimed at investigating how romantic love may affect the brain and its functional architecture during rest. Participants consisted of thirty-four people (the "in-love group") intensely in love for four to eighteen months, thirty-four people who ended their romantic relationship recently (two to seventeen months earlier), and thirty-two people who had never fallen in love. The "in-love group," in comparison to the control group, showed an increased ReHo (regional homogeneity) on the left dorsal anterior cingulate cortex (dACC), and an increased functional connectivity within both the reward network (caudate, nucleus accumbens, etc.) and the social cognition network (temporo-parietal junction, posterior cingulate cortex, etc.) (figure 2.2). All the mentioned increases were positively correlated with the duration of the "being in love" state (Song et al. 2015).

To summarize, the current literature increasingly supports the notion that love is regulated by neural systems belonging to the so-called social brain that involves specific areas and their interactions with neurotransmitters and hormones.

THE RISKS OF LOVE

Love is a natural strategy for creating new bonds with other, often unrelated people. However, there is a cost to pay due to the significant (and pathological, albeit transitory) changes in neurotransmitters and related structural changes in the brain: a greater risk of developing abnormal love-related conditions, such as jealousy, obsession manifested in stalking behaviors, or full-blown psychiatric disorders, like anxiety disorders, depression, OCD and even psychosis. In this section, we explore some of these pathological love-related conditions.

Jealousy

Jealousy is a complex emotion that involves a perceived threat that one might lose one's intimate partner to another (Klein 1975, Buss 1989). It is characterized by cognitive and behavioral emotional components. Jealousy is a heterogeneous condition ranging from normal to pathological expressions, with varying degrees of intensity, persistence, and insight (Mullen and Martin 1994; Marazziti, Di Nasso, et al. 2003; Robbins et al. 2012). Pathological jealousy, which might range in severity from obsessive to paranoid, is always predictive of stalking (Derntl and Habel 2011). It may easily reach delusional proportions when the threat is based on false beliefs and can lead to aggression and violence (Meloy 1998; Silva et al. 2000; Roberts 2002). Jealousy can also trigger a motivation to dominate and isolate the target before the beginning of stalking behaviors. The psychological defenses used by stalkers are denial, projection of guilt, and projective identification (Meloy 1992). If these fail, the stalker is vulnerable to develop feelings of persecution, which can be intensified by the intervention of a third party, who might be rendered as interference or threat (Meloy 1999).

The identification of the biological basis of jealousy, to date still unknown and poorly investigated, could have a significant impact on prevention of stalking behaviors (Hart and Legerstee 2010). Only one study reported that obsessive jealousy is associated with a specific alteration of the platelet 5-HT transporter, which may be suggestive of a possible involvement of the serotonergic system (Marazziti, Rucci, et al. 2003). In another functional-RNM study performed during a behavioral task involving jealousy-triggering scenarios, it has been observed that different areas of the brain were recruited in men and women (Takahashi et al. 2006). More recently, we proposed a theory that may explain the transition from normal to delusional jealousy, which is common among stalkers; the theory derives from the observation that dopamine agonists can induce delusional jealousy in patients with Parkinson's disease (Marazziti et al. 2013). This may be due to the fact that dopamine agonists can trigger the phenomenon of aberrant attribution of salience, a phenomenon that is hypothesized to underlie the development of delusions (Kapur 2003). In our opinion, delusional jealousy is likely to arise from at least three simultaneous conditions: an aberrant salience related to the relationship with the loved one, aberrant representations of the partner's feelings, thoughts and behaviors, and aberrant scenarios related to the potential loss of the relationship, provoked by an excess of dopamine, which can be primary or secondary to a low serotonergic tone. Excess activation of the dopamine system promotes the connections between the prefrontal cortex and dorsal striatum at the expense of those of the ventral striatum (Marazziti et al. 2013).

Stalking

Currently, there are no specific hypotheses to fully explain the phenomenon of stalking (Grattagliano et al. 2012), although the available studies suggest some common individual features, such as immaturity, loneliness or isolation, difficulty in social relationships or in attracting other people, and the presence of narcissistic personality traits. Other common features of stalkers are insecure or anxious attachment types. After an initial elation phase of feeling in love, the mood may shift toward irritability, resentment, anger, and sometimes aggressiveness and impulsivity, supported by an apparently neverending energy. At the cognitive level, the stalker may show manic thinking and obsessiveness, with a narrow focus on the victim, and little or no awareness of the consequences of their behaviors, with the possibility of psychotic drifts that can also be enhanced by jealousy.

The hypotheses on the neurobiology of stalking are virtually nonexistent, apart from the paper by John Meloy and Helen Fisher that represents one of the few comprehensive reviews on this topic, and our contribution (Meloy and Fisher 2005; Marazziti et al. 2015). Starting from what has already been published, we can make some very cautious general observations and suggestions, relying mainly on the characteristics of the phenomenon. If the stalking is due to altered brain processes, it is likely that these altered processes involve the systems regulating the so-called social brain, that is, a complex of brain areas and circuits. It is supposed that the social brain is the biological basis of any kind of human relationships, such as attachment, formation of the couple, falling in love, mother-infant interaction. Similar to an individual in love or a drug addict, the stalker is constantly anxious, hyperactive and obsessively thinking about the victim, regardless of whether or not their feelings are returned, or the consequences of their harassment.

Studies with fMRI in lovers showed an activation of brain areas involved in the regulation of emotions (amygdala, limbic lobe, hypothalamus) and a deactivation of certain cortical areas, which is also likely to be typical of the stalkers. However, compared to lovers, stalkers present an abnormal persistence of this pattern. From a biochemical point of view, these conditions may be explained by a hyperactivity of dopaminergic pathways and a reduction of the serotonergic tone. This particular neurobiological arrangement would provide a biochemical explanation of the peculiarities of the stalker, as mentioned above, and would account for the constant risk that the obsessive thoughts may become delusional and result in violence and aggression. A low serotonergic tone would represent a vulnerability factor toward the emergence of a broad range of behavioral disturbances, such as impulsive, compulsive, and aggressive acts (Berlin and Hollander 2008). The related high dopaminergic activity may thus contribute to the loss of behavioral control and insight.

There is no doubt that prevention of stalking should embrace comprehensive social, cultural and legislative projects; nevertheless, we believe that a better understanding of its neurobiological correlates or biomarkers may lead to early identification of at-risk individuals. This would enhance the chance of implementing appropriate measures to avoid those dramatic scenarios that increasingly and too often fill the media crime pages.

Psychiatric Disorders

As already explained, the systems involved in love processing are those regulating primary emotions, attachment, reward modulations and related neurotransmitters and brain areas. To fall in love and to love is a "sensitive" process from the neurobiological point of view, encompassing changes or change combinations generally occurring in different psychiatric conditions. Therefore, it is not surprising that these neurobiological changes might constitute triggers provoking full-blown disorders in vulnerable individuals. Indeed, a love relationship, its beginning, or its end can unleash depression, OCD, BD manic shifts or psychoses (Leckman et al. 1999; Berry and Worthington Jr. 2001; Price et al. 2016).

CONCLUSIONS

The present chapter is a review of some of the major findings on the neurobiology of love. This is an emerging and intriguing field of research that only recently has become the topic of intensive scientific investigations and has benefited from the application of the most advanced methods used in neuroscience. The scattered data that have been gathered and are accumulating at an increasing amount, albeit preliminary and fragmentary, allow us to set up an initial framework and hypotheses that need to be tested.

The neurobiology of love shows that love evolved to facilitate the bonding between two unrelated individuals. But this may collide with human rules, as it may provoke separations, family disruptions, or severe abnormal behaviors, such as suicides and murders.

In any case, our opinion is that a deeper understanding of the neurobiology of love would permit us to get access to our unique humanity, to love in a more rewarding and joyful way, and perhaps to prevent the suffering and dramatic consequences of unrequited love or separations.

REFERENCES

Acevedo, B. P., A. Aron, H. E. Fisher, and L. L. Brown. 2012. "Neural correlates of long-term intense romantic love." *Soc Cogn Affect Neurosci* 7 (2):145–59. doi: 10.1093/scan/nsq092.

Acher, R. 1996. "Molecular evolution of fish neurohypophysial hormones: Neutral and selective evolutionary mechanisms." *Gen Comp Endocrinol* 102 (2):157–72. doi: 10.1006/gcen.1996.0057.

Afifi, M. 2007. "Gender differences in mental health." *Singapore Med J* 48 (5):385–91.

Alfvén, G. 2004. "Plasma oxytocin in children with recurrent abdominal pain." *J Pediatr Gastroenterol Nutr* 38 (5):513–17. doi: 10.1097/00005176-200405000-00010.

Anderberg, U. M., and K. Uvnäs-Moberg. 2000. "Plasma oxytocin levels in female fibromyalgia syndrome patients." *Z Rheumatol* 59 (6):373–9. doi: 10.1007/s003930070045.

Anderson-Hunt, M., and L. Dennerstein. 1994. "Increased female sexual response after oxytocin." *BMJ* 309 (6959):929. doi: 10.1136/bmj.309.6959.929.

Anderson-Hunt, M., and Dennerstein, J. 1995 "Oxytocin and female sexuality." *Gynecol Obstet Invest* 40 (4):217–21. doi: 10.1159/000292340.

Aron, A., H. Fisher, D. J. Mashek, G. Strong, H. Li, and L. L. Brown. 2005. "Reward, motivation, and emotion systems associated with early-stage intense romantic love." *J Neurophysiol* 94 (1):327–37. doi: 10.1152/jn.00838.2004.

Bartels, A., and S. Zeki. 2000. "The neural basis of romantic love." *Neuroreport* 11 (17):3829–34. doi: 10.1097/00001756-200011270-00046.

Bartels, A., and S. Zeki. 2004. "The neural correlates of maternal and romantic love." *Neuroimage* 21 (3):1155–66. doi: 10.1016/j.neuroimage.2003.11.003.

Bergström, A., M. N. Jayatissa, A. Mørk, and O. Wiborg. 2008. "Stress sensitivity and resilience in the chronic mild stress rat model of depression; an in situ hybridization study." *Brain Res* 1196:41–52. doi: 10.1016/j.brainres.2007.12.025.

Berlin, H. A., and Hollander, E. 2008 "Understanding the differences between impulsivity and compulsivity." *Psychiatr Times* 25 (8):58.

Berry, Jack W., and Everett L. Worthington Jr. 2001. "Forgivingness, relationship quality, stress while imagining relationship events, and physical and mental health." *J Couns Psychol.* 48 (4):447–55. doi: 10.1037/0022-0167.48.4.447.

Blaicher, W., D. Gruber, C. Bieglmayer, A. M. Blaicher, W. Knogler, and J. C. Huber. 1999. "The role of oxytocin in relation to female sexual arousal." *Gynecol Obstet Invest* 47 (2):125–6. doi: 10.1159/000010075.

Brennan, Kelly A., Catherine L. Clark, and Phillip R. Shaver. 1998. "Self-report measurement of adult attachment: An integrative overview." In *Attachment theory and close relationships*, 46–76. New York, NY: The Guilford Press.

Buemann, B., Marazziti, D., and Uvnäs-Moberg, K. 2020. "Can intravenous oxytocin infusion counteract hyperinflammation in COVID-19 infected patients?" *World J. Biol. Psychiatry.* doi: 10.1080/15622975.2020.1814408

Buss, David M. 1989. "Sex differences in human mate preferences: Evolutionary hypotheses tested in 37 cultures." *Behav Brain Sci.* 12 (1):1–14. doi: 10.1017/S0140525X00023992.

Carmichael, M. S., R. Humbert, J. Dixen, G. Palmisano, W. Greenleaf, and J. M. Davidson. 1987. "Plasma oxytocin increases in the human sexual response." *J Clin Endocrinol Metab* 64 (1):27–31. doi: 10.1210/jcem-64-1-27.

Carmichael, M. S., V. L. Warburton, J. Dixen, and J. M. Davidson. 1994. "Relationships among cardiovascular, muscular, and oxytocin responses during human sexual activity." *Arch Sex Behav* 23 (1):59–79. doi: 10.1007/bf01541618.

Carter, C. S. 1992. "Oxytocin and sexual behavior." *Neurosci Biobehav Rev* 16 (2):131–44. doi: 10.1016/s0149-7634(05)80176-9.

Carter, C. S. 1998. "Neuroendocrine perspectives on social attachment and love." *Psychoneuroendocrinology* 23 (8):779–818. doi: 10.1016/s0306-4530(98)00055-9.

Carter, C. S., Kenkel, W. M., MacLean, E. L., Wilson, S. R., Perkeybile, A. M., Yee, J. R., Ferris, C. F., Nazarloo, H. P., Porges, S. W., Davis, J. M., Connelly, J. J., Kingsbury, M. A. 2020. *Pharmacol Rev.* 72 (4):829–61. doi: 10.1124/pr.120.019398

Cassano, G. B., S. Michelini, M. K. Shear, E. Coli, J. D. Maser, and E. Frank. 1997. "The panic-agoraphobic spectrum: a descriptive approach to the assessment and treatment of subtle symptoms." *Am J Psychiatry* 154 (6 Suppl):27–38. doi: 10.1176/ajp.154.6.27.

Changeux, Jean-Pierre. 1985. *L' homme neuronal*. Paris: Fayard.

de Boer, A., E. M. van Buel, and G. J. Ter Horst. 2012. "Love is more than just a kiss: a neurobiological perspective on love and affection." *Neuroscience* 201:114–24. doi: 10.1016/j.neuroscience.2011.11.017.

Derntl, B., and U. Habel. 2011. "Deficits in social cognition: a marker for psychiatric disorders?" *Eur Arch Psychiatry Clin Neurosci* 261 (Suppl 2):S145–9. doi: 10.1007/s00406-011-0244-0.

Enzo, E., P. Politi, M. Bianchi, P. Minoretti, M. Bertona, and D. Geroldi. 2006. "Raised plasma nerve growth factor levels associated with early-stage romantic love." *Psychoneuroendocrinology* 31 (3):288–94. doi: 10.1016/j.psyneuen.2005.09.002.

Fisher, H. E., A. Aron, D. Mashek, H. Li, and L. L. Brown. 2002. "Defining the brain systems of lust, romantic attraction, and attachment." *Arch Sex Behav* 31 (5):413–9. doi: 10.1023/a:1019888024255.

Fisher, H. E., X. Xu, A. Aron, and L. L. Brown. 2016. "Intense, passionate, romantic love: A Natural addiction? How the fields that investigate romance and substance abuse can inform each other." *Front Psychol* 7:687. doi: 10.3389/fpsyg.2016.00687.

Fisher, H. 1992. *Anatomy of love.* New York: Fawcett Columbine.

Forward, S., Buck, C. 1991. *Obsessive love: when passion holds you prisoner.* New York: Bantam Books Inc.

Gillath, O., S. A. Bunge, P. R. Shaver, C. Wendelken, and M. Mikulincer. 2005. "Attachment-style differences in the ability to suppress negative thoughts: exploring the neural correlates." *Neuroimage* 28 (4):835–47. doi: 10.1016/j. neuroimage.2005.06.048.

Grattagliano, I., R. Cassibba, R. Greco, A. Laudisa, A. Torres, and A. Mastromarino. 2012. "Stalking: old behaviour new crime. Reflections on 11 cases assessed in the judicial district of Bari." *Riv Psichiatr* 47 (1):65–72. doi: 10.1708/1034.11293.

Griffin-Shelley, E. 1991. *Sex and love: addiction, treatment and recovery.* New York: Praeger Publisher.

Hart, S. L., and Legerstee, M. 2010. *Handbook of jealousy: theory, research and multidisciplinary approaches.* West Suzzex, UK: Blackwell Publishing.

Heinrichs, M., Baumgartner, T., Kirschbaum, C., and Ehlert, U. 2003. Social support and oxytocin interact to suppress cortisol and subjective responses to psychosocial stress. *Biol. Psychiatry*, 54 (12), 1389–98. doi: 10.1016/s0006-3223(03)00465-7.

Hollander, E. 1993. Obsessive-compulsive spectrum disorders: An overview. *Psychiatric Annals*, 23 (7), 355–8. https://doi.org/10.3928/0048-5713-19930701 -05

Insel, T. R. 1997. "A neurobiological basis of social attachment." *Am J Psychiatry* 154 (6):726–35. doi: 10.1176/ajp.154.6.726.

Insel, T. R. 2003. "Is social attachment an addictive disorder?" *Physiol Behav* 79 (3):351–7. doi: 10.1016/s0031-9384(03)00148-3.

Insel, T. R., and L. J. Young. 2001. "The neurobiology of attachment." *Nat Rev Neurosci* 2 (2):129–36. doi: 10.1038/35053579.

Jankowiak, W. R., and Fischer, E. F. 1998 "A cross-cultural perspective on romantic love." In J. M. Jenkins, K. Oatley, & N. L. Stein (Eds.), *Human emotions: A reader* (pp. 55–62). Blackwell Publishing. (Reprinted from "Ethnology," 31, 1992, pp. 149–55)

Jenike, M. A. 1990. "Illnesses related to obsessive-compulsive disorder." In M. A. Jenike, L. Baer, and W. E. Minichiello (eds.), *Obsessive-compulsive disorders: Theory and management*, 39–60. Chicago: Year Book Medical.

Kane, J. M. 1987. "Treatment of schizophrenia." *Schizophr Bull* 13 (1):133–56. doi: 10.1093/schbul/13.1.133.

Kapur, S. 2003. "Psychosis as a state of aberrant salience: A framework linking biology, phenomenology, and pharmacology in schizophrenia." *Am J Psychiatry* 160 (1):13–23. doi: 10.1176/appi.ajp.160.1.13.

Kessler, R. C., M. B. Keller, and H. U. Wittchen. 2001. "The epidemiology of generalized anxiety disorder." *Psychiatr Clin North Am* 24 (1):19–39. doi: 10.1016/s0193-953x(05)70204-5.

Kirsch, P., Esslinger, C., Chen, Q., Mier, D., Lis, S., Siddhanti, S., Gruppe, H., Mattay, V. S., Gallhofer, B., and Meyer-Lindenberg, A. (2005). "Oxytocin modulates neural circuitry for social cognition and fear in humans." *J Neurosci* 25 (49):11489–93. doi: 10.1523/JNEUROSCI.3984-05.2005.

Klein, M. 1975. *Envy and gratitude.* New York: The Free Press.

Kosfeld, M., M. Heinrichs, P. J. Zak, U. Fischbacher, and E. Fehr. 2005. "Oxytocin increases trust in humans." *Nature* 435 (7042):673–6. doi: 10.1038/nature03701.

Leckman, J. F., L. C. Mayes, R. Feldman, D. W. Evans, R. A. King, and D. J. Cohen. 1999. "Early parental preoccupations and behaviors and their possible relationship to the symptoms of obsessive-compulsive disorder." *Acta Psychiatr Scand Suppl* 396:1–26. doi: 10.1111/j.1600-0447.1999.tb10951.x.

LeDoux, J. E. 2000. "Emotion circuits in the brain." *Annu Rev Neurosci* 23:155–84. doi: 10.1146/annurev.neuro.23.1.155.

LeDoux, J. E., J. Iwata, P. Cicchetti, and D. J. Reis. 1988. "Different projections of the central amygdaloid nucleus mediate autonomic and behavioral correlates of conditioned fear." *J Neurosci* 8 (7):2517–29. doi: 10.1523/jneurosci.08-07-02517.1988.

Lesch, K. P., and R. Mössner. 1998. "Genetically driven variation in serotonin uptake: is there a link to affective spectrum, neurodevelopmental, and neurodegenerative disorders?" *Biol Psychiatry* 44 (3):179–92. doi: 10.1016/s0006-3223(98)00121-8.

Liebowitz M. 1983. *The chemistry of love.* New York: Little Brown.

Marazziti, D. 2009. "Neurobiology and hormonal aspects of romantic relationships." In edited by Michelle de Haan and Megan R. Gunnar (eds.), *Handbook of developmental social neuroscience,* 265–80. New York, NY: Guilford Press.

Marazziti, D. 2015 "Beyond emotion: love as an encounter of myth and drive." by Lubomir Lamy. *Emotion Review,* 97–107. doi: 10.1177/1754073915594437.

Marazziti D. 2018. "La natura Dell'amore." Giovanni Fioriti editore, second edition.

Marazziti, D., Akiskal, H. S., Rossi, A., and Cassano, G. B. 1999 "Alteration of the platelet serotonin transporter in romantic love". *Psychol Med* 29(3):741–5. doi: 10.1017/s0033291798007946.

Marazziti, D., and Cassano, G. E. 2003. "The neurobiology of attraction." *J Endocrinol Invest* 26:58–60.

Marazziti, D., Di Nasso, E., Masala, Baroni, S., Abelli, M., Mengali, F., Mungai, F., and Rucci, P. 2003. "Normal and obsessional jealousy: a study in a population of young adults." *Eur Psychiatry* 18 (3):106–11. doi: 10.1016/s0924-9338(03)00024-5.

Marazziti, D., Rucci, P., Di Nasso, E., Masala, I., Baroni, S., Rossi, A., Giannaccini, G., Mengali, F., and Lucacchini, A. 2003. "Jealousy and subthreshold psychopathology: a serotonergic link." *Neuropsychobiology* 47 (1):12–6. doi: 10.1159/000068869.

Marazziti, D., Canale, D. 2004. "Hormonal changes when falling in love." *Psychoneuroendocrinology* 29 (7):931–6. doi: 10.1016/j.psyneuen.2003.08.006.

Marazziti, D., Bani, A., Casamassima, F., Catena, M., Consoli, G., Gesi, C., Iovieno, N., Massei, J., Muti, M., Ravani, L., Romano, A., Roncaglia, I., and Scarpellini, P. 2006. "Oxytocin: An old hormone for new avenues." *Clinical Neuropsychiatry* 3(5):302–21.

Marazziti, D., Dell'Osso, B., Baroni, S., Mungai, F., Catena, M., Pucci, P., Albanese, F., Giannaccini, G., Betti, L., Fabbrini, L., Italiani, P., Del Debbio, A., Lucacchini, A., & Dell'Osso, L. 2006. "A relationship between oxytocin and anxiety of romantic attachment." *Clin Pract Epidemol Ment Health*, 11(2):28. doi: 10.1186/1745-0179-2-28

Marazziti, D., Catena Dell'osso, M. 2008. "The role of oxytocin in neuropsychiatric disorders." *Curr Med Chem* 15 (7):698–704. doi: 10.2174/092986708783885291

Marazziti, D., Roncaglia, I., Del Debbio, A., Bianchi, C., Massimetti, G., Origlia, N., Domenici, L., Piccinni, A., and Dell'Osso L. 2009. "Brain-derived neurotrophic factor in romantic attachment." *Psychol Med* 39 (11):1927–30. doi: 10.1017/s0033291709990742.

Marazziti, D., Baroni, S., Giannaccini, G., Betti, L., Massimetti, G., Carmassi, C., Catena-Dell'Osso, M. 2012. "A link between oxytocin and serotonin in humans: supporting evidence from peripheral markers." *Eur Neuropsychopharmacol.* 22(8):578–83. doi: 10.1016/j.euroneuro.2011.12.010. Epub 2012 Jan 31.

Marazziti, D., Poletti, M., Dell'Osso, L., Baroni, S., Bonuccelli, U. 2013. "Prefrontal cortex, dopamine, and jealousy endophenotype." *CNS Spectr.*18 (1):6–14. doi: 10.1017/s1092852912000740.

Marazziti, D., Baroni, S., Giannaccini, G., Catena-Dell'Osso, M., Piccinni, A., Massimetti, G., and Dell'Osso, L. 2015. "Plasma oxytocin levels in untreated adult obsessive-compulsive disorder patients." *Neuropsychobiology*, 72(2), 74–80. doi: 10.1159/000438756.

Marazziti, D., Falaschi, V., Lombardi, A., Mungai, F., Dell'Osso, L. 2015. "Stalking: a neurobiological perspective."*Riv Psichiatr* 50 (1):12–8. doi: 10.1708/1794.19528.

Marazziti, D., Baroni, S., Giannaccini, G., Piccinni, A., Mucci, F., Catena-Dell'Osso, M., Rutigliano, G., Massimetti, G., and Dell'Osso, L. 2017. "Decreased lymphocyte dopamine transporter in romantic lovers". *CNS spectr.* 22(3):290–94. doi: 10.1017/S109285291600050X.

Marazziti, D., Baroni, S., Mucci, F., Piccinni, A., Moroni, I., Giannaccini, G., Carmassi, C., Massimetti, E., & Dell'Osso, L. 2019. "Sex-related differences in plasma oxytocin levels in humans." *Clin Pract Epidemiol Ment Health* 15:58–63. doi: 10.2174/1745017901915010058.

Meloy, J. Reid. 1992. *Violent attachments, violent attachments.* Lanham, MD: Jason Aronson.

Meloy, J. Reid. 1998. *The psychology of stalking: Clinical and forensic perspectives*, *The psychology of stalking: Clinical and forensic perspectives*. San Diego, CA: Academic Press.

Meloy, J. R. 1999. "Erotomania, triangulation, and homicide." *J Forensic Sci* 44 (2):421–4.

Meloy, J. R., and H. Fisher. 2005. "Some thoughts on the neurobiology of stalking." *J Forensic Sci* 50 (6):1472–80.

Meyer-Lindenberg, A., A. R. Hariri, K. E. Munoz, C. B. Mervis, V. S. Mattay, C. A. Morris, and K. F. Berman. 2005. "Neural correlates of genetically abnormal social cognition in Williams syndrome." *Nat Neurosci* 8 (8):991–3. doi: 10.1038/nn1494.

Mullen, P. E., and J. Martin. 1994. "Jealousy: a community study." *Br J Psychiatry* 164 (1):35–43. doi: 10.1192/bjp.164.1.35.

Murphy, C. R., and D. M. Dwarte. 1987. "Increase in cholesterol in the apical plasma membrane of uterine epithelial cells during early pregnancy in the rat." *Acta Anat (Basel)* 128 (1):76–9. doi: 10.1159/000146319.

O'Dwyer, A. M., and I. Marks. 2000. "Obsessive-compulsive disorder and delusions revisited." *Br J Psychiatry* 176:281–4. doi: 10.1192/bjp.176.3.281.

Panksepp, Jaak. 1982. "Toward a general psychobiological theory of emotions." *Behav Brain Sci* 5 (3):407–67. doi: 10.1017/S0140525X00012759.

Pitman, R. K., S. P. Orr, and N. B. Lasko. 1993. "Effects of intranasal vasopressin and oxytocin on physiologic responding during personal combat imagery in Vietnam veterans with posttraumatic stress disorder." *Psychiatry Res* 48 (2):107–17. doi: 10.1016/0165-1781(93)90035-f.

Porges, S. W., and S. A. Furman. 2011. "The Early Development of the Autonomic Nervous System Provides a Neural Platform for Social Behavior: A Polyvagal Perspective." *Infant Child Dev* 20 (1):106–18. doi: 10.1002/icd.688.

Prather, M. D., P. Lavenex, M. L. Mauldin-Jourdain, W. A. Mason, J. P. Capitanio, S. P. Mendoza, and D. G. Amaral. 2001. "Increased social fear and decreased fear of objects in monkeys with neonatal amygdala lesions." *Neuroscience* 106 (4):653–8. doi: 10.1016/s0306-4522(01)00445-6.

Price, M., Hides, L., Cockshaw, W., Staneva, A. A., and Stoyanov, S. R. 2016. "Young love: romantic concerns and associated mental health issues among adolescent help-seekers." *Behav Sci* 6 (2):9. doi: 10.3390/bs6020009.

Robbins, T. W., C. M. Gillan, D. G. Smith, S. de Wit, and K. D. Ersche. 2012. "Neurocognitive endophenotypes of impulsivity and compulsivity: towards dimensional psychiatry." *Trends Cogn Sci* 16 (1):81–91. doi: 10.1016/j.tics.2011.11.009.

Roberts, K. A. 2002. "Stalking following the breakup of romantic relationships: characteristics of stalking former partners." *J Forensic Sci* 47 (5):1070–7.

Sasahara, K., Shikimi, H., Haraguchi, S., Sakamoto, H., Honda, S., Harada, N., and Tsutsui, K. 2007. Mode of action and functional significance of estrogen-inducing dendritic growth, spinogenesis, and synaptogenesis in the developing Purkinje cell. *J Neurosci.* 27(28), 7408–17. doi: 10.1523/JNEUROSCI.0710-07.2007.

Silva, J. A., D. V. Derecho, G. B. Leong, and M. M. Ferrari. 2000. "Stalking behavior in delusional jealousy." *J Forensic Sci* 45 (1):77–82.

Song, H., Z. Zou, J. Kou, Y. Liu, L. Yang, A. Zilverstand, F. d'Oleire Uquillas, and X. Zhang. 2015. "Love-related changes in the brain: a resting-state functional magnetic resonance imaging study." *Front Hum Neurosci* 9:71. doi: 10.3389/fnhum.2015.00071.

Takahashi, H., M. Matsuura, N. Yahata, M. Koeda, T. Suhara, and Y. Okubo. 2006. "Men and women show distinct brain activations during imagery of sexual and emotional infidelity." *Neuroimage* 32 (3):1299–307. doi: 10.1016/j.neuroimage.2006.05.049.

Turner, R. A., M. Altemus, D. N. Yip, E. Kupferman, D. Fletcher, A. Bostrom, D. M. Lyons, and J. A. Amico. 2002. "Effects of emotion on oxytocin, prolactin, and ACTH in women." *Stress* 5 (4):269–76. doi: 10.1080/1025389021000037586-1.

Uvnäs-Moberg, K. 1997. "Oxytocin linked antistress effects--the relaxation and growth response." *Acta Physiol Scand Suppl* 640:38–42.

Uvnäs-Moberg, K. 1998. "Oxytocin may mediate the benefits of positive social interaction and emotions." *Psychoneuroendocrinology* 23 (8):819–35. doi: 10.1016/s0306-4530(98)00056-0.

Uvnäs-Moberg, K., I. Arn, T. Theorell, and C. O. Jonsson. 1991. "Personality traits in a group of individuals with functional disorders of the gastrointestinal tract and their correlation with gastrin, somatostatin and oxytocin levels." *J Psychosom Res* 35 (4–5):515–23. doi: 10.1016/0022-3999(91)90046-q.

Young, L. J. 2002. "The neurobiology of social recognition, approach, and avoidance." *Biol Psychiatry* 51 (1):18–26. doi: 10.1016/s0006-3223(01)01268-9.

Young, L. J., M. M. Lim, B. Gingrich, and T. R. Insel. 2001. "Cellular mechanisms of social attachment." *Horm Behav* 40 (2):133–8. doi: 10.1006/hbeh.2001.1691.

Young, L. J., and Z. Wang. 2004. "The neurobiology of pair bonding." *Nat Neurosci* 7 (10):1048–54. doi: 10.1038/nn1327.

Chapter 3

The Good and Bad of Love and Hate

Katherine Aumer and Michael A. Erickson

Love is all you need

—The Beatles

One word frees us of all the weight and pain in life.
That word is love.

—Sophocles

Hate, it has caused a lot of problems in this world,
but it has not solved one yet.

—Maya Angelou

Hate is too great a burden to bear. It injures the
hater more than it injures the hated.

—Coretta Scott King

Sentiments regarding the utility of love and the futility of hate have been
expressed in songs, speeches, plays, and books from historical to modern
times. The truth of these ideas seems unquestionable given the longevity and
consistency of these messages: hate is bad, and love is good. Even scholars
of emotion seem to resonate with this message categorizing hate as a destructive emotion (Royzman, McCauley, & Rozin 2005) and humanity's "biggest handicap as a social species" (Oatley, Keltner, & Jenkins 2006: p. 44),
whereas love is promoted as an emotion of utmost importance for the growth,
well-being, and functioning of humanity (Erikson 1963; Maslow 1954; Rogers
1961). It appears that the premise of love's goodness and hate's badness is,
at least historically, confirmed. Any suggestion to the contrary might be seen
as naive or even nefarious. What good could come from examining emotions

without the presumptions of their moral character? Why ignore years of historical evidence and rhetorical statements that have solidified the nature and consequences of love and hate? After all, the destructive nature of hate and the creative beauty of love seem self-evident. What possible insights and information could be gleaned from a systematic reexamination of love and hate?

Although the quotes cited above make a clear case that humanity should maintain love and eradicate hate, that does not seem to be easily achievable. People seem to find it difficult to find ways to love exclusively without feeling hate. Racism, sexism, and prejudice are burgeoning. People still struggle to cultivate love. Maybe it is just a part of the human experience to be in constant struggle with these two emotions, that humanity will never have only love without hate. These omnipresent messages lauding love and disparaging hate are, possibly, intended to remind people which path to take. However, it could also be that valuable information about love and hate is missing in a philosophy that only endorses the former and condemns the latter. By reviewing the academic literature on love and hate, we provide an analysis of both their positive and negative qualities with the goal of understanding their utility better and filling in these missing pieces. Both love and hate shape and distort perceptions and motivate people to actions that aid survival (Neese, 1990). This overview will help provide a more balanced analysis of these emotions to bring awareness of people's emotional capacity and control.

THE GOOD AND BAD OF LOVE

The study of love from philosophical (Plato and Aristotle), psychoanalytic (Freud), and humanistic (Jung) perspectives has a long history. Contemporary science has classified love in a variety of ways. The first quantitative analysis of love began in sociology and targeted romantic love via the "Belief Pattern Scale for Measuring Attitudes toward Romanticism" (Gross 1944). This scale was intended to measure American attitudes exclusively toward romantic love. Swensen (1961) introduced "The Scale of Feelings and Behavior of Love" that helped identify the thoughts and behaviors husbands and wives had toward each other, limiting the measure of love to romantic love in heterosexual marriages. Rubin (1970) created another love scale to measure the love experienced by "unmarried opposite-sex peers, of the sort which could possibly lead to marriage" (p. 266).

Subsequently, Hatfield and Walster (1978) identified two types of romantic love: passionate and companionate. Passionate love is an intense emotional state of longing for union with another whereas companionate love is a calmer emotion of friendly affection and deep attachment (Hatfield & Walster 1978). It was not until Hatfield and Sprecher (1986, 1990) constructed the

"Passionate Love Scale," however, that the study of romantic love became commonplace and could be applied to a variety of ages (Hatfield et al., 1988), ethnic groups (Easton 1985), and relationship statuses (Hatfield et al. 1984; Traupman & Hatfield 1981). The creation of the Passionate Love Scale (PLS) allowed people to report their phenomenological experience of passionate love in a relatively anonymous and quantifiable manner. Further studies would utilize this scale to enable psychologists to identify neural correlates of passionate love, specifically foci in the medial insula, the anterior cingulate cortex, the caudate nucleus, and the putamen (Bartels & Zeki 2000, 2004; Fisher, Aron, and Brown 2005). Additionally, this research drew attention to the similarity of the patterns of neural activation in passionate love and in sexual desire, providing evidence that love, at least passionate love, was intrinsically rewarding and positive. Further, establishing neurological evidence of passionate love was an important step in providing a material basis for an emotion that had often been characterized as ephemeral. However, these efforts could be conceived of as reductionistic. Additionally, not all love is passionate love. Many romantic relationships exist in which passionate love never existed or has fizzled away. Moreover, love is not confined just to romantic relationships. Love exists in a variety of relationships, and the love one has with one's parents, friends, or children is not the same love one has with a romantic partner.

The study of other types of love was springboarded by Lee's (1976) "Love Styles." Using Latin words and a color wheel, Lee theorized three primary (eros, ludos, and storge), three secondary (mania, pragma, and agape), and nine tertiary love styles (a combination of one primary and one secondary). Hendrick and Hendrick (1986) constructed the "Love Attitudes Scale" to explore and measure these different love styles. The love measured in the "Love Attitudes Scale" was an attempt to understand the components and shared features of different types of love better. Similarly, Sternberg's (1986) "Triangular Theory of Love" attempted to identify different types of love by measuring their components: passion, intimacy, and commitment. From these three components, Sternberg identified eight potential types of love.

Berscheid's (1986, 2010) work helped refine the study of love rather than just subdivide it. She identified four love taxa or types: attachment, compassionate, companionate, and romantic (Berscheid 2010). Within her framework, each love has different elicitors and is accompanied by a different temporal profile. Attachment love, which extends from the work of attachment styles, is characterized as a "strong affectional bond" (Bowlby 1977: p. 115) toward a person and can be seen in both children and adults (Harlow 1958; Bowlby 1977). This is the kind of love observed when a person under stress runs to a loved one for safety and security. However, adult attachment love is not the same as romantic love (e.g., Acevedo & Aron 2009; Shaver et al. 1988).

Compassionate love is a selfless all-giving love, sometimes characterized as charitable love or agape (Hendrick & Hendrick 1986). This type of love can be seen in a variety of relationships: friendship, romantic, parental, and communal in which there is no expectation of or demand for reciprocation.

Companionate love is "a comfortable, affectionate, trusting love for a likable partner, based on a deep sense of friendship and involving companionship and the enjoyment of common activities, mutual interests, and shared laughter" (Grote & Frieze 1994: p. 275). Companionate love, like compassionate love, can be observed in a variety of relationships whereas romantic love is specifically love in a romantic relationship. As described previously, according to Hatfield (1988), romantic love can be either passionate love or companionate love. Berscheid (2010), however, argues that romantic love is the combination of both passionate and companionate love. This conceptualization of romantic love as the combination of passionate and companionate love is a product of cultural changes in society (see Hatfield & Rapson, 2002). This does not mean, though, that the two do not exist independently. Instead, it may merely mean that under current standards, most people see that love in their romantic relationships should involve both passion and companionship. For the purposes of this chapter and going forward with this section, we treat passionate love, or an intense longing for union with another individual, as a separate type of love found only in romantic relationships. A variety of scales have been developed to measure these four types of love and have enabled researchers to identify correlations between them and other important psychological variables. Although the psychometric analysis of love is not without issue, the development of these measures has vastly improved the empirical study of love.

Before measures of love were developed, most psychologists discussed the importance of love within the framework of clinical psychology. Maslow (1954) discussed the motivation for affection-and-love relations as the third level of the hierarchy of needs. Love, for Maslow (1943, 1954), is a need that typically arises after physiological and safety needs are met, and if the love need is met, then the possibility of meeting other needs like esteem and self-actualization are possible. Essentially, for Maslow (1943, 1954), love is so important and positive because its fulfillment allows a person to become self-fulfilled and to reach their full potential. Additionally, for those who have reached their self-actualization (the last motivation), the love they are able to give is more empathetic and satisfying (Maslow 1953). Much of Maslow's work, which was based on biographical analysis and speculation, has been criticized for its lack of empirical evidence (McLeod 2020). Nevertheless, his work has found some support.

Before discussing some of this support, it is important to note that the evidence for the benefits or "good" of love is grounded in its reciprocation. Additionally, the benefits and detriments of love are typically discussed in the context of a relationship. Unrequited love is painful and can be considered a negative consequence of love. Even within a relationship, however, many negative aspects of love can still arise. Although songs, poems, and truisms highlight the benefits of love in the absence of context, it is important to recognize that empirical evidence for both the benefits and costs of love always occur within a context of a relationship. Whether or not love—or any emotion—could be studied in isolation of a relationship or context is in need of empirical investigation.

Attachment Love

Attachment or attachment love is considered a normal part of a healthy adult life (Bowlby 1977). Beginning in childhood, attachment love grows and typically revolves around parents (Ainsworth 1989), and over time, starting around college years, young adults begin to shift their targets of attachment love to best friends and romantic partners (Fraley & Davis 1997). Depending on the qualities of the attachment figure, different "styles" of attachment can develop: secure or insecure (avoidant and anxious/ambivalent) (Ainsworth et al. 1978/2015). Later research has further divided the insecure attachment styles as avoidant/dismissive, avoidant/fearful, and anxious/ambivalent (Bartholomew & Horowitz 1991). Additions to the insecure attachment styles have been identified; however, the main conclusion from most research is that those with secure attachment styles tend to lead happier and healthier lives than those with insecure attachment styles.

Secure attachment is considered to be the hallmark of a healthy love relationship. Children and adults who develop secure attachment styles tend to see their relationships as safe and see themselves as able to fully explore and be productive. The connection between styles of attachment and adult love were discovered by Hazan and Shaver (1987) who found that the styles of attachment could also be found in adult romantic relationships. Studies reveal that the majority of adults as well as children exhibit secure attachment styles (~59%) while the remaining adults and children usually exhibit insecure attachment styles, split between avoidant (~25%) and anxious (~10%) (Brennen et al. 1991; Hazan & Shaver 1987; Mickelson, Kessler, & Shaver 1997; Shaver & Hazan 1993). Hazan and Shaver (1987) found that those who classified their romantic relationships as secure tended to report more happiness, friendship, and trust in their romantic relationship than those who identified their romantic relationships to be avoidant or anxious/ambivalent. Additionally, those with secure attachment styles tended to think of themselves as being liked more and tended to think of the people around them as more trustworthy and well-intentioned than those with insecure attachment styles did.

Further research has confirmed that those with secure attachment styles tend to be more satisfied and have more trust, commitment, and interdependence in their relationships than those with insecure attachment styles (Collins & Read 1990; Kirkpatrick & Davis 1994; Simpson 1990). When looking at this research, it becomes clear that attachment styles and the attachment system are being treated as proxies for attachment love. When one considers that attachment styles and the attachment system are all measuring the quality of the relationship one has with someone, it is not surprising to see that certain attachment styles like "secure" are related to better relationship outcomes. All psychometric approaches to measuring love have the issue of including the elements that not only measure the construct of interest (e.g., attachment or passionate love) but also measure the outcomes that those constructs should be predicting.

Another way to demonstrate the benefits of attachment love is to consider the relationship between having and not having attachment love outside of a romantic relationship. Given Bowlby's claim (e.g., 1977: p. 115) that attachment with a familiar person creates a sense of safety and security, an attachment figure who is able to provide an individual with the necessary security and safety should fulfill the need for attachment love. Security and safety in attachment love encompass the overall feeling of having someone one can count on to go to in times of need and to seek to be with. Researchers have classified such people as having secure attachment. It would then follow that people without attachment love or who have insecure attachment styles may have less favorable outcomes when dealing with stress or possible threats to their own safety. Those with insecure attachment styles tend to be more likely to experience substance abuse disorders (Senchak & Leonard 1992) and depression (Hazan & Shaver 1990; Pettem et al. 1993; Zuroff & Fitzpatrick 1995). Mickelson and colleagues (1997) found that those with insecure attachment styles were more likely to exhibit personality disorders and other psychopathology. Thus, the benefits of attachment love seem more evident in its absence: those with insecure attachment styles also seem to have trouble coping with stressors, and this may result in issues like substance abuse or psychopathology. Given that no experiment could be done capably or ethically, by removing or inserting love into a situation, it would be prudent to refrain from drawing causal relationships between the presence/absence of any love and an outcome. After all, it could be that those who are more inclined to exhibit mental disorders are less likely to establish attachment. However, it would be safe to conclude that the presence of attachment love is related to benefits in one's relationship and mental health.

That being said, there are aspects of attachment love that are associated with bad outcomes, even if that attachment is relatively secure. Weiss (1975) found in couples who divorce, even after passionate love and liking of the partner has fled the relationship, that the attachment to the partner may still persist. People who find their ex-spouse neglectful, hurtful, or even abusive, may still find themselves inexplicably drawn to seek their ex-spouse or be with them out of attachment love. Because attachment love is indicated by seeking safety and support, especially during stressful events, it is understandable that many people may find themselves drawn to an ex-spouse, especially during a stressful time like a divorce. This seeking of ex-spouses or even current spouses who are neglectful and abusive for safety and comfort can be a very bad aspect of attachment love. It may contribute to the inability for many spouses to leave horrible and physically abusive relationships. Sullivan and Lasley (2010) have shown that children and abuse victims will often cling to and defend their abusers despite having opportunities to leave. According to the CDC (2020a), one in four women and one in ten men have experienced a form of intimate partner violence. Over half of female homicide victims have been killed by someone they loved or were in an intimate relationship with (Petrosky et al. 2017). Additionally, one in seven children have experienced some form of child abuse and neglect (CDC 2020b). Given the research and the rates, it appears that attachment love may contribute to many negative aspects of intimate relationships. Although there are many reasons (e.g., financial, situational, and fear of retaliation as cited by Anderson et al. 2003 and Craven 1997) why it is difficult to leave an abusive spouse or parent, the mechanisms of attachment love may make it difficult for some people to leave a person even if that person is causing them significant harm and damage. Attachment love is intended to provide a sense of safety and comfort with someone in one's environment. Despite clear evidence that an abuser is not providing the necessary safety and comfort one would expect from having cultivated attachment love with them, the feeling may persist and be difficult to overcome, preventing one from doing what is necessary to actually be safe and comfortable.

Finally, the research concerning attachment love often focuses on the one receiving the attachment love and rarely on the person who is the source or provider of attachment love. Caregivers and mothers who are often the sources of attachment love are typically less valued and penalized financially than those who do not have caregiving or parental responsibilities (Andersen 2018; England et al. 2016; Kmec 2011). Additionally, given that attachment love was argued to be fundamental to the future of a child's life and welfare puts considerable pressure and emotional demand on caregivers and mothers even today in many Western societies that still perceive mothers to be fundamental to a child's well-being (Vicedo 2011). Caregivers typically experience many negative consequences from the demands of being the primary provider of love, support, and comfort including stress, anxiety, burnout, and lack of socialization (Rahnama et al. 2017). The lack of focus and research on the negative consequences of being attachment figures is unfortunate given the large focus on and research emphasizing the importance of attachment love in the development of healthy relationships. This dearth of information may stem from the stereotypes and assumptions associated with motherhood and caregivers—that being secure and comforting safety figures should just come *naturally*, be uncompensated, and a reward in and of itself. If we are to be more objective in our analyses of emotions, the negative aspects of attachment love for both recipient and source should be further investigated.

Compassionate Love

Compassionate love is sometimes seen as similar to attachment love. Both are providing for the "care" of an individual, but there are some key differences. Hendrick and Hendrick (1986) identify compassionate love as selfless and giving love. This type of love has been characterized as "agape" in Lee's (1976) colors of love; it is also sometimes referred to as "altruistic love," as it centers on the good of the other. Underwood (2009) provides some distinct aspects of compassionate love that are not part of certain other forms of love. We focus on two of these here: (1) the free choice of the giver and (2) the accurate understanding of the needs of the recipient. In the first aspect of compassionate love, the person freely chooses to love the recipient. Unlike parental attachment love where there might be a drive or automatic need to love the child or in passionate love where one might feel a magnetic draw for the target of one's love, compassionate love is much more freely chosen. The giver of compassionate love decides often deliberately, to provide the recipient with compassionate love. Some may argue that this is a form of "support" or "care"; however, support and care can often be given without any emotional feeling, as a form of reciprocation or obligation, toward a person that may even be pitied. However, compassionate love, as Underwood (2009) describes, is inspired, and involves an investment of the heart toward a person who is valued and not necessarily pitied.

In the second aspect of compassionate love, the giver of compassionate love often has an accurate understanding of the needs of the recipient. It could be that the giver of compassionate love understands that the recipient needs patience, acceptance, generosity, or sacrifice. Whatever it is that the recipient of compassionate love needs, the giver of compassionate love accurately understands and freely gives. Unlike the other loves, compassionate love can be given regardless of the kind of love relationship: family members, friends, strangers, the whole of humanity, and so on. Fehr and Sprecher (2009) did find that participants gave higher ratings of compassionate love toward close family members and friends than strangers. They also found that compassionate love was given more freely to family members and friends. However, they showed both theoretically and empirically, the ability to show compassionate love to anyone.

The benefits of compassionate love are numerous. If one were to only imagine being the recipient of compassionate love, freely given and accurate care, one could experience increased happiness, relief, and/or satisfaction. Although the empirically documented benefits of compassionate love are rather scant, the budding literature has demonstrated that there are significant benefits from both giving and receiving compassionate love. Reis, Maniaci, and Rogge (2014) found that expressions of compassionate love between newlywed couples was a significant predictor of marital satisfaction even after controlling for the frequency of daily positive and negative interactions. In older married couples, Sabey, Rauer, and Jensen (2014) found that compassionate love mediated the relationship between sanctification of marriage and relationship satisfaction. Additionally, Neto and Wilks (2017) found that compassionate love for a significant other was positively related to subjective well-being across the adult life span.

These studies seem to indicate that there are significant benefits in being either the recipient or giver of compassionate love in a romantic relationship. Miller et al. (2015) found that compassionate love in parent–child relationships served as a buffer for many mothers when their children presented challenges. Mothers high in sympathetic dominance who were able to express compassionate love showed less negative and harsh parenting behaviors and more warmth toward their children than similar mothers with low compassionate love. In college-aged students, Sprecher and Fehr (2006) found increases in self-esteem, positive mood, self-awareness, and spirituality for both the recipient and receiver of compassionate love. Interestingly, the benefits of self-esteem, positive mood, and self-awareness were greater for the *recipients* of compassionate love than the givers (Sprecher & Fehr 2006). Additionally, the intensity of the experience of compassionate love (either as recipient or giver) was rated as higher in an established relationship than in an interaction with a stranger. Although Sprecher and Fehr's (2006) study may support the idea that "receiving" may be slightly better than "giving" compassionate love and that relational context matters, Ironson, Kremer, and Lucette (2018) found that being the *giver* of compassionate love was associated with a longer lifespan for those with HIV and that the type of relationship was not a significant predictor. All these studies demonstrate that compassionate love may be a beneficial emotion associated with increased marital and relationship satisfaction, warm parenting, positive sense of self, self-reflection, and longer lifespan.

Importantly, all these studies suggest that *both* giving and receiving compassionate love is beneficial. Given all the benefits of compassionate love, it is not surprising to see that many researchers suggest that compassionate love be more consciously and explicitly encouraged in a variety of relationships and settings. Van Dierendonck and Patterson (2015) have created a very compelling argument to utilize compassionate love in leadership of corporations and businesses, promoting the idea of servant leadership as a more responsible and community-centered approach to managing companies. In the medical industry, there is already evidence that compassionate love may protect nurses from burnout (Mersin et al. 2020) and that compassionate love (sometimes referred to as compassionate care) is an essential and moral dimension of nursing (Von Dietze & Orb 2000).

That being said, genuine compassionate love must be freely given. If one were to receive the same benefits of compassionate love on contingency or with certain strings attached, this would not be considered compassionate love, but more of a business transaction. Professions that attempt to employ compassionate love are essentially requiring emotional labor. Emotional labor is a more frequent requirement for service-related "people jobs" that entail interactions with customers or clients (e.g., nurses, restaurant servers, flight attendants, customer service, sales) and less likely to be encountered by certain "non-people" professions (e.g., construction workers, farmers, clerical staff). Because the empirical study of compassionate love is still in its infancy, any discussion of the negative or "bad" aspects of compassionate love must be theoretical.

Theoretically, the expression of compassionate love as part of one's employment may have several drawbacks. First, many who might naturally desire to give compassionate love and who become employed in giving it could fall prey to the overjustification effect (Deci, Koetsner, & Ryan 1999). With overjustification, the intrinsic motivation of loving for the sake of loving is replaced by the extrinsic motivation of loving for the sake of getting paid, thereby causing the compassionate love to lose its authenticity and possible benefits. Another theoretical drawback to employing compassionate love as emotional labor is burnout. Hochschild (1983) predicted that those professions that employ emotional labor in which the employees perform more surface-level acting of their positive emotions as opposed to sincere deep acting may be more likely to experience guilt and dissatisfaction with work. Other research has found support for these conclusions, suggesting that only those employees who express emotions sincerely and who do "people jobs" may be likely to actually benefit from the emotions they are expressing (e.g., Ashforth & Humphrey 1993; Brotheridge & Grandey 2002). If one were to employ compassionate love as a form of emotional labor, it would be important to ensure that the love they are feeling is actually sincere.

A more distressing yet theoretically "bad" aspect of compassionate love is exploitation. Although the above literature concerning the benefits of compassionate love did not find evidence of exploitation, they also did not specifically investigate this possibility. Compassionate love has many benefits for both the giver and the receiver; however, much of the research on compassionate love supposes that the intentions and motivations behind those giving and receiving the love are fair and considerate. The existence of inequity and exploitation is not uncommon in human behavior (Donnerstein & Hatfield 1982; Sprecher 1986; Utne et al. 1984). There are a variety of people who might take advantage of those who are so freely able to give compassionate love: those with personality disorders (e.g., dependent, narcissistic, borderline, histrionic, and antisocial), those who are just being opportunistic, and those with personality traits that are more sinister like the dark triad (Paulhus & Williams 2002; Jonason et al. 2009). It could be that even in these situations in which one is freely giving compassionate love to someone high in narcissism, Machiavellianism, and psychopathy, that both the giver and receiver are able to reap benefits and improve their positive mood and self-awareness. However, that research has not yet been done. Until then, it remains unclear whether compassionate love is always good. There may be more costs: relational, material, and financial that could result from providing compassionate love to those who may not fully appreciate or reciprocate. Given that one of the components of compassionate love is that it is "freely given," it may be safe to proceed with giving that love thoughtfully and carefully depending on the person and circumstances.

Passionate and Companionate Love

As described previously, romantic love has been found to be of two types: passionate and companionate. Considering the joint history of the study of passionate and companionate love and to avoid repetition, we discuss the good and bad of both emotions together. Much of the research concerning passionate and companionate love targets both emotions simultaneously. Passionate love embodies sexual desire, attraction, and longing for the romantic partner. Companionate love is a friendship-like love characterized as the "affection and tenderness we feel for those whom our lives are deeply entwined" (Hatfield & Rapson 1993: p. 9). Unlike compassionate love, which is not dependent on any current or future relationship, and which is given accurately and freely, passionate and companionate love are contingent upon a current or future relationship with expectations of reciprocation. In attachment love, there are delineated roles: one is the provider of protection, comfort, and security and the other is the receiver. These roles may change from day to day or moment to moment depending on the needs of the people within the relationship. Passionate and companionate love is predicated on the similarity of the people's roles in the relationship: both are trying to achieve similar objectives of desire and intimacy. Most of the research on passionate and companionate love focuses on couples (see Masuda 2003, for a meta-analysis). In the context of a romantic relationship, Hatfield and Walster (1978) have characterized passionate love as a "fragile flower" and companionate love as a "sturdy evergreen" (p. 125). Some stage theorists and laypersons have developed theories about how the two types of love work as the romantic relationship develops. It is theorized that at the beginning of a romantic relationship, passionate love is strong, while companionate love is just beginning. As time progresses, the passionate love begins to "wilt" or wane and the companionate love grows stronger (Cimbalo, Failing, & Mousaw 1976; Coleman 1977; Driscoll et al. 1972; Goldstine et al. 1977). However, studies do not always confirm this. Sprecher and Regan (1998) found that although passionate love tends to fade over time, companionate love remains unchanged. More recent studies have shown that both passionate and companionate love are strong at the beginning of the relationship (Hatfield et al. 2008; Regan, Lakhanpal, & Anguiano 2012), and that generally, both passionate and companionate love fade as the relationship progresses (Hatfield et al. 2008; Karney & Bradbury 1995; Tucker & Aron 1993; Sprecher 1999). That is not to say that all long-term relationships are doomed to have fading love, as some research has shown that it is possible for some couples in long-term relationships to have strong passionate love after many years (Acevedo et al. 2012). Thus, evidence suggests that both types of love are possible throughout the entire relationship even though both typically fade or are reported less over time. Additionally, as the expectations of relationships change, through either cultural shifts in the standards of relationships or changes in gender role expectations, the timeline of passionate and companionate love may look very different in the future. That being said, what are the benefits or the "good" of passionate and companionate love?

One may argue that both passionate and companionate love are good for their own sake. Having great passion for someone, as with passionate love is an ecstatic and joyful experience sometimes characterized as a "natural high" (Fisher et al. 2005; 2016). Similarly, having companionate love for someone, whom one can share values with, be intimate with, and be committed to, may be comforting and beneficial in and of itself (Hatfield & Rapson 1996; Hendrick & Hendrick 1986). Passionate love seems especially predictive of a happy and fulfilling romantic relationship. Several studies have found a strong consistent positive correlation between passionate love and relationship satisfaction (Masuda 2003). This is not too surprising considering that the ideal romantic relationship is often characterized in popular media as passionate and intense. Interestingly, although companionate love has not been found to be a consistent predictor of relationship satisfaction (Masuda 2003), it has been found to be positively related to life satisfaction in general (Kim & Hatfield 2004). As described previously, however, a difficulty with understanding the benefits of love is the high degree of similarity between these measures. Traupman, Eckels, and Hatfield (1982) created a model of love, life satisfaction, and relationship satisfaction based on a sample of older women, but this work has not been replicated or generalized. Some may argue that passionate and companionate love have intrinsic utility and that they are important, even essential, to helping the species bond and propagate. However, it is possible to have marriage, family, and offspring without passionate and companionate love, and for many centuries it has been done. It has only been within the past two centuries that love has been viewed as an essential requirement for marriage, family, and the bearing of offspring (Coontz 2005; Kephart 1967). Currently, many would not willingly choose such an arrangement (Sprecher et al. 1994), so the utility of passionate and companionate love may have increased over time as the culture has changed. What may be the most convincing evidence of love's benefits is that there are no psychological studies attempting to "banish" or "rid" the world of passionate or companionate love. There seems to be universal agreement that love is a beneficial emotion for the positive feelings (Kim & Hatfield 2004), companionship, and happiness it brings into people's lives.

However, that does not mean there are no downsides or "bads" of passionate and companionate love. It may be very easy for some to fall in love: to find someone that one wants to connect with, commit to, and care for. However, finding someone who also feels similarly—who reciprocates those feelings—is not as easy. Unrequited love is painful. Studies have shown that the pain of social rejection and heartbreak is similar to that of actual physical pain (Eisenberger & Lieberman 2004; 2005). Broken hearts may be more complicated, however, and that may be why some prefer to have a broken arm rather than a broken heart (e.g., Christie Brinkley as quoted by Oldenburg 2010). Studies have helped to illuminate these complicated issues. In unrequited love, there are two parties: the rejector and the would-be lover. (Broken arms do not require another party or person.) Baumeister and colleagues (1993) have shown that both parties find the experience to be negative with would-be lovers experiencing more humiliation and dips in their self-esteem, while rejectors experience more guilt, anger, and annoyance. Overall, the experience of passionate and companionate love, when it is not reciprocated, seems to be negative for all involved. Additionally, much of the research from Baumeister and colleagues (1993; 1994) was done using undergraduate students as participants. After a relationship deteriorates from many years of unreciprocated passionate and companionate love, the experience of loss is akin to significant grief (Najib et al. 2004). This grief also does not encompass the greater ramifications of relationship loss that can accompany the loss of passionate and companionate love, such as financial, social, and emotional loss.

Passionate love should also be considered within the context of individual differences, culture, and circumstances. People love differently depending on these factors, and this should be taken into account. Paris loved Helen of Troy very differently than all her other lovers and admirers. Much of that may have had to do with who Paris was, the culture of Troy, and his position of power (or lack thereof, as well as the influence of the goddesses; Hamilton 2017). That being said, his love for her and his subsequent actions to achieve this love sparked a war. The damage and loss of life were tremendous notwithstanding that his actions were inspired by love. The tale of Helen and Paris is not unique. Tales of the ruins of passionate love can be found in a variety of stories. Shakespeare's popular *Romeo and Juliet* ended in numerous, albeit fictitious, murders. Chikamatsu Monzaemon's *The Love Suicides at Sonezaki* was similarly popular and inspired actual suicides (Hoffman 2018). One may even argue that the literary convention of the "marriage plot" where passionately loving couples eventually disengage with the outside world to focus on each other and domestic bliss is a form of tragedy, a kind of modeling of love for the middle classes that provides unrealistic expectations and fantasy (Shaffer 1994). Considering that most marriages are likely based on love and that 40–50 percent of these marriages end in divorce (Amato 2010), or worse, domestic abuse or death (CDC 2020a), one may argue that the utility of passionate and companionate love is accompanied by substantial disutility.

Finally, it is important to mention the controllability of passionate love when one considers whether love is "good" or "bad." Unlike the other loves, passionate love has an element of uncontrollability and impulse as when one says, "Love at first sight." The ethical or moral considerations of passionate love also depend on the standards of the culture and time. This becomes most evident when one considers the target of one's passionate love. For example, most cultures find passionate love between consenting adult heterosexuals acceptable. However, the acceptability of passionate love between consenting adult homosexual partners has changed over time (Paglia 1990). The ethical considerations of passionate love challenge conventional norms when one considers that some cultures have accepted passionate love and marriage between an adult and a minor (Parsons et al. 2015). Serious legal and ethical questions about passionate love are raised when that passionate love is targeted at those that are viewed as culturally or ethically unacceptable. For example, toward a biological relative, a child, an animal that is not of one's species, or toward a thing that is not or is no longer alive. Depending on the behavior and possible "relationship," some may consider this kind of passionate love to be a minor violation of a cultural taboo (e.g., when a young person falls in love with their cousin), while in some cases, some may consider the behavior to be an extreme legal and ethical violation (e.g., when an adult seeks to marry or have sexual relations with a minor). Some may argue that these desires have nothing to do with passionate love, that these types of behaviors or feelings are something else, like a clinical disorder or disease. However, clinical disorders are also dependent on the prevailing attitudes of the time. The Diagnostic and Statistical Manual (DSM) by the American Psychiatric Association (APA) historically defines and provides the standards of psychological clinical disorders in the United States. Previously, the APA categorized homosexuality as a disorder in the DSM II until 1973 when it was removed with the introduction of the DSM III (Drescher 2015). Some may still argue that these desires are paraphilias that should not be conflated or even compared to passionate love.

However, there are those who would argue that the construction of paraphilias is similarly dependent on time and culture and creates opportunities for bias and pathologization of emotions (Moser & Kleinplatz 2020). Much of the "bad" that can be said about passionate love may stem not just from the standards of culture and time or its reciprocation or consequence, but from its controllability. Unlike other loves, passionate love is specifically seen to be less controllable, although some may view passionate love as a deliberate choice. That being said, when one says they have "fallen in love," it is typically a reference to passionate love, and it is rarely seen as a choice. After all, rarely do people purposefully "fall." However, viewing passionate love as controllable can influence the moral judgment of passionate love especially when it is given or targeted to certain individuals or objects. The issue of whether or not a condition or feeling is controllable is often a defining factor in its morality, with more controllable conditions and feelings being viewed as immoral when exhibited freely (Corrigan et al. 2002; Weiner Perry, & Magnusson et al. 2008). In modern Western cultures, if one were to "fall in love" with someone who is unable to give consent, this would be likely seen as bad. However, this may be truer for those who view love as controllable. Even if no action were directed toward that target, many may regard just the presence of the feeling to be improper. Therefore, whether one sees passionate love as controllable may contribute to one's view of this kind of love as a "good" or a "bad" thing.

To better understand the usefulness and purpose of love, objective studies must be done without assumption that one form of love is better than another or one is a disorder while the other is a form of grace. We propose using a signal detection theory framework (SDT; Green & Swets 1966) to help maintain a level of objectivity while studying both love and hate. Later, we discuss more of the usefulness of SDT when it comes to understanding hate. A key feature in SDT is that signals are ambiguous. The receiver typically cannot discern with 100 percent accuracy whether or not an event is a "signal" or just "noise." In the same way, one cannot know with certainty whether loving another will be beneficial (analogous to signal) or not (analogous to noise). Using SDT, there are two ways to be correct, and two ways to make an error. One kind of error is a "false alarm." This would be loving someone who is damaging or harmful in some way. The other kind of error is a "miss." This would be failing to love someone who would be beneficial or helpful to love. The two ways to be correct are a "hit," loving someone who is beneficial, and a "correct rejection," not loving someone who would have been damaging or harmful. Applying SDT to the study of love and hate involves two levels: (1) should/deserves to be loved and (2) actually loved. Just as with SDT, the objective truth is not known or not knowable. Predictions about the beneficence of relationships are notoriously inaccurate. The use of SDT may be especially helpful for emotions that specifically involve and target other people and objects. Unlike some emotions, love and hate are specifically felt in the context of relationships. SDT can help clarify consequences and outcomes of both emotions because SDT considers both the target of the emotion as well as the person experiencing the emotion. The SDT model can clarify not only the phenomenological experience of each emotion but also the subsequent ramifications. No theoretical approach to emotions will achieve perfect objectivity, nor is it without controversy. There is still the issue of defining who "should" and who "should not" be loved or hated. However, having an SDT framework as outlined below helps situate the approach one can take to examine love and hate. The following section discusses the good and bad of hate and uses the SDT model to help understand how a better understanding of hate can be achieved by using SDT.

THE GOOD AND BAD OF HATE

Unlike love, the study of hate is much more recent, and its scales have not been well established. Sternberg (2003) proposed the "Duplex Theory of Hate" that provided a hate scale analogous to the opposing components of love. Sternberg's scale of hate, although applicable to both individuals and groups, can be problematic when used for individuals. For example, many of our participants (Aumer, Bahn, & Harris 2015) found it difficult to apply items like: "We have to protect ourselves against (insert name of person hated) by every means" and "The public should be informed comprehensively about the danger of (insert the name of person hated)" to individuals that they hated. After all, if a person goes through a difficult breakup and ends up hating their ex, the last thing they may want to do is make this person's potential danger "public," especially if they have shared intimate details with the ex. Aumer-Ryan and Hatfield (2007), Brogaard (2020), and others have explored the components of hate and identified the reasons for hating and targets of hate; however, no scale has been produced. Roseman and Steele (2018) have been more systematic about the study of hate, identifying the specific components that lead to and characterize the experience of hate. Nevertheless, with the lack of a hate scale, most research regarding hate has allowed the participants themselves to define hate.

Many researchers have been empirically exploring definitions of hate. Aumer and Bahn (2016) have defined hate as a negative emotion aimed at destroying or incapacitating the target of hate when seeing the target as a threat. Unlike dislike or anger, which may be components of hate (Sternberg 2003; Brogaard 2020), Aumer and Bahn (2016) characterize hate as the feeling people have toward those they see as a threat to their own lives and well-being, or a threat to the lives and well-being of loved ones. Having negative thoughts of the target of hate and a strong desire to have the person out of one's life are all essential components of hate. Importantly, Halperin (2008) further supports this definition by specifying that, unlike fear or anger, the hater views the harm or threat from the target of hate to stem from a stable evil character. Unlike the different types of love which can be dependent on relationship and status, the current research on hate has been rather unidimensional and types of hate or specific relational aspects of hate have not been investigated. Contempt and dehumanization, which have received more psychological investigation, could be considered related to hate (Brogaard 2020), but it remains unclear exactly how or in what way they are related. In contempt, one sees the target of contempt with negativity and as beneath them or unworthy of consideration (Wagner 2000), and this emotion has been found (and debated to be found) across several cultures (Ekman & Heider 1988; Matsumoto 1992). Similarly, in dehumanization, one treats or perceives a human being as less than human, as animalistic and only worthy of being treated as an object (Haslam 2006). Both are similar in that they treat the target as low in status and with an amount of hostility and dislike; however, it is unclear if contempt or dehumanization are components or types of hate. The one distinction that has been made routinely, especially in studies by Halperin (2008; 2011) and Aumer and colleagues (Aumer & Bahn 2016; Aumer-Ryan & Hatfield 2007; Aumer et al. 2016; Aumer, Bahn, & Harris 2015) and later elucidated by Fischer and colleagues (2018) is that hate can either be targeted at a group (intergroup hate) or at an individual (interpersonal hate). This distinction is important as we investigate the "good" and "bad" of hate.

The negative ramifications of hate are very clear in the literature in that hate leads to destruction, discrimination, and discord in society (Sternberg 2005; Opotow & McClelland 2007; Staub 2005, 2011; Brogaard 2020). Unlike love, which has received some acknowledgment of its potentially negative aspects, most of the current research on hate is done with the presumption that it is entirely bad. When examining hate at the intergroup level, it is clear that hate is detrimental. Halperin and colleagues (2008, 2011; Halperin, Sharvit, & Gross 2011) have shown that hate prevents conflict-reducing behaviors and goals for establishing peace. Unlike anger, which can lead toward reconciliation and problem-solving (Fischer & Roseman 2007; Halperin et al. 2011), hate seems to banish all possibilities of establishing or fostering a positive relationship with the hated group, which makes sense. If one examines the precursors of hate, seeing an intentional threat from a group of people with intractable and stable evil characteristics (Roseman & Steele 2018), then the likelihood of establishing peace with these people seems small and any attempt would be irrational and likely self-defeating.

The phenomenological experience of hate is also one that is characterized as unpleasant and intense (Roseman & Steele 2018; Goodvin et al. 2018). Unlike love, hate is not a feeling one would typically admit to having (Ben-Ze'ev & Ben-Ze'ev 2001). The phenomenological experience of hate may incline one to see the goal of destroying, eliminating, or incapacitating the target of hate as the only reasonable way to also resolve the feelings of hatred (Rempel & Burris 2005; Brogaard 2020). Aumer and colleagues (2015) showed that people are more likely to harbor negative motivations toward their targets of hate when their hate was especially high on disgust and devaluation (as measured with Sternberg's Triangular Hate Scale, Sternberg & Sternberg 2008). These negative motivations could lead to violence and even murder. Congress passed the Hate Crime Statistics Act (1990/2009) to specifically measure crimes and destruction caused by hate. However, hate crimes do not cover all crimes involving hate but are attempting to measure crimes based on prejudices concerning race, religion, sexual orientation, and ethnicity. The hate crime rate from 2007 to 2018 has remained relatively high with about 7,000 annual cases reported for the past two years (FBI 2020). With interpersonal hate, there is significant evidence that couples conceive of hate with far more destructive scripts (Fitness & Fletcher 1993), that relationships with hate report less satisfaction and intimacy (Aumer & Bahn 2016; Aumer et al. 2016), and that hate (when seen as a form of contempt) is one of four good predictors of relationship dissolution (Gottman & Levenson 2000). There is a lot of evidence suggesting that hate is destructive and hurtful and seems to warrant its bad reputation. If that is true, what possible "good" can come from hate?

Bertrand Russell has said that "few people can be happy unless they hate some other person, nation, or creed" (Prochnow 1955). The happiness people may derive from hate has some evidence in the overlapping brain areas (i.e., the putamen and insula) seen in both love and hate (Zeki & Romaya 2008). However, as Russell hints, hate may play more than just a phenomenological role in human experience. The goal of hate is to destroy, be free of, or incapacitate the target of hate. There is evidence that hate is effective at preventing peace, and if there is consensual agreement that a target is evil and threatening (e.g., Hitler or Pol Pot), then cultivating peace with that target may be unacceptable or impossible. Preventing peace may be the first step in the process of incapacitating a target, but how effective is hate at actually eliminating threats? The casualties of war in the twentieth century of at least 108 million people (Hedges 2003) and more than 200 million victims of genocide (Roser & Nagdy 2013) in that same time period indicate that hate is frighteningly effective.

The ethical issue many may have regarding any usefulness or good of hate is that hate's effectiveness is too indiscriminate. The use of hate when viewed within the framework of signal detection theory has four possible outcomes: (1) *hit* (the target deserves to be hated and the person hates them), (2) *miss* (the target deserves hate, but the person does not hate them), (3) *false alarm* (the target does not deserve hate, but the person hates them), and (4) *correct rejection* (the target does not deserve hate and the person does not hate them) (Green & Swets 1966; see also Gable, Reis, & Downey 2003; Finkenauer et al. 2010). The current studies on hate focus primarily on "false alarms," which is understandable given the cost of innocent lives. However, the investigation of the "hits" and even the "misses" may be helpful in better understanding the human experience and the power of hate in general. Establishing any objective criteria of who deserves hate (or love for that matter) is controversial. Nevertheless, most research has aimed at eliminating hate (whether a hit or false alarm) before fully understanding its role and usage.

When it comes to interpersonal hate, forgiveness is offered as one possible eliminator of hate. Forgiveness can be tricky to define for both lay persons and scholars; however, McCullough et al. (2000) propose that forgiveness is an "intraindividual, prosocial change toward a perceived transgressor that is situated within a specific interpersonal context" (p. 9). When it comes to intergroup hate, there are numerous training protocols to help eliminate implicit bias and prejudice, all with very mixed results in terms of effectiveness (Lai et al. 2014). It may be that eliminating the bias and prejudicial feelings associated with hate are more complex. Aumer and Krebs-Bahn (2019) found that there is a difference between what one thinks will work to get rid of hate and what actually works. People currently hating a target were most likely to believe that if the target went away or asked for forgiveness, they could end their hate. However, people who no longer hated their targets were more likely to report that their hate ended because they, themselves, removed themself from that target's presence and learned to forgive them. What seemed to work for ending hate was a sense of agency and self-control.

Those who took it upon themselves to remove themself from the target's presence and learned to forgive the target (whether or not the target asked for forgiveness) found that their hate actually ended, while those currently in the throes of hatred believed that the answer to ending their hate was in the target's control. Aumer and Krebs-Bahn (2019) did not measure whether these incidents of interpersonal hate were "hits" or "false alarms." However, those whose hate had ended seemed to either have successfully removed themselves from their target or now perceived their target as someone who deserved prosocial behavior.

Probably the best argument for the "good" of hate stems from evidence that shared hate helps bring people together and increases social bonds. If the goal of hate is to eliminate a threat, then the effectiveness of hate can be enhanced when those who share that hatred come together to provide support and pool resources. When it comes to intergroup hate, shared hate facilitates the creation and maintenance of hate groups. Hate groups themselves are not good or positive for the wider general community; however, for the individuals within the hate group, they benefit from the social support and establishment of an identity (Swann et al. 2009). Similarly, with respect to interpersonal hate, people report that they are more intimate and feel closer to those who share their love or their hate, compared to those who do not share either (Aumer & Krebs-Bahn 2019). The sharing of any passionate emotion or attitude may be especially powerful for establishing relationships and social support (Bosson et al. 2014). Not all bonding over shared hate has to be as detrimental to society as forming a hate group. Bonding over shared hate can be as simple as sharing gossip and venting over issues at work or school (Ellwardt et al. 2012).

Hate has a very specific goal: eliminate or incapacitate the threat to protect the self and those one loves. Having a common enemy may help to reach that goal and if the current aim of research continues to be looking for effective ways to end hate, then one of the obvious challenges to that end is that one may also have to consider the social bonds created by the shared hate. For intergroup hate, there are the issues of identity, social support, and social context that comes with being part of those hate groups, and in any process of eliminating hate, one has to consider the kind of possible substitutes used to supplant the void of social significance and friendship created once hate is eliminated (Jasko et al. 2020).

SUMMARY

The all-positive sentiments regarding love and the all-negative sentiments regarding hate are unlikely to change dramatically anytime soon. There is a certain degree of truth in the reputations of both love and hate. However, the negative sides of love are often undervalued and the positive sides of hate are often frighteningly avoided. Much of this moral bias in the academic literature could be attributed to the fact that love and hate have only been recently studied.

As can be seen in this chapter, considerably more attention has been given to the study of love than hate. There are numerous scales to measure love and all its types. In this chapter, we covered the four primary types of love as detailed by Berscheid (2010): attachment, compassionate, companionate, and passionate. All four have incredible benefits or "goods." Attachment love, when securely formed, allows for tremendous human growth and potential. Attachment styles formed in childhood can also predict the attachment styles of adulthood relationships (Hazan & Shaver 1987). However, attachment love may also be dangerous because it is not let go of easily. There are people in one's life that one should probably *not* be attached to (e.g., abusive spouses or parents), and in those situations, attachment love can be detrimental (Weiss 1975). Attachment love also does not consider the hardships for the giver of attachment love; caregiver burnout is often ignored by both laypersons and scholars. Compassionate love has numerous benefits for both the giver and receiver: predicting relationship satisfaction (Reis, Maniaci, & Rogge 2014), life satisfaction (Neto & Wilks 2017), and providing a buffer for parental stress (Miller et al. 2015). However, compassionate love may also have, theoretically, its drawbacks, including emotional labor burnout and possible exploitation. Both passionate and companionate love are phenomenologically rewarding experiences with research consistently showing that passionate love is a good predictor of romantic relationship satisfaction (Masuda 2003) and that companionate love is a good predictor of life satisfaction (Kim & Hatfield 2004). However, when companionate and passionate love are unrequited, negative feelings of humiliation, anger, guilt, annoyance, and grief can complicate and endanger relationships (Baumeister et al. 1993; Baumeister & Wotman 1994). Much of the good and bad of love center on the relationships and who love is given to.

We did a similar analysis with hate using the framework of signal detection theory (Green & Swets 1966; see also Gable, Reis, & Downey 2003; Finkenauer et al. 2010). The signal detection framework helps highlight that the moral issues surrounding the investigation of any good of hate may come from the destruction that is often aimed at people who do not deserve hate ("false-alarms"). Hate is self-protective against a possible threat (Aumer & Bahn 2016) who is seen to be of a stable evil character (Roseman & Steele 2018). One of its primary goals seems to be to incapacitate or destroy the target of hate. Hate is a very destructive emotion (Sternberg 2005; Opotow & McClelland 2007; Staub 2005, 2011), preventing peace and any possible future prosocial relationship (Halperin 2008; 2011). However, what about people who deserve hate and that hate is given ("hit") or not given ("misses")? There is very little research in this area, possibly because the consensus surrounding hate from a variety of sources (e.g., poems, quotes, songs) suggests that hate should always be avoided. At the interpersonal level, hate is correlated with less intimacy and satisfaction in relationships (Aumer & Bahn 2016) and at the intergroup level hate prevents conflict resolution (Halperin 2008; 2011). However, hate also seems to help create bonds (Aumer & Krebs-Bahn 2019), and groups that are so bonded can help members find significance and identity (Jasko et al. 2020; Swann et al. 2009). Future research on hate will have to examine the significance of eliminating these "positive" aspects if or when hate ends.

If emotions are intended to help us adapt to our environments (Neese 1990), and we want to discover better ways to control both our capacity to love and hate then the removal of moral-laden values from the study of love and hate is necessary. The study of love is older and more thorough than the study of hate, and some of love's negative aspects have been brought to light. However, there is still significant progress to be made for both emotions. Most of the studies reviewed in this chapter assume the emotions being measured are in isolation, removed from the influence of other emotions. One of the challenges to this approach is that there is little evidence of the regularity with which love or hate are experienced in isolation. Often love and hate are situated within complex relationships that change over time and are influenced by the standards and mores of the culture. The current overview of love and hate in this chapter is intended to provide a springboard for future research to attempt more objectivity in the investigation of love and hate. By removing the moral biases and studying love and hate more objectively, we not only learn more about these emotions but about ourselves.

REFERENCES

Acevedo, B. P., & Aron, A. (2009). Does a long-term relationship kill romantic love?. *Review of General Psychology*, *13*(1), 59–65.

Acevedo, B. P., Aron, A., Fisher, H. E., & Brown, L. L. (2012). Neural correlates of long-term intense romantic love. *Social Cognitive and Affective Neuroscience*, *7*(2), 145–159.

Amato, P. R. (2010). Research on divorce: Continuing trends and new developments. *Journal of Marriage and Family*, *72*(3), 650–666.

Ainsworth, M. S. (1989). Attachments beyond infancy. *American Psychologist*, *44*(4), 709.

Ainsworth, M. D. S., Blehar, M. C., Waters, E., & Wall, S. N. (1978/2015). *Patterns of attachment: A psychological study of the strange situation.* Psychology Press.

Andersen, S. H. (2018). Paternity leave and the motherhood penalty: New causal evidence. *Journal of Marriage and Family, 80*(5), 1125–1143.

Anderson, M. A., Gillig, P. M., Sitaker, M., McCloskey, K., Malloy, K., & Grigsby, N. (2003). "Why doesn't she just leave?": A descriptive study of victim reported impediments to her safety. *Journal of Family Violence, 18*(3), 151–155.

Ashforth, B. E., & Humphrey, R. H. (1993). Emotional labor in service roles: The influence of identity. *Academy of Management Review, 18*(1), 88–115.

Aumer, K., & Bahn, A. C. K. (2016). Hate in intimate relationships as a self-protective emotion. In *The psychology of love and hate in intimate relationships* (pp. 131–151). Cham.: Springer.

Aumer, K., Bahn, A. C. K., & Harris, S. (2015). Through the looking glass, darkly: Perceptions of hate in interpersonal relationships. *Journal of Relationships Research, 6*(1), 4–11.

Aumer, K., Bahn, A. C. K., Janicki, C., Guzman, N., Pierson, N., Strand, S. E., & Totlund, H. (2016). Can't let it go: Hate in interpersonal relationships. *Journal of Relationships Research, 7*, 1–9.

Aumer, K., & Krebs-Bahn, A. (2019, July). Eliminating hate: What we think works vs. what does work. Paper presented at the International Society for Research on Emotions, Amsterdam, The Netherlands.

Aumer-Ryan, K., & Hatfield, E. C. (2007). The design of everyday hate: A qualitative and quantitative analysis. *Interpersona: An International Journal on Personal Relationships, 1*(2), 143–172.

Bartels, A., & Zeki, S. (November 27, 2000). The neural basis of romantic love. *Neuroreport, 11*, 3829–3834.

Bartels, A. & Zeki, S. (2004). The neural correlates of maternal and romantic love. *Neuroimage, 21*, 1155–1166.

Bartholomew, K., & Horowitz, L. M. (1991). Attachment styles among young adults: A test of a four-category model. *Journal of Personality and Social Psychology, 61*, 226–244.

Baumeister, R. F., & Wotman, S. R. (1994). *Breaking hearts: The two sides of unrequited love.* Guilford Press.

Baumeister, R. F., Wotman, S. R., & Stillwell, A. M. (1993). Unrequited love: On heartbreak, anger, guilt, scriptlessness, and humiliation. *Journal of Personality and Social Psychology, 64*(3), 377.

Ben-Ze'ev, A., & Ben-Ze'ev, A. (2001). *The subtlety of emotions.* MIT press.

Berscheid, E. (1986). Mea culpas and lamentations: Sir Francis, Sir Isaac, and "The slow progress of soft psychology." In S. Duck & R. Gilmour (Eds.), *The emerging field of personal relationships* (pp. 267–286). Erlbaum.

Berscheid, E. (2010). Love in the fourth dimension. *Annual Review of Psychology, 61*, 1–25.

Bosson, J. K., Johnson, A. B., Niederhoffer, K., & Swann Jr, W. B. (2006). Interpersonal chemistry through negativity: Bonding by sharing negative attitudes about others. *Personal Relationships, 13*(2), 135–150.

Brennan, K. A., Shaver, P. R., & Tobey, A. E. (1991). Attachment styles, gender and parental problem drinking. *Journal of Social and Personal Relationships, 8*(4), 451–466.

Brotheridge, C. M., & Grandey, A. A. (2002). Emotional labor and burnout: Comparing two perspectives of "people work". *Journal of Vocational Behavior, 60*(1), 17–39.

Bowlby, J. 1977. *The making and breaking of affectional bonds.* Tavistock

Brogaard, B. 2020. *Hatred: Understanding our most dangerous emotion.* Oxford University Press.

CDC (a2020, Aug. 8). *Preventing partner violence.* Center for Disease Control and Prevention. https://www.cdc.gov/violenceprevention/intimatepartnerviolence/fastfact.html

CDC (b2020, Aug. 8). *Preventing child abuse and neglect.* Center for Disease Control and Prevention. https://www.cdc.gov/violenceprevention/childabuseandneglect/fastfact.html

Cimbalo, S., Failing, V., & Mousaw, P. (1976). The course of love: A cross-sectional design. *Psychological Reports, 38*, 1292–1294.

Coleman, S. (1977). A developmental stage hypothesis for nonmarital dyadic relationships. *Journal of Marriage and Family Counseling, 3*, 71–76.

Collins, N. L., & Read, S. J. (1990). Adult attachment, working models, and relationship quality in dating couples. *Journal of Personality and Social Psychology, 58*(4), 644.

Coontz, S. (2005). Marriage, a history: From obedience to intimacy. *Viking.*

Corrigan, P. W., Rowan, D., Green, A., Lundin, R., River, P., Uphoff-Wasowski, K., White, K., & Kubiak, M. A. (2002). Challenging two mental illness stigmas: Personal responsibility and dangerousness. *Schizophrenia Bulletin, 28*(2), 293–309.

Craven, D. (1997). *Sex differences in violent victimization, 1994.* US Department of Justice, Office of Justice Programs, Bureau of Justice Statistics.

Deci, E. L., Koestner, R., & Ryan, R. M. (1999). A meta-analytic review of experiments examining the effects of extrinsic rewards on intrinsic motivation. *Psychological Bulletin, 125*(6), 627.

Donnerstein, E., & Hatfield, E. (1982). Aggression and inequity. In *Equity and justice in social behavior* (pp. 309–336). Academic Press.

Drescher, J. (2015). Out of DSM: Depathologizing homosexuality. *Behavioral Sciences, 5*(4), 565–575.

Driscoll, R., Davis, K. E., & Lipetz, M. E. (1972). Parental interference and romantic love: The Romeo & Juliet effect. *Journal of Personality and Social Psychology, 24*, 1–10.

Easton, M. J. (1985). Love and intimacy in a multi-ethnic setting (Doctoral dissertation, University of Hawaii at Manoa).

Eisenberger, N. I., & Lieberman, M. D. (2004). Why rejection hurts: A common neural alarm system for physical and social pain. *Trends in Cognitive Sciences, 8*(7), 294–300.

Eisenberger, N. I., & Lieberman, M. D. (2005). Why it hurts to be left out: The neurocognitive overlap between physical and social pain. *The Social Outcast: Ostracism, Social Exclusion, Rejection, and Bullying, 109*, 130.

Ellwardt, L., Steglich, C., & Wittek, R. (2012). The co-evolution of gossip and friendship in workplace social networks. *Social Networks, 34*(4), 623–633.

England, P., Bearak, J., Budig, M. J., & Hodges, M. J. (2016). Do highly paid, highly skilled women experience the largest motherhood penalty?. *American Sociological Review, 81*(6), 1161–1189.

Ekman, P., & Heider, K. G. (1988). The universality of a contempt expression: A replication. *Motivation and Emotion, 12*(3), 303–308.

Erikson, E. H. (1993). *Childhood and society.* WW Norton & Company.

FBI. (2020, Sept 11). Federal Bureau of Investigation, 2018 Hate Crime Statistics. https://ucr.fbi.gov/hate-crime/2018/hate-crime

Fehr, B. (1994). Prototype-based assessments of laypeople's views of love. *Personal Relationships, 1*, 309–331.

Fehr, B., & Sprecher, S. (2009). Prototype analysis of the concept of compassionate love. *Personal Relationships, 16*(3), 343–364.

Finkenauer, C., Wijngaards-De Meij, Reis, H. T., & Rusbult, C. E. (2010). The importance of seeing what is not there: A quasi-signal detection analysis of positive and negative behavior in newlywed couples. *Personal Relationships, 17*, 615–633.

Fischer, A., Halperin, E., Canetti, D., & Jasini, A. (2018). Why we hate. *Emotion Review, 10*(4), 309–320.

Fischer, A. H., & Roseman, I. J. (2007). Beat them or ban them: The characteristics and social functions of anger and contempt. *Journal of Personality and Social Psychology, 93*(1), 103.

Fisher, H., Aron, A., & Brown, L. L. (2005). Romantic love: An fMRI study of a neural mechanism for mate choice. *The Journal of Comparative Neurology, 493*, 58–62.

Fisher, H. E., Xu, X., Aron, A., & Brown, L. L. (2016). Intense, passionate, romantic love: A natural addiction? How the fields that investigate romance and substance abuse can inform each other. *Frontiers in Psychology, 7*, 687.

Fitness, J., & Fletcher, G. J. (1993). Love, hate, anger, and jealousy in close relationships: A prototype and cognitive appraisal analysis. *Journal of Personality and Social Psychology, 65*(5), 942.

Fraley, R. C., & Davis, K. E. (1997). Attachment formation and transfer in young adults' close friendships and romantic relationships. *Personal Relationships, 4*(2), 131–144.

Gable, S. L., Reis, H. T., & Downey, G. (2003). He said, she said: A quasi-signal detection analysis of daily interactions between close relationship partners. *Psychological Science, 14*(2), 100–105. doi: 10.1111/1467-9280.t01-1-01426.

Goldstine, D., Larner, K., Zuckerman, S., & Goldstine, H. (1977). *The dance-away lover.* Ballantine.

Goodvin, A. (2019). *Is hate a distinct emotion?* (Doctoral dissertation, Rutgers University-Camden Graduate School).

Gottman, J. M., & Levenson, R. W. (2000). The timing of divorce: Predicting when a couple will divorce over a 14-year period. *Journal of Marriage and Family, 62*(3), 737–745.

Green, D. M., & Swets, J. A. (1966). *Signal detection theory and psychophysics.* Wiley.

Gross, L. (1944). A belief pattern scale for measuring attitudes toward romanticism. *American Sociological Review, 9*(5), 463–472.

Grote, N. K., & Frieze, I. H. (1994). The measurement of Friendship-based Love in intimate relationships. *Personal Relationships, 1*(3), 275–300.

Halperin, E., Russell, A. G., Dweck, C. S., & Gross, J. J. (2011). Anger, hatred, and the quest for peace: Anger can be constructive in the absence of hatred. *Journal of Conflict Resolution, 55*(2), 274–291.

Halperin, E., Sharvit, K., & Gross, J. J. (2011). Emotion and emotion regulation in conflicts. In D, Bar-Tal (Ed.) *Intergroup conflicts and their resolution: Social psychological perspective* (pp. 83–103). New York: Psychology Press.

Halperin, E. (2008). Group-based hatred in intractable conflict in Israel. *Journal of Conflict Resolution, 52*(5), 713–736.

Halperin, E. (2011). Emotional barriers to peace: Emotions and public opinion of Jewish Israelis about the peace process in the Middle East. *Peace and Conflict, 17*(1), 22–45.

Hamilton, E. (2017). *Mythology: Timeless tales of gods and heroes.* Black Dog & Leventhal.

Harlow, H. F. (1958). The Nature of Love. *American Psychologist,* 13, 673–85.

Haslam, N. (2006). Dehumanization: An integrative review. *Personality and Social Psychology Review, 10*(3), 252–264.

Hate Crime Statistics Act, 28 U.S.C. § 534 (2009).

Hatfield, E. (1988). Passionate and companionate love. In R. J. Sternberg & M. L. Barnes (Eds.), *The psychology of love* (pp. 191–217). Yale University Press.

Hatfield, E., Bensman, L., & Rapson, R. L. (2012). A brief history of social psychologists' attempts to measure passionate love. *Journal of Personality and Social Psychology, 29,* 143–164. doi: 10.1177/0265407511431055.

Hatfield, E., & Rapson, R. L. (1993). *Love, sex, and intimacy: Their psychology, biology, and history.* HarperCollins College Publishers.

Hatfield, E., & Rapson, R. L. (1996). *Love and sex: Cross-cultural perspectives.* Allyn & Bacon.

Hatfield, E., & Rapson, R. L. (2002). Passionate love and sexual desire: Cross-cultural and historical perspectives. In A. Vangelisti, H. T. Reis, & M. A. Fitzpatrick (Eds.), *Stability and change in relationships,* (pp. 306–324). Cambridge, England: Cambridge University Press.

Hatfield, E., Rapson, R. L., & Aumer-Ryan, K. (2008). Social justice in love relationships: Recent developments. *Social Justice Research, 21,* 413–431.

Hatfield, E., Schmitz, E., Cornelius, J., & Rapson, R. L. (1988). Passionate love: How early does it begin? *Journal of Psychology and Human Sexuality, 1*(1), 35–51.

Hatfield, E., & Sprecher, S. (1986). Measuring passionate love in intimate relationships. *Journal of Adolescence, 9*(4), 383–410.

Hatfield, E., & Sprecher, S. (1990). The passionate love scale (PLS). In J. Touliatos, B. F. Perlmutter, & M. A. Straus (Eds.), *Handbook of family measurement techniques* (pp. 235–236). New York: Sage.

Hatfield, E., Traupmann, J., Sprecher, S., Utne, M., & Hay, J. (1984). Equity and intimate relations: Recent research. In W. Ickes (Ed.), *Compatible and incompatible relationships* (pp. 1–27). Springer-Verlag.

Hatfield, E., & Walster, G. W. (1978). *A new look at love.* University Press of America.

Hazan, C., & Shaver, P. (1987). Romantic love conceptualized as an attachment process. *Journal of Personality and Social Psychology, 52,* 511–524.

Hazan, C., & Shaver, P. R. (1990). Love and work: An attachment-theoretical perspective. *Journal of Personality and Social Psychology, 59*(2), 270.

Hedges, C. (2003, July 6). *What every person should know about war.* Retrieved September 17, 2020 from https://www.nytimes.com/2003/07/06/books/chapters/what-every-person-should-know-about-war.html#:~:text=At%20least%20108%20million%20people,men%20away%20from%20their%20wives.

Hendrick, C., & Hendrick, S.S. (1986). A theory and method of love. *Journal of Personality and Social Psychology, 50*(2), 392–402.

Hochschild, A. R. (1983). *The managed heart: The commercialization of human feeling.* Univ. of California Press.

Hoffman, (2018, Sept, 7). *Till death do us unite: Japan's dark tales of love.* https://www.japantimes.co.jp/news/2018/03/17/national/history/till-death-us-unite-japans-dark-tales-love/

Ironson, G., Kremer, H., & Lucette, A. (2018). Compassionate love predicts long-term survival among people living with HIV followed for up to 17 years. *The Journal of Positive Psychology, 13*(6), 553–562.

Jasko, K., Webber, D., Kruglanski, A. W., Gelfand, M., Taufiqurrohman, M., Hettiarachchi, M., & Gunaratna, R. (2020). Social context moderates the effects of quest for significance on violent extremism. *Journal of Personality and Social Psychology, 118*(6), 1165.

Jonason, P. K., Li, N. P., Webster, G. D., & Schmitt, D. P. (2009). The dark triad: Facilitating a short-term mating strategy in men. *European Journal of Personality: Published for the European Association of Personality Psychology, 23*(1), 5–18.

Karney, B. R., & Bradbury, T. N. (1995). The longitudinal course of marital quality and stability: A review of theory, methods, and research. *Psychological Bulletin, 118*(1), 3.

Kephart, W. M. (1967). Some correlates of romantic love. *Journal of Marriage and the Family, 29*(3), 470–474.

Kim, J., & Hatfield, E. (2004). Love types and subjective well-being: A cross-cultural study. *Social Behavior and Personality: An International Journal, 32*(2), 173–182.

Kirkpatrick, L. A., & Davis, K. E. (1994). Attachment style, gender, and relationship stability: A longitudinal analysis. *Journal of Personality and Social Psychology, 66*(3), 502.

Kmec, J. A. (2011). Are motherhood penalties and fatherhood bonuses warranted? Comparing pro-work behaviors and conditions of mothers, fathers, and non-parents. *Social Science Research, 40*(2), 444–459.

Lai, C. K., Marini, M., Lehr, S. A., Cerruti, C., Shin, J. E. L., Joy-Gaba, J. A., ... & Frazier, R. S. (2014). Reducing implicit racial preferences: I. A comparative investigation of 17 interventions. *Journal of Experimental Psychology: General, 143*(4), 1765.

Lee, J.A (1976). *Lovestyles*. Abacus.

Maslow, A. H. (1943). A Theory of Human Motivation. *Psychological Review*, 50, 370–396.

Maslow, A. H. (1953). Love in healthy people. In Montagu, A. (Ed.), *The meaning of love* (pp. 57–58). New York, NY: Julian Press.

Maslow, A. H. (1954). *Motivation and personality*. Harper & Row, Publishers.

Masuda, M. (2003). Meta-analyses of love scales: Do various love scales measure the same psychological constructs?. *Japanese Psychological Research, 45*(1), 25–37.

Matsumoto, D. (1992). More evidence for the universality of a contempt expression. *Motivation and Emotion, 16*(4), 363–368.

McCullough, M. E., Pargament, K. I., & Thoresen, C. E. (Eds.). (2000). *Forgiveness: Theory, research, and practice*. Guilford Press.

Mersin, S., İbrahimoğlu, Ö., Çağlar, M., & Akyol, E. (2020). Compassionate love, burnout and professional commitment in nurses. *Journal of Nursing Management, 28*(1), 72–81.

McLeod, S. A. (2020, March 20). *Maslow's hierarchy of needs*. Simply Psychology. https://www.simplypsychology.org/maslow.html

Mickelson, K. D., Kessler, R. C., & Shaver, P. R. (1997). Adult attachment in a nationally representative sample. *Journal of Personality and Social Psychology, 73*(5), 1092.

Miller, J. G., Kahle, S., Lopez, M., & Hastings, P. D. (2015). Compassionate love buffers stress-reactive mothers from fight-or-flight parenting. *Developmental Psychology, 51*(1), 36.

Moser, C., & Kleinplatz, P. J. (2020). Conceptualization, history, and future of the Paraphilias. *Annual Review of Clinical Psychology, 16*, 379–399.

Najib, A., Lorberbaum, J. P., Kose, S., Bohning, D. E., & George, M. S. (2004). Regional brain activity in women grieving a romantic relationship breakup. *American Journal of Psychiatry, 161*(12), 2245–2256.

Nesse, R. M. (1990). Evolutionary explanations of emotions. *Human Nature, 1*, 261–289.

Neto, F., & Wilks, D. C. (2017). Compassionate love for a romantic partner across the adult life span. *Europe's Journal of Psychology, 13*(4), 606.

Oatley, K., Keltner, D., & Jenkins, J. M. (2006). *Understanding emotions*. Blackwell publishing.

Oldenburg, A. (2010, June 2). Christie Brinkley: 'I'd rather have a broken arm than a broken heart'. *USA Today*. https://www.usatoday.com/

Opotow, S., & McClelland, S. (2007). The intensification of hating: A theory. *Social Justice Research, 20*, 68–97.

Paglia, C. (1990). *Sexual personae: Art and decadence from Nefertiti to Emily Dickinson* (Vol. 1). Yale University Press.

Parsons, J., Edmeades, J., Kes, A., Petroni, S., Sexton, M., & Wodon, Q. (2015). Economic impacts of child marriage: A review of the literature. *The Review of Faith and International Affairs, 13*(3), 12–22.

Paulhus, D. L., & Williams, K. M. (2002). The dark triad of personality: Narcissism, Machiavellianism, and psychopathy. *Journal of Research in Personality, 36*(6), 556–563.

Petrosky, E., Blair, J. M., Betz, C. J., Fowler, K. A., Jack, S. P., & Lyons, B. H. (2017). Racial and ethnic differences in homicides of adult women and the role of intimate partner violence—United States, 2003–2014. *MMWR. Morbidity and Mortality Weekly Report, 66*(28), 741.

Pettem, O., West, M., Mahoney, A., & Keller, A. (1993). Depression and attachment problems. *Journal of Psychiatry and Neuroscience, 18*(2), 78.

Prochnow, H. V. (1955). *Speaker's handbook of epigrams and witticisms.* Harper.

Rahnama, M., Shahdadi, H., Bagheri, S., Moghadam, M. P., & Absalan, A. (2017). The relationship between anxiety and coping strategies in family caregivers of patients with trauma. *Journal of Clinical and Diagnostic Research: JCDR, 11*(4), IC06.

Regan, P. C., Lakhanpal, S., & Anguiano, C. (2012). Relationship outcomes in Indian-American love-based and arranged marriages. *Psychological Reports, 110*(3), 915–924.

Reis, H. T., Maniaci, M. R., & Rogge, R. D. (2014). The expression of compassionate love in everyday compassionate acts. *Journal of Social and Personal Relationships, 31*(5), 651–676.

Rempel, J. K., & Burris, C. T. (2005). Let me count the ways: An integrative theory of love and hate. *Personal Relationships, 12*(2), 297–313.

Rogers, C. R. (1961). *On becoming a person: A therapist's view of psychotherapy.* Houghton Mifflin Harcourt.

Roseman, I. J., & Steele, A. K. (2018). Concluding commentary: Schadenfreude, Gluckschmerz, jealousy, and hate—what (and when, and why) are the emotions?. *Emotion Review, 10*(4), 327–340.

Roser, M. & Nagdy, M. (2013). *Genocides.* Retrieved September 17, 2020 from: 'https://ourworldindata.org/genocides'

Royzman, E. B., McCauley, C., & Rozin, P. (2005). From Plato to Putnam: Four ways to think about hate. In R. J. Sternberg (Ed.), *The psychology of hate* (pp. 3–35). American Psychological Association. doi: 10.1037/10930-001.

Rubin, Z. (1970). Measurement of romantic love. *Journal of Personality and Social Psychology, 16*(2), 265–273.

Sabey, A. K., Rauer, A. J., & Jensen, J. F. (2014). Compassionate love as a mechanism linking sacred qualities of marriage to older couples' marital satisfaction. *Journal of Family Psychology, 28*(5), 594.

Senchak, M., & Leonard, K. E. (1992). Attachment styles and marital adjustment among newlywed couples. *Journal of Social and Personal Relationships, 9*(1), 51–64.

Shaffer, J. A. (1994). The ideological intervention of ambiguities in the marriage plot: Who fails Marianne in Austen's sense and sensibility? In Hohne, & Wussow, H., *A dialogue of voices feminist literary theory and Bakhtin.* University of Minnesota Press.

Shaffer, J. A. (1994). The ideological intervention of ambiguities in the marriage plot: Who fails Marianne in Austen's sense and sensibility? In Hohne, & Wussow, H., *A dialogue of voices feminist literary theory and Bakhtin*. University of Minnesota Press.

Shaver, P. R., & Hazan, C. (1993). Adult romantic attachment: Theory and evidence. *Advances in Personal Relationships*, *4*, 29–70.

Shaver P.R., Hazan C., & Bradshaw D. (1988). Love as attachment: The integration of three behavioral systems. In R. J. Sternberg & M. L. Barnes (Eds.), *The psychology of love* (pp. 191–217). Yale University Press. (pp. 68–99)

Simpson, J. A. (1990). Influence of attachment styles on romantic relationships. *Journal of Personality and Social Psychology*, *59*(5), 971.

Sprecher, S. (1999). "I love you more today than yesterday": Romantic partners' perceptions of changes in love and related affect over time. *Journal of Personality and Social Psychology*, *76*(1), 46.

Sophocles, & Roche, P. (2004). *The oedipus plays of sophocles: Oedipus the king, oedipus at colonos, antigone*. Plume.

Sprecher, S. (1986). The relation between inequity and emotions in close relationships. *Social Psychology Quarterly, 49*(4) 309–321.

Sprecher, S., Aron, A., Hatfield, E., Cortese, A., Potapova, E., & Levitskaya, A. (1994). Love: American style, Russian style, and Japanese style. *Personal Relationships*, *1*(4), 349–369.

Sprecher, S., & Fehr, B. (2005). Compassionate love for close others and humanity. *Journal of Social and Personal Relationships*, *22*(5), 629–651.

Sprecher, S., & Fehr, B. (2006). Enhancement of mood and self-esteem as a result of giving and receiving compassionate love. *Current Research in Social Psychology*, *11*(16), 227–242.

Sprecher, S., & Regan, P. C. (1998). Passionate and companionate love in courting and young married couples. *Sociological Inquiry*, *68*(2), 163–185.

Staub, E. (2005). The origins and evolution of hate, with notes on prevention. In R. J. Sternberg (Ed.), *The psychology of hate* (pp. 51–66). American Psychological Association.

Staub, E. (2011). *Overcoming evil: Genocide, violent conflict and terrorism*. Oxford University Press.

Sternberg, R. J. (1986). A triangular theory of love. *Psychological Review, 93*(2), 119.

Sternberg, R. J. (2005). Understanding and combating hate. In R. J. Sternberg (Ed.), *The psychology of hate* (pp. 51–66). American Psychological Association.

Sternberg, R. J. (2003). A duplex theory of hate: Development and application to terrorism, massacres, and genocide. *Review of General Psychology*, *7*(3), 299–328.

Sternberg, R. J., & Sternberg, K. (2008). *The nature of hate*. Cambridge University Press.

Sullivan, R., & Lasley, E. N. (2010, September). Fear in love: Attachment, abuse, and the developing brain. In *Cerebrum: The Dana forum on brain science* (Vol. 2010). Dana Foundation.

Swann Jr, W. B., Gómez, A., Seyle, D. C., Morales, J., & Huici, C. (2009). Identity fusion: The interplay of personal and social identities in extreme group behavior. *Journal of Personality and Social Psychology, 96*(5), 995.

Swensen, C. H. (1961). Love: A self-report analysis with college students. *Journal of Individual Psychology, 17*(2), 167.

Traupmann, J., Eckels, E., & Hatfield, E. (1982). Intimacy in older women's lives. *The Gerontologist, 22*(6), 493–498.

Traupmann, J., & Hatfield, E. (1981). Love and its effect on mental and physical health. In Robert Fogel, Elaine Hatfield, Sara Kiesler & Ethel Shanas (Eds.), *Aging: Stability and change in the family* (pp. 253–274). Academic Press.

Tucker, P., & Aron, A. (1993). Passionate love and marital satisfaction at key transition points in the family life cycle. *Journal of Social and Clinical Psychology, 12*(2), 135–147.

Underwood, L. G. (2009). Compassionate love: A framework for research. The science of compassionate love: Theory, research, and applications, 3–25. In Fehr, Sprecher, & Underwood, *The Science of Compassionate Love: Theory Research and Applications*, Blackwell. Wiley-Blackwell. Malden Massachusetts, Oxford, England.

Utne, M. K., Hatfield, E., Traupmann, J., & Greenberger, D. (1984). Equity, marital satisfaction, and stability. *Journal of Social and Personal Relationships, 1*(3), 323–332.

Van Dierendonck, D., & Patterson, K. (2015). Compassionate love as a cornerstone of servant leadership: An integration of previous theorizing and research. *Journal of Business Ethics, 128*(1), 119–131.

Vicedo, M. (2011). The social nature of the mother's tie to her child: John Bowlby's theory of attachment in post-war America. *The British Journal for the History of Science, 44*(3), 401–426.

Von Dietze, E., & Orb, A. (2000). Compassionate care: A moral dimension of nursing. *Nursing Inquiry, 7*(3), 166–174.

Wagner, H. L. (2000). The accessibility of the term "contempt" and the meaning of the unilateral lip curl. *Cognition and Emotion, 14*(5), 689–710.

Weiner, B., Perry, R. P., & Magnusson, J. (1988). An attributional analysis of reactions to stigmas. *Journal of Personality and Social Psychology, 55*(5), 738.

Weiss, R. S. (1975). *Marital separation.* Basic Books.

Zeki, S., & Romaya, J. P. (2008). Neural correlates of hate. *PLoS One, 3*(10), e3556.

Zuroff, D. C., & Fitzpatrick, D. K. (1995). Depressive personality styles: Implications for adult attachment. *Personality and Individual Differences, 18*(2), 253–265.

Chapter 4

The Role of Ideals in Intimate Relationships

Robert J. Sternberg

When you enter an intimate relationship, you likely think of it as a relationship between two people. But it might be productive to think of it as a relationship involving at least four individuals, two material and two immaterial, or perhaps "spiritual."

The two material persons of course are the two partners in the relationship. Almost all of the literature on intimate relationships focuses on the two material beings as well as the persons and contexts surrounding them (see, e.g., Bradbury & Karney 2019; Sternberg & Sternberg 2019). But the other two persons, I will argue in this chapter, are perhaps as important as, or more important than, the material persons who are in the relationship. They are the ideals of each of the partners—the partner with which each person ideally would like to be. Much of people's behavior in reaction to each other is driven not only by the partner they have but also by the partner they wish they had. And people may have multiple ideals, so there actually may be more than two immaterial persons involved in the relationship.

WHAT IS AN IDEAL?

An ideal, basically, represents the romantic partner we wish we had, or equivalently, the romantic relationship we wish we were in. It is not simple to identify that ideal, because for most of us, our ideal partner, or relationship, is not fully accessible to consciousness. When my collaborators and I first started asking people to identify the stories they had about relationships—in particular, the stories they wish were true depictions of their actual relationships (if any)—many participants in our research drew a blank (see Sternberg 1998b). It was not until we started using Likert-scale responses (i.e., responses scaled from 1 = low to 9 = high, or similar) to questions about love stories that we obtained meaningful data (Sternberg 1998b; Sternberg, Hojjat, & Barnes 2001). Similarly, we found that people could characterize some of their feelings about ideal partners but did so much better using Likert scales (Sternberg 1997; 1998a). The bottom line is that people have ideals, despite not knowing on a conscious level exactly what they are.

Past Efforts to Understand Ideals

Although theorists have not always referred to ideals as such, the notion of ideals has played an important role in theory and research about intimate relationships. The review here is not exhaustive but covers some of the highlights.

Social Exchange Theory

Thibaut and Kelley (1959) introduced the concept of a comparison level (CL) in their social exchange theory of relationships. The comparison level is essentially the difference between what one has in a relationship and what one thinks one wishes one had—one's ideal. For example, one might wish that one were married to someone who is ravishingly beautiful but be married to someone whom one views as only average in attractiveness. One's satisfaction in a relationship is theorized to be higher, the lower the difference between the actual and the ideal. If people behaved only in terms of their comparison level, there would be a lot of very short-term relationships. Rather, the way people act is more determined by their comparison level for alternatives (CL_{alt}). This is the comparison level for what is realistically possible for them—whom they might be able to obtain as a partner in a relationship. In the real world, one often cannot have one's ideal, comparison-level partner.

Attachment Theory

Another theory that has dealt with ideals, in this case, indirectly, is attachment theory (Hazan & Shaver 1987; Mikulincer & Shaver 2019). According to attachment theory, individuals attach themselves to parents, and especially the mother, in one of several ways (Ainsworth 1973; 1989; Bowlby 2012). These ways then later show up in their adult relationships (Collins & Feeney 2004).

People may be securely attached in their adult relationships if they generally have a positive view of self and others. Or they may be insecurely attached, in one of three ways.

If someone has a negative view of the self but a positive view of others, they tend to show preoccupied attachment. They pursue closeness in intimate relationships, but because they have a low sense of self-worth, they are high in anxiety, always waiting for the other shoe to drop.

If someone has a positive view of the self, but a negative view of others, they tend to be dismissive of others. They cannot see others meeting their needs, and so they tend to seek distance and to remain self-sufficient.

If someone has a negative view of both themselves and others, they tend to have a fearful attachment style. They seek validation from others, but at the same time they expect others to reject them. As a result, they both want and do not want intimacy because of the pain it is likely to cause. They are conflicted.

Attachment styles create ideals, but not necessarily ideals that all people want from their partners. For example, if someone is dismissive—having a high view of themselves but a low view of others—they will be most comfortable with someone who wants distance and is happy in a relationship in which there is not so much closeness. If someone is preoccupied, they will want to be with someone who is constantly giving them reassurance. These ideals may not represent their conscious ideal for a relationship, but they are the preconscious ideals that work for them.

Relationships can serve as a source of self-actualization, helping to carry people to their full potential (Maslow 1943; 1954; 1962). But if one were to take attachment theory seriously, those most likely to be self-actualized through relationships are people with a secure style of attachment. They are the ones who most can take advantage of the relationships they are in, so long as their partner can give in like manner to what they get.

Evolutionary Theory

Evolutionary theory also deals with ideals, although in a way quite different from that of social exchange theory or attachment theory. According to evolutionary theory, people seek to maximize the successful reproduction of their genes (Buss 1994; 2019; Kenrick & Keefe 1992). Thus, men should seek out multiple partners, as they can thereby spread their genes widely and help to guarantee that at least some of their reproductive efforts are successful. Women, on the other hand, can have a child only, at most, once every so often, so they need to be very careful in their selection of a father for their future child. According to this theory, the ideals for men and women are somewhat different, therefore, with women being more selective than men in whom they will consider as a potential sexual partner with the goal of reproductive success. What constitutes an ideal of reproductive success may vary from one woman to another, but usually involves resources and some kind of assurance that the man will show fidelity so as to secure the future of any resulting children.

Of course, there are many other theories of love (see Sternberg & Sternberg 2019). But the three examples above should give a flavor of how theories of love can treat the search for the ideal partner.

PRE-THEORETICAL STUDIES OF LOVE

I have studied ideals in relationships in four different ways. The initial attempts were pre-theoretical. The later attempts were more clearly theory-based. These were through a triangular theory of love (Sternberg 1998a; 2019), a theory of love as a story (Sternberg 1998b; 2019), and through a model of jealousy and envy (Sternberg, Kaur, & Mistur 2019). The text below considers these programs of theory and research.

The Ideal as the Ideal Partner

Ideals Are Special

In our first study on intimate relationships, Susan Grajek and I asked participants to answer a number of questions about liking and loving using two scales (Sternberg & Grajek 1984), one devised by Zick Rubin (1970) and the other by Levinger, Rands, and Talaber (1977). At that point, I had not yet formulated my own theory of love. Rather, I applied three structural theories of intelligence to the love domain: that love cannot be decomposed but rather comprises a single general factor (analogous to Spearman's [1927] theory of intelligence), that love can be decomposed into a large number of bonds (analogous to Thomson's [1916] theory of intelligence), and that love can be decomposed into a set of primary factors (analogous to Thurstone's [1938] theory of primary mental abilities).

The participants were asked to describe their feelings toward not only their lover but also toward their mother, father, sibling, best friend, and for the Levinger scale, their ideal lover. In this way, from the present point of view, it was possible to compare ratings for ideal lovers to ratings for actual love relationships.

There were three kinds of results that were of interest. We can look at both means and correlations.

First, looking at means, we found that love for the ideal lover was statistically significantly higher than love for all others except the actual lover, but that result was marginally significant and the difference was almost 1 full point on the love scale (4.14 for mother, 3.35 for father, 3.23 for sibling, 4.41

for best friend, 4.46 for real love, 5.40 for ideal lover). So, it appears that there is something special about the ideal lover—something that sets them apart from other loves.

Second, the correlations reveal that patterns of responses are different for the ideal lover versus other loves. In particular, the correlation of responses for the ideal lover with the other lovers were .32 ($p < .01$) for mother, .23 for father (N.S.), .20 for sibling (N.S.), .50 ($p < .01$) for best friend, and .66 for lover ($p < .05$). (Not everyone had a lover, so the N for lover was lower than for other relationships.) Thus, people viewed their hypothetical relationship with an ideal lover in a way that was distinct from the way they viewed any other real relationship. The difference appears to be qualitative (correlations) as well as quantitative (means).

Third, the results supported Thomson's (1916) theory of bonds—that love comprises many disparate feelings, motivations, and thoughts, all of which combine to produce the single feeling that we call "love." The ideal love, therefore, is not a single thing, but rather a combination of many desired qualities. In our results, an overarching dimensional representation fit the data less adequately than did a representation with many clusters representing aspects of intimate love, such as of trust, communication, care, and respect.

This early study suggested that people do have some kind of identifiable conception of an ideal lover, and that the conception was apart from any relationship they had. In the next study, we sought to elaborate upon the role of ideals in relationships.

Ideals Affect Real Relationships

In a subsequent study (Sternberg & Barnes 1985), we found that not only do ideals matter; they matter in very specific ways. In this rather complex study, participants came to our laboratory at Yale University in couples. Each member of each couple filled out the Rubin Love Scale, as mentioned above. They filled out the questionnaire in four different ways: (a) how they felt about their partner, (b) how they thought their partner felt about them, (c) how they ideally would like to feel toward their partner, and (d) how they ideally would like their partner to feel toward them.

The findings of the study showed that ideals matter for the success and happiness of intimate relationships. Here were the main findings:

1. Five of six correlations of feelings for ideal others correlated with satisfaction in relationships. Thus, such feelings matter. However, the correlations for the ideal others with satisfaction were lower than the correlations for the real others. That is because what really matters is not

feelings for the ideals in themselves, but rather *differences* between feelings for real versus ideal others.

2. How one perceives one's partner to feel about oneself is just as important to relationship satisfaction as is how one feels about one's partner. In other words, one cares roughly equally about how one feels and how one perceives one's partner to feel.

3. More important than feelings toward the ideal is the *difference* between feelings regarding ideal others and feelings regarding actual others. Five of six correlations between difference scores and satisfaction were statistically significant. Interestingly, the absolute best predictor of satisfaction was not something one felt. Rather, it was the difference between how one ideally would like one's partner to feel about oneself and how one perceived that partner to feel about oneself. Notice, importantly, that the variable of interest is one's perception of how the other feels, not how the other actually feels.

4. How one's partner says they feel about oneself is of absolutely no importance in predicting satisfaction independent of one's perceptions of how the other feels toward oneself. In other words, one's satisfaction is a function not of how the other person states they feel, but rather of one's perceptions of their feelings. Put another way, if one doesn't feel the love, the love doesn't matter to one's satisfaction.

5. In general, how one feels toward the actual other, how one feels toward the ideal other, how one perceives the other to feel toward oneself, and how one ideally would like the other to feel toward oneself are all positively and significantly correlated. The greater the discrepancy among these feelings, the lower one's satisfaction with the relationship tends to be. In other words, congruence of the various feelings matters for satisfaction.

6. Feelings toward actual others are not as positive, on average, as feelings toward ideal others. In other words, one generally is less satisfied in one's relationship than one ideally would like to be.

The findings of the study with Barnes show that ideals play a powerful role in intimate relationships. It isn't just how you feel toward your partner that matters, but the difference between how you feel and how you would ideally like to feel, and similarly, it matters quite a bit not just how you perceive your partner to feel toward you but also how you ideally would like them to feel.

The most common problem is under-involvement. That is, you wish your partner loved you more than you perceive them to do. But the discrepancy also can go the other way. Sometimes, a partner is attempting to keep involvement at a fairly modest level. If one's partner is trying to increase the level of mutual involvement, one can become unhappy because one feels suffocated—that the partner is asking for more than one can provide.

THE ROLE OF IDEALS IN THE
DUPLEX THEORY OF LOVE

I have proposed a duplex theory of love (Sternberg 2006; 2019) that contains two parts: a triangular theory of love and a theory of love as a story that explains how love develops. These efforts are considered next.

The Triangular Theory of Love

I first presented the triangular theory of love some years back (Sternberg 1986). It has been updated over the years (Sternberg 2019). The theory has been shown to be valid across many cultures throughout the world (Sorokowski et al., 2020).

The basic idea of the triangular theory is that love has three basic components: intimacy, passion, commitment. Intimacy consists of feelings of communication, understanding, sharing, closeness, warmth, and compassion. Passion consists of motivations of need, lust, addiction, intense desire, longing, and inability to imagine life without someone. Commitment consists of thoughts of permanence, desire to stay with someone no matter what, and the decision that the love one feels is everlasting or, at least, long-lasting.

Different combinations of these components generate different kinds of love. Intimacy by itself produces *friendship love*. Passion by itself results in *infatuated love*. Commitment by itself results in *empty love*. Intimacy plus passion generates *romantic love*. Intimacy plus commitment yields *companionate love*. Passion plus commitment produces *foolish* or *fatuous love*. And intimacy, passion, and commitment together yield *consummate* or *complete love*.

There are different kinds of triangles in the triangular theory of love. These are not merely a matter of balance of components of love, but rather of expressions of love. A first triangle represents how an individual feels toward their partner. This is essentially a feelings triangle of the individual toward the partner. A second triangle is the feelings triangle of the partner toward oneself. A third triangle is an action triangle, representing how one acts, as opposed to just how one feels. A fourth triangle is the action triangle of the partner toward oneself.

For present purposes, particularly important is the set of ideal triangles. There are two of these, which correspond to the feelings studied in the Sternberg and Barnes (1985) study. These are, first, how one ideally would like to feel toward the other, in terms of intimacy, passion, and commitment; and second, how one would ideally like the other to feel about oneself, again in terms of intimacy, passion, and commitment.

Ideals are very important in the triangular theory. In particular, the closer one's actual triangle is to one's ideal triangle, in terms of intimacy, passion, and commitment, the more satisfied one tends to be with the relationship. I have found that relationships are happier and more satisfied to the extent that the triangle one has for a relationship matches one's ideal triangle (Sternberg 1997). In other words, as your real triangle departs from your ideal triangle, your relationship becomes less satisfactory to you.

There are five reasons related to triangles that relationships fail. Two of them pertain to relationship ideals.

The first cause of failure is that there just is not enough love. The levels of intimacy, passion, and/or commitment are not sufficient to commence or sustain a loving relationship. Either one is reluctant to get into the relationship because there is not enough love, or one is reluctant to stay in the relationship for the same reason.

The second cause of failure is mismatch between the perceived triangles of the two partners. One feels that one loves one's partner much more, or much less (!) than one's partner loves oneself. The asymmetry makes one too uncomfortable to start or stay in the relationship. The asymmetry can be of two kinds.

One kind of asymmetry is a matter of size, the other of shape, of the triangle. Consider each in turn. First, consider the size of triangles. One feels either that the other loves one too little or too much. Second, consider the shape of triangles. One feels a sense of mismatch. Perhaps you really value intimacy and your partner or potential partner hardly communicates with you. Or you value passion and your partner or potential partner is, well, on the chilly side when it comes to passion. Or you value commitment and your partner wants little or none of it. Any way you look at it, relationships are hard to sustain if people want different things.

A third cause of failure is when feelings triangles prove to be a poor match to action triangles. Feelings triangles concern how people feel; action triangles concern how people act or do not act upon their feelings. You may be with someone who feels intimacy but does not act intimate in the relationship, or who feels commitment but nevertheless has a wandering eye and rushes for the first person who seems to be available. If actions do not match words, it often is hard to stay in a relationship. It is even harder when you know the other means well but can't show it in action.

The fourth cause of failure, which is related to ideals, is a mismatch between your actual triangle and your ideal triangle. Perhaps you just aren't getting enough out of the relationship, relative to what you want. You may actually be getting a lot out of the relationship; it just is not enough for you. You want or need more. So, you always feel under-loved or under-appreciated, no matter how much love or appreciation the other has for you. Or it may be that you feel you are getting too much out of the relationship. You were looking for a light rain but ended up in a hurricane. You are overwhelmed. Whatever may be the case, the relationship is too far from your ideal, and you cannot make it work.

The fifth cause of failure is a mismatch between your ideal triangle and your partner's. What you both ideally want out of a relationship is too different, regardless of what you actually have in the relationship. In such cases, breakups can be sad. For example, you may feel that you need to have a child with a partner to consummate your love; your partner is uninterested or dreads the very thought of having children. To you, children would be a sign of the fulfillment of your intimacy, passion, and commitment. To your partner, children would be an abrogation of freedom. From their point of view, all those wonderful adventures you and the partner might have will be lost because you are both tied down by children. Or it may be matters pertaining to money, responsibilities to parents, or responsibilities to religion. Whatever may be the case, it is hard to make a relationship work when the ideals of the two partners clash.

Consider an example of partners who love each other but whose relationship nevertheless fails because of conflicting ideals held by the partners. This is a problem we actually have used in our research, with slight modifications.

Charles and Margaret are both engineers and have been married for five years. Three years ago, Charles was offered a job in Europe. Margaret agreed to quit her job in the United States and move to Europe with Charles. Margaret felt she was showing her love by agreeing to move to Europe with Charles. The job was an excellent career move for Charles. Soon after the move, they had a baby boy. After the birth, Margaret decided to start working again and, with effort, found a very exciting job that paid well and promised real security. Meanwhile, Charles was offered a transfer back to the United States. Margaret feels she needs another year or two in her new job to meaningfully advance her career. She is also tired of moving. She has already given up a lot of time following Charles around. She loves Charles but feels this time it is her turn. And she really is committed to her job, at least for the time being. Charles knows that his wife's job is as important as his own, but he thinks returning to the United States would help both their careers in the end. Moreover, he earns quite a bit more than Margaret and this is a chance to fulfill their financial dreams as well as to return home. Charles feels that if Margaret really cared about the relationship, and not just her job, she would move back to the United States with him. Margaret feels that if Charles really cared about the relationship, and not just his job, he would stay with her in Europe. What should Charles and Margaret do?

In this case, both Charles and Margaret have ideals about their love relationship in the future. Those ideals just are not the same. It will be hard for them to resolve the conflict in their future visions unless both of them make an effort to think dialogically—to see things from the other's point of view. Unless they do so—unless they think wisely—they may find themselves with a compromised future.

The Theory of Love as a Story

The theory of love as a story states that love can be understood as a series of stories that we carry within us (Sternberg 1998b). The stories are picked up from the environment as we observe the love stories around us—the story of our parents; of characters in novels, poetry, or music; love stories we see in movies; the love stories of friends, and eventually, of ourselves. These stories are so embedded in the common culture that people are hardly aware of them and that they even exist. Love stories, then, are socialized. You see your parents' love relationship, for example, and you take it as a model of what you would like to have. As an interaction between our personalities and our socialization, we resonate with some stories more than others. Some we internalize; others we reject. Eventually, we end up with a hierarchy of stories, some of which are more preferred and others of which are less preferred. Still others are not part of our hierarchy. The order in the hierarchy is a function of our socialization interacting with our personality.

Every love story has two roles—a protagonist and the loved one of the protagonist. The roles can be either symmetrical or asymmetrical. Table 4.1 shows a listing of the stories currently in the theory.

In a symmetrical story, the two partners have identical roles. For example, they may both be business partners, or they may both be equal participants in a democratic government story. In an asymmetrical relationship, the partners occupy complementary roles. For example, in an autocratic government story, one partner rules over the other. In an art story, one partner is a work of art and the other is an admirer.

Some stories are associated with failure in relationships, such as the horror story (see table 4.1)—those relationships are characterized by low satisfaction and often reduced longevity—but there are no stories that are uniformly associated with success (Sternberg, Hojjat, & Barnes 2001). In other words, no particular story comes even close to assuring success, no matter how well the story is executed. The reason appears to be, at least in part, that a story cannot succeed in a loving relationship unless one finds a partner who is a match for it.

Table 4.1 Taxonomy of Love Stories from the Theory of Love as a Story (Sternberg, 1998b)

1. *Addiction.* Strong and anxious attachment to a lover; clinging behavior toward the partner; anxiety at the thought of losing the partner.
2. *Art.* Love of the partner for the partner's physical attractiveness; importance to the individual of the partner's always looking his or her best.
3. *Business.* Relationships viewed as business ventures between two partners; money is often viewed as power; partners in close relationships are business partners who succeed or fail, depending on the success of their "business."
4. *Collection.* The partner is viewed as "fitting in" to some overall collection scheme; the partner is viewed in a detached way as befits an element of a collection.
5. *Cookbook.* Partners should do things a certain way (a recipe) so that their relationship is more likely to work out; departure from recipe for success can lead to increased likelihood of failure; there is one "right" way of conducting a relationship, namely, according to the recipe.
6. *Fantasy.* The individual often expects to save a princess or to be saved by a prince; or the individual may hope to marry a prince or a princess and then to live happily ever after.
7. *Game.* Love is viewed as a game or sport, with a winner and a loser (or more than one) loser.
8. *Gardening.* Relationships need to be treated like a garden, meaning they need to be continually nurtured and tended to.
9. *Government.* (a) *Autocratic.* One partner dominates over, or even controls the other. (b) *Democratic.* The two partners equally share power in the relationship.
10. *History.* Events occurring during the relationship form an indelible record; individuals keep a lot of records—mental or physical—which then become part of the ongoing relationship and its history.
11. *Horror.* Relationships become interesting and worthwhile when one partner terrorizes or is terrorized by your partner. Partners seek either to terrorize each other, or for one to terrorize the other.
12. *House and Home.* Relationships have their basis in the home, through its development and maintenance, and so the relationship centers around the home, both physically and spiritually.
13. *Humor.* Love funny and sometimes strange and a good relationship involves recognition of its humorous aspects.
14. *Mystery.* Love is mysterious and you shouldn't let too much about yourself be known, or at least known easily, because part of the thrill for the partner is figuring everything out.
15. *Police.* Love is like a relationship between a police officer and a lawbreaker. You must keep close tabs on your partner to make sure the partner is staying within the limits. Or you may feel you need to be kept under surveillance to ensure you behave properly.
16. *Pornography.* Love is dirty, and so to love is to degrade another person or to be degraded by that person. It is the degradation that creates excitement in the relationship.
17. *Recovery.* This story involves a survivor mentality; it encompasses the view that after past trauma, a person can get through practically anything and a partner can serve as a kind of life raft to bring the person to safety.

Table 4.1 Continued

18. *Religion.* The partners either view love itself as a religion, or view love as a set of feelings and activities dictated or guided by religion.
19. *Sacrifice.* To love is to give of oneself or for the benefit of someone else or for someone to give of themselves to you.
20. *Science.* Love is like any other natural phenomenon, and can be understood, analyzed, and dissected, just like any other natural phenomenon can be.
21. *Science Fiction.* This story involves the feeling that one's partner is like an alien—incomprehensible, strange, and nothing like the humans with whom one has dealt in the past.
22. *Sewing.* Love is whatever you make it out to be—you sew together your relationship into a new construction.
23. *Theater.* Love is scripted, much like a play, with predictable acts, scenes, and lines. Any relationship involves going through one or more scripts, with variations. Love is whatever the play script requires.
24. *Travel.* Love is a journey and the partners are on the journey together, trying to hew to the same path to the extent possible.
25. *War.* Love comprises a series of pitched battles, often carefully planned and executed, in a devastating but continuing war, where one person wins and the other loses. Who wins and loses depends on how well each fights the battles.
26. *Student-teacher.* Love is a relationship between a student and a teacher. The roles of student and teacher may reverse from time, but one person is almost always teaching the other. The roles may vary not only over time but over situations.

Ideals play into stories in four key ways. Let's consider each in turn.

First, each story represents an ideal for a relationship—a kind of prototype for what one would like a relationship to be. A real relationship may succeed to the extent that, for a given individual, the real relationship approximates the idealization of the story. For example, in a fairy tale story, a partner may feel that the relationship succeeds to the extent that the partner can view his or her significant other as occupying the role of prince or princess.

Second, when a partner departs from the ideal—which may be an initial departure or a departure that develops over time—the relationship may begin to fail because of the development of that departure from the ideal. The relationship may also become more open to external threat from another potential partner if some other potential partner fits the ideal story better than does the current partner.

Third, couples tend to be happy in relationships to the extent that they have matching hierarchical profiles of stories. That is, their hierarchies of stories tend to be more or less the same (Sternberg, Hojjat, & Barnes 2001). The stories they want more and want less, in general, roughly match, although an exact match is unlikely. The greater the discrepancy in the profile of more and less preferred stories, the less satisfied couples tend to be in their relationship.

Fourth, the chances of a couple having exactly matching hierarchies of stories when they first meet are negligible. So, an important element of success is a kind of flexibility. Can each of the partners develop or even modify their stories so as to suit the preferences and needs of their partner? If they cannot, the relationship is more susceptible to external threats.

In sum, stories represent idealized prototypes and people in relationships seek to match their stories in their life. When relationships do not quite match the stories, people will sometimes try to transform the relationships so as better to match the stories. In other words, people will try to match the stories, and if they do not, they may try to bring their stories more closely into alignment by modifying them. This is easier said than done, as stories have been socialized, interacting with personality, over a period of many years.

According to the theory, all relationships are observed and interpreted through stories. We never know any "objective" reality apart from our perceptions, but rather, only the subjective reality that the filter of our stories allows. For us, our perceptions seem "real." If the relationship does not match a preferred story, we may realize something is not working for us, but not know exactly what, because stories are largely preconscious. We feel the relationship is not quite what love should be, but for reasons that never quite clarify themselves to us. It is for this reason that using a love story scale can be useful to people—to clarify their own stories and how their current, past, and future, relationships fit into the schemas established by these stories (Sternberg 1998b).

Together, the triangular theory and the theory of love as a story constitute a "duplex" theory of love (Sternberg 2006; 2019). The triangular part of the theory deals with the structure of love and the theory of love as a story with the idealized stories that, in combination with lived experience, produced that triangle. Relationship ideals also show themselves in another way, through jealousy and envy. Consider these unwanted psychological constructs next.

Models of Jealousy and Envy

People sometimes experience jealousy and envy in their love lives. My colleagues and I have studied the factors that contribute to jealousy and envy, and also their relation to relationships ideals (Sternberg, Kaur, & Mistur 2019). In the context of a relationship, jealousy occurs when an individual becomes distressed because their partner seems interested in someone else, or someone else seems interested in their partner, or both. The interest may have originated with the partner or it may have originated with the individual external to the relationship. Either way, the individual sees a threat to their existing relationship—they are at risk of losing what they have. Envy, in contrast, occurs when the individual is interested in some other person with whom they are not in a relationship but with whom they would like to have a relationship. They envy the person who is in the relationship with the potential partner they covet. So, jealousy occurs when there is someone you have but are afraid of losing, whereas envy occurs when there is someone you want but you do not yet have and may never have.

Many people experience jealousy and envy as temporary problems. The feelings come and go. But other people chronically experience jealousy, envy, or both. They seem almost actively to seek out feelings of jealousy and envy. They may be hyper-alert, constantly looking for signs that their partner is interested in someone else, or constantly looking for a partner they desire more than the one they have, and then feeling envious of the individual who is perceived as lucky enough to be with that partner. They are never happy where they are in their relationships.

Navjot Kaur, Elisabeth Mistur, and I divided possible predictors of jealousy and envy into two groups: internal and external. Internal predictors are ones that exist within you. External predictors are ones that come from the outside. We then sought to model variables that were powerful predictors of jealousy and of envy.

Jealousy

With regard to jealousy, three predictors consistently proved to be important across different kinds of situations. First was an external variable—*threat to the existing relationship*: The individual perceives a threat to their relationship. The other two variables were internal. Second was the *need of the existing partner*: The individual feels like they need their partner. If they do not much need the partner, then the thought of someone going after the partner, or of the partner going after someone else, is not so threatening. The third predictor was *trust of your partner*. People are more likely to feel jealous if they don't trust their partner.

Envy

With regard to envy, an external variable, *threat* was again a good predictor. But here the threat was not to an existing relationship, but to the person's ideal for their life. There was one other external variable that mattered in prediction—*plausibility of the potential partner for a future relationship*. That is, someone might feel envy toward the partner of a famous celebrity because they are in a romantic relationship with the celebrity. But they likely will feel less envious to the extent that they understand that, realistically, they have little or no chance in hell of ever being with the actor or actress. It's just not plausible. The internal variables that best predicted envy were, first, *how much the individual wants the potential partner*, and, second, *how much the individual cares about the potential partner* (Sternberg, Kaur, & Mistur 2019).

Wanting someone as a partner and caring about that individual are not the same thing. An individual might want a potential partner because they are intensely attracted to the person's appearance or other qualities. But they do not necessarily care about the person. Indeed, they may never have met them and may never have had any communication with them. Or they might care about a potential partner but not want them all so much because they realize that they are happy and satisfied with the life they are living and are not prepared to leave it behind.

In the case of jealousy, one's ideal is to stay with what one has. In the case of envy, one's ideal is to gain the affection or the perceived possession of a person they do not have as a partner. (Of course, there are other kinds of envy besides that related to love, such as of possessions or achievements.) Either way, one tries to maintain an idealized state (jealousy) or obtain one (envy). The problem is that often the aspirations toward an ideal state are unrealistic and unlikely to be realized.

CONCLUSION

In conclusion, intimate relationships are between two material persons but also involve ideal persons who have no material substance. All partners have ideals, the nature of which they may not even be aware of. A further complexity is that each partner may have more than one ideal, with some ideals being more "ideal" than others. That is, they may have several hierarchically arranged stories that they prefer over other stories. Any of the preferred stories can result in a relationship, but that relationship can be knocked out by a future relationship that represents a more preferred story. These preferences do not necessarily remain entirely stable over time. In intimate relationships, therefore, there is always a note of uncertainty. Relationships between actual people may change, but so may ideals, resulting in a situation where the greatest key to success in intimate relationships may be flexibility in the face of relationship change resulting from constantly changing circumstances.

REFERENCES

Ainsworth, M. D. S. (1973). The development of infant–mother attachment. In B. M. Caldwell & H. M. Ricciuti (Eds.), *Review of child development research* (Vol. 3). University of Chicago Press.

Ainsworth, M. D. S. (1989). Attachments beyond infancy. *American Psychologist, 44,* 709–716.

Bowlby, J. (2012). *The making and breaking of affectional bonds.* Routledge.

Bradbury, T. N., & Karney, B. R. (2019). *Intimate relationships* (3rd ed.). W. W. Norton.

Buss, D. M. (1994). *The evolution of desire: Strategies of human mating.* Basic Books.

Buss, D. M. (2019). The evolution of love in humans. In R. J. Sternberg & K. Sternberg (Eds.), *The new psychology of love* (2nd ed., pp. 42–63). Cambridge University Press.

Collins, N. L., & Feeney, B. C. (2004). An attachment theory perspective on closeness and intimacy. In D. J. Mashek & A. Aron (Eds.), *Handbook of closeness and intimacy* (pp. 163–187). Erlbaum.

Hazan, C., & Shaver, P. R. (1987). Romantic love conceptualized as an attachment process. *Journal of Personality and Social Psychology, 2,* 511–524.

Kenrick, D. T., & Keefe, R. C. (1992). Age preferences in mates reflect sex differences in human reproductive strategies. *Behavioral and Brain Sciences, 15,* 75–133.

Levinger, G., Rands, M., & Talaber, R. (1977). *The assessment of involvement and rewardingness in close and casual pair relationships* (National Science Foundation Technical Report DK). University of Massachusetts, Amherst.

Maslow, A. H. (1943). A theory of human motivation. *Psychological Review, 50*(4), 370–396.

Maslow, A. H. (1954). *Motivation and personality.* Harper and Row.

Maslow, A. H. (1962). *Toward a psychology of being.* D. Van Nostrand Company.

Mikulincer, M., & Shaver, P. R. (2019). A behavioral systems approach to romantic to romantic love relationships: Attachment, caregiving, and sex. In R. J. Sternberg & K. Sternberg (Eds.), *The new psychology of love* (2nd ed., pp. 259–279). Cambridge University Press.

Rubin, Z. (1970). Measurement of romantic love. *Journal of Personality and Social Psychology, 16*(2), 265–273. https://doi.org/10.1037/h0029841

Sorokowski, P., Sorokowska, A., Karwowski, M., Groyecka, A., Aavik, T., ... Sternberg, R. J. (2020). Universality of the triangular theory of love: Adaptation and psychometric properties of the Triangular Love Scale in 25 countries. *Journal of Sex Research.* https://doi.org/10.1080/00224499.2020.1787318

Spearman, C. (1927). *The abilities of man.* Macmillan.

Sternberg, R. J. (1986). A triangular theory of love. *Psychological Review, 93,* 119–135.

Sternberg, R. J. (1997). Construct validation of a triangular love scale. *European Journal of Social Psychology, 27*(3), 313–335.

Sternberg, R. J. (1998a). *Cupid's arrow: The course of love through time.* Cambridge University Press.

Sternberg, R. J. (1998b). *Love is a story.* Oxford University Press.

Sternberg, R.J. (2006). A duplex theory of love. In R. J. Sternberg & K. Weis (Eds.), *The new psychology of love* (pp. 184–199). Yale University Press.

Sternberg, R. J. (2019). When love goes awry (Part 1): Applications of the duplex theory of love and its development to relationships gone bad. In R. J. Sternberg & K. Sternberg (Eds.), *The new psychology of love* (2nd ed., pp. 280–299). Cambridge University Press.

Sternberg, R. J., & Barnes, M. (1985). Real and ideal others in romantic relationships: Is four a crowd? *Journal of Personality and Social Psychology, 49,* 1586–1608.

Sternberg, R. J., & Grajek, S. (1984). The nature of love. *Journal of Personality and Social Psychology, 47,* 312–329.

Sternberg, R. J., Hojjat, M., & Barnes, M. L. (2001). Empirical aspects of a theory of love as a story. *European Journal of Personality, 15*(3), 199–218.

Sternberg, R. J., Kaur, N., & Mistur, E. J. (2019). When love goes awry (Part 2): Application of an augmented triangular theory of love to personal and situational factors in jealousy and envy. In R. J. Sternberg & K. Sternberg (Eds.), *The new psychology of love* (2nd ed., pp. 300–330). Cambridge University Press.

Sternberg, R. J., & Sternberg, K. (Eds.) (2019). *The new psychology of love* (2nd ed.). Cambridge University Press.

Thibaut, J. W., & Kelley, H. H. (1959). *The social psychology of groups.* Wiley.

Thomson, G. H. (1916). A hierarchy without a general factor. *British Journal of Psychology, 8,* 271–281.

Thurstone, L. L. (1938). *Primary mental abilities.* University of Chicago Press.

Section II

RELATIONSHIPS AND NORMS

Chapter 5

Love for One?

Romantic Love and Altruism in Pair-bonds

Bianca P. Acevedo

LOVE FOR ONE VERSUS LOVE FOR ALL

The moral psychology of love encompasses a wide array of topics as evidenced in this volume. This chapter focuses specifically on the moral psychology of love in the context of romantic pair-bonds. Romantic/passionate love is typically defined as "a state of intense longing for union with another" (Hatfield & Rapson 1996, p. 5), also referred to as "being in love" (Meyers & Berscheid 1997), "infatuation" (Fisher 1998), and "limerence" (Tennov 1999). All these conceptualizations include an obsessive element, characterized by intrusive thinking, intense focus on the partner, uncertainty, and mood swings. Other definitions of romantic love in the context of pair-bonds suggest that it includes "intensity, engagement, and sexual interest" (Acevedo & Aron 2009), as well as rapid inclusion of other in the self (Aron & Aron 1986). In recent times, research has shown that high levels of romantic love can exist in long-term marriages (Acevedo & Aron 2009; Acevedo et al. 2012; O'Leary et al. 2012).

However, it is interesting to note that in many earlier societies romantic love and marriage were not usually paired. This may have been due to strong religious norms. For example, in many Christian traditions, it was deemed to be immoral to love another person more than God (Coontz 2006; Hendrick & Hendrick 1992). Intense love was to be devoted to God, not another human. In these societies, marital unions were mostly reserved for practical matters such as exchange of wealth, land, power, raising children, and taking care of a household. Certainly, being highly passionate in a marriage could undermine familial, social, and other responsibilities. Thus, romantic love was seen as a threat to social norms and was mostly suppressed (Bataille 1962). Many

Eastern philosophies also minimize the role of romantic love as they apply a broader, more inclusive definition of love. For example, in Eastern traditions, love is defined as a desire to give unselfishly to another being, free of attachment and craving (i.e., Bstan-'dzin-rgya-mtsho & Hopkins 2006). In sum, in earlier times in both the East and the West, many societies undermined the role of romantic love in relationships. Instead, these traditions suggested that love ought to be reserved for God or devoted as a wish for the well-being of others. As a result, romantic love played, and continues to play, a minimal role in some societies where the focus is on responsibility, devotion, and the larger social structure (Riela et al. 2010).

In contrast, in modern Western times, romantic love plays a central role in marriages. Many people marry for love and see the disappearance of love as grounds for divorce (Simpson, Campbell, & Berscheid 1986). For many couples, marriage is viewed as a source of fulfillment and self-expression (Dion & Dion 1991). The modern couple may come together to fulfill functional duties, but many also simply marry for love in the hopes of building a life together to enjoy each other's company and support each other in reaching individual life goals (Rusbult, Finkel, & Kumanshiro 2009). Pleasure, joy, meaning, and intensity are the focus for many modern couples. As such, in many Western societies, romantic love and marriage have become strongly intertwined.

Another factor contributing to our emerging perspectives on the role of love in long-term relationships are the scientific advances in the biology of love, attachment, and pair-bonding. Recent studies suggest that there are underlying biological factors, including genetic variants, which play a role in attachment bonds and romantic love, and the processes that support their maintenance. Indeed, ascribing "special meaning" to specific others is the basis of mammalian "attachment." Attachment bonds serve important functions, including reproduction, raising of offspring, caregiving, and long-term companionship (Bowlby 1982; Conroy-Beam et al. 2015). Similarly, cooperation and altruistic tendencies are thought to have contributed to the success of our species and others (Wilson 1975). As such, attachment processes and their biological correlates, with corresponding social systems (marriage, raising children, and the family unit) have taken front stage in modern times, and provide one lens to consider a moral psychology of love.

Recent theoretical and scientific advances suggest that the mammalian system is intricately wired for attachment. This work includes investigations on pair-bonds, which are characterized by partner preference (over others), proximity-seeking, biparental care of offspring, sharing of a nest (or cohabitation), aggression toward strangers, and highly coordinated behaviors between couple pairs such as the tendency to travel together (e.g., Curtis et al. 2006; Mendoza & Mason 1986). Behaviors that characterize attachment bonds are caregiving and altruistic acts which are thought to have evolved to promote fitness of the species (Batson 2011; Preston & de Waal 2011). As such, the ascribing of special meaning to and focus on the well-being of a specific individual, over others, is consistent with depictions of attachment bonding. It is proposed that these complex social behaviors (with corresponding neural systems) evolved for the care of helpless offspring, but are also applied more broadly toward those we care for or develop attachments to, such as a spouse or a close friend (Preston 2013).

In sum, attachment is innate, efficient, and a condition of mammalian functioning, that is thought to have evolved for the success of the species. Inherent in attachment is a preference for specific others which includes loving behaviors, care, and proximity. With respect to social norms, it is indeed typically considered immoral for a person not to behave in a caring and nurturing way toward a loved one, for example, to provide them with care and support, especially in times of need. Also, it may be perceived as inappropriate for an individual to display the same level of affection toward a stranger as they would toward their child, spouse, or friend. Thus, herein I suggest that it is socially accepted and beneficial for individuals to ascribe special meaning to a specific other, including nonkin, such as a beloved romantic partner.

Building on this introduction, this chapter discusses two aspects that are central to the morality of romantic pair-bonds: monogamy and altruism. The chapter is organized in two sections. First, I will provide some background information on conceptualizations of pair-bonds and romantic love. Next, I will discuss three key interrelated topics on a moral psychology of love within pair-bonds: romantic love, monogamy, and altruism.

LOVE FOR ONE? THE SPECIAL CASE OF ROMANTIC LOVE IN PAIR-BONDS

As noted earlier, pair-bonds are characterized as a select partner preference where the couple shares territory, co-habits, and engages in coordinated behaviors together such as grooming, feeding, and mating (Walum & Young 2018). In humans, romantic love is thought to be an evolutionarily conserved strategy for reproduction, the biparental care of offspring, and long-term companionship (Acevedo et al. 2019). Psychological theories of romantic love propose that it is "an intense longing for union with another individual" (Hatfield & Rapson 1996). One widely accepted model of romantic love distinguishes between passionate love and companionate love, defined as a warm attachment where the individual experiences feelings of warmth, friendship, and nurturance toward the partner, but not necessarily sexual attraction. This model has been useful in explaining why passionate love often fades over time in relationships. Decreases in love are nontrivial because they often coincide with decreases in relationship satisfaction and relationship transgressions, such as devaluing of the partner and infidelity (Zak et al. 2002), which often result in divorce and diminished well-being (Huston et al., 2001; Jacobs & Lyubomirsky 2013). However, recent research suggests that high levels of romantic love can exist in long-term marriages with both passionate love (without infatuation) and companionate love (Acevedo & Aron 2009).

Somewhat similarly, other models have characterized different types of love within pair-bonds. For example, Love Attitudes Style (LAS) theory suggests that six different love styles—romantic love (Eros), infatuation (Ludus), pragmatic love (Pragma), friendship love (Storge), and altruistic love (Agape)—may be present, to different degrees, in any given relationship and relationship stage (Hendrick & Hendrick 1986). The LAS model has been useful in explaining why romantic love fluctuates as a function of human and relationship development. According to LAS theory, infatuation (Mania) and romantic love (Eros), which tend to appear in the early stages of relationships and in youth, are most susceptible to moral transgressions. Although there is some evidence that the level of each love style is partly a function of age and relationship stage, case studies and empirical research with individuals in love suggest that romantic love may appear at any life or relationship stage (Acevedo & Aron 2009; Tennov 1999). Also, altruistic, selfless, unconditional love does not only appear in the later stages of life and relationships in but may also appear at any relationship stage, including in the context of first-time newlywed marriages (Acevedo et al. 2019; Acevedo & Aron 2009).

Somewhat differently, and based in Eastern perspectives, the self-expansion model suggests that it is a basic human motivation to expand the self. According to this model, romantic relationships provide a unique opportunity to expand the self, through the inclusion of the partner in the self (for review see Aron et al. 2013). Using the Inclusion of Other in the Self (IOS) Scale (Aron et al. 1992), numerous studies over recent decades have shown that the rapid inclusion of the partner in the self coincides with feelings of romantic love (Aron et al. 1995). Somewhat similar views suggest that love is a function of increases in intimacy in couples, whereby rapid increases in intimacy are related to feelings of love (Baumeister & Bratslavsky 1999). In more recent times, researchers examining the possibility that love can last in long-term relationships have proposed that romantic love (without infatuation) is characterized by intensity, engagement, and sexual desire (Acevedo & Aron 2009). All of these models have corresponding scales that have been validated and widely used over recent decades.

EVIDENCE OF THE SPECIAL NATURE OF
ROMANTIC LOVE IN PAIR-BONDS

A common theme among models of romantic love is that it includes characterizations of pair-bonds in nonhuman mammals as a "select" partner preference, where the "partner" takes on special meaning and becomes the intense
focus of the lover's attention. Often in committed, romantic relationships,
the partner becomes integrated into the self as shown by numerous studies of
self-expansion using the IOS Scale (for review see Branand, Mashek, & Aron
2019). Merging with the partner is a cardinal feature of romantic relationships, including psychological, emotional, cognitive, and social union (Cuber
& Harroff 1965).

Somewhat related to the intense focus and ascribing of special meaning to
the partner is idealization, where the lover places a high value on the beloved
and fails to see any flaws (Murray, Holmes, & Griffin 1996). Incidentally,
behaviors related to idealization of the partner are known as "positive illusions." Positive illusions are associated with a variety of relationship benefits
including higher levels of relationship satisfaction, love, and trust; and less
conflict and ambivalence in both dating and marital relationships (Murray &
Holmes 1997). Positive illusions also predict increases in later relationship
satisfaction. Moreover, longitudinal studies have shown that couples with
higher initial levels of positive illusions tended to have more stable, in-love
marriages measured over thirteen years (Miller, Nuehuis, & Huston 2006).
Correspondingly, studies of individuals in love have shown that romantic
love is positively associated with thinking about the partner, having positive
thoughts about the partner, and percentage of an average day spent thinking
about the partner (Fisher, Aron, & Brown 2006; O'Leary et al. 2012).

In sum, positive thinking about a partner that takes on special meaning and
is the focus of the lover's attention is a cardinal feature of romantic love in
adaptive pair-bonds. Positive illusions and focus on the partner provide relationship benefits, and serve to conserve the pair-bond. Also, focused, positive
thinking about the partner has important implications for pair-bonds as they
promote fidelity, trust, positive emotions, care, and stability in marriages. As
such, the special and positive meaning that a partner takes on promotes relationship quality and stability.

Brain imaging studies have confirmed self-report research suggesting that
in pair-bonds, the partner takes on special meaning. For example, numerous
studies have shown that in response to face images of the partner (versus
controls for facial familiarity and closeness), individuals in love showed
marked activation in brain regions that mediate reward, motivation, euphoria, attention, and higher-order cognitive processes (Acevedo et al. 2012;
Aron et al. 2005; Xu et al. 2011). Also, activation in dopamine-rich, reward

regions—namely, the ventral tegmental area (VTA) and striatum, were associated with commitment and relationship longevity as shown in a two-year study with young adults in China (Xu et al. 2012). Importantly, activation of dopamine-rich reward regions (i.e., the VTA) was also associated with sustained levels of romantic love as shown in a study of newlyweds scanned over the first year of marriage (Acevedo et al. 2020).

In addition to dopamine-rich activations, romantic love is also correlated with enhanced activity in brain regions that are rich in oxytocin and vasopressin in response to images of the romantic partner (Acevedo et al. 2012; Acevedo et al. 2020). Oxytocin is involved in a variety of complex social behaviors including trust, eye gaze, parental nurturing, empathy, and pair-bonding (for review, see Feldman 2012). Some researchers have termed oxytocin the "moral molecule" because it is involved in a variety of prosocial behaviors (Zak 2013). Vasopressin is also critical for pair-bonding and other social behaviors, such as social recognition, territorial behaviors, and aggressive behaviors toward outsiders, which coincidentally also serve pair-bond conservation (Walum & Young 2018).

In sum, self-report and brain imaging studies on romantic love provide evidence that for individuals in love, the partner takes on special meaning. Researchers have provided various conceptualizations and scales to measure the special nature of romantic love in pair-bonds. For example, some work has focused on positive illusions, idealization, and inclusion-of-other in the self. More recently, researchers have started to focus on the neural and genetic correlates of romantic love in dating relationships and marriages. Brain imaging studies of romantic love have shown that in response to face images of the beloved (versus familiar persons or a close friend), individuals in love show increased activation in brain regions associated with attention, motivation, reward, and higher-order cognitive processes. Also, activation of the dopamine-rich regions, implicated in motivation and attention, was associated with relationship longevity. In sum, these studies all confirm the conceptualizations of the beloved as taking on "special meaning." Also, this body of work suggests that the special meaning that a partner takes on helps to promote the conservation of the pair-bond, as love and positivity are associated with relationship quality, love, trust, fidelity and relationship stability.

MONOGAMY

In marriages, there are several expectations related to prosocial behaviors. The one that is most often cited and that causes many tensions in marriages is infidelity. Perhaps this is because infidelity provides a serious threat to the pair-bond, often resulting in relationship dissolution and divorce. Indeed, research suggests that only a small percentage of marriages survive infidelity (Shackelford 1998; Zare 2011). Also, infidelity results in other issues such as the redirection of resources outside of the family unit, which may result in competition and negative sentiments such as anger, punishment, and violence (Conroy-Beam et al. 2015). Therefore, we will begin with a discussion of monogamy in pair-bonds.

The expectation of monogamy in relationships, when there is a deviation from this norm, can be the source of much suffering for individuals and their families. Indeed, many relationships and marriages often fail because of breaches in trust and the expectation of monogamy. In nature, two types of monogamy are observed: social monogamy and sexual monogamy. Social monogamy is a mating system that is characterized by partners cohabiting, sharing in the biparental care of offspring, and preferential mating but not sexual exclusivity (Walum & Young 2018). Sexual monogamy is where the conditions of social monogamy are met, but sexual mating is reserved exclusively for the pair-bond partner. It's interesting to note that only 9 percent of mammals are sexually monogamous, while 90 percent of bird species display some form of monogamy (Lukas & Clutton-Brock 2013). Humans, however, are the exception to other mammals as they are mostly socially monogamous, showing a strong inclination for pair-bonding in nearly all cultures and societies (Jankowiak & Fischer 1992).

Sexual monogamy is another part of the pair-bonding story. Sexual monogamy is rare in nature, but the expectation of social and sexual monogamy is common for human pair-bonds. However, many individuals engage in sexual acts outside the pair-bond. *Infidelity*, defined as a breach in the promise of sexual exclusivity, is the leading cause of divorce in the United States. Some statistics suggest that more than 50 percent of "committed" dating people "cheat" on their partner, at least 20 percent of "monogamous" married people "cheat," and many individuals think about sex with someone other than their partner but don't act on their impulses (Rosenberg 2018). Infidelity gives rise to a variety of negative sentiments and behaviors including jealousy, hatred, suicide, intimate partner violence, and homicide.

Given these weighty repercussions, some individuals restrain their impulses to be unfaithful for various reasons. Some may fear reprisal, shame, and disappointment by their partners, peers, and/or community; or contracting a disease. Others may refrain from engaging in infidelity for more practical reasons such as reserving resources and investments for their partner and/or offspring (Conroy-Beam et al. 2015). Yet, for others, the decision to remain sexually faithful to the pair-bond partner may arise from compliance with social norms. For some individuals, the motivation to refrain from cheating, despite the impulse to do otherwise, may stem from care, empathy, and consideration for the partner's feelings and well-being. Finally, for others, the impulse to engage in sex outside the pair-bond may not be there at all. These individuals are likely to be in love and/or true "monogamous" types.

Recent research suggests that there may be genes that underlie sexual monogamy. For example, the *DRD4-7R* gene variant, associated with dopamine function, has been shown to predict short-term pair-bonding strategies (Minkov & Bond 2015), novelty-seeking (He et al. 2018, meta-analysis; Munafò et al. 2008, meta-analysis), and a desire for a wider variety of sexual behaviors (Halley et al. 2016). Notably, the *DRD4-7R* variant has also been associated with higher rates of promiscuous behavior and infidelity in humans (Garcia et al. 2010). Interestingly, the *DRD4-7R* variant was also shown to be associated with sustained feelings of romantic love in newlyweds measured in their first year of marriage (Acevedo et al. 2020). This particular dopamine gene variant appears not only to play a role in infidelity and sexual behaviors, but also importantly in sustaining feelings of romantic love. Indeed, romantic love has been shown to buffer couples from infidelity and attention to alternative partners (Gonzaga et al. 2008; Maner, Gailliot, & Miller 2009).

Although only some individuals appear to have a predisposition to be sexually monogamous and remain in love, many humans continue to pair-bond and marry despite the odds. Indeed, this is a Catch-22 because although many couples may enter their marriage with the hope of living happily ever after, it is not uncommon for couples to experience decreases in love which often coincide with a higher probability for infidelity, dissatisfaction, and divorce (Huston et al. 2001). Thus, does it seem just to legally condemn sexual infidelity in marriages if some individuals may simply not be "wired for monogamy"? (see Piemonte et al. in this volume for a discussion).

Answering this question is beyond the scope of this chapter because it would require considering not only individual differences for monogamy, but also varying cultural and societal norms. Luckily, there are other options beyond infidelity. For example, humans have a relatively large cortical brain surface (compared to other mammals) that coordinates complex, higher-order thinking, including self-reflection, empathy, moral processing, and the communication of complex ideas (Sun & Hevner 2014). Also, mind–body practices including yoga and meditation, psycho/cognitive/behavioral therapy, and biofeedback strengthen high-order circuits necessary for self-regulation, empathy, and perspective-taking. As such, these techniques benefit individuals' well-being (see Acevedo, Pospos, & Lavretsky 2016; Fischer, Baucom, & Cohen 2016) and also couple well-being (e.g., Mclean et al. 2013; Whitebird et al. 2013; Acevedo et al. 2021).

Humans are creative, so some couples have adopted their own social norms for sexual behavior in their relationships/marriages. For example, some couples engage in what is known as consensual non-monogamy (CNM), whereby both partners consent to nonexclusive sexual partnerships. Although there is still some moral stigma against CNM, couples that practice CNM report similar or better sexual health practices relative to a monogamous couple. Also, couples that engage in CNM have more diversified needs fulfillment, greater social opportunities, and more fluid sexual expression (for review, see Mogilski et al. 2019); and these benefits are associated with enhanced relationship satisfaction (Levine et al. 2018). Thus, although there is still a moral stigma around CNM, these communities appear to have comparable relationship satisfaction, added benefits, and perhaps they circumvent issues around infidelity such as partner jealousy, partner/child abandonment, and risk of divorce.

In sum, sexual monogamy is the exception, not the rule, in most mammals. However, humans are unique such that pair-bonds are observed in nearly every society around the globe. Sexual monogamy, however, is rare in nature but remains a critical expectation of human romantic partnerships. Most societies endorse strong social norms for sexual fidelity in pair-bonds, most notably in marriages. Indeed, a cardinal characteristic of marriage is sexual monogamy, whereby many societies shun infidelity and have instilled legal repercussions for extra-pair copulation.

However, due to recent advances in the science of pair-bonding and attachment behaviors, it has become clear that individual differences in neurobiology, including genetic variance, underlie the propensity to a pair-bond, remain in love, and be sexually monogamous. Nevertheless, strong social norms for sexual monogamy prevail in many human societies despite there being alternative, progressive options, such as CNM, that are perhaps better aligned with scientific data on individual differences in pair-bonding neurobiology and couple well-being.

ALTRUISM

Another common expectation of romantic pair-bonds is caring, empathy, and altruistic behaviors. Although this facet is somewhat more variable and lenient (many couples may not consider a partner that would not be willing to die for them a "deal-breaker"), kindness is one of the top variables that both women and men find desirable in a partner (Buss & Barnes 1986). However, altruism is different from monogamy in that it is commonly applied widely, beyond the pair-bond. Altruism is thought to be rooted in neurobiological mechanisms to promote offspring care, being observed most prominently in kin and close relationships but also extending to others (Preston 2013). However, evolution is thought to have conserved altruism to respond to others' needs, even at a cost to the self, with the function of promoting species survival and fitness (Batson 2011; de Waal 2008).

Social psychologists have considered the existence of altruistic love (Agape) as an important factor for relationships. Indeed, a large survey study conducted at the National Opinion Center in Chicago showed the greater self-reported altruism towards a partner was associated with more marital happiness (Smith 2005). Also, this survey showed that altruism was associated with commitment, as 40 percent of married individuals ranked near the top of the altruism scale, 25 percent of divorced and separated respondents endorsed high levels of altruism, and only 20 percent of those who had never married endorsed high levels of altruism. In sum, altruism may support pair-bond establishment, happiness, and conservation.

In the only neurobiological study of altruism in marriages (Acevedo et al. 2019), findings showed that altruism (measured with the Agape Scale) was positively associated with passionate love (measured with the Passionate Love Scale) and an oxytocin gene variant (*OXTR* rs53576—a greater number of G-alleles), which is associated with complex social behaviors including empathy (Buffone & Poulin 2014; Uzefovsky, Döring, & Knafo-Noam 2016), empathic accuracy (Rodrigues et al. 2009), sensitive parenting (Bakermans-Kranenburg & van Ijzendoorn 2008), and overall greater empathic ability (Gong et al. 2017) and sociality (Li et al. 2015). In one study, newlyweds were shown various empathy/emotion (happy and sad)-inducing and neutral face images of the partner and a stranger. Results showed that in response to partner happy and sad images, newlyweds showed greater brain response in the ventral pallidum (VP), an area of the brain that is critical for attachment and pair-bonding (see Acevedo et al. 2019, for review), as a function of greater altruism and OXTR G-alleles. However, participants did not show significant VP activity in response to strangers' face images. Moreover, specifically in response to happy partner faces, participants showed enhanced responsivity in regions implicated in reward- (the nucleus accumbens) and emotion- (amygdala and septum) processing, as a function of increasing altruism scores and OXTR G-alleles. Also, specifically in response to sad partner faces, participants showed enhanced responsivity in the amygdala and decreased response in the dopamine-rich reward region of the VTA. Only the amygdala showed a similar pattern of response to stranger sad images.

In sum, results from brain imaging studies suggest that altruism in marriages is associated with higher passionate love scores: an OXTR genotype associated with social behaviors including pair-bonding; and the activation of brain regions that support pair-bonding (VP), reward, and emotional responsivity (septum and amygdala) in response to partner images. It's interesting to note that many of these activations did not appear in response to strangers' emotional expressions (except for the amygdala showing activity to sad stranger images) suggesting that on a very basic level, humans ascribe special meaning to their loved ones.

Moreover, contrary to many Eastern and spiritual perspectives it appears that the social mind discriminates, ascribing special meaning to those we are close to and thus responding more strongly in response to their needs. More importantly, this work suggests that beyond romance and sexual monogamy, selfless caring for a partner also plays a pivotal role in the happiness and conservation of the pair-bond.

FUTURE DIRECTIONS

The current state of knowledge on the science of pair-bonding provides promising evidence for the nature of love, monogamy and altruism, but work remains to be done. For example, many of the neuroimaging studies to date have used rather small and constrained samples, limiting the generalizability of the results. Nevertheless, many of the key findings, most notably the activation of the reward system in the context of romantic love and pair-bonding processes, were replicated across human studies of early-stage and long-term romantic love, and in newlyweds, as well as across cultures (United States, China, and the United Kingdom), in homosexual and heterosexual pair-bonds, and in studies using a variety of stimuli (for review, see Acevedo 2015). Also, these findings were confirmed across species, appearing in the context of monogamous pair-bonding in rodent mammals and primates, as well (for review, see Walum & Young 2018). Moreover, in newlywed brain imaging studies, findings were replicated within individuals scanned twice, with functional MRI, over the first year of marriage (Acevedo et al. 2020). Furthermore, taking into account the point made by Goetz et al. (2019), suggesting that human research participants are often nonrepresentative and WEIRD (Western, Educated, Industrialized, Rich, and Democratic), it is important for future studies to make concerted efforts to recruit more representative samples.

In the emerging field of the "science of pair-bonding," only a small number of genes have been examined. For example, the dopamine receptor variant DRD4-7R has been associated with promiscuous behavior and infidelity (Garcia et al. 2010), as well as the propensity to sustain romantic love (Acevedo et al. 2020). However, there are other possibilities to explore. It will be critical for future research to examine a wider array of genetic polymorphisms underlying pair-bonding with larger samples, both with genome-wide association studies (GWAS) and more directed approaches with predicted polymorphisms. It has been shown that in many cases single genes have very small effect sizes (for review, see Fox & Beevers 2016). However, GWAS studies are limited in that they require very large sample sizes (Landefeld et al. 2018). Other important genetic variants may also be examined in future studies, for example, the 5-HTTLPR VNTR of the serotonin transporter gene that has been associated with differences in life history strategy and risk acceptance in mating competition (Minkov & Bond 2015). Also, it is important to note that although identifying biological markers for pair-bonding in group studies is helpful, individual differences must be accounted for. For example, in recent years, OT has received significant attention for strengthening pair-bonds (e.g., Quintana et al. 2019). However, responses to OT may vary according to some oxytocin genetic polymorphisms and gender (e.g., Pearce et al. 2019; Xu et al. 2020).

CONCLUSIONS

Historically, many spiritual and Eastern traditions have minimized the role of romantic love, defined as a desire for union with a specific individual, in relationships. However, recent scientific advances provide evidence for the special nature of the pair-bond. As such, this chapter builds on the idea that the tendency to form a pair-bond is rooted in mammalian biology for reproduction, attachment, and long-term companionship. Next, the chapter focused on two key issues centered around the morality of pair-bonds: monogamy and altruism. I highlighted recent evidence suggesting that although humans show a proclivity for pair-bonding, there are individual differences in how pair-bonding behaviors are expressed. For example, recent neuroimaging and genetic studies suggest that dopamine, oxytocin, and vasopressin genes modulate individuals' propensity to stay in love, be sexually monogamous, and express altruism toward their partner. Although many of these behaviors appear to be out of our control, humans have the advantage of a large cortex which allows them to engage in complex thinking and behaviors which may facilitate the overriding of impulses or developing new systems that are better aligned with their individual biology. Yet, another possibility resides in future technologies which may allow humans to manipulate their own biology (through epigenetics) to meet their individual needs and standards.

REFERENCES

Acevedo, B. (2015). Neural correlates of human attachment: Evidence from fMRI studies of adult pair- bonding. In Zayas, V. & Hazan, C. (Eds.). *Bases of adult attachment: From brain to mind to behavior*. NY, NY: Springer.

Acevedo, B. P., & Aron, A. (2009). Does a long-term relationship kill romantic love? *Review of General Psychology*, *13*(1), 59–65.

Acevedo, B. P., Aron, A., Fisher, H. E., & Brown, L. L. (2012). Neural correlates of long-term intense romantic love. *Social Cognitive and Affective Neuroscience*, *7*(2), 145–159. https://doi.org/10.1093/scan/nsq092.

Acevedo, B. P., Aron, A., Fisher, H. E., & Brown, L. L. (2012). Neural correlates of marital satisfaction and well-being: reward, empathy, and affect. *Clinical Neuropsychiatry, 9*(1), 20–31.

Acevedo, B.A, Marhenke, R., Kosik, K. S., Zarinafsar, S., Santander, T. (2021). Yoga improves older adults' affective functioning and resting-state brain connectivity: Evidence from a pilot study, *Aging and Health Research, 10018.* https://doi.org/10.1016/j.ahr.2021.100018.

Acevedo, B. P., Pospos, S., & Lavretsky, H. (2016). The neural mechanisms of meditative practices: Novel approaches for healthy aging. *Current Behavioral Neuroscience Reports, 3*(4), 328–339. https://doi.org/10.1007/s40473-016-0098-x.

Acevedo, B. P., Poulin, M. J., Collins, N. L., & Brown, L. L. (2020). After the honeymoon: Neural and genetic correlates of romantic love in newlywed marriages. *Frontiers in Psychology, 11*, 634. https://doi.org/10.3389/fpsyg.2020.00634.

Acevedo, B. P., Poulin, M. J., Geher, G., Grafton, S., & Brown, L. L. (2019). The neural and genetic correlates of satisfying sexual activity in heterosexual pair-bonds. *Brain and Behavior, 9*(6), e01289. https://doi.org/10.1002/brb3.1289.

Acevedo, B., Poulin, M., Brown, L. (2019a). Beyond romance: Neural and genetic correlates of altruism in pair-bonds. *Behavioral Neuroscience, 133*(1), 18–31.

Aron, A., & Aron, E. N. (1986). *Love and the expansion of self: Understanding attraction and satisfaction.* Hemisphere Publishing Corp/Harper & Row Publishers.

Aron, A., Aron, E. N., & Smollan, D. (1992). Inclusion of Other in the Self Scale and the structure of interpersonal closeness. *Journal of Personality and Social Psychology, 63*(4), 596–612. https://doi.org/10.1037/0022-3514.63.4.596.

Aron, A., Fisher, H., Mashek, D. J., Strong, G., Li, H., & Brown, L. L. (2005). Reward, motivation, and emotion systems associated with early-stage intense romantic love. *Journal of Neurophysiology, 94*(1), 327–337. https://doi.org/10.1152/jn.00838.2004.

Aron, A., Lewandowski Jr, G., Mashek, D., & Aron, E. (2013). The self-expansion model of motivation and cognition in close relationships. *The Oxford Handbook of Close Relationships*, 90–115.

Aron, A., Paris, M., & Aron, E. N. (1995). Falling in love: Prospective studies of self-concept change. *Journal of Personality and Social Psychology, 69*(6), 1102–1112. https://doi.org/10.1037/0022-3514.69.6.1102.

Bakermans-Kranenburg, M. J., & van Ijzendoorn, M. H. (2008). Oxytocin receptor (OXTR) and serotonin transporter (5-HTT) genes associated with observed parenting. *Social Cognitive and Affective Neuroscience, 3*(2), 128–134. https://doi.org/10.1093/scan/nsn004.

Bataille, G. (1962). *Death and sensuality.* Walker.

Batson, C. D. (2011). *Altruism in humans.* Oxford University Press.

Baumeister, R. F., & Bratslavsky, E. (1999). Passion, intimacy, and time: Passionate love as a function of change in intimacy. *Personality and Social Psychology Review, 3*(1), 49–67. https://doi.org/10.1207/s15327957pspr0301_3.

Bowlby, J. (1982). *Attachment* (2. ed.). *Attachment and loss: / John Bowlby; Vol. 1.* Basic Books.

Branand, B., Mashek, D., & Aron, A. (2019). Pair-bonding as inclusion of other in the self: A literature review. *Frontiers in Psychology, 10*, 2399. https://doi.org/10.3389/fpsyg.2019.02399.

Bstan-'dzin-rgya-mtsho, & Hopkins, J. (2006). *How to expand love: Widening the circle of loving relationships* (1st Atria books trade paperback ed.). Atria Books.

Buffone, A. E. K., & Poulin, M. J. (2014). Empathy, target distress, and neurohormone genes interact to predict aggression for others-even without provocation. *Personality & Social Psychology Bulletin, 40*(11), 1406–1422.

Buss, D. M., & Barnes, M. (1986). Preferences in human mate selection. *Journal of Personality and Social Psychology, 50*(3), 559–570. https://doi.org/10.1037/0022-3514.50.3.559.

Conroy-Beam, D., Goetz, C. D., & Buss, D. M. (2015). Why do humans form long-term mateships? An evolutionary game-theoretic model. In J. M. Olson & M. P. Zanna (Eds.), *Advances in experimental social psychology* (Vol. 51, pp. 1–39). Academic Press. https://doi.org/10.1016/bs.aesp.2014.11.001.

Coontz, S. (2006). *Marriage, a history: How love conquered marriage.* Penguin Books.

Cuber, J., & Harroff, P. (1965). *The Significant Americans: A Study of Sexual Behavior Among the Affluent* (1st ed.). Century.

Curtis, J. T., Liu, Y., Aragona, B. J., & Wang, Z. (2006). Dopamine and monogamy. *Brain Research, 1126*(1), 76–90. doi:10.1016/j.brainres.2006.07.126

de Waal, F. B. M. de (2008). Putting the altruism back into altruism: The evolution of empathy. *Annual Review of Psychology, 59*, 279–300.

Dion, K. K., & Dion, K. L. (1991). Psychological individualism and romantic love. *Journal of Social Behavior and Personality, 6*(1), 17.

Feldman, R. (2012). Oxytocin and social affiliation in humans. *Hormones and Behavior, 61*(3), 380–391. https://doi.org/10.1016/j.yhbeh.2012.01.008.

Fischer, M. S., Baucom, D. H., & Cohen, M. J. (2016). Cognitive-behavioral couple therapies: Review of the evidence for the treatment of relationship distress, psychopathology, and chronic health conditions. *Family Process, 55*(3), 423–442. https://doi.org/10.1111/famp.12227.

Fisher, H. E., Aron, A., & Brown, L. L. (2006). Romantic love: A mammalian brain system for mate choice. *Philosophical Transactions of the Royal Society of London. Series B, Biological Sciences, 361*(1476), 2173–2186. https://doi.org/10.1098/rstb.2006.1938.

Fox, E., & Beevers, C. G. (2016). Differential sensitivity to the environment: Contribution of cognitive biases and genes to psychological wellbeing. *Molecular Psychiatry, 21*(12), 1657–1662. https://doi.org/10.1038/mp.2016.114.

Garcia, J. R., MacKillop, J., Aller, E. L., Merriwether, A. M., Wilson, D. S., & Lum, J. K. (2010). Associations between dopamine D4 receptor gene variation with both infidelity and sexual promiscuity. *PLoS One, 5*(11), e14162. https://doi.org/10.1371/journal.pone.0014162.

Goetz, C. D., Pillsworth, E. G., Buss, D. M., & Conroy-Beam, D. (2019). Evolutionary mismatch in mating. *Frontiers in Psychology, 10*, 2709. https://doi.org/10.3389/fpsyg.2019.02709.

Gong, P., Fan, H., Liu, J., Yang, X., Zhang, K., & Zhou, X. (2017). Revisiting the impact of OXTR rs53576 on empathy: A population-based study and a meta-analysis. *Psychoneuroendocrinology, 80*, 131–136. https://doi.org/10.1016/j.psyneuen .2017.03.005.

Gonzaga, G. C., Haselton, M. G., Smurda, J., Davies, M. s., & Poore, J. C. (2008). Love, desire, and the suppression of thoughts of romantic alternatives☆. *Evolution and Human Behavior, 29*(2), 119–126. https://doi.org/10.1016/j.evolhumbehav .2007.11.003.

Halley, A. C., Boretsky, M., Puts, D. A., & Shriver, M. (2016). Self-reported sexual behavioral interests and polymorphisms in the dopamine receptor D4 (DRD4) Exon III VNTR in heterosexual young adults. *Archives of Sexual Behavior, 45*(8), 2091–2100. https://doi.org/10.1007/s10508-015-0646-6.

Hatfield, E., & Rapson, R. L. (1996). Stress and passionate love. In C. D. Spielberger & I. G. Sarason (Eds.), *Stress and emotion: Anxiety, anger, and curiosity* (Vol. 16, 29–50). Hemisphere Publ. Corp.

He, Y., Martin, N., Zhu, G., & Liu, Y. (2018). Candidate genes for novelty-seeking: A meta analysis of association studies of DRD4 exon III and COMT Val158Met. *Psychiatric Genetics, 28*(6), 97–109. https://doi.org/10.1097/YPG .0000000000000209.

Hendrick, S. S., & Hendrick, C. (1992). *Romantic love.* Sage.

Hendrick, C., & Hendrick, S. (1986). A theory and method of love. *Journal of Personality and Social Psychology, 50*(2), 392–402. https://doi.org/10.1037/0022 -3514.50.2.392.

Huston, T. L., Caughlin, J. P., Houts, R. M., Smith, S. E., & George, L. J. (2001). The connubial crucible: Newlywed years as predictors of marital delight, distress, and divorce. *Journal of Personality and Social Psychology, 80*(2), 237–252. https://doi .org/10.1037/0022- 3514.80.2.237.

Jacobs Bao, K., & Lyubomirsky, S. (2013). Making it last: Combating hedonic adaptation in romantic relationships. *The Journal of Positive Psychology, 8*(3), 196–206.

Jankowiak, W. R., & Fischer, E. F. (1992). A cross-cultural perspective on romantic love. *Ethnology, 31*(2), 149. https://doi.org/10.2307/3773618.

Landefeld, C. C., Hodgkinson, C. A., Spagnolo, P. A., Marietta, C. A., Shen, P.-H., Sun, H., Zhou, Z., Lipska, B. K., & Goldman, D. (2018). Effects on gene expression and behavior of untagged short tandem repeats: The case of arginine vasopressin receptor 1a (AVPR1a) and externalizing behaviors. *Translational Psychiatry, 8*(1), 72.

Levine, E. C., Herbenick, D., Martinez, O., Fu, T.-C., & Dodge, B. (2018). Open relationships, nonconsensual nonmonogamy, and monogamy among U.S. adults: Findings from the 2012 National Survey of Sexual Health and Behavior. *Archives of Sexual Behavior, 47*(5), 1439–1450. https://doi.org/10.1007/s10508 -018-1178-7.

Li, J., Zhao, Y., Li, R., Broster, L. S., Zhou, C., & Yang, S. (2015). Association of Oxytocin Receptor Gene (OXTR) rs53576 Polymorphism with Sociality: A Meta-Analysis. *PLoS One, 10*(6). https://doi.org/10.1371/journal.pone.0131820.

Lukas, D., & Clutton-Brock, T. H. (2013). The evolution of social monogamy in mammals. *Science (New York, N.Y.)*, *341*(6145), 526–530. https://doi.org/10.1126/science.1238677.

Maner, J. K., Gailliot, M. T., & Miller, S. L. (2009). The implicit cognition of relationship maintenance: Inattention to attractive alternatives. *Journal of Experimental Social Psychology*, *45*(1), 174–179. https://doi.org/10.1016/j.jesp.2008.08.002.

Mclean, L., Walton, T., Rodin, G., Esplen, M., & Jones, J. (2013). A couple-based intervention for patients and caregivers facing end-stage cancer: Outcomes of a randomized controlled trial. *Psycho-oncology*, *22*(1), 28–38.

Mendoza, S. P., & Mason, W. A. (1986). Parental division of labour and differentiation of attachments in a monogamous primate (Callicebus cupreus). *Animal Behaviour 34*, 1336–1347.

Meyers, S. A., & Berscheid, E. (1997). The language of love: The difference a preposition makes. *Personality and Social Psychology Bulletin, 23*(4), 347–362.

Miller, P. J. E., Niehuis, S., & Huston, T. L. (2006). Positive illusions in marital relationships: A 13-year longitudinal study. *Personality and Social Psychology Bulletin*, *32*(12), 1579–1594. https://doi.org/10.1177/0146167206292691.

Minkov, M., & Bond, M. H. (2015). Genetic polymorphisms predict national differences in life history strategy and time orientation. *Personality and Individual Differences*, *76*, 204–215. https://doi.org/10.1016/j.paid.2014.12.014.

Mogilski, J. K., Mitchell, V. E., Reeve, S. D., Donaldson, S. H., Nicolas, S. C. A., & Welling, L. L. M. (2019). Life history and multi-partner mating: A novel explanation for moral stigma against consensual non-monogamy. *Frontiers in Psychology*, *10*, 3033. https://doi.org/10.3389/fpsyg.2019.03033.

Munafò, M. R., Yalcin, B., Willis-Owen, S. A., & Flint, J. (2008). Association of the dopamine D4 receptor (DRD4) gene and approach-related personality traits: Meta-analysis and new data. *Biological Psychiatry*, *63*(2), 197–206. https://doi.org/10.1016/j.biopsych.2007.04.006.

Murray, S. L., & Holmes, J. G. (1997). A leap of faith? Positive illusions in romantic relationships. *Personality and Social Psychology Bulletin*, *23*(6), 586–604. https://doi.org/10.1177/0146167297236003.

Murray, S. L., Holmes, J. G., & Griffin, D. W. (1996). The benefits of positive illusions: Idealization and the construction of satisfaction in close relationships. *Journal of Personality and Social Psychology*, *70*(1), 79–98. https://doi.org/10.1037/0022-3514.70.1.79.

O'Leary, K. D., Acevedo, B. P., Aron, A., Huddy, L., & Mashek, D. (2012). Is long-term love more than a rare phenomenon? If so, what are its correlates? *Social Psychological and Personality Science*, *3*(2), 241–249. https://doi.org/10.1177/1948550611417015.

Pearce, E., Wlodarski, R., Machin, A., & Dunbar, R. I. M. (2019). Genetic influences on social relationships: Sex differences in the mediating role of personality and social cognition. *Adaptive Human Behavior and Physiology*, *5*(4), 331–351. https://doi.org/10.1007/s40750- 019-00120-5.

Preston, S. D. (2013). The origins of altruism in offspring care. *Psychological Bulletin*, *139*(6), 1305–1341. https://doi.org/10.1037/a0031755.

Preston, S., & de Waal, F., 2011. Altruism. In J. Decety & J. T. Cacioppo (Eds.), *The Oxford handbook of social neuroscience* (pp. 565–585). Oxford University Press.

Quintana, D. S., Rokicki, J., van der Meer, D., Alnæs, D., Kaufmann, T., Córdova-Palomera, A., Dieset, I., Andreassen, O. A., & Westlye, L. T. (2019). Oxytocin pathway gene networks in the human brain. *Nature Communications, 10*(1), 668. https://doi.org/10.1038/s41467-019- 08503-8.

Riela, S., Rodriguez, G., Aron, A., Xu, X., & Acevedo, B. (2010). Experiences of falling in love: Similarities and differences in culture, ethnicity, gender, and speed. *Journal of Social and Personal Relationships, 27,* 473–493.

Rodrigues, S. M., Saslow, L. R., Garcia, N., John, O. P., & Keltner, D. (2009). Oxytocin receptor genetic variation relates to empathy and stress reactivity in humans. *Proceedings of the National Academy of Sciences, 106*(50), 21437–21441.

Rosenberg, K. P. (2018). *Infidelity: Why men and women cheat* (First edition). Da Capo Press, Hachette Book Group.

Rusbult, C. E., Finkel, E. J., & Kumashiro, M. (2009). The Michelangelo Phenomenon. *Current Directions in Psychological Science, 18*(6), 305–309. https://doi.org/10 .1111/j.1467-8721.2009.01657.x.

Simpson, J. A., Campbell, B., & Berscheid, E. (1986). The association between romantic love and marriage: Kephart (1967) twice revisited. *Personality and Social Psychology Bulletin, 12*(3), 363–372. https://doi.org/10.1177/0146167286123011.

Shackelford, T. K. (1998). Divorce as a consequence of spousal infidelity. In V. C. de Munck (Ed.), *Romantic love and sexual behavior: Perspectives from the social sciences* (pp. 135– 153). Praeger.

Smith, T. W. (2005). *Altruism and empathy in America: Trends and correlates.* Chicago, IL: National Opinion Research Center, University of Chicago.

Sun, T., & Hevner, R. F. (2014). Growth and folding of the mammalian cerebral cortex: From molecules to malformations. *Nature Reviews. Neuroscience, 15*(4), 217–232. https://doi.org/10.1038/nrn3707.

Tennov, D. (1999). *Love and limerence: The experience of being in love* (2nd ed.). Scarborough House; ProQuest Ebook Central.

Uzefovsky, F., Döring, A. K., & Knafo-Noam, A. (2016). Values in Middle Childhood: Social and Genetic Contributions. *Social Development, 25*(3), 482–502. https://doi.org/10.1111/sode.12155.

Walum, H., & Young, L. J. (2018). The neural mechanisms and circuitry of the pair bond. *Nature Reviews. Neuroscience, 19*(11), 643–654.

Wilson, D. S. (1975). A theory of group selection. *Proceedings of the National Academy of Sciences of the United States of America, 72*(1), 143–146. https://doi .org/10.1073/pnas.72.1.143.

Whitebird, R. R., Kreitzer, M., Crain, A. L., Lewis, B. A., Hanson, L. R., & Enstad, C. J. (2013). Mindfulness-based stress reduction for family caregivers: a randomized controlled trial. *Gerontologist, 53*(4):676–86. doi: 10.1093/geront/gns126.

Xu, L., Becker, B., Luo, R., Zheng, X., Zhao, W., Zhang, Q., & Kendrick, K. M. (2020). Oxytocin amplifies sex differences in human mate choice.

Psychoneuroendocrinology, 112, 104483. https://doi.org/10.1016/j.psyneuen.2019
.104483.

Xu, X., Aron, A., Brown, L., Cao, G., Feng, T., & Weng, X. (2011). Reward and
motivation systems: A brain mapping study of early-stage intense romantic love
in Chinese participants. *Human Brain Mapping, 32*(2), 249–257. https://doi.org/10
.1002/hbm.21017.

Xu, X., Wang, J., Aron, A., Lei, W., Westmaas, J. L., & Weng, X. (2012). Intense
passionate love attenuates cigarette cue-reactivity in nicotine-deprived smokers:
An FMRI study. *PLoS One, 7*(7), e42235. https://doi.org/10.1371/journal.pone
.0042235.

Zak, A., Coulter, C., Giglio, S., Hall, J., Sanford, S., & Pellowski, N. (2002). Do his
friends and family like me? Predictors of infidelity in intimate relationships. *North
American Journal of Psychology, 4*(2), 287–290.

Zak, P. J. (2013). *The moral molecule: The source of love and prosperity*. Dutton.

Zare, B. (2011). *Review of studies on infidelity: 3rd International Conference on
Advanced Management Science* (1st ed.). IACSIT Press.

Chapter 6

"I Am Glad That My Partner Is Happy with Her Lover"

On Jealousy, and Compersion

Aaron Ben-Ze'ev

INTRODUCTION

The self-other relation is central to all emotions, particularly emotions concerning the good or bad fortune of others. Other people interest us more than anything else, because the things that people do and say have the greatest impact on us. The self-other relation is significant because it highlights the social nature of emotions.

Emotions centering on the fortune of others encompass an important comparative concern, wherein we compare the desirability of another's situation to that of our own. Such emotions involve two basic evaluations: the value of the other's fortunate impact on us and on them. Sometimes the two evaluations are not correlated, as in the case of envy, jealousy, and schadenfreude (pleasure-in-another's-misfortune); sometimes they are correlated, as in the case of compersion, compassion, happiness for the other, and admiration. The comparative concern becomes competitive when there is a conflict between the two evaluations; when the evaluations are correlated, the comparative concern becomes a cooperative concern.

In this chapter, I discuss two major opposing emotions toward the beneficial romantic fortune of another person: jealousy, which negatively evaluates this fortune, and compersion, which positively evaluates it. The first section briefly discusses the group of emotions relating to the good fortune of others, while focusing on jealousy. The second section discusses the emotion of compersion, while arguing that it can be perceived as involving sexual and romantic generosity. The third section describes various forms of polyamory and examines major issues related to polyamory, such as the hierarchy between different partners, whether polyamory spreads love too thin and the overall quality of polyamorous relationships. The fourth section discusses the nature of jealousy and compersion in polyamory. Both emotions are present in polyamory—though more typically, a mild form of jealousy can be seen, while compersion takes a more enhanced form.

EMOTIONS TOWARD THE GOOD FORTUNE OF OTHERS

He that is not jealous, is not in love.

—Saint Augustine

Emotions are personal, involved attitudes; we are not indifferent or neutral when experiencing them. Typically, emotions, therefore, have a positive or a negative valence. The other's good fortune, or well-being—in other words, their auspicious state resulting from favorable outcomes—is of great concern for us. When we compare someone else's good fortune in a way that conflicts with the evaluation of our own fortune, emotions like envy and jealousy may arise. At other times, the two evaluations are in harmony, and we may wind up with the emotions of sympathetic joy (happy-for) or admiration (Ben-Ze'ev 2000: 92-103; Ortony, Clore, & Collins 1988).

Envy involves a negative evaluation of our undeserved inferiority, whereas jealousy involves a negative evaluation of the possibility of losing something—typically, a favorable human relationship—to someone else. Envy and jealousy would seem to address a similar concern: in envy we wish to obtain something that the other has and in jealousy we fear losing something that we already have to someone else. However, this is not a minor distinction: the wish to obtain something is notably different from the wish not to lose it. In contrast to envy, which is essentially a two-party relationship, jealousy is basically a three-party relationship. Jealousy concerns the partner's relationship with another person, since it may threaten one's favorable and exclusive relationship with one's partner. Jealousy is more personal and generates greater vulnerability than envy, as it touches on far more significant aspects of our self-esteem (Ben-Ze'ev 2000; 2010; Ben-Ze'ev & Goussinsky 2008).

The personal comparative concern is central in emotions. We may compare our current, novel state to a different state in which we have been or to the state of our significant others. This different state might be a previous actual state, an ideal state in which we desire to be, or a state in which others think we ought to be. The different states of others can also be actual states, ideal states, or states in which we think they ought to be. Emotions are generated when a significant discrepancy arises between our current personal state and the compared state, to the state of our significant others. This different state might be a previous actual state, an ideal state in which we desire to be, or a state in which others think we ought to be. The different states of others can also be actual states, ideal states, or states in which we think they ought to be. Emotions are generated when a significant discrepancy arises between our current personal state and the compared state.

The comparative concern is vividly expressed in jealousy. Jealousy increases when the domain of the rival's achievements is comparable, and hence relevant, to our self-esteem. Thus, individuals who place great importance on physical attractiveness are more likely to be jealous when their rival is unusually attractive. In jealousy, the significance of the rival's achievements depends not only on their relevance to how we desire to be but also on what we believe our partner finds desirable. Our jealousy would be intensified if we knew that our partner likes clever people and our rival is clever. When the rival is compatible with our partner's preferences, the threat to the relationship is increased (Salovey & Rodin 1989; DeSteno & Salovey 1996).

The importance of the comparative concern is also expressed in the painful nature of romantic rejection. Two major types of romantic rejection are: (1) a comparative rejection of leaving you because of someone else, and (2) a noncomparative rejection involving no one else. Empirical findings indicate that participants who experienced, recalled, or imagined a comparative rejection felt significantly worse than those who did the same for a noncomparative rejection (Deri & Zitek 2017).

Unlike envy and jealousy, the emotions of sympathetic joy and admiration involve a positive evaluation of the other's good fortune. I use the term "sympathy" not in the sense of "feeling pity and sorrow for another's misfortune," but rather, akin to "supporting their shared feelings or opinions" (*Oxford English Dictionary*).

Some people doubt that an emotion like sympathetic joy is possible. Thus, Jean-Jacques Rousseau (1762: 221) argued that nobody can share anyone's happiness—even one's best friend—without envy. Only the friend's neediness, which poses no threat to us, can bring out our generous emotions. Rousseau's claim is wrong when someone is so close to us that we consider her success our own, and hence, it poses no threat to our self-esteem. This is known as "basking in reflected glory": the other's glory shines on us, enhancing our self-esteem. This is so in parental love and in the admiration of sport fans for their winning teams (Cialdini et al. 1976). Whether we admire or envy another person depends, among other things, on the relevance of that person's good fortune to our self-esteem.

Jorge Ferrer (2019) argues that in Buddhism, sympathetic joy (*mudita*) is regarded as one of the four qualities of an enlightened person. (The others are kindness, compassion, and calmness.) Ferrer indicates that many religions have attempted to develop sympathetic joy toward all sentient beings, including, of course, our partners. However, in intimate relationships, the required selfless sympathetic joy is turned into selfish jealousy. Ferrer rightly claims that "compersion can be seen as a novel extension of sympathetic joy to the realm of intimate relationships and, in particular, to interpersonal situations that conventionally evoke feelings of jealousy" (2019: 4).

COMPERSION

Love is when the other person's happiness is more important than your own.

—H. Jackson Brown

Sometimes, my wife wants to compare. On the one hand, she wants that my lover is not better than she is, that she is not a threat, and on the other hand that she is not a few levels below her because that creates a certain disdain.

—A polyamorous man (Cited in Carmi & Sade-Saadon 2022).

Compersion is the feeling of being happy for your partner's romantic affair with someone else. As such, compersion is a specific form of sympathetic joy. Compersion falls on the opposite end of the spectrum to jealousy: jealousy involves a negative attitude toward your partner's romantic affair with someone else while compersion adopts a positive attitude toward these same circumstances. Jealousy and compersion refer to the emotional experience itself, regardless of its cause. Accordingly, you can be jealous of your spouse merely because it wounds your self-esteem and not because you are actually in love with them. Compersion, which is a type of sympathetic joy, focuses on joy toward one's romantic partner in intimate relationships. In the same manner that jealousy does not imply love toward one's partner, compersion does not imply love, or at least not intense love, while being in intimate relationships. It merely implies that people perceive their partner's affair positively, regardless of whether they love or do not love their partner. For example, one can be happy with one's spouse's affairs, because it makes one's own affair easier to conduct, or it leaves more time for work or hobbies. The motives underlying compersion may influence the nature of an experience of compersion, though not its characterization as compersion.

Genuine mutual love is believed to enhance the well-being of both partners. But what happens when the needs of the two lovers are incompatible? A long tradition maintains that love has less to do with the lover's own needs and more with the beloved's needs (e.g., Levinas 1998: 105: 228–29). Yet, a different approach emphasizes the needs of the lover, not necessarily as a secondary concern (Wonderly 2017). This is obvious in the dialogical approach to romantic love, which considers the interaction between the two partners to be essential to love (Krebs 2014; 2015).

Profound romantic love encompasses genuine care toward the beloved; however, it is not a general concern for the beloved's happiness in all circumstances (Ben-Ze'ev 2019). Frequently, the lover desires the beloved's happiness in a conditional manner—only insofar as the lover is either a part or the cause of this happiness. In particular, many people do not want their beloved to be sexually happy with another person.

A few major attitudes toward the happiness of one's partner when they are having a sexual or emotional affair with another person are (1) jealousy, (2) emotional neutrality, (3) compersion, and (4) emotional ambivalence. Jealousy seems to be the most common, while emotional neutrality is likely to be present when there is hardly any romantic connection between partners.

Having discussed jealousy and compersion, I will briefly describe emotional neutrality and emotional ambivalence. Emotional neutrality is a kind of indifference. In these cases, people are neither jealous nor happy about their partner's affair with someone else. They may take it as a natural, common phenomenon that does not trigger any emotional reaction. Emotional ambivalence, where a person simultaneously experiences positive and negative reactions, exists, for example, when a widow attending the wedding of her daughter feels joy, but also sadness that her late husband, the father of the bride, is not present (Ben-Ze'ev 2019). In such circumstances, emotional ambivalence consists of both jealousy and compersion. Thus, Masha Halevi, a polyamorous therapist, writes that the usual perception of compersion in the poly-community is equivalent to the joy of a little child feeding a hungry duck. In actuality, for Halevi, "it is different. I feel mixed emotions" (Halevi 2021: 256–258). I believe that this is the case for many other polyamorist people. I will argue that in polyamorous relationships, all possible attitudes are present, while the percentage of compersion, emotional neutrality, and ambivalence is higher than in monogamous relationships.

Compersion as Sexual and Romantic Generosity

For it is in giving that we receive.

—Francis of Assisi

Compersion, which expresses our happiness for our partner's romantic affair with another, is a type of sexual and romantic generosity—of giving more than is expected. A dictionary definition of a generous person is "showing a readiness to give more of something, such as money or time, than is strictly necessary or expected" (*Oxford English Dictionary*). We should not confuse generosity with sacrifice. As Francis of Assisi emphasizes, we get a lot while giving.

Many religions and moral traditions praise generosity. This praise is not unjustified: studies show that generosity is good for us, physically and mentally. Generosity can decrease blood pressure, reduce stress, help you live longer, boost your mood, promote social connections, and improve the quality of your marriage (Whillans et al. 2016). Thus, one study found that generosity, which is defined in the study as "giving good things to one's spouse freely and abundantly," was positively associated with marital satisfaction and negatively associated with marital conflict and the likelihood of perceived divorce (Dew & Bradford Wilcox 2013).

Whether or not generosity within marriage stems from merely altruistic motives or from a wish to be treated generously in return is an open question. It is probably associated with both—kindness and reciprocity are high on the list of desired qualities in a romantic partner. Conversely, when people are asked to name three negative qualities that would make them shun a prospective partner, stinginess appears on most lists. Generosity is an essential positive framework for prosperous marital relationships: it is natural to be generous toward the one you love (Ben-Ze'ev 2019).

Generosity is very valuable for our well-being and health. Is this also true of sexual generosity? And should we aim to be more sexually generous? Sexual generosity has come to refer primarily to caring about the pleasure of one's sexual partner. The generous lover is often perceived as someone who takes pleasure in giving pleasure—a phrase that is often used with regard to oral sex. Two major types of sexual generosity within a committed relationship are: (1) taking part in undesired sexual interactions with one's partner, and (2) passively allowing one's partner to obtain sexual satisfaction with someone else. Passive generosity is most relevant to compersion.

The first type of sexual generosity concerns the willingness to engage in sexual interactions with one's partner even when lacking a real desire to do so and with little prospects of enjoying it. A few major kinds of such one-sided sex are pity sex, charity sex, and peace-inducing sex. In the second type of sexual generosity, one is passive, allowing the partner to be active in seeking sexual satisfaction somewhere else. This can occur, for example, in polyamory, open marriages, or when one spouse is unable or unwilling to have sexual interactions. The first type—in which the generous person tries to fulfill the unfortunate spouse's desire for sex—is more common than the second—in which the fortunate spouse is allowed to be even more fortunate.

Somehow, being kind to an unfortunate spouse is easier and feels better than being kind to a fortunate spouse, perhaps because the first is less threatening in the sense that there is no risk of negative comparison, competition, and envy.

The moral evaluation of these two types of generosity is complex. The positive and negative consequences of active sexual generosity are more limited. It might temporarily alleviate the situation, as an aspirin does, but it does not substantially improve the overall state of affairs. The negative impact is also minor.

Sexual generosity is also present in the context of aging and sick people. An extreme case is that of a seriously ill husband, who cannot function sexually. People, who are deeply in love with each other, may ask their partners to promise them that if they will be incapacitated in such a manner, then the partner will find sexual satisfaction elsewhere. In some such cases, the third person may be helping the caregiver taking care of the sick spouse at their home.

This type of generous compersion can be found in many cases of aging and Alzheimer's disease (and other types of sickness). John Portmann (2013) claims that the unaffected spouse in Alzheimer's disease is often required to exhibit both active and passive sexual generosity. Having sexual interactions with a spouse suffering from Alzheimer's can be considered active sexual generosity. Portmann (2013) cites research indicating that many ill spouses make incessant sexual demands. However, healthy spouses are often disturbed by the idea of having sex with someone who cannot recognize them. They can feel guilty about withholding sex from their spouse but feel conflicted about granting it. This is a variant of pity sex. Healthy spouses may choose to exhibit the passive sexual generosity of letting sick spouses have sexual interactions with other patients—a common phenomenon, as sick spouses might no longer recognize their partners.

To sum up, two major claims of mine are relevant here: (a) at the basis of generosity is giving more than expected, and generosity is different from sacrifice, and (b) compersion, which is a kind of sympathetic joy, refers to intimate relationships and does not presuppose love, for the same reasons that jealousy does not presuppose love. Many different personal circumstances can generate jealousy or compersion. Given these two claims, it is easier to understand the above cases of generous sexual compersion. Like other types of generosity, active and passive sexual generosity involve giving more than expected, and in some cases, generous people are happy about it—in other cases, they can be emotionally neutral or ambivalent while doing so. (See also Alice Munro's wonderful story, "The bear came over the mountain.")

POLYAMORY

> Only you and you alone can thrill me like you do, and fill my heart with love for only you.
>
> —The Platters

> Thousands of candles can be lit from a single candle, and the life of the candle will not be shortened. Happiness is never reduced by being shared.
>
> —Buddha

Monogamous romantic relationships often involve a trade-off between the romantic intensity prompted by change and novelty, on one hand, and the romantic profundity of a connection with one person, on the other. This trade-off rests on the premise that increasing the one inevitably decreases the other. Is this premise correct? Can nonmonogamous relationships offer both romantic intensity and romantic profundity? (Ben-Ze'ev & Brunning 2018; Brunning 2018).

Polyamory and Open Sexual Relations

Consensual nonmonogamy comes in different flavors. Open sexual marriages (and other committed relationships) and polyamory are prime examples, and each has many variations on its main theme. Both relationships are open, though in different ways. In open sexual relationships, the major aspect that is "open" is the sexual realm, which includes sex with other people—and possibly swinging. More comprehensive in nature, polyamory is open not merely in the sexual realm but also in the more general romantic one. Even though polyamory is characterized by having multiple lovers, it can also involve single sexual encounters, such as one-night stands. The commitments and rights of such partners are minor.

A basic attitude in open sexual marriages is that marriages are essentially fine, while a most acute problem is the declining sexual desire. This is taken care of by adding new sexual partners. The basic attitude in polyamory is more radical: the essential problem is in the prevailing assumption in romantic ideology that one person can fulfill all of our romantic needs (Ben-Ze'ev 2019). Hence, we cannot be satisfied with "merely" adding one or a few sexual partners; we need to add (at least) another romantic partner, who can also satisfy our sexual needs. Whereas open sexual marriages are perceived as a solution to the monotony of a monogamous marriage, polyamory seeks to replace, rather than fix, marital monogamy. In any case, the claim that polyamory is only about sex is wrong; it is also about love in which sex is significant (Brake 2017; Jenkins 2017).

Although an increasing number of polyamorous couples do not adopt the primary–secondary configuration—approximately half of couples are either co-primary and non-primary configurations (Balzarini et al. 2017; Balzarini et al. 2019b, 2019c), I believe that the complex and dynamic nature of polyamory and open marriages make the need for an order of priorities in these relations rather urgent. Such a hierarchy is obvious in open sexual relationships, where a clear difference exists between the primary relation and the secondary one. Primary and secondary relationships differ with respect to, for example, time spent together, physical cohabitation, child rearing, and finance. Primary partners share not only sexual intimacy but typically also children, finances, and a home. Secondary partners are often "more like girlfriends or boyfriends than spouses" (Pincus & Hiles 2017).

Moreover, individuals reported experiencing less stigma as well as more long-term rewards, satisfaction, commitment, and greater communication within the primary relationship (as opposed to the secondary relationship). Secondary partners are less accepted by friends and family, are less satisfying, and involve less commitment, less investments, greater relationships secrecy, and greater proportion of time spent on sex. Hence, it seems that people may be getting different things out of different relationships, all while maintaining their already established relationships (Balzarini et al. 2017; Balzarini et al. 2019b).

The co-primary and non-primary configurations in polyamory have considerably increased their share in polyamorous relationships. Nevertheless, the differences between the two partners still exist, though to a lesser extent. Rhonda Balzarini and colleagues (2017) argue that this indicates that "despite attempts at equality, many relationship qualities differ among partners in non-hierarchical relationships similar to the differences that emerge for those who make formal primary–secondary partner classifications." In other words, in this case, the egalitarian ideology has some impact, but typically cannot completely change reality, for example, when taking into account a limited amount of total resources, such as time (Balzarini et al. 2017).

When arranging consensual nonmonogamous relations in light of their closeness to the monogamous configuration, open sexual marriages are closest, followed by primary–secondary configuration of polyamory, with the most distant being co-primary and non-primary configurations. Open sexual marriages differ from monogamy "merely" in the sexual aspect, while leaving intact the rest of the monogamous configuration. Polyamory is more distant from monogamy in that it enlarges the "free zone" for other romantic purposes. The configurations that lack a hierarchy, namely, the co-primary and the non-primary, considerably reduce the uniqueness of the romantic bond between the two partners. This is expressed in cases where polyamorists categorize their relationships as "nesting" (living together) and non-nesting (living separately) (Pincus & Hiles 2017).

The lack of hierarchy in romantic relationships is problematic, since emotional and romantic experiences are complex and discriminative. Emotions are *partial* in the sense that they are focused on a *narrow* target, such as one person or a few people, and in the sense that they express a *personal and interested* perspective. Emotions direct and color our attention by selecting what attracts and holds it. We cannot assume an emotional attitude toward everyone or toward those with whom we have no relationship whatsoever. We cannot conduct our lives properly if we treat everything as equally important; we must have some order of priority. We must learn to be insensitive to some issues and more sensitive to others; otherwise, our mental system will become overwhelmed. Accordingly, we should examine whether having several nonhierarchical romantic relationships is in conflict with the discriminatory nature of love, or whether it is similar to having several children.

Love involves being sensitive to the beloved. Too much sensitivity, however, can ruin love. Conversely, indiscriminate sensitivity, like indiscriminate freedom, disrupts our normative order of priorities, as shown, for instance, in our commitments to those who are close to us. Both innate and learned characteristics are involved in developing romantic sensitivity. A sensitive partner will focus on the most meaningful and relevant aspects needed for a relationship to thrive. Without such focus and prioritization, sensitivity can become toxic. If we deal with a penny as we would a million dollars, sensitivity overloads us with irrelevant and even destructive noise (Ben-Ze'ev 2019).

The ideal of lacking hierarchy is compatible with the emphasis on polyamorous ideology, which values romantic freedom. Lacking any type of hierarchy is obviously erroneous. We are limited creatures, bound by barriers such as the length of our life and our inability to fulfill all our wishes and values. In this sense, I disagree with the verse from the unforgettable song by Kris Kristofferson (sang by Janis Joplin), "Me and Bobby Magee": "Freedom's just another word for 'nothing left to lose'." When there is nothing left to lose, your actions are not determined by your own values, but rather by external forces that chaotically push you in various directions. Our autonomy is best expressed when there is no conflict between what we desire to do and what our values prescribe. In fact, it comes into play both when we behave according to our profound values, as well as when we follow transient desires that represent less entrenched values. Polyamory may increase romantic freedom, but also increase boundaries and rules associated with polyamorous way of living.

Falling in love is easier than staying in love, and we fall out of love more slowly than we fall in it. Staying in love—or more precisely, maintaining loving relationships—requires much conscious efforts. While almost everyone should invest conscious effort to maintain their relationship, not everyone has to invest equally to keep their loving relationship alive (Ben-Ze'ev 2019). It seems that in polyamory, the required maintenance work is much more extensive and profound. And often, as Laura Kipnis tells us, "good relationships may take more work, but unfortunately, when it comes to love, trying is always trying too hard; work doesn't work" (Kipnis 2003: 18).

The increased need for maintenance work in polyamory may ruin the relationship or some aspects of it, such as investing time in family, children, and personal flourishing. As a polyamorous woman said, "But at some point, the relationship becomes oppressive to me; I don't have time to get anything done as it is, and now I need to make time for another relationship? At first, it was worth it, but then it wasn't anymore." Similarly, another polyamorous woman said, "I was full of guilt about the fact that my kids were still young, that I wasn't present enough . . . Consequently, I try not to date single guys, and preferably not divorced ones, either. Married men with children are my top preference. I feel like there's something about it that protects me, that he also has a family with kids and another love, that I'm his secondary and not his primary" (both citations are from Carmi & Sade-Saadon 2022).

There can, of course, be many types of priorities, though embracing none, while bestowing equal value to several partners, undermines common values, such as having greater moral obligations to those who are close to you. A colleague of mine once said that he loves all children in the world as he loves his son. I responded that it follows that he does not love his son. Fulfilling my moral obligations to my children requires time and various mental and financial resources that are not sufficient for all children in the world, or even all those in my neighborhood.

An order of priority should be given when considering our investment in our career, family and relationships. Some normative order of priority, which is part and parcel of human existence, is required and exists also in the emotional attitudes of people within consensual nonmonogamous relationships, toward their primary and secondary partners. Indeed, one study found that polyamorous people experienced greater distress when imagining their primary, rather than their secondary partner, violating consent (Mogilski et al. 2019).

We live in a complex world that demands compromise. An order of priorities can guide us as to when we should concede something of lower value for something of higher value. The equal status of partners within a couple should not be a mechanical equality and symmetry, in which the comparative concern is central and each partner receives and gives precisely the same. The relationship should be based upon each partner's needs.

Spreading Love Too Thin

A major criticism of polyamory is that it spreads love too thin. As a lover has limited resources, spreading them over several lovers may reduce the resources given to each lover, consequently making them insufficient for each loving relationship. In reply, we may compare love to happiness, which, as Buddha said, "is never reduced by being shared." In this sense, the heart can expand when you love more. Is spreading love around like spreading limited butter or like expanding happiness? The first option assumes a resources-competition, or a contrast model, which essentially involves a zero-sum game. The second option presupposes an expanding, additive resources model.

It seems that both options have a valid point. Love is not an entity with a fixed energy, but an emotional capacity that, when used, generates increasingly positive energy. This does not mean that love is not limited. Hence, the danger of spreading our love too thin is a real one.

A few basic psychological capacities might be involved in expanding the loving heart: (1) the broadening capacity of positive emotions (Fredrickson 2001), (2) the expanding nature of the self (Aron et al. 2013), and (3) the ability to be generous.

In her influential broaden-and-build theory, Barbara Fredrickson (2001) claims that positive emotions, such as happiness and love, *broaden* people's momentary thought-action repertoire, which in turn serves to build their enduring personal resources, ranging from physical and intellectual strengths to social and psychological capabilities. Fredrickson further argues that positive emotions do not merely signal flourishing—they also produce flourishing. Positive emotions are valuable not just as end states in themselves but also as a means to enhance psychological growth and improve our well-being over time.

Another capacity facilitating the growth of the heart is *self-expansion*. The "self-expansion model" holds that we are hardwired to expand ourselves through relationships with other people. This is because relationships enable us to incorporate the resources and perspectives of others within ourselves. Over time, and because of their interpersonal relationships, people can "expand" by internalizing perspectives and resources that were previously unavailable to them (Aron et al. 2013: 95–98).

The broadening capacity of positive emotions and the expanding nature of the self are both highly relevant for understanding how polyamory provides a context in which one's heart can expand by participating in more than one loving relation. Polyamory is a form of romantic life that is significantly self-expansive since an intimate relationship expands the self, and having a few such relationships expand the self in a greater degree. One can further claim that the expanded nature of love may be due to the inclusive manner of certain romantic activities. Indeed, not all meaningful romantic activities must be done in the intimacy of merely two people. Thus, activities such as shared talking and walking can be done with more than one person, thereby expanding the impact of such activities.

An additional capacity that expands our heart is *generosity*. Loving two people can be described as a kind of romantic generosity, which, like other types of generosity, increases the flourishing of the person. Generosity is an essential positive framework for prosperous marital relationships (Dew & Wilcox 2013). Extending romantic generosity from one person to two people can in principle further enhance one's good feelings while expanding the heart. In this regard, Berit Brogaard argues that since sexual and emotional satisfaction is a good (possibly intrinsically valuable), "denying one's partner this value outside of the narrow context of a monogamous relationship is inconsistent with the core feature of romantic love, which is a genuine concern for one's partner's agency, autonomy and well-being" (Brogaard 2017: 56).

Even if we assume, as we should, that romantic energy can expand, it is still limited. A relevant metaphor here is comparing love to a muscle: as exercise can make muscles stronger, "exercising" love with various people can make capacities for love stronger. However, in engaging in too many activities, the muscle may become tired and with too little activity, the muscle loses its strength. Mildly tired athletes can indeed manage to summon their strength for a major exertion, but after a certain point, fatigue becomes insurmountable. Athletes begin to conserve their remaining strength when their muscles begin to tire (Baumeister, Vohs, & Tice 2007). I believe that in this sense, lovers, including polyamorous ones, are similar to athletes.

Numerous difficulties still face polyamory. One is the presence of limiting factors—the most obvious one being time. Another difficulty is how the assumed expansion of love is divided. The primary partner may receive less than was given before, and less than the secondary partner gets. Nevertheless, it might be possible that both the primary and secondary partner come to gain more than before (Jenkins 2017).

Overall Quality: Intensity, Profundity, Length

There are various ways to assess the overall quality of a romantic relationship. Two such ways are intensity and profundity. Romantic intensity is a snapshot of a momentary peak of passionate, often sexual, desire. Romantic profundity goes beyond mere romantic intensity and refers to the lover's broader and more enduring attitudes (Ben-Ze'ev 2019; Ben-Ze'ev & Krebs 2018).

A somewhat related distinction is that between eroticism and nurturance. Eroticism is characterized by desire, lust, sexual excitement, and bodily pleasure. Nurturance, for its part, is marked by a strong sense of security, emotional attachment, deep commitment, and warmth and comfort. One study suggests that people in polyamorous relationships experience greater nurturance with primary partners (compared to secondary and monogamous partners) and greater eroticism with secondary partners (compared to primary and monogamous partners) (Balzarini 2019a).

Clearly, polyamory increases overall *romantic intensity*, which is highly dependent on change and novelty. The sexual aspect is dominant in polyamorous relations—at least toward the secondary partner (Conley et al. 2018; Rubel & Bogaert 2015; Wood et al. 2018). The glowing intensity in the secondary relationship often be reflected in increasing intensity in the primary relationship and this may enhance the overall value of the polyamorous relationship. However, as the secondary relationship may be volatile, it often includes sadness and frustration, especially when in crisis and separation. Such negative emotions are also reflected in the behavior of the spouse in the primary relationship. Thus, a polyamorous wife told her husband, whose current secondary relationship was unstable, "Don't take me on this roller-coaster. These are your choices—they should stay outside the home. Come tell me if you want, but it can't affect the mood, our Saturday daytrips, the fact that you don't feel like talking and don't have the energy for the kid's shenanigans" (Carmi & Sade-Saadon 2022).

The relationship between polyamory and *romantic profundity* is multifaceted, mainly because profound love requires a strong investment in quality time. Whereas time decreases emotional intensity, the same factor enhances emotional profundity. Accordingly, it is natural to assume that having several romantic partners reduces the quality time available for each. Nonetheless, polyamory increases complexity, which underlies romantic profundity (Brunning, this volume). Living in complex circumstances requires a profound understanding of the other partners. Hence, it would be a mistake to think of polyamory and emotional profundity as mutually exclusive. Polyamorous relationships can provide ongoing opportunities for self-expansion through romantic engagement with more than one person. However, on occasion, such quantitative expansion runs the risk of reducing the quality of the present relationship (Balzarini et al. 2019a; Ben-Ze'ev & Brunning 2018).

In monogamous relationships, there is some association between romantic intensity (sexual satisfaction) and romantic profundity (that can be expressed in overall relationship quality). One study found that in polyamory (and consensually nonmonogamous relations in general), individuals who were more sexually fulfilled in their primary relationship reported greater relationship satisfaction with their secondary partner (Muise et al. 2019). Men who were more sexually fulfilled in their secondary relationship reported greater relationship satisfaction with their primary partner, but women who were more sexually fulfilled with their secondary partner reported lower sexual satisfaction in their primary relationship. The addition of another partner in polyamory has elements of both the contrast model, in which the addition creates more conflicts, and the self-expansion model, in which the addition of another person benefits all parties involved (Muise et al. 2019).

Relationship quality also relates to the overall length of the relationship. Time is typically a necessary condition for the creation and enhancement of profound romantic love. However, it is not a sufficient condition. So only in some cases, but not in all, does loving longer mean loving more (Ben-Ze'ev 2017). It has been claimed that the greater complexities of nonmonogamous relationships "have the significant potential to offer increased structural stability to nonmonogamous romantic lives" (Brunning, this volume). The issue is more complex. Polyamorous relationships include features that are negatively associated with enduring relationships, such as that of being existentially dependent on someone you have not chosen (for instance, the partners of your partners); the increased likelihood of feeling that you are second best; managing the great intensity associated in being with a new partner; the potential pitfalls of choice fatigue when faced with many potential partners; complications in family life, reduced privacy and the complex wish to abolish jealousy (Brunning 2018; Sheff 2014).

Indeed, though the quality of polyamorous relationships is similar to that of monogamous relationships, their duration is typically briefer. While there are no definite empirical studies in this regard, there are some indications that this is so (Jankowiak & Gerth 2012). Indeed, it was found that participants in a polyamorous relationship were more likely to report divorce (polyamorous, 22.3%; monogamous, 14.1%) or separation. Because individuals in polyamorous relationships have more relationships than individuals in monogamous relationships, it is plausible that there are more divorces and separations among polyamorous participants (Balzarini et al. 2019b).

I believe that the assumed briefer duration of polyamorous relationships relates to lesser commitment. *Commitment theory* describes several major factors underlying romantic commitment: the degree of satisfaction, the cost of separation, and the availability of an alternative. Commitment is strengthened by the amount of satisfaction and the extent of the cost, and it is weakened by possible alternatives to that relationship. Satisfaction level is significantly more predictive of commitment than is the quality of alternatives or the cost of separation. However, when satisfaction is not high, the extent of the cost and the attractiveness of the alternatives can carry greater weight (Benjamin & Agnew 2003). In the case of polyamory, the cost of separation is lower than in monogamous relationships. Changing a partner when being romantically dissatisfied is more central in polyamorous ideology than in monogamous ideology. Moreover, this ideology approves of romantic alternatives, and in doing so makes these alternatives more feasible and the polyamorous relationships less robust as well as less committed.

COMPERSION AND JEALOUSY IN POLYAMORY

> At first, it had a very positive effect. I experienced an awakening that I also brought home with me. It did exactly what we wanted it to do; it was a real honeymoon. But very quickly, it went in a different direction. It wasn't polyamory, since the more I fell in love with him and wanted him, the less I wanted my husband.
>
> A polyamorous woman (Carmi & Sade-Saadon 2022).

Is Jealousy a More Natural Emotion?

There are various factors determining whether a certain emotion is more or less natural. Two such major factors concern the linguistic (and cultural) and developmental realms. The linguistic factor is clear: many languages do not have a specific term for sympathetic joy, while all languages have terms for jealousy. Sympathetic joy in the romantic realm is also nameless—and the recent need to invent a word for it, namely, "compersion," testifies for such a void. Similarly, cultures in various periods and places frequently deal with jealousy, while compersion is less discussed—though in recent years it has received much media attention, one reason being its unique nature.

Children's behavior and experiences are also relevant in determining the natural aspect of jealousy and compersion. Indeed, there is ample evidence for the presence of jealousy, even in infancy. In Sybil Hart's and Heather Carrington's study on the origin of jealousy, six-month-old infants were exposed to their mothers attending, in turn, to a lifelike baby doll and a book. Infant negativity was greater when maternal attention was directed toward the social object, suggesting the presence of an early form of jealousy by six months of age (Hart & Carrington 2002). Jealousy is also evident in the children of polyamorous parents. Thus, one polyamorous mother talks about her nine-year-old daughter, who keeps asking whether daddy loves her mother or his girlfriend more.

The emotion of schadenfreude (pleasure-in-another's-misfortune), which is the opposite of sympathetic joy, is also present in childhood (though it manifests later in life than jealousy). Thus, Simon Shamay-Tsoory and colleagues (2014) examined whether schadenfreude develops as a response to inequity aversion, through assessing the reactions of children to the termination of unequal and equal triadic situations. They found that children as early as twenty-four months show signs of schadenfreude, following the termination of a situation involving both inequality and unfairness.

Sympathy is found in infants, but it typically refers to the object's suffering, rather than to the object's success, as is in the case of compersion. One study found that humans have a remarkable ability to share the distress of others, but may react less strongly to the joy of others. However, intense positive empathy is evident in our attitudes toward winning sports teams and our children (Cialdini et al. 1976; Perry, Hendler, & Shamay-Tsoory 2012).

Empirical research indicates that although sexual or emotional relationships with others are not prohibited within consensual nonmonogamous relationships, individuals may still experience jealousy, restrict their partner's extradyadic behaviors, or otherwise engage in mate guarding, that is, behaviors that thwart partner defection (Mogilski et al. 2019). This study also found that consensually nonmonogamous individuals often report experiencing jealousy, but process and manage this jealousy by communicating openly with their partner about these experiences and negotiating agreements about what types of extradyadic sexual or romantic behaviors are acceptable (Mogilski et al. 2019).

Another interesting finding is that monogamous individuals reported greater emotional jealousy and distress toward a partner's imagined extradyadic involvement, whereas consensually nonmonogamous individuals reported thinking about their partner's extra-pair relationships more frequently (Mogilski et al. 2019). These findings imply that jealousy among monogamous individuals is more intense and distressing, while consensually nonmonogamous individuals are more frequently concerned about circumstances associated with jealousy. The lower intensity and lower impact of jealousy in consensually nonmonogamous individuals may be due to the possibility that such relationships are better suited for people who are naturally less jealous. It may also be due to the influence of nonmonogamous ideology.

Another relevant point in this regard is that while many people in monogamous relationships perceive low intensity of jealousy as a positive element, such jealousy is perceived as highly negative in polyamorous relationships. Thus, it is common for individuals in polyamorous relationships to leave a partner if controlling behaviors or consistent patterns of jealousy are exhibited (Ziegler et al. 2014). This may be due to the more common and vivid opportunities for generating jealousy.

The more natural character of jealousy as compared to compersion is evident in the fact that the experience of compersion must be developed, sometimes through hard work. Thus, Masha Halevi, a polyamorous therapist, writes "For me personally compersion is not necessarily this effortless joyful feeling . . . yes, I would like to feel it naturally, but I don't. I get scared and jealous on occasions" (Halevi 2021: 256–258). By contrast, no one needs a tutorial in jealousy. It is a spontaneous reaction that we can merely try to moderate.

The different attitudes in monogamy and polyamory toward an additional intimate relationship are also expressed in different attitudes toward former lovers. Reviving past romantic experiences may have a devastating effect on current monogamous relationships. In polyamory, the situation is different since the attitude in polyamory toward an additional partner is essentially positive. Hence, whereas in monogamous contexts, friendship with former partners typically ends once new romantic relationships are formed, in polyamorous contexts, friendships are often maintained after relationship dissolution. Therefore, the beginning of one relationship need not signal the end of another relationship or friendship for those who practice polyamory (Conley & Moors 2014).

Katherine Aumer and colleagues (2014) found that women scored higher on jealousy and lower on compersion than men. They further found that those in monogamous relationships are happier when they perceive their partners as jealous, which may be seen as a sign of faith and desire to maintain exclusive bonds. In contrast, a partner's level of compersion positively predicts relationship satisfaction in nonmonogamous relationships. Jealousy in monogamous relationships and compersion in nonmonogamous ones indicate that the chosen relationship is more likely to last longer. It was further found that for women who are successful in their monogamous relationships, jealousy increases satisfaction; for women whose monogamous relationships have failed, jealousy and lack of compersion are detrimental (Aumer et al. 2014).

Emotional experiences are a package deal that includes both positive and negative emotions. We should not wage war against jealousy—when jealousy is moderate, it can contribute to romantic relations. Similarly, while compersion is not a miracle cure, it is also not a poison. In some (more limited) circumstances, compersion can be a valuable emotion. Making our partner happy is, after all, what underlies profound love (Brunning 2019; de Sousa 2018).

Compersion in Polyamory

> When the lover of my husband sits on his knees, I melt: "They're sooooo cute!"
>
> Swann, in Hypatia from Space, *Compersion*

As I argued above, jealousy is more common and natural than compersion. This is in accordance with the negativity bias, in light of which negative emotions are more common and noticeable than positive ones (Baumeister et al. 2001). However, although occasional episodes of jealousy might have certain benefits in romantic relationships, jealousy should not be cultivated as an enduring character trait (Brunning 2019a).

Compersion, which is at the heart of polyamorous ideology, is more common in polyamory than in monogamy. Nevertheless, since jealousy is more natural, experiencing compersion is still an achievement.

I now turn to discuss three major groups of factors influencing the emergence of compersion in polyamory: (a) circumstantial features of polyamory; (b) individual differences between the partners; and (c) personal features.

Circumstantial features, which refer to general conditions of a polyamorous environment, include, for example, greater vividness and feasibility of factors relevant to the emergence of jealousy or compersion. The coexistence of multiple parallel romantic relationships makes comparison more vivid and feasible in polyamory since you are surrounded by people who are tied up with your flourishing and self-esteem: the lover of your spouse, the spouse of your lover, and others in this romantic network. Nevertheless, you are obliged to put less weight on the comparative concern, as the polyamorous ideology favors parallel relationships and welcomes compersion. The very essence of romantic jealousy—your partner's affair with someone else—is not perceived as something bad and hence these supposed rivals are normatively not rivals at all, and the comparison between them is less significant and less poisonous.

Individual differences between the various partners are important for the emergence of either jealousy or compersion, as comparison is more common and powerful when people are more similar to each other. The Greek poet Hesiod wrote that "the potter is furious with the potter and the craftsman with the craftsman, and the beggar is envious of the beggar and the singer of the singer." Indeed, jealousy and envy are more likely to emerge when it concerns those similar to us. Accordingly, it is more likely for compersion, rather than jealousy to emerge when there are significant differences between the various partners, for example, in age, gender, appearance, character, or occupation.

Personal traits and circumstances determine, no doubt, the likelihood of jealousy or compersion in polyamorous relationships. I focus here on several factors: one's self-esteem, the state of infatuation, and whether one's sexual needs are fulfilled.

I have suggested that self-esteem is central to the emergence of envy and jealousy. Is it central to compersion as well? Self-esteem, which is our subjective overall evaluation of our worth as a person, is measured by one's level of agreement with statements like "I like myself just the way I am";

"On the whole, I am satisfied with myself"; and "I feel worthless at times." Self-esteem partly depends on the way others, including romantic partners, evaluate us. However, it is unhealthy for our self-esteem to depend solely on our partner. Indeed, high self-esteem is not based on constant comparison with others—it includes self-acceptance, calmness, humility, generosity, gratitude, and a lack of feeling superior to others (Erol & Orth 2016; Orth, Erol, & Luciano 2018).

Self-esteem is also central to polyamory. There is a stigma suggesting that polyamorous relationships must involve low self-esteem. However, this only seems to be the case for the partner who hesitates to embark on a new relationship, not the one initiating it. In any case, being in a polyamorous relationship requires high self-esteem since comparison with other people (e.g., those sharing your partner) is vivid and feasible. It will be difficult, though not impossible, for people with low self-esteem to maintain a high-quality polyamorous relationship. Thus, people with low self-esteem are more likely to become jealous, which is, as I have claimed, poisonous for polyamorous relationships.

Another personal factor determining the likelihood of compersion concerns infatuation, or as it is called in the polyamorous vocabulary, the "new relationship energy," experienced at the beginning of sexual and romantic relationships, which typically involves intense feelings and excitement. High romantic intensity may decrease the likelihood of compersion by people who feel infatuated.

Consider the following self-description of Masha, a polyamorist married woman, who has just begun a new relationship, and is highly infatuated with her new boyfriend:

> My boyfriend was always really cool about me being with other men, especially with him being so far away. He never used his given right to be with other women in the new city he moved to. And then he came to visit for a few days and enthusiastically told me that he'd started talking to that woman to make some concrete plans. It's clear that there's a mutual attraction, and he thinks he's going to act on it. And I felt like I wanted to die. I felt a debilitating fear, suffocation and a knife in my heart. And immediately I felt horrible. Completely horrible. How is this possible if we're in an open relationship? How dare I feel this way? (Halevi 2021: 284)

Masha provides the following explanation to her behavior:

> After some thought, I realized that what was bothering me was the fact that now he would have to split the little time we have together every time he comes north. I wait impatiently for him for months, and when he finally comes for two or three

days, I suddenly have to share him with someone else? I can't do it. So I asked him to help me with this. I told him I'm working on myself and attempting to cope with jealousy, but in the meantime, as long as this is the situation, I ask if he could be satisfied with women from his area (and if that particular woman he wanted to go see goes there, that's also perfectly fine) when he's far from me. But when he finally comes to my area, I want to have him all to myself (Halevi 2021: 284–285).

As suggested above, other cases where compersion, rather than jealousy is common, are those in which the spouse can only partially satisfy his spouse's sexual needs. This takes place in cases such as aging and sickness, where one partner cannot fulfill the other's sexual needs, and other cases where healthy people who cannot, or do not want to, fulfill their partner's sexual needs.

Concluding Remarks

To sum up, I claim the following:

(1) Compersion is not a new emotion, as it is a form of sympathetic joy;
(2) Jealousy is both natural and largely unavoidable, since it is essentially a response to threats to self-esteem;
(3) Jealousy and compersion are typically incompatible; compersion is rarer than jealousy;
(4) The quality of polyamorous relationships is not lower than that of monogamous ones;
(5) The feasibility and value of compersion depends on the specific extent to which threats to self-esteem can be mitigated in a given relationship.

Polyamory and jealousy can be a lethal mix. Eliminating, or at least reducing jealousy, is essential for polyamorous relations. An emotional attitude like compersion can be, therefore, beneficial for enduring polyamorous relationships. However, in light of the difficulties associated with polyamory and compersion, such experiences are unsuitable for most people.

The above considerations indicate that the appearance of jealousy or compersion in polyamory is context- and personality-dependent. Nevertheless, it seems that compersion is indeed more common in polyamory than in monogamy. Although jealousy is not absent in polyamorous relationships, it tends to be less severe in intensity and the related behavior tends to be less hostile than in monogamy.*

*I would like to thank Arina Pismenny and Berit Brogaard for their great insights and corrections of the text. The chapter would be of considerably lower quality without their helpful suggestions.

REFERENCES

Aron, A., Lewandowski Jr, G. W., Mashek, D., & Aron, E. N. (2013). The self-expansion model of motivation and cognition in close relationships. *The Oxford handbook of close relationships*, 90–115, Oxford: Oxford University Press.

Aumer, K., Bellew, W., Ito, B., Hatfield, E., & Heck, R. (2014). The happy green eyed monogamist: Role of jealousy and compersion in monogamous and non-traditional relationships. *Electronic Journal of Human Sexuality, 17*, 77–88.

Balzarini, R. N., Campbell, L., Kohut, T., Holmes, B. M., Lehmiller, J. J., Harman, J. J., & Atkins, N. (2017). Perceptions of primary and secondary relationships in polyamory. *PLoS One, 12*(5), e0177841.

Balzarini, R. N., Dharma, C., Muise, A., & Kohut, T. (2019a). Eroticism versus nurturance: How eroticism and nurturance differs in polyamorous and monogamous relationships. *Social Psychology, 1*, 1–16.

Balzarini, R. N., Dharma, C., Kohut, T., Holmes, B. M., Campbell, L., Lehmiller, J. J., & Harman, J. J. (2019b). Demographic comparison of American individuals in polyamorous and monogamous relationships. *The Journal of Sex Research, 56*, 681–694.

Balzarini, R. N., Dharma, C., Kohut, T., Campbell, L., Lehmiller, J. J., Harman, J. J., & Holmes, B. M. (2019c). Comparing relationship quality across different types of romantic partners in polyamorous and monogamous relationships. *Archives of Sexual Behavior, 48*, 1749–1767.

Baumeister, R. F., Bratslavsky, E., Finkenauer, C., & Vohs, K. D. (2001). Bad is stronger than good. *Review of General Psychology, 5*, 323–370.

Baumeister, R. F., Vohs, K. D., & Tice, D. M. (2007). The strength model of self-control. *Current Directions in Psychological Science, 16*, 351–355.

Ben-Ze'ev, A. (2000). *The subtlety of emotions*. Cambridge, MA: MIT Press.

Ben-Ze'ev, A. (2010). Jealousy and romantic love. In S. Hart, & M. Legerstee (eds.), *Handbook of jealousy*. Chichester: Wiley-Blackwell, 40–54.

Ben-Ze'ev, A. (2017). Does loving longer mean loving more? On the nature of enduring affective attitudes. *Philosophia, 45*, 1541–1562.

Ben-Ze'ev, A. (2019). *The arc of love: How our romantic lives change over time*. Chicago: University of Chicago Press.

Ben-Ze'ev, A., & Brunning, L. (2018). How complex is your love? The case of romantic compromises and polyamory. *Journal for the Theory of Social Behaviour, 48*, 98–116.

Ben-Ze'ev, A., & Goussinsky, R. (2008). *In the name of love*. Oxford: Oxford University Press.

Ben-Ze'ev, A., & Krebs, A. (2018). Love and time. In C. Grau, & A. Smuts (eds.), The *Oxford handbook of philosophy of love*. Oxford: Oxford University Press.

Benjamin, L., & Agnew, C. (2003). Commitment and its theorized determinants: A meta-analysis of the Investment Model. *Personal Relationships, 10*, 37–57.

Brake, E. (2017). Is "loving more" better? The values of polyamory. In R. Halwani, A. Soble, S. Hoffman, & J. M. Held (eds.), *The philosophy of sex*. Lanham: Rowman & Littlefield, 201–219.

Brogaard, B. (2017). The rise and fall of the romantic ideal. In R. Grossi & D. West (eds.), *The radicalism of romantic love*. London: Routledge, 47–63.

Brunning, L. (2018). The distinctiveness of polyamory. *Journal of Applied Philosophy*, *35*, 513–531.

Brunning, L. (2019). *Imagine there's no jealousy*. Aeon.

Brunning, L. (2020). Compersion: An alternative to jealousy? *Journal of the American Philosophical Association*, *6*, 225–245.

Brunning, L. (this volume). *Multiple loves and shaped selves*.

Carmi, Z. & Sade-Saadon, L. (2022). *A few is the new two*. Tel-Aviv: eBookPro.

Cialdini, R. B., Borden, R. J., Thorne, A. & Sloan, L. R. (1976). Basking in reflected glory: Three (football) field studies. *Journal of Personality and Social Psychology, 34*, 366–375.

Conley, T. D., & Moors, A. C. (2014). More oxygen please!: How polyamorous relationship strategies might oxygenate marriage. *Psychological Inquiry*, *25*, 56–63.

Conley, T. D., Piemonte, J. L., Gusakova, S. & Rubin, J. D. (2018). Sexual satisfaction among individuals in monogamous and consensually non-monogamous relationships, *Journal of Social and Personal Relationships*, *35*, 509–531.

de Sousa, R. (2018). Love, jealousy, and compersion. In C. Grau & A. Smuts (eds.), *Oxford handbook of philosophy of love*. Oxford: Oxford University Press.

Deri, S., & Zitek, E. M. (2017). Did you reject me for someone else? Rejections that are comparative feel worse. Personality and Social *Psychology Bulletin*, *43*, 1675–1685.

DeSteno, D. A., & Salovey, P. (1996). Jealousy and the characteristics of one's rival: A self-evaluation maintenance perspective. *Personality and Social Psychology Bulletin*, *22*, 920–932.

Dew, J., & Bradford Wilcox, W. (2013). Generosity and the maintenance of marital quality. *Journal of Marriage and Family*, *75*, 1218–1228.

Erol, R. Y., & Orth, U. (2016). Self-esteem and the quality of romantic relationships. *European Psychologist*, *21*, 274–283.

Ferrer, J. N. (2019). From romantic jealousy to sympathetic joy: Monogamy, polyamory, and beyond. *International Journal of Transpersonal Studies*, *38*, 1–17.

Fredrickson, B. L. (2001). The role of positive emotions in positive psychology: The broaden-and-build theory of positive emotions. *American Psychologist, 56*, 218–226.

Halevi, M. (2021). *The freedom to choose: Rethinking Monogamy, Marriage and Relationships*. Kindle Edition. Pro Publishing.

Hart, S., & Carrington, H. (2002). Jealousy in 6-month-old infants. *Infancy, 3*, 395–402.

Jankowiak, W., & Gerth, H. (2012). Can you love more than one person at the same time? *Anthropologica*, *54*, 95–105.

Jenkins, C. (2017). *What love is: And what it could be*. New York: Basic Books.

Kipnis, L. (2003). *Against love*. New York: Pantheon.

Krebs, A. (2014). Between I and Thou–On the dialogical nature of love. In C. Maurer, T. Milligan, and K. Pacovská (eds.), *Love and its objects*. London: Palgrave Macmillan, 7–24.

Krebs, A. (2015). *Zwischen Ich und Du. Eine dialogische Philosophie der Liebe*. Frankfurt: Suhrkamp.

Levinas, E. (1998). *On thinking-of-the-other: Entre nous*. New York: Columbia University Press.

Mogilski, J. K., Reeve, S. D., Nicolas, S. C., Donaldson, S. H., Mitchell, V. E., & Welling, L. L. (2019). Jealousy, consent, and compersion within monogamous and consensually non-monogamous romantic relationships. *Archives of Sexual Behavior, 48*, 1811–1828.

Muise, A., Laughton, A. K., Moors, A., & Impett, E. A. (2019). Sexual need fulfillment and satisfaction in consensually nonmonogamous relationships. *Journal of Social and Personal Relationships, 36*, 1917–1938.

Orth, U., Erol, R. Y., & Luciano, E. C. (2018). Development of self-esteem from age 4 to 94 years: A meta-analysis of longitudinal studies. *Psychological Bulletin, 144*, 1045–1080.

Ortony, A., Clore, G. L. & Collins, A. (1988). *The cognitive structure of emotions*. Cambridge: Cambridge University Press.

Perry, D., Hendler, T., & Shamay-Tsoory, S. G. (2012). Can we share the joy of others? Empathic neural responses to distress vs joy. *Social Cognitive and Affective Neuroscience, 7*, 909–916.

Pincus, T. & Hiles, R. (2017). *It's called "polyamory": Coming out about your non-monogamous relationships*. Portland: Thorntree Press.

Portmann, J. (2013). *The ethics of sex and Alzheimer's*. London: Routledge.

Rousseau, J. J. (1762/1979). *Emile: or on education*. New York: Basic Books.

Rubel, A. N., & Bogaert, A. F. (2015). Consensual nonmonogamy: Psychological well-being and relationship quality correlates. *The Journal of Sex Research, 52*, 961–982.

Salovey, P., & Rodin, J. (1989). Envy and jealousy in close relationships. In C. Hendrick (ed.), *Review of personality and social psychology*, Vol. 10. *Close relationships* (pp. 221–246). Thousand Oaks: Sage.

Shamay-Tsoory, S. G., Ahronberg-Kirschenbaum, D., & Bauminger-Zviely, N. (2014). There is no joy like malicious joy: Schadenfreude in young children. *PLoS One, 9*(7), e100233..

Sheff, E. (2014). *The polyamorists next door*. Lanham: Rowman & Littlefield.

Whillans, A. V., Dunn, E. W., Sandstrom, G. M., Dickerson, S. S., & Madden, K. M. (2016). Is spending money on others good for your heart? *Health Psychology, 35*, 574–583.

Wonderly, M. (2017). Love and attachment. *American Philosophical Quarterly, 54*, 232–250.

Wood, J., S. Desmarais, Burleigh, & Milhausen, M. (2018). Reasons for sex and relational outcomes in consensually nonmonogamous and monogamous relationships: A self-determination theory approach. *Journal of Social and Personal Relationships, 35*, 632–654.

Ziegler, A., Matsick, J. L., Moors, A. C., Rubin, J. D., & Conley, T. D. (2014). *Does monogamy harm women? Deconstructing monogamy with a feminist lens*. Orange, CA.: Chapman University Digital Commons.

Chapter 7

Multiple Loves and Shaped Selves

Luke Brunning

Romantic relationships are one of the most significant and transformative experiences for many people.[1] People are said to be "completed" or "made whole" by a romantic partner, to have found their "better half," to "become one" with someone else. Although tired, these expressions describe a valued dimension of romantic love. Specifically, reciprocated love embedded in a relationship, love which shapes lives and selves.[2]

But what happens when romantic life is plural, and romantic love is not confined to one person at a time? In the common imagination, metaphors of completion, wholeness, or unity are rarely associated with nonmonogamy. Nor is the idea of a transformed self. The reticence to think about nonmonogamy in these terms, parallel to monogamy, is partly due to the lingering impact of union views of romantic love, and partly due to unimaginative attitudes toward nonmonogamy.

In this chapter, I resist both forms of reticence. I will argue for a shift of emphasis away from notions of romantic union toward notions of romantic *fashioning*, then I shall explain how nonmonogamy can fashion people in beneficial ways.

A few points of clarification will be useful. First, I am not providing an account of romantic *love*. Instead, I will describe the transformative dynamics of romantic *life* while leaving open the connection between those dynamics and romantic love. A romantic relationship may fashion someone even when they are not strictly in love with their partner. They might be falling in or out of love, for instance.

Second, I am not arguing that nonmonogamous romantic life is always better than monogamous life. Instead, my aim here, as in my other research, is to consider the skepticism stacked against nonmonogamy in a balanced way. Full appreciation of nonmonogamy must also recognize how it can sustain distinct harms, unrealistic ideals, and forms of intimate privilege (Brunning 2018: 527–8; forthcoming).

Finally, I remain neutral about the connection between romantic life and morality. I lack the space to consider whether many of the benefits I consider are moral, nonmoral, or a mixture of both, although many do seem to be at least partly moral (especially when we consider how character is shaped in romantic life). Similarly, I am not blind to the possibility that romantic life could make people worse, and morally worse, perhaps by miring them in forms of partiality that lead them to neglect other obligations (Jollimore 2011: 4–6; see also Pismenny 2021, and Pismenny and Brogaard in this volume).

The chapter has the following structure. In the first part, I orient my discussion by briefly describing different forms of nonmonogamous romance. In the second part, I consider union views of romantic love and suggest that they are compatible with nonmonogamy. I then echo Marilyn Friedman's autonomy critique of the union view, which also applies to nonmonogamous relationships. Full appreciation of Friedman's critique motivates my shift of emphasis, in the third part, toward a fashioning view of romantic life. Instead of forming unions with people, we are open to being fashioned by them. This fashioning view has two distinct but related dimensions: the shaping of our self-conception and the shaping of our capacities. In the fourth part, I then describe the ways in which *nonmonogamous* life fashions people in distinct ways, often for the better.

PLURALITY IN ROMANTIC LIFE

Romantic life can admit of plurality in numerous ways. I will only focus on forms of *consensual* nonmonogamy like polyamory (Anapol 2010). It can be useful to distinguish between dyadic and non-dyadic relationships, and between exclusive and nonexclusive relationships. A romantic triad is non-dyadic but may be exclusive if all three people are faithful to each other. An open relationship between two people may be dyadic but nonexclusive if they pursue additional relationships.

We can also distinguish between sexual and emotional exclusivity. A married couple may have a nonexclusive open relationship when it comes to sexual activity but avoid emotional bonds. Or the members of a romantic triad may be free to form close romantic bonds with other people, but reserve sexual activity for each other. Polyamory, where people love several people at once, is often both sexually and emotionally nonexclusive.

Practically speaking, nonmonogamous lives differ in other ways. Some people adopt more formal structures of hierarchies to organize their time, activities, and domestic spaces (Veaux & Rickert 2014). A married couple might have secondary partners who do not share their domestic life. Or a polyamorous person with two loves might be eager to ensure their time and attention is divided equally between partners. In those cases, the key organizational norms are *primacy* and *equality*, respectively. So-called romantic anarchists, however, look to challenge received norms about romantic relationships, especially when compared to friendship, and so they often resist the idea of formal structure or hierarchy between different people (De las Heras Gómez 2019).

I will focus primarily on nonmonogamous relationships that admit of both sexual and emotional intimacy, such as polyamorous relationships. Those cases most closely resemble monogamous romantic life, and they arguably transform people to the greatest extent. They certainly provoke the most skeptical reactions when people are asked to consider whether nonmonogamous is a viable form of romantic life.

This focus means I will overlook so-called casual sex. This is not to deny some of the similarities between casual sex and polyamory, or to deny the former may shape people. Casual sex can be pursed with consideration and is arguably compatible with a virtuous life (Halwani 2003: ch. 3).

MERGERS AND ACQUISITIONS

Some philosophers have taken seriously the idea that romantic love and relationships involve a kind of union or merger with another person (Fisher 1990; Solomon 2006; Nozick 1989). Elke Schmidt distinguishes usefully between three versions of this claim: (1) the strong ontological model, (2) the striving model, and (3) the moderate ontological model (2018). On the strong ontological model, romantic lovers *literally* merge into a new entity, or something like that, with their individual forms of autonomy and decision making, say, being replaced with a new joint or fused agent (Schmidt 2018: 708). On the striving model, lovers are *trying* to become a new entity, although this may not be literally possible. On the moderate ontological model, lovers retain their separate existence, but a *new* entity, the couple or relationship, is formed alongside them.

There is room for disagreement about *what* is unified or merged when lovers merge, or try to merge. Typical candidates might include a merger of desires, interests, projects, and identities. On this view, lovers come to want the same things, enjoy the same activities, have identical projects, and think of themselves in the same ways. Marilyn Friedman, who adopts a moderate ontological view of romantic merging, offers us a broader list of what might be merged. The additional features on her list include lover's care and protection, mutual familiarity, attention, agency, labor, awareness, and evaluative perspective (2003: 122–24).

Although these union views were intended to make sense of the common feeling of being "completed" or "becoming one with" someone in a monogamous relationship, they cannot be restricted to monogamous life. In principle, if two people can merge, or try to merge, then so can three, or four, or more; and if a union theory of love explains what goes on in monogamous romantic life, it may explain what goes on in nonmonogamous romantic life as well. Many nonmonogamous people are as welcome to the romantic clichés outlined in the first paragraph of this chapter as anyone.[3] The three members of a romantic triad, for example, could come to have, or strive to have, merged desires, interests, and projects; a unified sense of agency; a distinct idiolect and mode of expression; a unified sense of attention and evaluative perspective; and a shared sense of care. Similarly, the desire for union can stretch beyond the boundaries of an existing relationship. A couple may *strive* to unify with a third party; the triad may want a new member, and so on.[4]

Attempts to reserve the potential benefits of union, to monogamous couples look strained or *ad hoc*. Sigmund Freud struggled with this tension. At one point in *Civilisation and Its Discontents*, a work exploring the connections between individual human drives and social organization, he writes that the purpose of Eros "is to gather together individuals, then families and finally tribes, peoples, and nations in one great unit—humanity. Why this has to happen we do not know: it is simply the work of Eros" (2002: 58).

Understood in this way, Eros seems to tend to ever-larger unions between people. One might think this applies to romantic relationships, too. Yet, elsewhere in the same work, he describes Eros in the context of romantic life:

> When a love relationship is at its height, the lovers no longer have any interest in the world around them; they are self-sufficient as a pair, and in order to be happy they do not even need the child they have in common. In no other case does Eros so clearly reveal what is at the core of his being, the aim of making one out of more than one; however, having achieved this proverbial goal by making two people fall in love, *he refuses to go any further.* (2002: 45 emphasis added)

As a description of what love can feel like, this may be accurate. But in many cases, of course, Eros *does* indeed go further, as many nonmonogamous people can attest. Freud is drawn into trying to explain away an unnecessary restriction and he does not consider the normative potential of embracing this possibility.[5]

Philosophers in recent literature also try to restrict their conception of the romantic union to the monogamous couple. Perhaps one of the best examples is from Robert Nozick, an exponent of the union view who flatly asserts that "it is not feasible for a person simultaneously to be part of multiple romantic couples (or a trio) even were the person to desire this" (1989: 84). But assertion is clearly no argument, and the romantic lives of nonmonogamous people once again bring pressure to bear directly on these claims.

These contortions and assertions are interesting not for what they establish, but because their lack of argument shows how difficult it is to embrace a union view of romantic life while restricting it to two people. If the union view of romantic love is plausible, it can apply easily to nonmonogamous life. This is not to deny that nonmonogamy may require unique psychological and practical considerations, but simply to note that the underlying idea of "making one out of more than one" cannot be arbitrarily restricted to two. And if someone thinks a union of two is *good*, for whatever reason, it is possible that a union of three, or more, is better, for the same reason.

Union views are flawed, however. All versions of it are subject to problems (see, e.g., Brogaard 2015; Schmidt 2018). On the strong ontological model, we end up with a new union that supersedes the independent existence of the two lovers. This seems metaphysically and psychologically questionable and does not tally with the phenomenology of even the closest loving relationships. On the striving model of union, people seem to be trying to bring about an end that is not possible to achieve, which may be irrational, or generate perpetual frustration. More problematically, the striving model seems to retain two issues shared with the moderate ontological model. The first is that the desire for union seems in tension with being *robustly concerned* for the other person, for their own sake (Soble 1997). The second is that the desire for a union or merger appears to undermine individuals' *autonomy* (Friedman 2003).[6]

Friedman develops an influential version of the autonomy critique. She draws on Neil Delaney's analogy between romantic lovers and political states in a federal union (1996). The individual states retain their identities but merge some core powers.[7] For Friedman, romantic life is a more flexible equivalent of this kind of merger, where some aspects of personal life, decision making, and competence, are merged:

> Merged lovers are, on my view, partly separate selves and also partly merged beings. They constitute an "interpersonal federation." Thus we should ask what impact these romantic partial mergers of identity have on the personal autonomy of lovers. (2003: 121)

We saw above that Friedman has an expansive conception of what can be merged in romantic love. Her primary concern, however, is not that mergers might be extensive, but that they might be *unfair*. Fundamentally, romantic mergers "can yield asymmetries that affect differently the identities and individual autonomies of two people who love each other" (2003: 124). Particularly important asymmetries include the extent to which one person has to make an adjustment to their identity or way of life in order to pursue the relationship; the extent to which someone is able to enter the relationship in a voluntary way; and the differences in "autonomy competences" within the relationship.

Friedman's core concern is that *women* have historically suffered along all three of these dimensions, among others; that the romantic merger is asymmetric in ways which predominantly benefit men. She also thinks this extends into the modern era, where egalitarian norms of romantic life are slowly taking hold, because women

> experience more cultural pressure than men to change what is deeply defining of who they are, for the sake of heterosexual love, rather than simply being permitted to build their heterosexual relationships in accord with whatever happens already to define their identities. (2003: 132)

Although these issues are the contingent product of contemporary social norms, they have a real impact on the autonomy of women within romantic life. This impact is sufficient to be wary of romantic union as a practical ideal because the ideal emphasizes the merger of functions, competences, and features of identity, as opposed to their development or improvement.

Friedman's conclusion also applies to romantic union as a nonmonogamous ideal. Nonmonogamy is hard to pursue openly in most social contexts, and people are subject to suspicion and stigma. The social aversion to nonmonogamy amplifies the intimate privilege of the socially dominant partner, or partners, relative to the other partners. How this intimate privilege is constructed will depend on the context, but affluent, educated, upper class, white, heterosexual, men will typically be more able to live nonmonogamously than people from less privileged backgrounds (Rambukkana 2015; Sheff & Hammers 2011). Less privileged people, typically women, will have to make significant identity-distorting adjustments, or relinquish autonomy, in order to embrace their nonmonogamous relationships over time as they are constrained by more privileged partners.

Given the assumption that autonomy is an important value to preserve, then the above concerns are sufficient to be wary of union as a romantic ideal. But is this to condemn the spirit of those notions of unity, completion, wholeness and so on which appear to many people to capture the texture of romantic relationships No. But a change of emphasis is needed.

ROMANTIC FASHIONING

In this section, I start with a discussion of an objection which Friedman entertains and then tries to answer. Considering this objection helps motivate a different approach to the transformative character of romantic relationships.

Friedman asks: might relationships actually *enhance* our capacities, including our autonomy, and change us in positive ways? Initially she is receptive to this thought, acknowledging that romantic relationships can increase self-knowledge, personal individuality, self-esteem, and other constituents of autonomy such as the ability to reflect and consider alternative points of view. She also notes that romantic relationships often center on projects which lead to forms of extended group agency (2003: 133–34).

In themselves, these remarks might suggest a general shift of emphasis away from the ideal of romantic unions and toward an ideal of romantic fashioning, in which people are open to being influenced and changed by others while retaining their separateness. Instead of developing this idea, however, Friedman offers a few remarks by way of rejoinder:

> Whether or not love permits such growth in the less autonomous lover, however, depends on many factors, not the least of which is the support and encouragement of the more dominant or directive partner. My larger concern is with individual, and particularly women's, losses of autonomy over the whole course of a romantic love relationship, not merely with isolated occasions of it. (2003: 134)

I understand these brief remarks in the following way. First, the connections between romantic relationships and autonomy enhancement are fragile. They depend on positive background conditions, especially the character of a partner. Second, although romantic relationships may enable some women to flourish by becoming more autonomous, in general they erect *structural* barriers to such flourishing.

Both of these ideas warrant discussion. In the next section, I consider the possibility that relationships might also offer structural *benefits* to the people within them, not just barriers. For now, however, I will consider Friedman's first point: that the benefits of romantic relationships are fragile or contingent on a supportive partner.

Friedman is certainly right that the degree to which romantic relationships change people in positive ways may depend on their partner. But we must resist a simplistic interpretation of this idea. Support and encouragement are neither necessary nor sufficient to help people become more autonomous.

Some forms of support and encouragement are smothering. They can prevent someone from learning through experience, or coming to terms with their ambivalent feelings (Brogaard 2020: ch. 2). Similarly, people can learn about themselves; about their identity, desires, values, and feelings, in noticing how they diverge from, or even conflict with, a partner. Moments of disagreement, even resistance, can help people find their voice. Of course, extreme hostility is inimical to flourishing in romantic life, but our acceptance of that fact should not blind us to the common ways that dissention and divergence shape people.

This point is important for two reasons. First, it further highlights the inadequacy of union views, for they neglect the ways that romantic relationships can be deepened through tension, not only harmony. Second, it should alert us to the ways that romantic life can fashion people *indirectly*.

Friedman's objection to her own view should be taken seriously. Not only can romantic relationships enhance the autonomy of lovers, they change them in other ways too. We can develop this thought, and capture what was implied in our initial metaphors of "completion" or "being made whole," while jettisoning ideas of union and merger. This is just as well, as the desire to merge with someone can often reflect an evasion of identity or an abdication of responsibility for one's character.

To consider how people fashion each other, consider an analogy. Imagine a group of academic colleagues researching the philosophy of sex and love. Although they produce individual books and articles, these academics share a common philosophical narrative: a sense of which questions are significant, and an understanding about how those questions might be examined.

These academics differ in talent, effort, quirks of imagination, and methodology. Their group dynamic is also shaped by luck as they benefit from unexpected grants or learn to avoid hostile journals. These variations in ability, working practices, and luck, influence each academic differently. One may adapt their writing style in recognition of another's success at a prestigious journal. Another might revise their argument in response to helpful objections. Another might finally start having confidence in their research project, after hearing their colleague's excited praise.

Some of these influences are explicit. They can be traced back to specific bits of advice or inspiring conversations. But other influences are more subtle. Hours spent listening at workshops, animated discussions, lingering disagreements, mutual enthusiasm: these features of a shared *environment* can change these academics.

In turn, these changes differ in character. On the one hand, these academics might alter their sense of self and research identity. They might learn to think about their subject in a new way, refine their research project, restructure an article, or develop a renewed sense of their academic personality. On the other hand, their character might change, as positive feedback boosts their self-esteem, or they come to adopt new roles. Working together changes who these academics are, but also what they are capable of doing.

These academics are not trying to copy, compete, or merge with each other. Instead, they are individuals who are *permeable* to each other's thinking and academic practice. Their interests, arguments, and academic decisions are molded by each other, and their individual writings are shaped by their companions' research. In turn, these mutual influences, both the explicit and environmental, fashion their collective narrative sense of what they are doing. What might have started as a response to the historical neglect of a topic, say, might develop into a positive research project.

Similar dynamics are visible within romantic relationships, albeit with greater intimacy and intensity. Lovers are permeable to each other and develop as individuals in response to mutual influence around a loose, shared, narrative sense of what they are doing. Some of those influences are explicit, as partners advise each other. Other influences are more subtle, and arise due to shared environments and practices. Cutting across that distinction is the further fact that some of those influences shape lovers' sense of self, or shared narrative, whereas others shape their practical abilities. Taken together, we can say that romantic relationships *fashion* people.[8] Let us explore this idea in general terms, before considering how nonmonogamous relationships in particular can fashion people.

Take, first, the idea that lovers shape each other's sense of self. Pilar Lopez-Cantero explores this idea in developing her "mutual self-shaping" model of being in love (2020; Lopez-Cantero and Archer 2020).[9] Although applied to lovers, the model captures the general way that romantic life can shape self-concepts and broader identity.

For Lopez-Cantero, romantic lovers are in love when they are: (1) open to having their interests, choices, and emotions directed by their lover (2) their self-concept is sensitive to their lover's reasonably accurate *interpretations* of them, in a way that is (3) dynamically permeable and (4) shaped by their *narrative understanding* of themselves as on a loving *trajectory* with each other (Lopez-Cantero 2020: ch. 4).

On this view, lovers are lovers because they are open to each other in a reciprocal way. Whether explicit or otherwise, they are receptive to the passions and desires of the other, and actively receptive to being interpreted, evaluated, and guided by the other person, from their distinct agential perspective. Their relationship has momentum, that is, they are likely to act in ways which continue the relationship, because they share a narrative sense of themselves on a loving trajectory. This trajectory is analogous to the sense of intellectual purpose shared by the academics; it may be loose and change over time, but they understand themselves, and the changes they experience, in reference to it dynamically.

When active and explicit, this self-shaping can help align people with their ideal conception of who they are, that is, their "best self." In the psychological literature, this process is called "the Michelangelo Phenomenon," because lovers face each other as the sculptor faced the marble (Drigotas et al. 1999; c.f. Ben-Ze'ev 2019: 57). These shaping influences can expand someone's *ideal* sense of themselves, too, especially if their imagination is limited or they lack confidence or self-esteem.

The academic analogy, however, helps us see how Lopez-Cantero's account only captures part of romantic fashioning. First, people are not only shaped by explicit forms of evaluation and interpretation in romantic life, but also by practical interaction and simple proximity within a certain environment. Second, it is not just their identity and self-concept that are changed, but also their *characters*, understood broadly to include habits, skills, and traits (including emotion traits). Lovers may find they become more patient, better listeners, more adept at compromise, or happier, for example, in addition to developing new desires or honing their appreciation of certain values, and thus fashioning their self-concepts. (As with changes to a person's self-concept, characters are shaped by disagreements and differences, not just positive interactions.)

To take one example which brings out both additional features of romantic fashioning, Barbara Fredrickson argues that the experience of positive emotions enables people to resist momentary responses to negative situations, react more creatively, become more resourceful, and, ultimately flourish (Fredrickson 2001). If this is right, then if romantic relationships are sources of positive emotions, as is usually the case, they can help people "broaden and build" their psychological resilience. This is a change of character that happens through exposure to certain kinds of emotion, not explicit direction from another person.

The distinction between changes to self-concept and to broader character is useful because these changes can conflict or can lag behind each other. Someone's ability to be more patient, for example, may lag behind their openness to being fashioned in that direction by a lover; or someone's persistent perception of themselves as timid might fail to reflect their emerging courage. A lover's active attempts to beneficially "sculpt" their partner may also undermine the indirect benefits of a supportive environment; the benefits of companionate sympathy can outweigh those of explicit "advice."

Let us take stock. In thinking about change or transformation in romantic life, I have suggested we shift emphasis. We should reject union views and talk instead of romantic fashioning. I have sketched the outlines of a romantic fashioning approach. Romantic fashioning encompasses both changes to individuals' self-conceptions, and to their broader character, and involves both explicit interpretation and direction by a partner, and more indirect environmental effects. These changes, to self-conception and character, need not happen at once, and can conflict with each other.

Unlike the union approach, the romantic fashioning approach begins and ends with the individual; romantic partners are not aiming to subsume themselves in the other. This approach also emphasizes the reciprocal, cocreated nature of romantic interactions. People fashion *each other*, and their narrative understanding of their relationship is coauthored.

In contrast to Friedman's view, however, I have also suggested that valuable forms of romantic fashioning can be the consequence of difference and disagreement, not just encouragement and support. Romantic relationships fashion people in extensive, messy, and nonlinear ways.

Friedman seemed to suggest that although some relationships can change people for the better, there are structural barriers to this happening. In adopting the romantic fashioning approach, we have reason to look again at this idea. We can acknowledge that romantic relationships are sites of power and privilege, but also ask whether there can be structural *benefits* to certain relationship forms. Different kinds of relationship may produce distinct dynamics of interaction and unique guiding narratives which, in turn, may benefit the people involved in noticeable ways. In the next section, I explore this idea in connection with nonmonogamy.

NONMONOGAMY AND ROMANTIC FASHIONING

The romantic fashioning view helps us attend to the structural features of romantic life. Some relationships may encourage certain forms of guiding narrative and practical dynamics which benefit the people involved. These benefits may not outweigh the harms of indifferent or abusive partners, and they are certainly not sufficient for romantic flourishing but they may be substantial, and they deserve consideration. In this section, I suggest nonmonogamous relationships have such beneficial structural dynamics.

I will focus on consensual nonmonogamous relationships which involve emotional bonds with other people, such as a domestic triad, or polyamorous people with several concurrent loving relationships. I shall assume there is significant interaction between these people, but much of what I say will apply, to a lesser extent, to other kinds of nonmonogamous life.

Some of the claims below are contingent on the current shape of romantic norms and attitudes. If those norms and attitudes were different, and the gap between monogamous and nonmonogamous life was smaller, then nonmonogamous lovers would be fashioned in a different way. Some of the claims, however, are more structural, and would survive changes to contingent social norms.

Two core features give nonmonogamous romantic life its particular structure. First, and more contingently, there are few social exemplars or narratives for this kind of relationship. Second, and more substantively, people have to contend with the active influence of more than one other romantic partner. I will consider both in turn.

Lack of Exemplars

Consider first the lack of exemplars or commonplace narratives. Nonmonogamous life differs greatly from the established romantic norm because there are very few clear norms, ideals, or shared stories to influence and structure people's romantic aspirations and practice. Instead, people may experience hostility or suspicion. Even if they are lucky, they are likely to experience disorientation and ambivalence about how, exactly, to have several romantic partners.

As a result, nonmonogamous relationships cannot run on default, especially initially. Instead of falling into a common romantic trajectory, one modeled against parents or common social examples, nonmonogamous people have to define their lives against the grain of existing social structures and forge their own narrative sense of what they are doing. They need some sense of how their amorous entanglements fit together, and how they might develop.

To coauthor such a narrative, nonmonogamous people have to develop what Karen Stohr calls a "moral neighbourhood," which is a "shared normative space" in which people interact, provide evaluative perspectives on each other's actions, and support each other's developing "aspirational moral identities" from the position of a "shared evaluative outlook" (2019: 108).

This evaluative outlook consists of the norms and ideals which guide nonmonogamous life, for example, norms of radical honesty (Emens 2004: 322–34), or the emotional ideal of compersion (joy at a partner's intimate flourishing with another person, Brunning 2020; see also Ben-Ze'ev, this volume), as well as the specific practices in which these norms and ideals have expression, for example, nonconfrontational relationship "check-ins," or meetings with partners of partners.

In practice, people vary greatly in their approaches to nonmonogamy. Some people deviate more widely from existing norms and practices, others embrace similarities with familiar forms of romantic life. Irrespective of how far they travel, however, all nonmonogamous people need to navigate themselves some distance away from the norm.[10]

In itself, this unpredictable and ongoing process exercises individual autonomy, and in many cases it does so extensively. Conversation, negotiation, setting boundaries, processing emotions, developing ideals, and revising practices are all good contexts for the expression and improvement of autonomy.

These processes also provide an opportunity for nonmonogamous people to undertake a more extensive examination of romantic life, at least compared to conventional relationship contexts. On reflection, perhaps they come to reject modern individualism, or the equation of romantic worth with personal appearance and sexual competence, or "whole life ethics" in which people have to evaluate what they are doing in reference to some kind of life plan (Walker 2007: ch. 6): a form of reflection that accords nicely with the romantic escalator, that is, a teleological notion of romantic life as "progressing" from dating, through to cohabitation, marriage, and a family, but which is less suited to other forms of romantic relating.

Multiple Romantic Partners

Having several romantic partners, or being open to this, also introduces a distinct dynamic which has practical impacts on relationships. This dynamic requires management, but also confers structural benefits to nonmonogamous people. In many cases, these benefits arise simply from being forced to confront the realities of relating romantically to more than one person.

First, consider the emotional currents nonmonogamous people have to navigate. All relationships are potential sources of difficulty or conflict. But this risk increases when there are more people to accommodate, and thus more personal boundaries to establish and maintain. As a result, nonmonogamous relationships involve substantial amounts of communication and reflection, especially around emotions like jealousy and insecurity, to which nonmonogamous relationships are exposed explicitly.

Faced with these currents, nonmonogamous people need to reflect on the form of their romantic interactions; they need to listen carefully to each other, and find ways of de-escalating conflicts; they need to be able to contain and cope with the emotional disorientation of other people, and to actively try and see the best in situations which could ordinarily provoke jealousy (Brunning 2020); they need to take responsibility for mistakes and misunderstandings. The latter requirement is especially important as mistakes and misunderstandings are likely in a social context that is not receptive to nonmonogamy and in which few exemplars exist.

Some of these demands, such as the need to navigate the kinds of insecurity that arise when a partner is in love with someone else, are arguably unique to nonmonogamy. Other demands, those around communication, say, are common to monogamous romantic life too, but are exacerbated when there are more people.

To say that nonmonogamous relationships generate these unique structural demands is not to imply that nonmonogamous people are better at handling them well from the outset. Instead, I am suggesting that it is hard to live as part of a triad, say, or to openly pursue two loving relationships at the same time, without engaging in this kind of work.

Over time, however, the need to do this work will fashion people. They will get better in virtue of having to do it. Some improvements will be through explicit reflection on their situation and sensitivity to positive inputs by other people; other improvements will arise indirectly, as a result of continued exposure to situations where conversation is needed, insecurity is likely, and so on. Some nonmonogamous people will try to avoid having to communicate with others or reflect on themselves, and so may not be fashioned much by their romantic life, but these people are also less likely to sustain successful romantic relationships over time.

Now consider how nonmonogamous relationships equip people with valuable resources. In close romantic relationships, people internalize each other. They are able to explore and adopt the perspective of another person, and incorporate that person's presence into their self-concept and the shared narrative sense of their relationship. This process can be quite extensive. As Arthur Aron and colleagues put it:

> When we include another person in the self, our cognitive construction of the other overlaps with (or shares activation potentials with) our cognitive construction of the self. . . . Thus, to the extent we include another in the self, we take on the resources, perspectives, and identities of that person, and we share that person's outcomes. The other person then informs who we are, enhances the tools we feel we have at our disposal, shapes how we see the world, and affects the costs and benefits we perceive ourselves to incur. (2013: 102)

A key difference between monogamous and nonmonogamous romantic life is that people in the latter adopt and internalize the perspectives of more than one lover at once. This fact fashions people in distinct ways.

Importantly, nonmonogamous people are subject to more than evaluative perspectives *as lovers*. Their sense of romantic identity, and how they see themselves in the context of their romantic relationship, is fashioned by more than one person at a time. People form their sense of self in relation to other people; they need others to corroborate their self-image, and help to "hold" them in established roles (Lindemann 2016) or with respect to aspirational identities (Stohr 2019). When someone has multiple lovers, their identity is held in place and corroborated by more than one person.

There are advantages to these expanded perspectives. Romantic relationships are often the site of intense defensiveness and insecurity. People are motivated to present themselves well and avoid confronting more troubling aspects of their character. Self-knowledge is, therefore, often hard to attain. But since being seen by others, particularly in close relationships, is a good way of coming to know about oneself, the more lovers someone has the more they may come to know about themselves, especially as it is harder to ignore similar remarks from multiple people. Such knowledge can aid their ability to act well and to continue, and flourish within, their relationships.

The increased intimate perspectives provided by multiple loves also bear upon the narrative understanding guiding nonmonogamous life. This narrative trajectory, the sense of what these lovers are doing, why it matters, and where it is going, is coauthored between several people. In itself this can be advantageous. First, it enlarges someone's "narrative ecology"; that is, the features from which they can forge a narrative understanding of themselves and their relationships (McLean 2015: 5–6). Different people can articulate one situation using different concepts, idioms, and genres. Second, different coauthors will have different skills. Some may be imaginative, skilled in envisaging how a story could go, and what it might mean to love this way over time; others may be good at "holding" a narrative and ensuring continuity of understanding over time, through periods of uncertainty.

Although nonmonogamous life may increase the *amount* of emotional work people do, which can be burdensome and require practical compromise, the fact that more people are involved may arguably reduce the pressure on any specific individual to live up to demanding ideals or compromise their identities. People do not have to be "the other half" to the other. By default, nonmonogamous relationships are more permeable and open to outside influence. This reduces some tensions between individuals as their contribution to the shared narrative is reduced somewhat, and they are less likely to have to make identity-shaping *changes* in order to accommodate the desires of other people.[11]

Nonmonogamous relationships can expand and hold someone's sense of self, and the narrative guiding their relationship. But this is not a static or uncritical process. As I mentioned above, relationships are also sites of productive disagreement and critical evaluation. Romantic partners hold each other to account in many different ways, some more explicit than others. At times these challenges are serious: to moral values and practical commitments. But most often these challenges address the daily distortions of defensiveness, anxiety, anger, or jealousy, the hard feelings which are most visible in intimate life. Or else they help confront people mired in what Iris Murdoch called the "fat relentless ego" (Hopwood 2018: 489).

To explore the dynamic, critical, aspect of romantic life, we can develop Friedman's political metaphor. She compared romantic relationships to a federal configuration of individual states. But we might think, instead, of partners as akin to the different branches of government within a state. These branches are independent, and may conflict, but they must function together to make and implement decisions.

This analogy helps us recognize that some nonmonogamous relationships may have advantages over monogamous ones because they are not bipartite. As a result, there are greater *checks and balances* within romantic life since there are additional perspectives from which individual actions and emotional responses can be evaluated. Disagreements or tensions between two people can always be evaluated by a third, or more, just as an impasse between executive and legislature can be adjudicated by a court.

Nonmonogamous relationships are structured around the possibility that interactions between two people can be evaluated by a third party who is romantically invested in one or both people directly and indirectly involved in the narrative they all share. Structurally, it is harder for any one person to be complacent in a nonmonogamous relationship because defensive and distorting dynamics are harder to sustain when people are also answerable to a third romantic partner. Of course, romantic relationships do not just involve dour reflection or critical evaluation. These checks and balances, the presence of a third party, can also help people open out to each in moments of vulnerability, growth, and joy.

This is not to assume that these evaluative dynamics are always *equal* in nature, no matter how ideal that may be. In hierarchical nonmonogamous relationships, this is particularly unlikely to be the case, just as the executive branch of government often has undue influence over the legislature (Balzarini et al. 2019). Equal forms of evaluation are not required, however, to establish the claim that there are more checks and balances in a tripartite or quadripartite form of romantic life.

Taken together, the increased evaluative perspectives, opportunities for self-knowledge, richer narrative ecology, and the checks and balances of an additional loving gaze have the significant potential to offer increased *structural stability* to nonmonogamous romantic lives. The recognition, perspectives, and narrative competence of more people mean the narrative trajectory at the heart of such a relationship is more able to survive lapses in attention, or disagreements, tensions, and confusion. This stability is important in intimate interpersonal contexts where people are trying to relate well to each other. It is even more important when there are few ideals of what good relating might look like, and so disorientation is a constant possibility.

It may be argued that I am overstating what is particular to nonmonogamous romantic life. Might friendship confer similar benefits? This suggestion overlooks some important differences. Although intimacy, sexual attraction, desire, and activity, and domestic proximity might not be sufficient or necessary to distinguish all friendships and romantic relationships, they make the difference for most people. Friends and lovers also organize their lives according to different narrative trajectories and self-conceptions and, unlike nonmonogamous romance, friendship is an accepted social institution with clear exemplars and norms.

Having an extra romantic partner is not the same as having a friend. The romantic lover evaluates someone *as a lover*, from the *perspective* of a lover, and relative to their *shared* narrative sense of themselves as lovers. Friends offer external perspectives on the romantic life of each other, lovers offer an internal perspective; they inhabit different moral neighborhoods.

CONCLUSION

People equate romantic relationships with personal change. These changes can be understood in terms of the ideal of romantic union. In principle, non-monogamous relationships can be thought of in this way too. But union views are implausible. Few people want to become one with another; still fewer achieve this. Romantic fashioning is a more productive romantic model. People are fashioned in two ways. Their self-conceptions change, and their wider character changes. These changes occur due to overt direction and the subtler effects of ongoing proximity or practical entanglement with others. Nonmonogamous relationships create unique dynamics which mean people are often fashioned beneficially.

Someone may object that for the benefits I have described to obtain, the romantic lovers concerned must *already* be competent, that they have to be communicative, reasonable, and emotionally resilient. But that would be to misunderstand my argument. Interpersonal skills develop over time as a result of exposure to other people and the desire to be open to their evaluative direction. Nonmonogamy generates the urgent demand for such skills, and it is hard to evade the need to develop them for long. This is no guarantee that the way people are fashioned in nonmonogamous relationships is always for the better, but the deck is stacked slightly in their favor and, arguably, more so than that of monogamous people.[12]

NOTES

1. Some people are aromantic and experience no desire for romantic relationships. Friendships and parenthood can be as, or more, important as romantic love.

2. In recent years, the phrase "transformative experience" has been given technical treatment by Laurie Paul (2014). Paul thinks an experience like becoming pregnant is transformative in this sense if you can only come to *know* what it is like by undergoing it, and if it *changes who you are* in the process by altering your preferences. Here, my appeals to transformation are looser. But I think it is plausible that specific romantic relationships may yield transformative experiences in this technical sense, and will explore this idea in future work.

3. With the exception, perhaps, of "my other half," which can be substituted for an appropriate fraction: "I've found my other third."

4. Not all nonmonogamous configurations need think of themselves in this way, of course. A V-shaped network, where X is in a relationship with Y, Y in a

relationship with Z, but Z not in a relationship with X, for example, could reject notions of union at the level of their network (although they may share many desires, and a common outlook).

5. Herbert Marcuse takes up that task in *Eros and Civilisation*.

6. Schmidt also points out that union views of romantic love, even in their moderate forms, seem to proliferate entities and appear incapable of saying what is *distinctive* about romantic love because other relationships, like friendship, seem to generate similar unions (2018: 713–14).

7. We could envisage a version of this analogy running in the opposite direction, where lovers merge their identities but retain some core powers. I lack space to consider whether this would sidestep concerns about compromised autonomy, but it seems plausible that Friedman's concerns about unequal accommodation apply to such fused identities, also.

8. I use "fashioning" here rather than Lopez-Cantero's notion of "self-shaping" to reflect the fact that romantic relationships can change people in a variety of ways; some involve the active, interpretive, input of other people, but other transformative aspects of romantic life are situational or environmental. I did not use "transformational" more broadly to avoid confusing my view with the literature on transformational experience.

9. Lopez-Cantero draws upon Dean Cocking and Jeanette Kennett's "drawing" theory of friendship (1998); Amélie Rorty's sense of love as "dynamically permeable" (1987), and Karen Jones's conception of loving trajectories (2008) in suggesting that love can shape how people regard themselves. In the psychological literature, a very similar view has been defended by Aron & Aron (1986; 1996).

10. This process is part of what might make the pursuit of nonmonogamy a transformative experience in Paul's sense, for once reflection begins, it is unclear where it will lead.

11. The extent to which this is true is in need of empirical study, and is likely to depend on broader structural features of romantic life, such as gender norms (cf. Overall 1998).

12. My thanks to Aaron Ben-Ze'ev, Pilar Lopez-Cantero, and Joe Saunders for their helpful comments on this chapter.

REFERENCES

Anapol, D. 2010. *Polyamory in the 21st century: Love and intimacy with multiple partners*. Rowman & Littlefield Publishers.

Aron, A., & Aron, E. N. 1986. *Love and the Expansion of Self: Understanding Attraction and Satisfaction*. Hemisphere Publishing Corp/Harper & Row.

Aron, E. N., & Aron, A. 1996. Love and expansion of the self: The state of the model. *Personal Relationships, 3*, 1, 45–58.

Aron, A., Lewandowski, G. W., Jr., Mashek, D., & Aron, E. N. (2013). The self-expansion model of motivation and cognition in close relationships. In J. A.

Simpson & L. Campbell (Eds.), Oxford library of psychology. The Oxford Handbook of Close Relationships. Oxford University Press: 90–115.

Balzarini, R. N., Dharma, C., Muise, A., & Kohut, T. 2019. Eroticism versus nurturance how eroticism and nurturance differs in polyamorous and monogamous relationships. *Social Psychology, 1*, 1–16.

Ben-Ze'ev, A. 2019. *The arc of love: How our romantic lives change over time.* University of Chicago Press.

Brake, E. 2012. *Minimizing marriage: Marriage, morality, and the law.* Oxford University Press.

Brogaard, B. 2015. *On romantic love.* Oxford University Press.

Brogaard, B. 2020. *Hatred: Understanding our most dangerous emotion.* Oxford University Press.

Brunning, L. 2022. Polyamory: The Future of Love? in A. Grahle, N. McKeever, & J. Saunders (eds.) *Philosophy of Love in the Past, Present, and Future*, Routledge: 163–78.

Brunning, L. 2020. Compersion: an alternative to jealousy? *American Journal of Philosophy 6*(2), 225–245.

Brunning, L. 2018. The distinctiveness of polyamory. *Journal of Applied Philosophy, 35*(3), 513–531.

Cocking, D., & Kennett, J. 1998. Friendship and the self. *Ethics, 108*(3), 502–527.

Delaney, N. 1996. Romantic love and loving commitment: Articulating a modern ideal. *American Philosophical Quarterly, 33*, 375–405.

Drigotas, S. M., Rusbult, C. E., Wieselquist, J., & Whitton, S. W. 1999. Close partner as sculptor of the ideal self: Behavioral affirmation and the Michelangelo phenomenon. *Journal of personality and social psychology, 77*(2), 293.

Emens, E. 2004. Manogamy's law: Compulsory monogamy and polyamorous existence. *NYU Review Law & Society Change, 29*, 277–376.

Fisher, M. 1990. *Personal love.* Duckworth.

Fredrickson, B. L. 2001. The role of positive emotions in positive psychology: The broaden-and-build theory of positive emotions. *American Psychologist, 56*, 3: 218–226.

Freud, S. 2002 [1930]. *Civilization and its Discontents,* (trans. McLintock, D.) London: Penguin Press.

Friedman, M. 2003. *Autonomy, gender, politics.* Oxford University Press.

De las Heras Gómez, R. 2019. Thinking relationship anarchy from a queer feminist approach. *Sociological Research Online, 24*(4), 644–660.

Halwani, R. 2003. *Virtuous liaisons: Care, love, sex, and virtue ethics.* Open Court Publishing.

Hopwood, M. 2018. 'The extremely difficult realization that something other than oneself is real': Iris Murdoch on love and moral agency. *European Journal of Philosophy, 26*(1), 477–501.

Jollimore, T. 2011. *Love's vision.* Princeton University Press.

Jones, K. 2008. How to change the past. In K. Atkins, and C. Mackenzie (eds.), *Practical identity and narrative agency.* Routledge.

Lindemann, H. 2016. *Holding and letting go: The social practice of personal identities*. Oxford University Press.

Lopez-Cantero, P. 2020 *Being in Love: A Narrative Account,* PhD Thesis, Manchester University.

Lopez-Cantero, P., & Archer, A. 2020. Lost without you: The value of falling out of love. *Ethical Theory and Moral Practice, 23,* 515–529.

McLean, K. C. 2015. *The co-authored self: Family stories and the construction of personal identity*. Oxford University Press.

Nozick, R. 1989. Love's bond. In R. Nozick (ed.), *The examined life. Philosophical meditations* (pp. 68–86). Simon & Schuster.

Overall, C. 1998. Monogamy, nonmonogamy, and identity. *Hypatia, 13*(4), 1–17.

Paul, L.A. 2014. *Transformative experience*. Oxford University Press.

Rambukkana, N. 2015. *Fraught intimacies: Non/monogamy in the public sphere.* UBC Press.

Pismenny, A. 2021. "The amorality of romantic love." In R. Fedock, M. Kühler, and R. Rosenhagen (eds.), *Love, justice, and autonomy: Philosophical perspectives,* 23–42. Routledge.

Pismenny, A., & B. Brogaard. 2021. "Vices of Friendship" THIS VOLUME.

Rorty, A. O. 1987. The historicity of psychological attitudes: Love is not love which alters not when its alteration finds. *Midwest Studies in Philosophy 10,* 399–412.

Sheff, E., & Hammers, C. 2011. The privilege of perversities: Race, class and education among polyamorists and kinksters. *Psychology & Sexuality, 2*(3), 198–223.

Schmidt, E. E. 2018. Are lovers ever one? Reconstructing the union theory of love. *Philosophia, 46*(3), 705–719.

Soble, A. 1997. Union, autonomy, and concern in *love* analyzed (ed. Roger E. Lamb). Boulder, CO: Westview Press, 65–92.

Solomon, R. C. 2006. *About love: Reinventing romance for our times*. Hackett Publishing.

Stohr, K. 2019. *Minding the Gap: Moral Ideals and Moral Improvement*. Oxford University Press.

Veaux, F., & Rickert, E. 2014. *More than two: A practical guide to ethical polyamory*. Thorntree Press, LLC.

Walker, M. U. 2007. *Moral understandings: A feminist study in ethics*. Oxford University Press.

Chapter 8

Being Trans, Being Loved

Clashing Identities and the Limits of Love

Gen Eickers

INTRO

Jake: You okay?
Margot: Did you hear what that lady said to me at the bakery?
Jake: About our kids?
Margot: Yeah, she thought we were straight, Jake!
Jake: So? She thought we were straight.
Margot: You're excited!
Jake: No I'm not.
Margot: You're passing and you're excited.[1]

(*Tales of the City*, 2019: season 1, episode 1)

In the television series *Tales of the City* (2019), one of the first scenes shows a young couple in a bakery, picking up a cake they ordered for a birthday. One of them, Margot, starts talking to two children who are fascinated by the cakes on display. The mother of the children then approaches the couple asking if they had children of their own. Margot is obviously uncomfortable being asked this question, and abruptly says "not yet."

The couple portrayed is Margot and Jake. Margot is a cis woman; Jake is a passing trans man.[2] Margot ascribes excitement to Jake about being perceived as a heterosexual couple. As it turns out in the scene described as well as throughout the episode, Margot is not content with being perceived as heterosexual. Later in the series, it becomes clear that Margot identifies as lesbian. As is apparent from the dialogue, the couple is facing an issue: since Margot is a woman who is into women, and Jake is a trans man, their sexual and gender identities do not seem to match. Margot and Jake had been together for a while when Jake came out as trans. That is, initially, the relationship was based on the belief that Jake was a woman and that the two were in a lesbian relationship. When Jake came out as a trans man, this belief turned out to be wrong.

Tales of the City (2019) here depicts a narrative many trans people have experienced: being romantically involved with someone when coming out as trans. Sometimes, this presents the individuals in love with a challenge. Their sexual and gender identities now clash.[3] If, for example, a trans woman comes out to her heterosexual cis wife, the wife might not be able to adapt, and the trans woman might not be able to cope. That is, the heterosexual wife is into men and thus might not feel attracted to her wife any longer after she comes out, and the trans woman might not want to be with a heterosexual woman since that makes her feel like she will be perceived as a man. These are the kinds of examples I focus on in this chapter. The examples and arguments do not intend to show, however, that all romantic love between a trans person and other people (trans or cis) is doomed to fail. There are, of course, cases where someone's being trans is not an issue to the romantic love in question, for example, when a cis partner does not understand their sexual identity as rigid or definable in only one way, and the romantic love therefore remains unimpeded by one partner coming out as trans (see, e.g., Morris 1974). But in this chapter, I want to shed light on the specific complications trans people face when in love, falling in love, or being loved. This chapter considers those complications to delineate the limits of romantic love. There are normative restrictions to who and how we love, and those are the ultimate limit of romantic love for some of us—for example, for trans people. Some of the restrictions I frame as normative here include psychological responses such as sexual attraction. I consider sexual attraction to be influenced by norms, and thus possibly limited by normative restrictions, too. In this sense, a limit to romantic love means that the identity clashes I present in this chapter are (perceived to be) insurmountable obstacles to love. The obstacles are insurmountable insofar as they present challenges to the people in question that make them (a) no longer feel romantic love or (b) unable to consider (the exhibition of) romantic love to be an option. These include different cases, such as, not being open to falling in love with certain genders, not being open or able to adjust one's own sexual identity when a partner comes out as trans, not being open or able to deal with the identity struggles a partner might have after coming out as trans.

The ethics and politics around trans love are complicated.[4] This chapter argues that when it comes to trans love, analyzing what love is and looking at the moral psychology and philosophy of love requires considering different aspects of gender and sexual identity than when considering love between only cis people (which is the default in the moral psychology and philosophy of love literature). If we theorize romantic love without considering trans narratives, then the issue of clashing gender and sexual identities remains unaddressed, occluding our attention to the specific kinds of restrictions that can play a role in love for trans people specifically.

First, this chapter does some brief terminological work around the terms "trans" (including an insight into how this chapter conceives of gender) and "love." In doing the terminological work, the chapter will already start highlighting issues in trans love. The core ideas and arguments will be presented in the fourth and fifth sections, where I analyze the issue of identity clashes, and discuss the limits of love through such clashes. Overall, the chapter aims to provide descriptive insights rather than formulate prescriptive claims. The conclusions I draw are as follows: Romantic love is not equally accessible to everyone. Trans people face specific challenges when it comes to romantic love. In romantic love relationships, they often have to deal with their gender identity clashing with their partner's sexual identity.[5] Such identity clashes are commonly perceived as insurmountable obstacles to romantic love. The identity clashes illuminate normative restrictions of romantic love that often remain un(der)examined in theorizing about love.

BEING TRANS

Let me first clarify a few basic concepts surrounding gender and trans identities and point out the commitments I make in this chapter. I do not intend to argue for or against metaphysical claims about gender here. Some of the explications of gender I rely on are typically considered to be derivative of (social) constructionist theories about gender that are widely accepted in both community-based literature and practical guides (e.g., Altadonna 2011; Hill-Meyer & Scarborough 2014) and in trans theory (e.g., Hamm 2020; Bettcher 2007; 2012).

Gender or gender identity is the gender a person identifies as, for example, being a man, a woman, or nonbinary. There are, in addition, gender roles, or behaviors that are associated with gender identities. These are said to be "performed" in the sense that they are not instincts, but rather socially and culturally informed, and (often unconsciously) enacted through conditioned behaviors and bodily responses (see, e.g., Butler 1988).[6] It used to be common to distinguish gender from sex, which was associated with "biology" (and often used synonymously with "genitals") but, depending on where we look in the discourse, that distinction is no longer regarded as tenable, since biological differences are themselves contingent on social and cultural classification schemes and biology is heavily impacted by social factors (behavioral norms, life experiences, skills, diet, hormones, etc.) (see Ásta 2011;

Fausto-Sterling 2000a; 2000b; Serano 2007).[7] In this sense, gender encompasses sex. This is not to say that all physical characteristics are sufficiently explained by gender since, for example, the specific functions of reproductive organs could not be sufficiently explained by gender categories and it would not be inclusive or conceptually correct to do so—for example, calling all people who give birth "women" is a conceptual and ethical error. However, constructing a separate category—sex—as an umbrella category under which physical and biological characteristics get taxonomized does not do justice to the variety of bodies and embodiments that exist.

In short, being trans means not identifying with the gender/sex one was assigned at birth.[8] Sex, in this respect, refers to the medical category we get assigned at birth (typically "male" or "female") and gender is the social analog (typically "man" or "woman") we get implicitly assigned.[9] Being trans can be understood as a move away from the gender/sex one was assigned—be that move social, performative, or embodied. Transitioning can be social—for example, performing gender differently via clothing or behavior, using a different name or pronouns—and legal—for example, changing one's gender category on the ID, official name changes, and medical—for example, undergoing hormone replacement therapy or other gender-affirming medical care like surgeries. Transitioning can encompass all or any combination of these aspects. There are different ways to be trans and to live as a trans person. Being trans is often contrasted with being cis—"cis" refers to people who identify with the gender they were assigned at birth, for example, a woman who was assigned "female/woman" at birth and identifies as a female/woman is a cis woman.

Talia Mae Bettcher (2017) explains trans identities via sex/gender categories and the way one deals with the sex/gender category one was assigned: "Many trans people do not self-identify with the sex and gender categories assigned to them at birth. Consequently, they may wish to change various things about themselves and their lives. They may decide to transition from one sex/gender category to another" (Bettcher 2017: 120). Transition does not necessarily mean moving from one binary gender category to another but includes many other possibilities, for example, nonbinary and gender-nonconforming identities.

There are, of course, certain characteristics and functions bodies have that are not changeable per se—for example, if your body is not equipped with a uterus, you are not able to conceive. But understanding bodies as non-fixed entities is central to understanding trans identities (and to understanding gender in general). Certain bodily limitations might need to be accepted (e.g., not everyone can grow a beard, no matter the amount of testosterone in their blood), however, those limitations are far fewer than what is typically portrayed in cis-hetero-normative societies and literature. Consider how trans people embody their identities: some trans people reinterpret and rename their genitals in ways that are gender-affirming (see Hamm 2020). For example, a trans man might refer to his genitals as "boypussy" or "t dick" (see also Bauer 2015). Also, external devices that are typically referred to as sex toys are often considered detachable parts of one's body instead of sex toys. Bauer (2015) describes trans-masculine people who reinterpret and rename dildos as their "cocks." These are not to be understood as replacements but rather as integral to people's bodies and body images (see Bauer 2015; Hamm 2020).

It becomes clear that the emphasis here is on identities determined via self-identification. I consider this to be integral to understanding trans realities. Focusing on self-identification provides us with the opportunity to look at the struggles trans people face; and relying on trans narratives will bring us closer to understanding how love can be experienced and approached by trans people. In this chapter, I aim to examine trans love from the viewpoint of different trans identities in order to explore the many different identity clashes trans people can face when in love. What might be some issues here? Let me point them out briefly. Morty Diamond describes the issues with loving while being trans as follows:

> Transgender people maneuver in a world that seemingly offers little hope of finding love . . . or even good sex. If they aren't ignored and rendered invisible by mainstream narratives of romance, trans and gender-variant folks are consistently portrayed as deviants unsuitable to love. (Diamond 2011: 7)

The reasons for why trans people face difficulties and challenges with love are manifold. What Diamond describes revolves around finding love. Finding love as a trans person is complicated. A trans person who is out as trans, in transition, and not living stealth, for example, might face trans-exclusion and trans-fetishizing in dating (see Blair & Hoskin 2018).[10] Often, the reasons for why trans people face difficulties accessing romantic love boil down to transphobia. Transphobia has a broad scope that ranges from more subtle, everyday cases (like access to romantic love) to more obvious and explicit cases (e.g., bathroom bills targeting trans people). The understanding of transphobia this chapter relies on and makes use of is Bettcher's understanding. She explains transphobia as a basic denial of authenticity, meaning that trans people's self-identifications are not recognized (Bettcher 2006). She argues that this understanding of transphobia can account for the variety of inappropriate behavior trans people have to endure on a daily basis; for example, being asked questions about surgeries, pointing to a misalignment between someone's gender and sex, and even violence.

Furthermore, there can be psychological burdens for trans people that arise from knowing about the negative or otherwise problematic attitudes toward dating trans people. Knowing about transphobia can make it harder for trans people to establish a willingness to date, and to trust enough to love. Second, when coming out as trans while being in love or being about to fall in love, one might face the issue of a clash between one's (new) gender identity and the partner's sexual identity.[11]

Before I dive deeper into what a clash of identities means for romantic love, let me first take a look at how this chapter conceives of romantic love.

BEING LOVED (ROMANTICALLY)

Romantic love is among the trickiest concepts in emotion theory. The debate about whether romantic love can even be considered an emotion is not settled (Pismenny & Prinz 2017). This chapter does not aim at establishing what love is, or at providing insights into the question whether love is a basic emotion (Ekman & Cordaro 2011) or a social emotion (Hareli & Parkinson 2008) or an emotion at all (Pismenny & Prinz 2017). Rather, this chapter aims to illuminate aspects of romantic love through a more practical lens, through the narratives of the lived experiences of people who have faced difficulties with romantic love due to their identity and the struggles this identity seems to evoke and provoke. That is why I regard it as appropriate to consider romantic love within frameworks that place emphasis on normative entanglements that come with being in love or falling in love. In what follows, I will discuss Averill's (1985) account of love, which emphasizes social norms. I will provide a brief summary of this account, and spell out why I think it can help elucidate how identity and love hang together, and the ways in which love might be limited in that respect.

Averill (1985) conceives of emotions in general "as socially constituted syndromes (transitory social roles) that include a person's appraisal of the situation and that are interpreted as passions rather than as actions" (Averill 1985: 98). Syndromes, according to Averill, are accumulations of behavioral, cognitive, and physiological reactions. The components syndromes consist of are neither fixed nor arbitrary: "the component processes that make up an emotional syndrome are constrained (. . .) by the prototypic features of the paradigm" (Averill 1985: 98). That is, we are not necessarily sad every time we feel unwell—feeling unwell is a component that needs to be put in context in order to be understood as sadness or otherwise. For example, we might feel unwell after someone stepped on our feet or we might feel unwell after having experienced the loss of a loved one—these are different contexts that provide our phenomenological experience with different objects. "The object of an emotion," in turn, "is dependent on an individual's appraisal of the situation" (Averill 1980: 310). Emotional appraisals, according to Averill, are individuals—that is, the instances in which your friends get angry might differ from the instances in which you get angry.

Romantic love, according to Averill, consists of the following components (where no component on its own is necessary or sufficient): romantic idealization, sudden onset, physiological arousal, commitment. These components are certainly debatable, but I want to look at one of those aspects—idealization—in a little more detail. Looking at what Averill means by romantic idealization can first help clarify constructionist views on love, and second help us understand why considering gender identities matters for understanding romantic love.[12] A consideration of love as consisting of many different components might help to think about love through a trans narrative. Gender identity can be considered one of the components contributing to establishing a love relationship. In this sense, it is not surprising that when the gender of one partner seems to shift, the entire relationship and the way the love is understood shift too. Before analyzing Averill's notion of romantic idealization, let me briefly explain the other components.

When defining the components of love, Averill draws on folk usages of romantic love terminology and thereby explains how romantic love is socially constructed. First, according to Averill, "a person does not enter into love gradually but 'falls', 'tumbles', or is 'struck' by love" (Averill 1985: 102). Averill also states that most instances of romantic love do not actually feature a sudden onset; this point emphasizes that there seems to be a folk belief about the sudden onset of romantic love. Second, the category "physiological arousal" seems to be structured similarly, according to Averill. Averill criticizes many theories of love naturalizing love by defining it through physiological arousal but points out that this seems to be a further folk belief about romantic love that plays into how love manifests through its social constructions (cf. Averill 1985: 103). A third component of love, according to Averill, is a "commitment to the welfare of the other" (Averill 1985: 104). He explains that when we declare our love to someone, we are not describing how we feel about the other person just for the sake of communicating; rather, we express our commitment: we express that the bond we share comes with obligations and norms that should not be violated (Averill 1985: 105).

Having explored three of Averill's components of romantic love, I now turn to Averill's fourth component: romantic idealization. A consideration of Averill's notion of romantic idealization opens up to a broader discussion about the role of norms for romantic love. When speaking about romantic idealization, a lot of people take idealization in romantic love to mean casting the beloved in the most favorable light or perceiving them as the most exciting, interesting, awesome, or even perfect person. This might be a feature of love and a part of its phenomenology. Averill, however, does not only consider an individual's psyche and their tendencies to idealize someone romantically but also societal aspects that contribute to romantic idealization. These societal aspects are typically about the social status or looks of a person that render the person lovable in society's eyes (Averill 1980; 1985).

It is this rendering someone lovable that comes into play when thinking about how gender identities influence who we consider to be someone we could fall in love with. First, think of how sexual identities are conceptualized. Sexual identities come with rules, so to speak, about who we can fall in love with (Sedgwick 1990; Foucault 1990). Hall points out that, "following Foucault, the categorization of erotic acts and desires into discrete sexualities that form the foundation of sexual identities is an historical occurrence rather than an innate (and thus inevitable) characteristic of human nature" (Hall 2017: 243). Hall and Foucault both challenge the "born this way" narrative, according to which people's sexual identities are innately given.[13] These perspectives clarify how sexual identities can be considered to come with rules and norms about who we can fall in love with. In more practical terms, think of it this way: If I conceive of myself as a heterosexual woman, it is unlikely that I will fall in love with a woman. If I do fall in love with a woman, I might quickly realize that heterosexuality is not the right concept to elucidate my sexual identity. This gets more complicated in the case of trans identities since, often, trans people are excluded from people's sexual identities. Being trans is often considered to be "an extra gender" rather than an umbrella category for a variety of different genders (i.e., people often fail to differentiate between trans men and trans women and thus fail to recognize them as women or men).[14] This view also ignores a very basic truth mentioned in earlier: trans people can inhabit all sorts of sexual identities, be it queer, straight, gay, homosexual, heterosexual, asexual, bisexual, or pansexual.

In this sense, falling in love cannot be conceived of in terms of having the possibility of falling in love with just anyone. Falling in love and being in love come with normative restrictions—to formulate it less pessimistically: with normative entanglements. Someone understanding themselves to be straight but experiencing queer desires for the first time might struggle with accepting or exploring these desires (Sedgwick 1990). This does not only concern desires but might also concern someone realizing they fell in love or are about to fall in love with a person of the same gender/to fall in queer love.

Framing the phenomenon of love through Averill's account helps to focus on the normative entanglements that come with love since the account is built on an understanding of love that incorporates norms and context. The account of love summarized here points to how social aspects of identity contribute to how we conceive of romantic love and to how those aspects shape our loving and being loved. This is why they are especially useful for understanding romantic love through a gender identity lens. By emphasizing different components of love and the norms enabling them, the account of love considered here also shows us that understanding and recognizing someone for who they are might be pivotal to romantic love. Recognizing someone for who they are, as Averill suggests, enables us to render someone as lovable.

In the following section, I will look at different cases of trans love and clashing identities and thereby analyze the normative entanglements of love. This will enable me to argue that clashing identities in love connections are often perceived to be insurmountable obstacles, that is, limits to love.

CLASHING IDENTITIES

As noted, trans people often face exclusion in dating. Trans-exclusion can manifest on different levels: some people might get rejected for being trans early on (e.g., when trying to flirt with someone in a bar or online), and others might get rejected for being trans later on (e.g., when a relationship was about to be established). While some of the examples we are able to imagine here can be applied to marginalized people in general (e.g., exclusion before starting to date someone on the grounds of a specific social identity like race or disability), others are specifically about trans identities (e.g., breaking up a romantic relationship because the partner comes out as trans). Both factors contribute to trans people having a more limited access to romantic love than cis people. Let me give some more insights and examples here to clarify what it means to have (limited) access to romantic love.

Flirting might be experienced as stressful by trans people because we often have to worry about being categorized as a gender we do not identify with or about having to come out as trans to the person we're flirting with. One aspect we can look at more closely here is that of passing. Passing, again, is understood to mean that you are being read as the gender you identify as (cf. Bettcher 2017). The concept of passing is strongly intertwined with many trans people's identities, especially when sexuality and love enter the picture. Dating as a gay trans man, for example, is easier if you pass and if you are, therefore, more likely to be considered desirable (since many cis gay men don't date trans gay men). Passing, thus, might give trans people a glimpse of access to being desired for who they are (e.g., a trans man being desired for his being a man)—I am speaking of a glimpse here since that desirability might change once one's being trans is brought to the table. If a trans man passes as a man and is flirting in a bar, for example, there might be a moment (spanning from seconds to hours) that allows them to experience what it is like to be desired as a man, and what it's like to be considered a potential romantic partner. But that moment might be over once the trans man comes out as trans, depending on the reaction of the person they are flirting with.[15] I'd also like to add that passing, in the sense I describe here, is not an option for many trans people, especially gender-nonconforming or nonbinary people. Passing depends on whether being perceived as a binary gender is affirming or invalidating for a trans person. Passing will not solve the problems trans people face in dating and pursuing romantic love relationships. Whether you pass or not, once it is known you are a trans person, the pool of people willing to date you, that is, the pool of people thinking of you as desirable and as lovable will shrink considerably (see Blair & Hoskin 2018).

The reasons for trans-exclusion in dating are multifold but eventually share a common variable: transphobia. For example, someone might not date trans people because they are afraid of the stigma they might face when dating a trans person. But fears of stigma are central parts of phobias: think of men over-performing masculinity because they are afraid of being perceived as gay: this is typically classified as internalized homophobia. Likewise, fear of facing stigma when dating a trans person seems to be rooted in transphobia. Another possible reason is someone being confused about their sexual identity or sexual orientation. As pointed out in an earlier section, often, trans people are excluded from people's sexual identities because people have an incorrect understanding of trans identities. I consider this to be a case of clashing identities since trans people, here, are not conceived of in terms of who they are, since their identities (as men or women, for example) including their sexual identities are not fully seen and recognized. As a consequence, trans people are not considered as lovable as cis people. Thus, trans identity comes with limited access to romantic love.

In what follows, I want to look at three specific examples of trans love that portray clashes between gender and sexual identities. The examples all revolve around romantic love relationships and thus explore a trans-specific perspective on the limits of love (rather than a more general take on the limits of love). I will first look at the examples and describe the kind of identity clash I consider them to display. After having discussed each, I will turn to a more optimistic outlook on trans love.

Let me first consider the case of an already established romantic love relationship:

I came out as a trans woman while I was in a gay relationship with a cis man. While he was supportive of my identity, at some point I started questioning whether I really wanted to be in a relationship with a gay man. We began discussing and he would not move away from identifying as gay, even as I asked him how he thinks that goes together with me being a woman. Eventually, I decided our identities did not match and ended the relationship. Being with a gay man who was supportive but did not reflect upon his own sexuality while attempting to stay with me after my coming out did not feel affirmative of my gender. (Anonymous Personal Report)

In this case, a trans woman came out while being in an already established romantic love relationship. This example presents an identity clash between someone's gender identity (A) and another person's sexual identity (B) because A is a (trans) woman and B is a (cis) gay man. In the example, this clash led to the end of the romantic love relationship.

First, it might seem like B fails to recognize the trans woman as a woman because he insists on identifying as gay despite being with her.[16] If the trans person in question is not recognized for who they are, this presents a limit of love. However, B might indeed recognize A's gender but is staying with her anyways. As reflected in A's thoughts depicted above, this is not the kind of relationship A imagines for herself since she has a desire for being represented through her relationship. B might also recognize A's gender and recognize that A's gender does not fit his sexual identity. Both these options lead to the trans person not being able to continue a relationship and thus present limits to love.

Let me consider another example that portrays a romantic love relationship that seems about to be established rather than being already in place. The example is told by a gay trans man and is about an experience of falling in love with a gay cis man. The cis man is seemingly in love with the trans man as well. However, the cis man cannot imagine being with a gay trans man who has not had particular gender-affirming surgeries:

> When I finally ended up in his bed, still fully clothed, he lost the courage (and with that the physical ability) to go through with it. I had fallen for him so hard that when he turned his own impotency into my issue I totally took that on. I felt disgusting. And when he told me that he believed he could love me if only I were different, I owned that, too. And lastly, as he cried and said he wished I would go away, have surgery, and then come back to him so we could be together, I held him. I stayed there and held him all night long. (Hero 2011: 28)

This example, too, might be considered to be a failure to recognize the trans man for what he is (i.e., a man) since the only aspect the cis man is not content with in his potential partner is the genitals.[17] One might also say that the cis man does see the trans man as a man but nevertheless is unable to represent and express that via his sexual identity. Even if the cis gay man can't change his attraction, this still limits the access of the trans person in question to love: if he were not trans, the issue discussed wouldn't be present. Either way, the cis man seems unable to overcome his binary and cis-normative understanding of sex and gender, even in the face of romantic love. In this case, romantic love is not enough to bring them together even though the gender and sexual identities seem to match. However, the cis man's sexual identity is entangled with cis-normative ideals (i.e., his partner having cis male genitalia) and thus clashing with the reality of the person he is in love with (i.e., the person being trans and not having undergone specific gender-affirming surgeries). Love, in this case, is experienced as limited since both the cis man and the trans man seem confronted with obstacles they are not able to overcome: for the cis man, the obstacle is the genitals of the trans man; for the trans man, it is the resulting negative feelings of the cis man rejecting him because of his genitals.

Let me turn to a third example. Transitioning can also mean, for somebody involved in romantic love, that the love relationship starts being perceived differently by other people and by society. That is, if a trans woman who is, for the first time, in a relationship with another woman, she might find herself suddenly being a member of another marginalized group since she has a history of being perceived as straight. Altadonna describes this as follows:

> Suddenly becoming a member of a minority, straight culture seemed to be everywhere. It was a little overwhelming to stand outside the heterosexual matrix and look in. Once people started perceiving me as female, there was the concern of how affectionate we ought to be in public or amongst our families. This was something we never thought about when we were perceived as straight. (Altadonna 2011: 40)

It is possible, of course, for a relationship to shift from being conceived of as a straight relationship to being conceived of as a queer/gay/lesbian relationship or the other way around. However, what needs to be kept in mind here is that this is an identity shift (in terms of sexual identities) that can come with different forms of hardship. First, as described, society will react differently depending on whether they perceive the romantic love to be of the straight or of the queer kind. When shifting to being perceived as involved in queer love, one might be subject to experiencing a kind of discrimination one has not experienced before (e.g., one might be stared at in public). When shifting to being perceived as involved in straight love, one might have to adapt to not being discriminated against anymore because of sexual identity and to not being perceived as queer anymore. People in trans love relationships might also conceive of themselves as queer despite their straight-passing, and might experience frustration with being perceived as straight (consider the scene from *Tales of the City* again where one of the characters continued to understand the relationship as queer). When one of those involved in a romantic relationship transitions, and the relationship nevertheless holds, the people around them have to transition to a certain extent too. They have to adjust to the new sexual and gender identities those involved in the love relationship might inhabit, and to the new roles that get assigned to those involved through societal norms. For example, when the partner of a straight cis man transitions and starts being perceived as a man by other people, the couple will be perceived differently (i.e., as gay/homosexual/queer). That might be something they have not experienced before, thus they (both) have to adjust to being perceived differently. In that sense, the partner of someone transitioning may experience a transition too.

In addition, outsiders might fail to understand how their friend or family member can be with a trans person or how they can be in a queer/straight relationship. In cases where romantic love seems to transition along the transition of the involved trans person, love might explore its social limits through being confronted with conformity to social norms (e.g., being perceived as performing queer love now instead of straight love).

None of the three examples portrayed here mean to suggest that trans love is always limited through identity clashes and is thus not possible. When considering the fluidity of sexual identities, we are given the chance to look at trans love more optimistically. For many, including trans people who might decide to end a relationship due to an identity clash, adjusting one's sexual identity is not an option. This inability to adjust need not be rooted in problematic attitudes regarding gender or sexual identities but can merely be due to the person's strong identification with a particular (sexual) identity (e.g., a trans woman who identifies as lesbian has good reasons not to pursue love with a heterosexual woman or a man). The ability of some people to conceive of their sexual identity as fluid nevertheless presents a more optimistic example when looking at trans love. Trans love is not always limited. There are many examples where the relationship is able to adapt to a new identity, where partners of trans people are able to question their own sexual identity and not conceive of gender and sexuality as something rigid. Trans love can be liberating, in a sense, when identity clashes are not perceived as insurmountable obstacles but rather as something one can work through. This is not meant to suggest that any trans person should adjust their gender identity—whatever that would look like—but rather meant to describe a reality: there are trans women, for example, who are happy to date gay men or even keep identifying as gay after coming out as trans. There are also trans men and trans masculine and nonbinary people who keep identifying as lesbians after coming out as trans. My claim here is that neither gender, nor sexual identity *inherently* presents us with any limits regarding how and who we love; rather, the limits depend on the individual and often come with good reasons. That is, the limits are largely socially imposed or structured (and thereby influence individuals), and partly stem from the (unjust) hermeneutical exclusion of trans identities from theories of love and sexuality. However, how individuals deal with these imposed limits will differ; as shown, not all individuals are able to question their sexual identity.

LIMITS OF LOVE?

Do the described identity clashes limit love? In this section, I will provide concluding thoughts on the normative entanglements and limits of love.

This chapter has established that there are normative restrictions for trans people when it comes to romantic love. I have pointed out that "limits of love" are meant to address issues that are considered to be insurmountable obstacles by those in love. I argued that the obstacles are sometimes insurmountable since they present challenges to the people in question that make them (a) no longer feel romantic love or (b) unable to consider (the exhibition of) romantic love to be an option.

In the fourth section, I presented different example cases of trans love—each of which comes with limits that are due to normative entanglements (i.e., expectations and norms around how and who we love). These entanglements present differently in different individuals. While one person might be able and willing to conceive of their gender and sexual identity as something fluid, another person might not be able to do so.

As pointed out in the third and fourth sections, romantic love is not accessible to the same extent to everyone. This is a factor we also need to keep in mind when researching romantic love since it enables us to think about how romantic love and social identities interact and intertwine. Depending on factors such as being trans, someone's ability to access love or someone's possibilities for love can be limited. As mentioned, trans people can face exclusion from other people's dating pools that are specifically related to their trans identities, and moreover, trans people can also face limits of love that are due to clashes of gender and sexual identities in romantic love relationships.

Behrensen (2018) describes trans people (and other marginalized people) as often subject to being sexually desired but not considered lovable. But the rejection of trans people might even start at desirability and not only at lovability. This is especially obvious in the example where a trans man is falling in love with a cis man and the cis man seems to reciprocate loving feelings but cannot conceive of being with a trans man who has not had particular gender-affirming surgeries (he might also not want to be with a trans man after those surgeries; the example rather suggests he wants the person he is falling for to be a cis man). Examples like this illustrate how clashes between one person's gender identity and another person's sexual identity limit the possibility of romantic love for the involved individuals and that sometimes this is due to trans people not being considered desirable or trans people being excluded from consideration as a potential partner by someone's conception of their own sexual identity. This also shows how narrow conceptualizations of sexual identity can interfere with romantic love. If society's understandings of gender and sexuality were more expansive, and more inclusive of trans gender identities, to begin with, perhaps we would not have to think about the limits identity struggles and clashes present to romantic love.

But we need not confuse understanding sexual identities as trans-inclusive with the claim that trans identities are or trans love is inherently queer. I think that, on the surface, this seems to make sense since being trans questions expectations prevalent in certain societies about gender and about gendered bodies. But embracing trans identities also means creating and keeping space for trans individuals who do not identify as queer or who want to achieve cis- and straight-passing. I do not think the desire for cis- and straight-passing and one's legitimate self-conception as straight or not-queer needs any justification, especially since that is what cis people have been doing since the dawn of time.

Trans people can inhabit all sorts of sexual identities, be it queer, straight, gay, homosexual, heterosexual, bisexual, or pansexual.[18] For that, it does not matter whether the trans person in question is a binary or a nonbinary trans person. There are nonbinary folks who are gay, just like there are nonbinary folks who are straight (i.e., many nonbinary people have strong ties to a sexual identity—such as lesbian, gay, straight—and continue to embrace that identity; also, some nonbinary people might additionally be trans-masculine or trans-feminine and thus embrace a sexual identity that reflects this part of their gender). Sexual identity need not necessarily reflect one's own gender, from an observer's perspective, even though it often does.

Requiring all nonbinary people to describe their sexual orientation as queer, likewise, ignores the fact that the category "nonbinary" contains multitudes and cannot be boiled down to one particular essence. Some nonbinary people are agender, some are trans men/women, some are simply nonbinary. If someone describes their gender identity as a nonbinary trans man, this might seem like a contradiction, as "nonbinary" seems to reject the categories "man" and "woman." However, identifying as a nonbinary trans man/woman might mean that the person in question rejects the social norms associated with being a man/woman or that their gender identity depends on the social contexts they are part of (meaning: perhaps in some contexts they are nonbinary, and in other they are a man/woman). In this sense, phrasing trans identities as "inherently queer" and "taking us beyond the binary" actually misrecognizes the variety of trans identities.

Finally, let me reconsider the normative entanglements of romantic love presented in the second section. In the second section, I spelled out how Averill's account of love (1985) makes sense of how societal aspects, mostly social norms, play into our understanding of romantic love and our practicing romantic love. Norms, as pointed to, guide us not only in terms of how our relationships are supposed to look (e.g., a monogamous relationship versus a nonmonogamous relationship) but also tell us what kind of people we are supposed to find desirable and lovable (Brunning & McKeever 2021; Sedgwick 1990; Behrensen 2018). Social norms affect our gender identities and also our sexual identities, both of which are central to romantic love. Bringing together these theoretical considerations about the normative entanglements of romantic love with some of the examples portrayed earlier in this chapter, one might arrive at a rather pessimistic conclusion: namely, that romantic love is not accessible and thus not possible for some of us, that is, that the limits these normative restrictions present to who and how we love are the ultimate limit of romantic love for some of us (e.g., trans people). But we have also considered more optimistic examples in this chapter, where those in love were ready and willing to commit to a transition of their sexual identity that goes along with the gender transition of the person they are in love with.

Further optimistic examples include trans for trans (t4t) relationships. Malatino (2019) offers a vivid analysis of t4t love:

> It is cynical, skeptical; t4t is set up to fail, about aiming high and taking what one can get. It embraces ethical imperfection and complexity. It dwells in difficulty without the expectation that such difficulties will cease by and through a t4t praxis of love. It is about being with and bearing with; about witnessing one another, being mirrors for one another that avoid some of the not-so-funhouse effects of cisnormative perceptive habits that frame trans folk as too much, not enough, failed, or not yet realized. (Malatino 2019: 656)

T4t can be considered a strategy that's empowering by way of being cynical: the term "t4t" critically refers to the often transphobic or, at the very least, trans-exclusive, attitudes trans people have to encounter in dating: "it sequesters trans folks from Ms and Ws (as in M4M, W4W), partaking of the kind of trans-exclusionary (not to mention cisnormative [. . .]) logic that misconstrues trans as a sexualized gender category unto itself" (Malatino 2019: 653). Many of the specific challenges with romantic love discussed in this chapter are rooted in transphobia (e.g., trans-exclusion on the basis of [assumed] genitals, trans-fetishization). This is one of the reasons many trans people prefer or at least desire t4t relationships. Trans people loving each other romantically, t4t, is one way we can expand the limits of love or move beyond the limits of love. Romantic love can be liberating when it occurs between trans people who aren't constrained by narrow conceptions of body parts determining sexual identity and gender identity. As Malatino points out, t4t is a way to invest in self-love by investing in one's own community and freeing oneself from cis-hetero-normative norms (cf. Malatino 2019: 654) since, in t4t, we no longer have to rely on cis people and their approval of our genders and how we embody them.

ACKNOWLEDGMENTS

Many thanks for extremely helpful feedback on earlier versions of this chapter to the editors and reviewers of this volume, Zoey Lavallee, and the Network for Critical Emotion Theory (Ditte Marie Munch-Jurisic, Imke von Maur, Ruth Rebecca Tietjen, Marie Wuth, Henrike Kohpeiß, Laurencia Sáenz, Laura Silva, Millicent Churcher, Janna Hilger).

NOTES

1. Passing is defined by Bettcher as "passing as a member of the gender category one has transitioned into and fading into the mainstream" as a non-trans person (2017: 122). See the fourth section in this chapter for a more detailed exploration of "passing."

2. "trans" means not identifying with the gender assigned at birth; "cis" means identifying with the gender assigned at birth. More in section 2.

3. Throughout the chapter, when I use the word "love," I will be referring to romantic love specifically. The definition of romantic love I am using here includes both cases of "infatuation" and cases of "being in love" as well as forms of love we can subsume under "companionate love"; that is, love that is experienced by partners who have been together for a while and that is phenomenologically different than passionate, newly inflamed love. The definition of romantic love this chapter relies on focuses on *that* the people involved feel love rather than *how* exactly the love manifests or what it feels like.

4. I will use the term "trans love" throughout this chapter to refer to romantic love between at least one trans person and other (possibly, but not necessarily trans) people.

5. I'm using the term "sexual identity" here in the "sexual and romantic orientation" sense. I'm referring to "identity" and not "orientation" since, for this chapter, it is central to look at how the person has identified in their life rather than wondering whether they misunderstand their own sexual orientation. See also Bettcher (2017): "By sexual identity I mean how a person conceives of themselves with respect to their sexual orientation. So sexual orientation and sexual identity are not the same thing. A man could be sexually oriented to men, but he might not have come out to himself yet; he might not yet (or ever) self-identity as gay. His sexual identity would be 'straight' while his sexual orientation would not" (Bettcher 2017: 120).

6. When talking about gender roles, we think of certain behaviors we consider to be typical for certain genders: for example, it used to be (more) common to think that women were the only people wearing make-up, and that men were the only people being technicians. Gender roles come with an array of expectations that often carry heavy normative demands; consider for example how damaging the make-up example is for young boys who like to dress up (e.g., they might suppress that desire as a consequence and develop shame around that desire).

7. For a discussion on the "natural attitude about sex" and the transphobia resulting from it see Bettcher (2012). For a discussion on the naturalization of bodies and sex see Gregor (2015).

8. While I rely on Bettcher's understanding of trans identities, one could also make use of Serano's understanding (2007), or the understandings other scholars have provided (e.g., Hale 1998; Salamon 2010).

9. I want to point out here that trans experiences are diverse; some may describe their trans identities in terms of being "trans," others in terms of being "transgender," and others in terms of being "transsexual." In theory, most positions nowadays provide understandings of trans identities that are inclusive of the variety of experiences.

10. Living stealth as a trans person means not disclosing one's being trans. Some people (can) choose to be stealth in certain contexts, but not in others. Not every trans person is able to live stealth and some are only able to do so in some contexts; that is why trans people who usually live stealth might still face exclusion and fetishizing in dating upon coming out.

11. While the second point is the prime example of this chapter and the narrative through which the arguments in this chapter are told, the first point need not be omitted. The point about finding love as a trans person ultimately plays into how we conceive of trans love. For trans people who belong to multiple social identities that are sexually marginalized (e.g., disabled, fat, racialized), the challenges of finding love can be further compounded by multiple aspects of discrimination and sexual/gender-based violence.

12. For a discussion of the role of idealization and ideals in romantic love see Sternberg in this volume.

13. For a detailed discussion of the social construction of sexual orientation and identity, see Hall (2017) and Foucault (1990).

14. This might be due to cis people not having the proper hermeneutic equipment to "see" transness beyond the stereotypes/ rigid cis-normative concepts (see, e.g., Fricker & Jenkins 2017).

15. I want to add here that I do not think there is any obligation for trans people to out themselves. However, especially considering one's status of medical transition, it might not be possible to not come out as trans at some point.

16. The claim about the refusal or impossibility to adjust one's sexual identity I make here is descriptive, not prescriptive. I have no intention of implying that everyone involved in trans love ought to question their sexual identity.

17. See also Bettcher (2012) for work on genital fixation.

18. See, for example, Kuper, Nussbaum, & Mustanski (2012) for an online survey for trans people about gender identity and sexual orientation. In this survey, 14 percent of the participants said they were heterosexual.

REFERENCES

Altadonna, A. (2011). Shifting Sexuality or How I Learned to Stop Worrying and be a Bisexual Tranny Dyke. In M. Diamond (Ed.), *Trans/Love. Radical Sex, Love, and Relationships Beyond the Gender Binary*, 38–42, Manic D Press.

Ásta (2011) (published under "Ásta Sveinsdóttir"). The Metaphysics of Sex and Gender. In C. Witt Dordrecht (Ed.), *Feminist Metaphysics*, Springer.

Averill, J. R. (1980) A constructivist view of emotion. In R. Plutchik & H. Kellerman (Eds.), *Emotion: Theory, Research and Experience, Vol. 1: Theories of Emotion*, 305–340, Academic Press.

Averill, J. R. (1985). The Social Construction of Emotion: With Special Reference to Love. In K. J. Gergan & K. E. Davis (Eds.), *The Social Construction of the Person*, 89–109, Springer.

Bauer, R. (2015). Trans* Verkörperungen in queeren BDSM Praktiken. *Zeitschrift für Sexualforschung, 28* (01), 1–21.

Bauer, R. (2018). Cybercocks and Holodicks: Renegotiating the Boundaries of Material Embodiment in Les-bi-trans-queer BDSM Practices. *Graduate Journal of Social Science*, 14 (2), 58–82.

Behrensen, M. (2018). Queer Bodies and Queer Love. In A. M. Martin (Ed.), *The Routledge Handbook of Love in Philosophy*, 93–104, Routledge.

Bettcher, T. M. (2006). Understanding Transphobia: Authenticity and Sexual Abuse. In Krista Scott-Dixon (Ed.), *Trans/Forming Feminisms: Transfeminist Voices Speak Out*, 203–210, Sumach Press.

Bettcher, T. M. (2007). Evil Deceivers and Make-Believers: On Transphobic Violence and the Politics of Illusion." *Hypatia*, 22 (3), 43–65.

Bettcher, T. M. (2009). Trans Identities and First-Person Authority. In L. J. Shrage (Ed.), *You've Changed: Sex Reassignment and Personal Identity*, 98–120. Oxford University Press.

Bettcher, T. M. (2012). Full-Frontal Mortality: The Naked Truth about Gender. *Hypatia*, 27 (2), 319–337.

Bettcher, T. M. (2017). Trans 101. In R. Halwani, A. Soble, S. Hoffman, & J. M. Held (Eds.), *The Philosophy of Sex: Contemporary Readings*, 7th ed., 119–137. Rowman & Littlefield.

Blair, K. L., & Hoskin, R. A. (2018). Transgender Exclusion from the World of Dating: Patterns of Acceptance and Rejection of Hypothetical Trans Dating Partners as a Function of Sexual and Gender Identity. *Journal of Social and Personal Relationships*, 36 (7), 2074–2095.

Brunning, L., & McKeever, N. (2021). Asexuality. *Journal of Applied Philosophy, 38*(3), 497–517.

Butler, J. (1988). Performative Acts and Gender Constitution. An Essay in Phenomenology and Feminist Theory. *Theatre Journal*, 40 (4), 519–531.

Diamond, M. (2011). *Trans/Love. Radical Sex, Love, and Relationships Beyond the Gender Binary*. Manic D Press.

Ekman, P., & Cordaro, D. (2011). What Is Meant by Calling Emotions Basic. *Emotion Review*, 3, 364–370.

Fausto-Sterling, A. (2000a). *Sexing the Body. Gender Politics and the Construction of Sexuality*. Basic Books.

Fausto-Sterling, A. (2000b). *The Five Sexes, Revisited. The Sciences, 40*(4), 18–23.

Foucault, M. (1990). *The History of Sexuality Volume 1: An Introduction*, translated by Robert Hurley, Vintage.

Fricker, M., & Jenkins, K. (2017). Epistemic Injustice, Ignorance, and Trans Experiences. In A. Garry & S. Khader & A. Stone (Eds.). *The Routledge Companion to Feminist Philosophy*, 268–278, Routledge.

Gregor, A. (2015). *Constructing Intersex. Intergeschlechtlichkeit als soziale Kategorie.* Transcript Verlag.

Hale, Jacob C. (1998). Tracing a Ghostly Memory in My Throat: Reflections on the Feminist Voice and Agency. In T. Digby (Ed.). *Men Doing Feminism*, 99–129, Routledge.

Hall, K. (2017). Thinking Queerly about Sex and Sexuality. In R. Halwani, S. Hoffman, and A. Soble (Eds.). *The Philosophy of Sex: Contemporary Readings*, 7**th** ed., 241–256, Rowman and Littlefield.

Hamm, J. (2020). *Trans* und Sex. Gelingende Sexualität zwischen Selbstannahme, Normüberwindung und Kongruenzerleben.* **Psychosozial-Verlag.**

Hareli, S., & Parkinson, B. (2008). What's Social About Social Emotions? *Journal for the Theory of Social Behaviour*, 38, 131–156.

Hero, J. (2011). Out of the Darkness. In M. Diamond, M. (Ed.), *Trans/Love. Radical Sex, Love, and Relationships Beyond the Gender Binary*, 26–31, Manic D Press.

Hill-Meyer, T., & Scarborough, D. (2014). Sexuality. In L. Erickson-Schroth (Ed.), *Trans Bodies, Trans Selves: A Resource for the Transgender Community*, 355–389, Oxford University Press.

Kuper, L. E., Nussbaum, R., & Mustanski, B. (2012). Exploring the Diversity of Gender and Sexual Orientation Identities in an Online Sample of Transgender Individuals. *Journal of Sex Research*, 49(2), 244–254.

Malatino, H. (2019). Future Fatigue: Trans Intimacies and Trans Presents (or How to Survive the Interregnum). *Transgender Studies Quarterly*, 6(4), 635–658.

Morris, J. (1974). *Conundrum.* Harcourt Brace Jovanovich.

Pismenny, A., & Prinz J. (2017). Is Love an Emotion? In C. Grau & A. Smuts (Eds.), *The Oxford Handbook of Philosophy of Love,* Oxford University Press.

Salamon, G. (2010). *Assuming a Body: Transgender and Rhetorics of Materiality.* Columbia University Press.

Sedgwick, E. (1990). *Epistemology of the Closet.* University of California Press.

Serano, J. (2007). *Whipping Girl: A Transsexual Woman on Sexism and the Scapegoating of Femininity*, 2**nd** ed., Seal Press.

Serano, J. (2009). *Psychology, Sexualization and Trans-Invalidations.* Keynote lecture presented at the 8th Annual Philadelphia Trans-Health Conference.

Tales of The City. (2019). TV series. Netflix.

Section III

LOVE AND MORALITY

Chapter 9

The Possibility of a Duty to Love

Lotte Spreeuwenberg

In *The Right to Be Loved*, Matthew Liao claims that children have a right to be loved (2015). He argues that children, as human beings, have rights to the primary essential conditions for a good life and that being loved as children *is* a primary essential condition for a good life: children need to be loved in order to be adequate, functioning individuals. Therefore, he claims, children have a right to be loved. Liao furthermore argues that all human beings have a moral duty to provide that love, addressing objections that there would be no appropriate obligation-holder if parents die while a child is young.

This moral obligation to provide love is considered controversial. Could there be such a thing as a duty to love? Mhairi Cowden criticizes Liao by arguing that there might be a right to care, but not to love (2012). This raises questions about what "love" entails. Whether love can be the object of an obligation might depend on what kind of love one has in mind. Some philosophers think of love as an emotion (Brogaard 2015; Liao 2015; Solomon 1993; Velleman 1999), or a syndrome (de Sousa 2015; Pismenny and Prinz 2017; Pismenny 2018), others think of love as a volitional disposition (Frankfurt 2009), still others think of love as a way of looking (Jollimore 2011; Murdoch 2013). What kind of love one has in mind is not what the debate about Liao's claim focuses on.

The debate about a moral duty to love surrounding Liao's claim centers on the practical question of regulation (e.g., Cowden 2012) or the question of what happens when children are not loved (e.g., Ferracioli 2014; Liao 2015). Cowden focuses on what kind of obligations and responsibilities such a duty would imply, the regulation of such a right, and the boundary between public and private spheres, and concludes there cannot be a duty to love. Liao and Laura Ferracioli focus on the child's need for attention, care, and affective bonds to achieve healthy development or, in Ferracioli's terms, in order to lead a "meaningful life" (2014), and conclude that children have a right to be loved. In an effort to answer worries related to both regulation and children's development, Mar Cabezas adds to the debate that "the right to be loved can be translated into a right to be *well*-loved and to love *well*" (2016, italics in text).

The questions they pose, however, are not the only philosophical questions one can ask regarding the possibility of a moral duty to love. Even if Cowden is correct in pointing out how a right formulated in Liao's way would imply many difficulties in the discourse of rights and duties, we do not need to throw the baby out with the bathwater. What if we zoom out? We do not need to focus on regulation, or what "providing love" entails, to say something about a duty to love. Similarly, we do not need to focus on love particularly for *children*, or the consequences of a lack of love.

Zooming out from this discussion, this chapter examines four objections to the idea that we have duties to love. Some philosophers take issue with love being something that we can claim or control (Darwall 2017; Kant 1797 [2017]). Love should not be something that we can claim, because we find "free" love particularly valuable, or so they argue. Being able to control emotions, such as love, is furthermore a fantasy, others object.[1] Another objection turns on the idea that love is not responsive to reasons, and, therefore, is not able to serve as the object of an obligation (Frankfurt 2009). Others object to the compatibility of motivations: doing something out of love for the beloved is not compatible with being motivated for the sake of duty (Stocker 1977; Williams 1981).

For the purposes of this chapter, I will not commit to any particular conception of love and will remain neutral about its meaning.[2,3] This paper seeks out conceptions of love which render the moral duty to love more plausible. The conceptions it focuses on are conceptions following from questions such as "does love have reasons" or "what is love's motivation," not so much on conceptions following from questions such as "what is the object of the love" (e.g., parental or romantic love). The latter is irrelevant for discussing the four objections. For example, whether we have parental or romantic love in mind is irrelevant to the opposition between the reasons-for-love view and the no-reasons-for-love view.[4] The question of whether there can be an obligation to love does not depend solely on the interpretation of love we have.

This chapter will neither provide a positive defense of Liao's claim or other claims for a moral duty or obligation to love. The goal is solely to rebut the four objections and to show that, on particular conceptions of duties and particular conceptions of love, a duty or obligation to love may appear more plausible.[5] Like many philosophers, including Frankfurt (1998), I will adopt the way of speaking that opposes love and duty as referring to the purported limits of the authority of morality.

First, I will argue that a moral obligation to love may appear more plausible on conceptions of moral obligations that are detached from the notion of making claims and demanding things from one another. In the second and third part of this chapter, I will argue respectively that conceptions of love that depict love as responsive to reasons, and emotions involved in love as commandable, also contribute to the plausibility of a moral obligation to love. Finally, I argue that conceptions of the motivation of moral duty as at least compatible with, or even constitutive of a motivation of love, also contribute to the possibility of a moral obligation to love.

A DIFFERENT CONCEPTION OF OBLIGATIONS

In *The Second-Person Standpoint*, Stephen Darwall argues that moral obligations are essentially interpersonal and presuppose mutual accountability (2009). This second-person standpoint is "the perspective you and I take up when we make and acknowledge claims on one another's conduct and will" (2009, p. 3). For example, standing in line for a food truck, you ask the woman next to you—who is unaware of her foot being on top of your toes—to remove herself from your foot. According to Darwall, moral claims are defined by their origin in another person's will. You are not informing the woman of something or calling her attention to some fact, but you are making a moral claim on the woman's conduct. Claims are understood by Darwall to be sources of a distinctive kind of reason for action, which Darwall refers to as second-personal. "What makes a reason second-personal is that it is grounded in (*de jure*) authority relations that an addresser takes to hold between him and his addressee" (2009, p. 4). These distinctive reasons are created by second-personal address, whereby a person with the relevant authority, for example, you standing in line for a food truck, issues a demand to a specific addressee, the woman stepping on your toes. On the basis of such a Darwallian conception of moral obligations, an obligation to love becomes somewhat problematic. Darwall argues that love is "something we cannot earn but that can only be freely given" (2017). We want love to be freely offered to us, and we do not want a debt to return it. If love is something we want to be freely offered, love cannot be the object of a second-personal address, whereby someone issues a demand for love to a specific addressee. Unlike respect, Darwall argues, love cannot arise through acceptance of a claim for love. "Even if there could be a legitimate claim to love, the most that could arise through accepting the claim's legitimacy would be respect for someone's authority to make it and for them as having this authority"

(2017, p. 99). For Liao, this would imply that children cannot lay claim to love, because love should be given freely, to children, too, and we therefore cannot have an obligation to love them.

However, on a different, non-Darwallian, conception of moral obligations, an obligation to love may appear more plausible. R. Jay Wallace takes issue with the idea that a claim or demand is the source of the obligation. Darwall refers to an example by David Hume (2006) in which a person with a gouty toe protests that you should remove your foot from atop his inflamed and painful digit (2009, pp. 6–8). If we take seriously the idea that it is the addressing of a claim or demand that is the source of distinctively second-personal reasons, we would not have a second-personal reason to refrain from stepping on the victim's toe until the protest was issued. Surely this cannot be right, as R. Jay Wallace has pointed out (2007). We want to say that we have a reason not to step on someone's gouty toe, that is (to some degree), prior to and independently of any complaint that might be issued after the toe has actually been stepped on. Such a conception of moral obligations also makes possible that we owe things to people who are not in the position to claim anything from us, like the severely disabled, future generations, or, relevant in Liao's case, small children. One's reason not to step on the gouty toe of one's neighbor seems to obtain independently of whether the victim of the condition orders one not to tread on him. Moreover, it seems equally independent of whether the victim, or anyone else, is in fact disposed to respond to one's treading on his toes with accountability reactions (Wallace 2007, p. 7).

R. Jay Wallace proposes an alternative to Darwall's voluntarist model to avoid the apparent disadvantage of the requirement that when (explicit or implicit) commands that one does *x* are absent, one cannot have second-personal reasons or obligations to do *x*. Wallace's alternative is to understand second-personal reasons in essentially relational terms (2007; 2019). On his approach, what makes a reason second-personal is not that it derives from the command of another person but that it is implicated in a structure of relational or "bipolar normativity."[6] This means that in the gouty toe example, we might say that one's reason not to tread on the other person's foot is second-personal, insofar as it is connected with a series of characteristic assumptions about the normative relations one stands in to the other person. For Wallace, these normative relations are not limited to special relationships, like the ones we have with friends or family. Much like Darwall's second-personal reasons, Wallace's relational reasons are broader: we have normative relations with persons beyond these special relationships. All these persons have a right not to be harmed or made to suffer, which warrants a demand not to be treated in these ways. Wallace argues that one's obligation in this matter has a similarly relational aspect; it is an obligation to the gout victim *not to disregard his well-being*. Its violation would not merely be something that is impersonally wrong or incorrect, but an act that wrongs the person who is thus made to suffer (Wallace 2007, p. 28). The second-personal reason for one to remove one's foot is not created by the protest of one's victim, but by the fact that stepping on someone's gouty toe is *wronging someone.*

Wallace allows us to speak of moral obligations without claims but is still relying on the notion of second-personal reasons. Is any relation or interaction between people necessary to see that "toe-stepping" is wrong? Isn't toe-stepping wrong independently of the normative relations we stand in to the other person? We could disregard second-personal reasons altogether. Besides, a second-personal reason to remove one's foot, Darwall also introduces what he calls a "third-personal reason": a "state-of-the-world-regarding reason" for anyone to effect displacement of the foot, which is provided by the fact that the person whose toe is being stepped on is in pain (Darwall 2007; 2009).[7] Perhaps third-personal reasons suffice to determine our duties. As Gopal Sreenivasan has argued, the relational aspect is not necessary on a different account of duties or obligations. Sreenivasan draws a distinction between directed and nondirected duties: a duty is a *directed duty* if there is someone to whom it is owed; it is a *nondirected duty* if there is no one to whom it is owed (Sreenivasan 2010, p. 467). Sreenivasan compares it to Judith Jarvis Thomson's distinction between "duty" and "ought" (Thomson, 1990). By "ought," Thomson means what morality requires someone, all things considered (ATC), to do. By "duty," she means that which can be claimed by one person from another. There is similarity here between Thomson's ought ATC and Sreenivasan's nondirected duty, and between Thomson's duty and Sreenivasan's directed duty. Although someone's claim-right against one will often coincide with what one ought ATC to do, these are two distinctive kinds of obligations. We do not need a relational reason for an obligation to come into place. Sreenivasan distinguishes directed from nondirected duties, but both are grounded in nonrelational, objective facts. To return to the gouty toe example, if the victim claims you desist, you have a directed duty to remove your foot. Independently of this directed duty, you have a nondirected duty: after balancing all moral considerations and interests, you ought ATC to remove your foot.

Both Wallace and Sreenivasan show conceptions of moral obligations that are detached from the notion of making claims and demanding things from one another. If we accept that love should be freely given, both Wallace and Sreenivasan could argue for a moral obligation to love children without the child making a moral claim on our conduct. Wallace could argue that we are obliged to love a child, because we are obliged not to disregard their well-being; not loving the child would wrong the child. But such a relational aspect is not even necessary here, since Sreenivasan shows us that we can have a nondirected duty that is not owed to anyone. We could have a moral obligation to love children, not because we owe this to the particular child, but because after balancing all moral considerations and interests, this is what we—all things considered—ought to do.

REASONS FOR LOVE

A different objection to there being a moral obligation to love comes from Harry Frankfurt, who famously argued that love is not a response to reasons but is in fact the basis of all reasons (2009). On this account, an obligation to love is impossible: we cannot have an obligation that is not reason-respon-sive.[8] Frankfurt argues that love is not a response to the value of the beloved but rather a bestowal of value on them: we love someone and through our love that person becomes valuable. Other philosophers, for example, Nick Zangwill (2013) and Aaron Smuts (2013), have defended similar positions. Although these positions differ in detail and argument, they have in common the claim that love is not a response to reasons.

The first and most common objection to this view is that it makes love unintelligible. Why do we feel we have reasons to love the particular person we love? If there is nothing about the particular person we love that could be a reason for our love, there would be no reason for us to love this person rather than anyone else (Velleman 1999; Stump 2006; Shpall 2020). This seems quite counterintuitive. Eleonore Stump writes, if there is no reason for love, then "it seems as if the lover could just as easily have loved some other person. Since there is nothing about the particular person he loves which is the reason for his love, there is also no reason why he should love her rather than anyone else" (Stump 2006, p. 2). Loving particular persons seems to require loving for reasons tied to the beloved.

Another objection comes from Niko Kolodny (2003): Frankfurt's view fails to show why some kinds of love strike us as appropriate and others as inappropriate. From the first-person perspective of someone who loves, the constitutive emotions and motivations of love make reflexive sense, argues Kolodny (2003, p. 137). Love seems appropriate to the person who experiences it. Furthermore, from the third-person perspective of an adviser or critic, we often find love or its absence inappropriate: "Consider our reactions to the wife who loves her abusive and uncaring husband, or to the parent who is emotionally indifferent to her child" (2003, p. 137). Even if we hold a conception of love as involuntary, as Kolodny does, it does not follow that there cannot be normative reasons for love, that love cannot be assessed as appropriate or inappropriate to its object (2003, p. 138). Frankfurt's view does not distinguish between love of things that are unworthy and love of things that are worthy of our love (Baier 1982; Wolf 2002). Some things seem to be valuable or to lack value, independently of whether or not we love them. Love sometimes seems inappropriate to us, and the appropriateness of love seems to be a response to such independent values.

While the previous objection to there being an obligation to love was countered by looking at a different conception of obligations, objections like Frankfurt's could be countered by looking at our conception of love. Several philosophers argue that love *is* a response to reasons. David Velleman (1999), for example, famously argues that love is a moral emotion and a response to the dignity of the beloved. He claims that love is an attitude of appreciation: an awareness of the incomparable value in a person as a rational being, who can be actuated by reasons and appreciate ends. In Liao's case, this means that we have a reason to love children by responding to their dignity. But children (at least until a certain age) cannot be considered to be fully rational beings, actuated by reasons and appreciating ends. One could argue for a potentiality account: children have the potential to become rational beings, and therefore we can respond to their dignity providing a reason for love. But unless we take up the potentiality perspective, Velleman's conception of love, although a reason-responsive account, does not work for the duty to love that Liao is arguing for.

Another conception of love is the quality view, which claims that what justifies our love are the *qualities* or *properties* we value in the object of our love (see, e.g., Brogaard 2015; Keller 2000). Simon Keller, for instance, argues that attractive or desirable qualities are those the lover values in anyone; and my love for my beloved is justified by the beloved having these properties (2000). The biggest objection to a quality view like Keller's is that if we love for qualities, we would trade our beloveds for people who possess these qualities to an even greater degree (the fungibility or tradability problem). This consequence seems counterintuitive to what we think love is. Love does not seem to be transferable to someone else with the same characteristics, even to one who "scores" higher for these characteristics (Nozick 1974).

Due to this and similar critiques, quality views have had to refine their position in order not to fall prey to problems, such as: "if I love a particular person B for value V, I should love everyone who has value V" (the promiscuity problem), or "if my beloved B no longer possesses this value V, I should stop loving her" (the inconstancy problem). Another worry is that if reasons are universal, and if my love for B is a response to those reasons, then everyone is justified, or even obligated to love B (the universality problem).[9] These supposed consequences seem all quite counterintuitive to what we think love is and does.

Besides these general problems, the quality view might seem counterintuitive, especially for parental love: parents often claim to love their children unconditionally, or in general that could be considered an ideal worth pursuing. We consider it constitutive of romantic love that we choose our romantic partners on the basis of what properties we find attractive, explaining why we love this person rather than anyone else. In parental love, however, the aspect of choice for a particular person with particular properties seems irrelevant, because we cannot choose the people that become our children. Once we have children, we could of course compare their qualities, but that seems more irrelevant to parental love than it is to, for example, romantic love. Even if we would consider it appropriate that people have "a favorite child" because of particular properties this child has, this does not mean that they do not love their other children. Qualities might be less relevant as a reason for love in parent–child relationships than they are in romantic or friendship relationships. However, since Keller's proposal, the quality view has come a long way. Shpall argues convincingly that some of these arguments are fallacious (2020). They paint a naïve, or perhaps outdated, picture of the quality view. These objections should rather be seen as a way to refine the quality view as to reject it completely. To avoid comparing qualities and the aforementioned problems, one could argue that one's reason for loving a person is one's relationship to them: the ongoing history of shared concern and activity between individuals (Kolodny 2003).[10] One could argue that the parent–child relationship is valuable and renders love appropriate. The absence of love would then be inappropriate because there is a relationship that calls for it. This view holds that lovers view relationships as reasons for valuing both the relationship and the person with whom one has the relationship. Several philosophers have argued for a combination of the quality and relationship view. Thomas Hurka argues they are often intertwined: when we share a valuable history with a person, we come to admire qualities because they belong to someone with whom we share this history (2017). Conversely, we feel more attached by a history if it involves someone whose qualities we admire (Hurka 2017, p. 168). This is similar to an argument from Troy Jollimore who argues that love is justified by the valuable qualities of the beloved which are only valued as a result of the love relationship (2017). When we ask a father why he loves his child he might just say "because she is my daughter," revealing that the relationship they share is a reason for their love. Sharing this valuable relation with the child, the qualities of the child also become valued by the father. Thus, several kinds of reasons for love can become intertwined.

If one accepts that love is reason-responsive, one could then argue that, because we have reasons to love such as a person's qualities or the history we share with them, we should love particular people because of these particular qualities or relationships. I do not intend to argue for such a claim, but only to expose its possibility.

What this debate seems to ignore is that we could not only have a reason to love "person x," we could independently have a reason to love (period).

Focusing on why we love and what love is in general, enables us to look at what we find meaningful in love and loving, instead of what we find valuable in the beloved. Although arguing for an obligation or moral duty to love seems to be unpopular in contemporary analytic philosophy, such a duty is not a novel idea. For example, a commandment to "love thy neighbor" has a central place in almost every religion. Throughout philosophical, spiritual, or religious traditions, loving is often seen as a virtue: a loving person is more virtuous than an indifferent person. Could contemporary philosophy make room for an ethical reason to love, regardless of the beloved? Iris Murdoch lays out such a moral framework in which love is the center of morality (1971 [2013]). She argues that loving teaches us how to be better people. Focusing on the reason for *loving* instead of focusing on the particularities of beloved "x," might make arguing for a moral obligation to love a whole lot easier. Focusing on the *lover* instead of the beloved could furthermore improve the way we love in general, improving our relationships with all those particular x's. It could help us categorize better and worse forms of loving.

The objection to an obligation to love is that we cannot have an obligation to love because love is not responsive to reasons. However, it is not at all decided that love is not responsive to reasons. If love is responsive to reasons, the duty to love becomes more plausible. Furthermore, we do not have to focus on accounts of "reasons to love x" and their accompanying criticisms. Focusing on "reasons to love, period" might give us possibilities in arguing for a duty to love.

CONTROLLING EMOTIONS

A third argument against the possibility of a moral obligation to love is the commandability objection. It is generally accepted, after the Kantian point of "ought implies can" that to have a duty to do something, the action must be commandable. One must be able to bring about the action with success or, as some would say, at will. Love, so this argument goes, is not commandable, because it is an emotion, and emotions are not commandable. Therefore, there cannot be a duty to love. Immanuel Kant writes, "love is a matter of feeling, not of willing, and I cannot love because I will to, still less because I ought to (I cannot be constrained to love); so a duty to love is an absurdity" (Kant 1797 [2017], p. 172). Similarly, Richard Taylor argues that "love and compassion are passions, not actions, are therefore subject to no terms of duties or moral obligations . . . Love, as a feeling, cannot be commanded, even by God, simply because it is not up to anyone at any given moment how he feels about his neighbor or anything else" (Taylor 1970, pp. 252–253).

There are three controversial key concepts at play: emotion, love, and duty. There are opposing conceptualizations for all of them. The controversy around duty and obligations was covered in the first section. In connection to Kant's objection, one should bear in mind fundamentally different conceptualizations of the nature of love and emotion. His objection would work only if we thought of love as an emotion and viewed emotions as physiological uncontrollable conditions. Again, a different conception of love could do the trick. Love is not a bodily feeling like hunger. There is an explanatory but never a justificatory reason for why someone is hungry. According to reason-based accounts, there are reasons for love, because love is not like hunger. Love is not an urge or a drive, and hence this cannot be an argument to support that we cannot have an obligation to love. We can have reasons for love in a way that we cannot have for a sensation like hunger. At most we can *explain* why we are hungry, and this explanation is one of physiological causation. Furthermore, love distinguishes from hunger because we can talk about it in terms of loving better or worse: while we cannot be better or worse in being hungry, we can try to be better at loving.

What about the view that love is not a sensation, but an emotion? Would that still render love unfit to be object of an obligation? Whatever conception of love we choose, love does at least *involve* emotions (Brogaard 2015). Love without emotions would be a cold and undesirable phenomenon. If love involves emotions, does that pose a threat to the duty or moral obligation to love? Liao thinks it does not, because there are plausible conceptions of emotions according to which they are controllable (2015). He argues that we can bring about this emotional component of love by several methods: (1) internal control, (2) external control, and (3) cultivation. Internal control means that we motivate ourselves to have certain emotions by using reasons: (a) we can give ourselves reasons to have particular emotions and (b) we can reflect on reasons why we have particular emotions in particular circumstances or toward particular persons (2015, p. 106). By appealing to these reasons and reflecting on them, we might begin to view people differently. In *The Sovereignty of Good* (2013), Iris Murdoch gives an example where a mother-in-law (M) feels contempt for her daughter-in-law (D). M decides to reflect on the reasons why she feels contempt for D, and realizes that her reason is that she is jealous that D will threaten M's relationship with her son. After critical self-reflection, she decides that her feelings of contempt for D are not supported by good reasons. Through reflecting on the reasons why she feels a certain way toward D and deciding that her emotions are not well-supported, M makes way for developing affection for D.

Liao's second method for bringing about particular emotions is one of external control: deliberately placing ourselves in situations in which we know that we would probably experience particular emotions (2015, p. 108).

For example, if we know that we tend to feel compassion when we see homeless people, then we have a reasonable chance of feeling compassion if we deliberately visit a homeless shelter.

A third method is to cultivate our emotions, for which Liao names several strategies (2015, p. 108). One strategy for cultivating our emotions is to behave *as if* we have particular emotions. Liao argues that by doing so, we cultivate our emotional capacities such that we would be more likely to have particular emotions in appropriate circumstances. Through engaging in these forms of behavior repeatedly over time, and cultivating the capacity for an emotion, it is likely that we increase that particular emotional response in the future. Other strategies for cultivating particular emotions are repeatedly using the methods of internal and external control.

Finally, cultivating does not merely involve a repetition of internal and external control over time but also a deep reflection on the reasons why we tend to have particular emotions and whether we have good reasons for continuing or not continuing to have these emotions. In the case of parental love, we could reflect on the reasons why we tend to feel a certain way toward a particular child. Moreover, we can successfully bring about the emotional aspect of love for a child through external control by deliberately placing ourselves in situations in which we would have a good chance of feeling affection and warmth toward the child. Finally, we can cultivate loving emotions for a child through behavioral inducement: we might try to act affectionately and warmly toward a child, even if we do not initially feel that way. In the case of parental love, by repeatedly acting as if, there is a reasonable chance that we cultivate the capacity for feeling affection and warmth for the child.

It may be argued that at best there is a duty to *try* to love, but not a duty to love, since the success of bringing about emotions is not guaranteed. Even if we try to love, we cannot directly control whether or not we succeed. But since ought implies can, one might argue that we cannot have a duty to love, because we cannot guarantee love. However, this is a wrong depiction of what it means to have a duty. The ought-implies-can requirement does not exclude the possibility that someone has a duty while not fulfilling it. Moreover, the requirement leaves room for conditions that do not annul the duty, but the blameworthiness for failing to meet the duty. In other words, we can have valid excuses for not fulfilling our duty: a cook has a duty to provide guests with good food but should not be blamed when the waiter secretly poisons it.[11] Similarly, we can have a duty to love, even when we do not have direct control over whether we succeed. A mother with postnatal depression who is trying to love her child, but who does not succeed because of her mental illness, does not fulfill her duty (which is a duty to love, not a duty to try to love), but she is also not blameworthy because she has a valid excuse.

But this last example is not very satisfying. It relies on a conception of love in which we do not attribute love to the depressed mother. Now some would say that indeed a mother who suffers from postnatal depression cannot love her child. But is it really incoherent to conceive of someone who is too depressed to make loving gestures or expressions, but who would still say of themselves that they love their children or spouses? Can we make room for a conception of love in which someone does not perform loving actions, but who still loves or continues to love? Arguing that there is at best a moral obligation to *try* to love but not to love does not only depend on a particular conception of duty, it also depends on a particular conception of love. It seems to depend on a behaviorist view of love, a view of love in which there must be some sort of *expression of love* to count as love. Some philosophers argue, for example, that when someone is unable to have sex or to care about the feelings of the other person (e.g., in depression), then they do not longer love the other (Earp & Savulescu 2020, p. 60, see, however, Naar 2017). On a different conception of love, however, we can make room for someone who continues not to perform loving actions, but who still continues to love. We could view love as a *practice* that can happen in the inner life: it does not need to be something that is measured by expressions, for example, verbal expression of feelings or sex (Spreeuwenberg 2021; Spreeuwenberg & Schaubroeck 2020). Iris Murdoch argues for love as focused attention (2013). Looking, attending, and focusing our direction all takes place in the *inner life*. The example of M and D shows that the practice of loving is something that takes place in M's mind. Instead of expressing a feeling that "overcame her," M reflects and looks at D, carefully attends to D. She is trying to see D in a way that goes beyond her own projections and her initial assumptions, a way that is not guided by her ego. Loving in this sense is shifting our focus, a practice of transcending the self, but it is not measured by proof of expression. Love then is not a practice that can fail or succeed, since engaging in this practice *is what loving is*. On such a conception of love, an obligation to love might be more plausible: we would be obliged to engage in loving practice.

THE MOTIVATION FOR LOVE

Some theories put love at the center of a well-lived life and present duty as a lesser, or even morally deficient, motivation (Grenberg 2014, p. 210). They argue that duty is that upon which we act when we do not have enough—or the right kind—of love, that is, when we don't have enough—or the right— positive attraction toward ourselves, other persons or issues of concern outside of ourselves. This brings up an interesting point of whether love and duty are at all compatible. This fourth objection for a duty to love consists in arguing that love and duty are incompatible, because its *motivations* are incompatible.

This objection focuses on one's motivations to act lovingly. Our motivations in love are focused on the beloved: out of love we act for the beloved's sake. We buy them flowers, cook them dinner, or, following somewhat grittier but famous examples, visit them in the hospital (cf. Stocker 1977) or rescue them when they are drowning (cf. Williams 1981). If one had a duty to love, it follows that one could fulfill this duty by loving someone out of duty. Yet, loving a person out of duty rather than for the person's own sake does not seem equivalent to really loving a person. Following this line of thought, duty has no place in love, and love has no place in the world of moral obligations.

This objection from motivation is rooted in criticism of Kant's moral theory. Kant argues that an action has moral worth only if it is done for the sake of duty (1797 [2017]). Critics of Kant argue that at least in personal relationships, we should act out of a direct concern for others, but a Kantian agent cannot do this, because he is acting out of a concern for a moral principle. In Michael Stocker's (1977) example, Smith is visiting you in the hospital and alleges that he is your friend. You are thankful for his visit, but when you express your gratitude, Smith tells you that he came to visit you because he thought it was his duty, not essentially because you are friends (1977). Stocker argues that Smith is not really a friend, because Smith appears to be motivated to visit you for the sake of some impartial rule but not for *your* sake. Smith is doing the right thing, but for the wrong reason. Bernard Williams (1981) famously makes a similar point with his example of the drowning wife and the rescuing husband having "one thought too many" when he considers whom to save among the two people drowning: one being his wife and the other being a stranger (Williams 1981, p. 18). Similarly, looking at Liao's argument, a child who discovers that his parents love him out of a sense of duty might feel that they do not really love him.

What to make of this objection? There are three ideas at play, of which only the third is controversial. First, we should do the right thing with the right motivation; a right action that is done for the wrong reason has less moral worth than an action done for the right reason. Second, in personal relationships, we should be motivated to do things for the other person's sake. We would not be motivated to do something for the other person's sake if we were motivated to perform the action out of self-interest. The third idea with which Liao takes issue is that in personal relationships, when we are motivated to do our duty for duty's sake, it inevitably undermines the relationship, because as with being motivated to do things out of self-interest, we would not be motivated to do things for the other person's sake. This idea presupposes that being motivated to do the right thing for the sake of duty and being motivated to do something for the other person's sake are incompatible motivations (2015). However, Liao argues that we can be motivated to do something for the sake of moral duty, and, *at the same time*, for the person's sake (2015, p. 126). In Stocker's example, Smith could have been motivated to see you both for the sake of duty and because he wants to see you. The two motives need not always be distinct, argues Liao: "The content of the duty is just to be motivated for the other person's sake" (2015, p. 126). We can specify the content of the duty as partial: Smith would have a duty to be motivated for your sake to visit you in the hospital.

One might respond that in personal relationships, a person should only have one motive for action, the motive to do things for the other person's sake. One might even go further and say that it is wrong to have any other motive but the motive to do things for the other person's sake: that is the upshot of Williams's one thought too many' objection against impartial justifications for helping one's beloved. Brook Sadler takes up the opposite stand and argues not just that the motives are compatible, but that modern moral notions of respect, duty, and obligation help us to determine how to act out of concern for the particular person who is the friend or beloved (2006). She argues that in considering and choosing how to act with regard to my friend, I open myself to moral deliberation or more broadly, to practical reasoning. Despite the fact that we sometimes act toward our friends and loved ones in ways that appear unmediated by moral deliberation, it is nonetheless true that moral considerations ultimately constitute a large part of our conceptions of love and friendship and even our motives for action. If we were shown that acting a certain habitual way toward a friend was morally indefensible, we would no longer see that as what friendship requires.

> If our actions are motivated by an appeal to duty, or obligation, or a concern for doing the right thing, we do not have one thought too many; rather, we have mustered up the strength of will to fulfil a duty. And it is the fact that one has been morally steadfast that reveals the genuineness of one's love or friendship. One should be admired for adhering to one's commitment to the other. (2006, p. 235)

Sadler argues that Stocker's complaint against modern ethical theories does not seem so cutting. Notions of duty, obligation, or rightness taken as motives, are not only consistent or compatible with relationships of love and friendship, but can be seen to be *constitutive* of them, she argues. Moral obligations can aid us in determining what it is that we are to do with respect to the other; comprise our commitment to the friend or beloved; and help us to fulfil that commitment. Sadler argues that "I did X because I love you" does not necessarily differ from "I did X because it is the right thing to do." If Smith is a good friend, it is because he has been attentive to the fact that your illness in the hospital is an occasion on which he ought to uphold his commitment to you. In Liao's case, if one is a loving parent, it could be because one has been attentive to the fact that the position of the child and one's relationship with it is an occasion on which one ought to love the child. The child who is disturbed upon hearing that his parents love him out of moral duty would make a mistake if he inferred that the parents do not truly love him: being motivated to act for duty's sake is *constitutive* of the parents being concerned for the child's sake, argues Sadler.

The answers offered above all reject the motivation objection within a Kantian perspective. Another possibility comes up in rejecting the Kantian perspective altogether and rejecting the idea that an action has moral worth only if it is done for the sake of duty. In that case, we do not have to act *out of a sense of duty* but just have to act *in accordance with the duty*. Solely being motivated for the other person's sake could then have moral worth on its own. While Kantians deem impartiality most important, Murdoch (1971 [2013]) argues that the route to become a morally better person is precisely via the particular. Murdoch would probably agree with Liao's claim that we can be morally motivated and, at the same time, for the sake of the other, like Sadler does, but she takes the opposite route to Sadler's toward being both a better person and lover. While Sadler argues that notions of duty, obligation, or rightness taken as motives make us better lovers, Murdoch argues the other way around: loving is what makes us morally better people. She places love at the center of morality and considers love a virtue. In her view of love and morality, there is no incompatibility between claiming that one's motivation for doing "x" was love, or claiming that one's motivation for "x" was moral insight. In this sense, Murdoch argues that love is constitutive of being a good person, which is the opposite of the route Sadler takes, who starts with being motivated to be a good person and ends up with being a good lover.

These routes do not have to be incompatible, though: Murdoch would not object to the claim taking up moral responsibilities can make us better lovers. While believing that moral responsibilities make us better lovers, we could at the same time accept that engaging in the practice of loving attention makes us better people. In some kind of circular motion, moral motivation and loving practice could positively influence each other, building upon each other. Smith knows that you being in the hospital is an occasion on which he ought to uphold his commitment to you, and this causes his attentiveness, which is Sadler's argument. At the same time, Smith can become aware of his moral responsibilities and becomes a morally better person precisely because of being attentive to you, which is Murdoch's argument.

Both Sadler's and Murdoch's position, as well as a hybrid position of these two intertwined, do away with the motivation objection for a moral duty to love. Here, again, with different conceptions of both love and morality, a moral obligation to love appears more plausible.

CONCLUSION

The four objections that have been raised against a moral obligation to love have been rejected by looking at different conceptions of obligations and different conceptions of love. On conceptions of moral obligations that are detached from the notion of making claims and demanding things from one another, a moral obligation to love may appear more plausible. Conceptions of love that depict love as responsive to reasons, and emotions involved in love as commandable, also contribute to the plausibility of a moral obligation to love. Finally, conceptions of the motivation from moral duty as at least compatible with, or even constitutive of a motivation from love, also contribute to the possibility of a moral obligation to love. Similarly, conceptions of love as constitutive of moral practice contribute to this possibility, taking a different route. Now that the obstacles have been removed and an obligation to love seems at least possible, one could take up the task of arguing whether we *have* such an obligation.

NOTES

1. Whether or not love involves emotions is a matter of controversy. For discussion, see, for example, Brogaard (2015) and Pismenny (2018).

2. I will remain neutral about the meaning of love as long as it is taken to mean more than "showing the right kind of behavior." I take "love" to refer to at least some kind of mental state, be it a sentiment, concern, perception, emotion, or other.

3. Throughout this chapter, I will solely talk about love for people. Not because I render love for other objects impossible, but because most authors in the discussed literature only talk about love for people, and this is sufficient to make my claim.

4. I follow Esther Kroeker's (2019) discussion of this debate, which includes among other things romantic love, love of parents for children, and friendship.

5. I am aware that there are technical differences between the concepts of "duty" and "obligation," however, these differences are irrelevant for this particular contribution. I will use "duty" and "obligation" somewhat interchangeably here, since I adopt the relevant word usage of major sources in the debate, such as Matthew Liao, Stephen Darwall, Harry Frankfurt, and Immanuel Kant.

6. On bipolar normativity, see Michael Thompson (2004).

7. In *The Second-Person Standpoint* (2009), Darwall writes that it is possible that there are different kinds of reasons for action involved in the gouty toe case. In his "Reply to Korsgaard, Wallace and Watson" (2007), Darwall elaborates on that statement by saying that he meant to say that there are two different kinds of reason, one

consisting in the fact that you are in pain and that this is bad for you (and a bad thing agent neutrally), and the other consisting in the fact that you warrantedly demand that the agent not be on your foot (2007, p. 60).

8. That something must be responsive to reasons to be the object of an obligation is a claim held by Harry Frankfurt (2009) among others. However, there are a few philosophers who take up the position that love can be an object of an obligation while not being responsive to reasons. Nick Zangwill (2013), for example, claims that a lack of parental love can be a moral flaw while not being a rational flaw. He claims love can be assessable as more or less appropriate without being more or less rational (2013, p. 310).

9. Distinction and names of these four problems are derived from Troy Jollimore's *Love's Vision* (2011).

10. I follow Esther Kroeker's (2019) classification of recent accounts of the relationship between love and practical reasons, which classifies Kolodny as a reasons-for-love-view.

11. This example is a variation of an example given by Liao (2015, p. 115).

REFERENCES

Baier, A. C. (1982). Caring about caring: A reply to Frankfurt. *Synthese*, 53 (2): 273–290.

Brogaard, B. (2015). *On romantic love: Simple truths about a complex emotion*. New York: Oxford University Press.

Cabezas, M. (2016). The right to love during childhood and the capability approach: beyond the Liao/Cowden debate. *Ethical Perspectives, 23*(1), 73–99.

Cowden, M. (2012). What's love got to do with it? Why a child does not have a right to be loved. *Critical Review of International Social and Political Philosophy, 15*(3), 325–345.

Darwall, S. (2007). Reply to Korsgaard, Wallace, and Watson. *Ethics, 118*(1), 52–69.

Darwall, S. (2009). *The second-person standpoint: Morality, respect, and accountability*. Cambridge, MA: Harvard University Press.

Darwall, S. (2017). Love's second-personal character. In K. Schaubroeck & E. Kroeker (Eds.), *Love, reason and morality* (pp. 93–109). New York: Routledge.

de Sousa, R. (2015). *Love: A very short introduction*. New York: Oxford University Press, USA.

Earp, B. D., & Savulescu, J. (2020). *Love Drugs: The chemical future of relationships*. Redwood City, CA: Stanford University Press.

Ferracioli, L. (2014). The state's duty to ensure children are loved. *Journal of Ethics & Social Philosophy, 8*, iv.

Frankfurt, H. G. (1998). Duty and love. *Philosophical Explorations*, *1*(1), 4–9.

Frankfurt, H. G. (2009). *The reasons of love*: Princeton, NJ: Princeton University Press.

Grenberg, J. M. (2014). All you need is love? In A. Cohen (Ed.), *Kant on emotion and value* (pp. 210–223). London: Palgrave Macmillan.

Hume, D. (2006). *An enquiry concerning the principles of morals: a critical edition* (Vol. 4). New York: Oxford University Press.

Hurka, T. (2017). *Love and reasons: The many relationships. Love, Reason, and Morality,* Routledge.

Jollimore, T. (2011). *Love's vision*: Princeton University Press.

Jollimore, T. (2017). Love: The vision view. *Love, Reason and Morality,* 1–19.

Kant, I. (1797 [2017]). *Kant: The metaphysics of morals (*M. Gregor, Trans. L. Denis Ed. 2nd ed.). Cambridge University Press.

Keller, S. (2000). How do I love thee? Let me count the properties. *American Philosophical Quarterly, 37*(2), 163–173.

Kolodny, N. (2003). Love as valuing a relationship. *The Philosophical Review, 112*(2), 135–189.

Kroeker, E. (2019). In A. M. Martin (Ed.), *The Routledge Handbook of Love in Philosophy*: Routledge.

Liao, S. M. (2015). *The right to be loved*: Oxford University Press.

Murdoch, I. (2013). *The sovereignty of good*: Routledge.

Naar, H. (2017). Love as a disposition. In *The Oxford handbook of philosophy of love*. Oxford University Press, available at: https://www.oxfordhandbooks.com/view/10.1093/oxfordhb/9780199395729.001

Nozick, R. (1974). *Anarchy, state, and utopia* (Vol. 5038). Basic Books.

Pismenny, A., & Prinz, J. (2017). Is love an emotion? In C. Grau & A. Smuts (Eds.), *The Oxford handbook of philosophy of love*. Oxford University Press.

Pismenny, A. (2018). *The syndrome of romantic love* [Doctoral dissertation, City University of New York, The Graduate Center]. CUNY Academic Works. https://academicworks-cuny-edu.ezproxy.gc.cuny.edu/gc_etds/2827

Sadler, B. J. (2006). Love, friendship, morality. *The Philosophical Forum, 37*(3), 243–263. https://doi.org/10.1111/j.1467-9191.2006.00241.x

Shpall, S. (2020). Against Romanticism. *Ergo*, 7(14). https://doi.org/10.3998/ergo.12405314.0007.014

Smuts, A. (ms.). In defense of the no-reasons view of love.

Solomon, R. C. (1993). The philosophy of emotions. *Handbook of emotions, 2*, 5–13. Guilford Press.

Spreeuwenberg, L. (2021). 'Love' as a practice: Looking at real people. In S. Cushing (Ed.), *New philosophical essays in love and loving*. Palgrave Macmillan.

Spreeuwenberg, L., & Schaubroeck, K. (2020). The non-individualistic and social dimension of love drugs. *Philosophy and Public Issues, 10*(3), 67–92.

Sreenivasan, G. (2010). Duties and their direction. *Ethics, 120*(3), 465–494.

Stocker, M. (1977). The schizophrenia of modern ethical theories. *The Journal of philosophy, 73*(14), 453–466.

Stump, E. (2006, November). Love, by all accounts. *Proceedings and Addresses of the American Philosophical Association*, 80(2), 25–43. American Philosophical Association.

Taylor, R. (1970). *Good and Evil. A forceful attack on the rationalistic tradition in ethics*. The Macmillan Company.

Thompson, M. (2004). What is it to wrong someone? A puzzle about justice. In R. J. Wallace, P. Pettit, S. Scheffler, & M. Smith (Eds.), *Reasons and value: Themes from the moral philosophy of Joseph Raz* (pp. 333–384). Clarendon.

Thomson, J. J. (1990). *The realm of rights*. Harvard University Press.

Velleman, J. D. (1999). Love as a moral emotion. *Ethics, 109*(2), 338–374.

Wallace, R. J. (2007). Reasons, relations, and commands: Reflections on Darwall. *Ethics, 118*(1), 24–36.

Wallace, R. J. (2019). *The moral nexus*. Princeton University Press.

Williams, B. (1981). Persons, character, and morality. In B. Williams (Ed.), *Moral luck: Philosophical papers 1973-1980* (pp. 1–19): Cambridge University Press.

Wolf, S. (2002). *The true, the good, and the lovable: Frankfurt's avoidance of objectivity* (pp. 227–244). The MIT Press.

Zangwill, N. (2013). Love: gloriously amoral and arational. *Philosophical Explorations, 16*(3), 298–314.

Chapter 10

Love and Integrity

Raja Halwani

Love and morality have various interesting connections, both conceptual and causal. For example, love might conceptually be tied to well-being, in that for X to love Y, X must be concerned for Y's well-being for its own sake.[1] Another connection is whether to act from love is to act from reasons of love, or whether from reasons of morality but in the context of love.[2] A third connection is whether love is a virtue of sorts.[3] A fourth is that people often love others on the basis of the latter's moral properties.[4] My focus in this chapter is on the relationship between love and integrity, specifically on the conditions under which love and integrity conflict. I will argue that given specific features of love and of integrity, the two conflict when five conditions obtain: (1) the lover's integrity tracks real and worthwhile values, (2) the values reflected in the lover's integrity are important to the lover, (3) the beloved has values contrary to those of the lover's integrity, (4) the beloved acts on these values, and (5) the lover cannot justify the beloved's values.[5] I shall argue that the presence of all five is sufficient for a genuine clash between the lover's integrity and the love.[6]

After discussing a plausible conception of integrity in the first section, I lay out, in the second section, some moral features of love that I gather from the literature. I then provide, in the third section, two detailed cases of potential conflicts between love and integrity, explaining the conditions under which such conflicts occur. In the fourth section, I discuss mistaken integrities. I conclude in the fifth section with some remarks about the actual frequency of such conflicts and what these frequencies might imply for the philosophical arguments of this chapter. My focus throughout is on the kind of love that has the features I discuss in the first section, mostly exemplified by romantic (erotic, sexual) love and close friendships (which can be between siblings and between parents and their adult children). For brevity's sake, I will use

213

the terms "lovers," "lover," and "beloved" to refer to the parties in all such close relationships.

INTEGRITY

I will sketch a conception of integrity that borrows from the various conceptions of it offered in the literature.[7]

Integrity, as Lynne McFall (1987) convincingly argues, involves at least three kinds of coherence, each of which is necessary for having integrity: (a) among one's principles, commitments, or values; (b) between one's principles and one's actions; and (c) among one's motives, principles, and actions (1987, 7–8). To see the differences between the three, consider (a) first, suppose that Juan is committed to the principle of not causing harm. Integrity requires coherence between this commitment and his other commitments—if he is a serious hunter, for example, then one of the two commitments needs to yield to the other or be revised. Now consider (b), that integrity requires coherence between Juan's value of no harm and his actions: Juan must refrain from, say, killing animals since it causes harm to animals. Finally, (c), integrity requires that his motives for what he does cohere with his commitments—Juan should not refrain from hunting just to signal his virtue to his friends. He should be motivated by the value itself. As McFall puts it, "If one values not just honesty but honesty for its own sake, then honesty motivated by self-interest is not enough for integrity" (1987, 8).

The above three kinds of coherence—among the agent's values, actions, and motives—are internal to the agent, which might not be sufficient for integrity if integrity is also about *which* values the agent adopts. We cannot, with a "straight face," claim some things about integrity, such as the following: "Sally is a person of principle: pleasure"; "Harold demonstrates great integrity in his single-minded pursuit of approval"; and "John was a man of uncommon integrity. He let nothing—not friendship, not justice, not truth—stand in the way of his amassment of wealth" (McFall 1987, 9). The idea is that there are particular things—pleasure, wealth, approval, money, status, and personal gain in general—that people with integrity resist, so it is difficult to conceive of integrity's values as reflecting them. Something other than those things must be at stake for the person if she is to have integrity. Someone who is committed to seeking pleasure might resist the temptation to yield to it on a particular occasion, but this is not enough to show that she has integrity, because having integrity is not just about resisting temptation, but also about *why* someone resists the temptation.

Typically, those things for which people with integrity stand are moral.[8] People with integrity are not willing to do just anything if the action is unjust, (directly?) harmful to the innocent, or a betrayal of a spouse or friend. In other words, integrity involves a commitment not just to any value or principle, but to moral ones. Moreover, people with integrity often stand up or speak out for what is worthwhile, which can be done passively or actively. The former is a refusal to do certain things—to refuse to sign a petition that makes outrageous demands or to join a mob that wants to "cancel" someone. The latter goes beyond the refusal to do something to further act in particular ways—to speak out against the petition being circulated, to stand up to the mob.

This discussion of integrity, especially in its active role, brings out the important point that integrity has both personal and social aspects. As Cheshire Calhoun (1995) argues, "Integrity . . . seems tightly connected to viewing oneself as a member of an evaluating community and to caring about what that community endorses" (1995, 254). The artist, according to Calhoun, who changes his work to suit a tasteless public not only fails himself, he "lacks integrity because he does not regard his best aesthetic judgment as important to anyone but himself" (1995, 258). This social aspect of integrity explains why we regard hypocrites as not having integrity: they lack it not because (or, not only because) they show lack of coherence between what they avow and what they do, but because they mislead others. This is because when we act with integrity we affirm before others what we believe about worthwhile matters—matters of worth to ourselves as fellow co-deliberators. Hypocrites mislead because what they affirm before others is a lie, for it does not cohere with their true beliefs (Calhoun 1995, 258–259).

Integrity, then, involves coherence among one's values, actions, and motives, such that the values reflect worthwhile things, and are typically moral in nature. Moreover, because integrity is not always a matter of not dirtying one's hands but also actively standing up for what one believes, integrity has a social dimension to it, signaling the importance of speaking our minds among and with fellow co-deliberators.

One additional feature of integrity is the *importance to the agent* of the values that his integrity reflects. People's moral values can be about many subjects, not all of which have priority to them. Andrea might care about criminal justice reform in the United States, but the issue of universal health care is what resonates with her the most—it is the latter issue about which she enters into heated debates with others, on the basis of which she votes for politicians, and that might act as a deal-breaker as far as whom she is willing to date or befriend. Moreover, although one *can* have integrity about issues that are not very important to one—thus, whenever an opportunity arises, Andrea would act regarding issues of criminal justice; one's integrity typically is about values that are very important to one, as is the case with Andrea's concern about universal health care. Integrity, then, reflects one's *core* values, those that are part of one's moral *identity*.

Given these features of integrity, people can have, so to speak, mistaken integrities. Beyond internal coherence, one's integrity can reflect nonmoral values (if we assume that integrity is about moral questions), or superficial moral values. In addition, one can be wrong to care about some worthwhile values more than others *in a given context* (e.g., standing up for the individual liberty of refusing to wear masks while in the midst of a pandemic). In such cases, when one perceives threats to one's integrity, one's perception might be mistaken (more on this in the fourth section).

I now turn to four features of love that, along with the above conception of integrity, can give rise to conflicts between love and integrity.

FOUR FEATURES OF LOVE

The following four features of love especially stand out as related to morality and so relevant to integrity.

The first is the openness and willingness to be changed by one's beloved ("mutual drawing"). This idea was defended by Dean Cocking and Jeannette Kennett (2000) and more recently by Dirk Baltzly and Kennett (2017).[9] Mutual drawing involves two aspects. First, lovers are motivated and have reason to do things, to develop new interests, and to be open to new ideas and beliefs on each other's recommendation. Second, lovers are open and willing to see themselves the way their beloveds or friends see them. The nature of love is such that to be a lover is to have this kind of openness and willingness. Moreover, it is the love itself that supplies the reason for why a friend would be willing to, say, take up Russian literature: the friend or beloved's recommendation is reason enough.

Almost all the examples given by Baltzly and Kennett involve openness to nonmoral things and activities (going bowling, seeing oneself as looking good when dressed in red).[10] But the connection to morality here is clear: the lovers, through the process of mutual drawing, open themselves up to moral change, whether for the better or for the worse.

The second feature of love—defended by Ward E. Jones (2012)—is the tendency for lovers to see each other as morally good. The idea is that "to love someone . . . involves a persistent expectation that she lives as a good person does," and that "loving involves something like the desire that one's beloved be a good person, and that she live a good life" (616). This is a pervasive feature of love in that lovers typically think of themselves as being in love with good people; it is rare that a lover claims that their beloved is bad, and lovers tend to resist the admission by using various tactics, such as disbelief in, making light of, or explaining away the badness of the beloved (Jones 2012, 622–23). This does not mean that the lover's beliefs that her beloved is good are always true, only that lovers tend to think of their beloveds under such descriptions.

The third feature, also from Jones, is the idea of moral endorsement. Jones claims that lovers morally *endorse* their beloveds: "The lover vouches for his beloved with his belief that she is good and his placing his well-being, as it were, at her mercy" (2012, 624). Lovers not only tend to see their lovers as good, but they also, *in being lovers*, endorse their beloveds' goodness. This endorsement occurs from a combination of the tendency to see their beloveds as good and incorporating the beloved's well-being with the lover's well-being (624). In endorsing or vouching for their beloveds' goodness, lovers put their own moral well-being at stake, so to speak: if the beloved acts wrongly, this reflects badly on the lover, which induces reflexive shame—the beloved, in acting wrongly, brings shame to the lover (626).

The fourth feature is a descendant of union theories of love, according to which the lovers somehow pool their identities or well-beings, as in Robert Nozick's (1991) *we*. Because union theories face serious criticisms,[11] philosophers have tried to capture what is true about them while avoiding these criticisms. Whereas on the third feature, there is no necessary connection between a lover's vouching for or endorsing his beloved's moral goodness and his *adopting* her values (accepting them as his and being motivated to act on them), Bennett Helm's (2010) account does have this strong feature. On Helm's view, love is intimate identification: "Loving someone . . . involves valuing what she values for her sake" (2010, 161), such that valuing is a "mode of self-love in which one understands the thing valued to have a place within the kind of life worth one's living" (2010, 149). To love someone is to share the beloved's values for the beloved's sake, and to endorse these values in a strong, evaluative way: not only do they motivate the lover to act, but the lover makes them part of his life and part of his conception of the worthwhileness of his life. If these values are part of the identity of the beloved, then when the lover takes them up, he will share her identity.[12] I will call this the adoption of the beloved's values.

All these features can conflict with integrity, though the nature of the conflict is different with some than with others. (I will assume in what follows, up until the fourth section, that there are no mistaken integrities.) The first and second features contingently conflict with integrity: under the first feature, the lover opens herself to being changed by the beloved, and although the change can be moral, it need not be. Under the second feature, the lover will tend to see the beloved as good, even if the beloved is not, but this need not involve a revision of the lover's own values. The reason for the contingent conflict is that both these features are descriptive, so whether they apply depends on the case at hand. It is the third and fourth features that pose genuine threats to integrity because under both features some sort of identification is going on between the lover's and the beloved's values, an identification that seems to be a necessary feature of love. When these values are opposed, the identification can rupture: the lover would not be able to endorse the beloved's goodness (the third feature) or would not be able to adopt the beloved's values (the fourth feature).

TWO CASES

Talk of maintaining one's integrity is easy when the discussion is at an abstract level: we are all committed to justice, peace, and kindness. And although this level of discussion allows us to handle some cases, fine-grained values and commitments are needed to think through more complex or realistic cases. Consider two.[13]

Sandra and Kamal

Sandra and Kamal have been together for a good ten years. Recently, Sandra has slowly changed her dietary regimen to become a vegetarian and then a vegan. Sandra has become a committed vegan because of animal welfare (though the health advantages are a plus). She has come to believe that animals, much like their human counterparts, have their own lives to lead and to flourish, so are not resources of nutrition or medicine, let alone of pleasure, for human beings. Thus, to Sandra, our relationship with animals does not revolve merely around lessening or obliterating their suffering, but also about letting them be—in the case of animals in the wild to let them live and die as nature prescribed, and in the case of farm animals to stop breeding them for our purposes.

These changes in her beliefs and habits have strained somewhat the practical aspect of Sandra's relationship with Kamal, but they were able to work things out. They have always alternated when it comes to cooking, so that each cooks three times a week (with one night dedicated to a weekly date out somewhere), and Sandra did not (at first) have a problem cooking meat dishes for Kamal.

Lately, however, she has been immersing herself more and more in the literature about and activism for veganism, and she has started finding herself less tolerant of people who eat meat and consume animal products. She started, and Kamal was happy to go along, changing all the household products to cruelty-free products. But Sandra has also started finding herself not wanting to cook meat dishes for Kamal, so she cooked only vegan meals, and, more troublingly, when Kamal cooked a meat dish for himself, she has started to find herself less able to be with him and watch him eat meat without thinking to herself that he is doing something deeply wrong.[14] In addition, she has started to not be able to abide having meat in the fridge or in the house in general.

They talk it through and Kamal is sympathetic to her concerns. He tells her that though he will not stop eating meat, he will make sure to buy it from ethical sources, such as local farms that treat their animals humanely until they are killed for meat. Sandra appreciates this but has lingering concerns, for she has doubts about the so-called humane treatment of animals and about killing them for their meat, especially since they are killed at a young age. To Sandra, death is a harm, and a serious one at that when it comes at a young age. So killing a young animal for the taste of its meat is a clear moral wrong, and so is abetting this practice.

Clearly, Sandra feels a conflict. She loves Kamal but she also worries about what being with him means for her being vegan. The conflict she feels is between being vegan and being with a beloved who is not. She is motivated to act and shape her life by the values of veganism, but this acting and shaping are in tension with being motivated to endorse Kamal's goodness and adopt his values. Her moral reasons and her reasons of love are in conflict; or, if we consider reasons of love to ultimately be moral reasons, then Sandra's conflict is between two sets of moral reasons.[15]

One response is to shrug off the conflict and claim that many couples have to make compromises, so that if Kamal is willing to eat and use only humanely sourced animal products, then surely Sandra's reasons for love ought to persuade her to compromise on her part and just drop the issue. This, however, is an easy way out because it targets the practical aspect of their relationship and does not go into the theoretical issues that create the conflict for Sandra—the issue here is not compromising on how many nights a week to go out for a movie, but of how one can have an integrated self when two of its parts pull away from each other.

To see this point clearly, change the case to a couple X and Y, in which X buys products made by slaves. Now imagine Y having qualms about what this means to Y and to the relationship, given that Y is an abolitionist. Would it do to compromise by saying that X can buy slave-made products but only from places where slaves are treated humanely (given that non-slave-made products are available)? No, for the issue is not practical, but concerns Y's ability to maintain Y's moral compass while also loving X. The only reason why we would accept the compromise in Sandra's case is the social (and lamentable) fact that we do not take animals' lives seriously enough. And indeed this is how Sandra, plausibly, thinks about it. So there is a conflict that goes beyond figuring out a workable arrangement for the two of them.

Let us flesh out the conflict more. To Sandra, animal lives are intrinsically valuable, and she cannot see herself participating in the practice of exploiting them, no matter how humanely it is done. But she also has a difficult time accepting the fact that she is with someone who is willing to benefit from the exploitation of animals. In this regard, and unlike the relationships between coworkers, neighbors, roommates, and people who are neither strangers nor intimates, intimate relationships, as we have seen, involve features such as adopting the beloved's values and endorsing the beloved's moral goodness. Lovers (and friends) like each other and enjoy each other's company, because, often, the liking and enjoyment occur against a backdrop of, and are enhanced by, shared values. I have a close relationship with Betty because, like me, she loves and respects animals. I have a close relationship with Satya because, like me, she is committed to the Palestinian cause. And I have a close relationship with Jerome because, like me, he is committed to racial justice in America. Although lovers and friends need not share all their values together, having *opposed* values or commitments puts a strain on their relationship (which many navigate by "not going there"). My relationship with Seth is sometimes put to the test when his commitment to not invite some speakers to campus clashes with my commitment to expose our students to various ways of thinking.

Going back to the four features of love in the second section, note that Sandra's openness to Kamal might lead her to change her views on animals, and her tendency to see Kamal as a good person might be threatened to some extent by his continued eating of meat. I say to "some extent" because unless Sandra's view of Kamal is completely colored by his consumption of animal products, Sandra will continue to see Kamal as a good person in other aspects. Nonetheless, neither of these two features pose any obvious threat to her integrity—his lack of goodness as such is not connected to her integrity, because she might foreclose change as far as animals are concerned; and her tendency to see Kamal as not good has no bearing, as such, on her own integrity. If anything, these two features might prompt her to try to change Kamal to become vegan himself, as a way of promoting his moral well-being.

It is the other two features that threaten Sandra's integrity, because they directly involve Sandra *as Kamal's lover*. If love requires that the lover endorse the moral goodness of the beloved, per Jones's view, it is unclear how Sandra can do this without violating her integrity: she cannot be committed to the welfare of animals while endorsing the moral goodness of someone, even if he is her beloved, who not only eats meat but thinks that it is perfectly permissible to do so under certain conditions (e.g., the meat is humanely obtained). More damningly, it is unclear how, on Helm's view, Sandra can share and adopt Kamal's values as part of her own conception of her life, without violating her integrity.

Thus, in this case, the five conditions outlined in the introductory paragraph are satisfied: Sandra's integrity tracks real and worthwhile values; animal welfare is a crucial, identity-forming value to Sandra; Kamal has values contrary to those reflected in Sandra's integrity; Kamal acts on these values; and Sandra cannot justify the beloved's values: given that early death is a serious harm to animals, given that this harm cannot justify the pleasures of eating meat, Kamal's view seems to be indefensible.

Sandra can do one of three things as far as her values and being with Kamal are concerned: set her qualms aside (turn a blind eye to them), revise her values on animals, or not be with Kamal.

Set aside the actual ability to pull off any one of the three options. Assume (plausibly) also that Sandra's values are correct—that she is right to value what she does about animals, and that this commitment to their well-being is based on moral facts about their lives. Then each of the three options would leave Sandra morally compromised. The first option requires a violation of her integrity insofar as turning a blind eye to being with Kamal is a failure to live up to her ideals. It severs the ties between what she believes and values and her actions. She would be willing to not only tolerate but to actively allow herself to love (care, support, comfort, make happy) someone whose actions help maintain a practice that is morally abhorrent by her own lights.

The second option requires a revision of her values, which in some cases is the right thing to do (if one's values were mistaken) but which in Sandra's case is not. Note that the process by which a lover decides to revise or not to revise her values need not exclude the beloved. Sandra, for instance, owes it to Kamal and to herself to discuss the issue, not (only) with an eye to changing his (or her) mind, but out of epistemic and moral openness to another, especially to someone who is her beloved. The point regarding the second option is not so much about the process of revision, as much as it is the cost of the revision, given that the revision would mean changing (Sandra's) correct values.

The third option keeps Sandra's integrity intact, and it conforms with what integrity requires: standing up for her beliefs. It confirms not only that integrity is a personal matter, something inside Sandra and between her and herself, concerning the coherence among her values, motives, and actions, but also that it is about a worthwhile matter for which Sandra is willing to take a public stance. "Public" does not mean an announcement to all and sundry, but, per Calhoun, standing up for her values as something that she does before others—it is an issue of importance and sticking by it demonstrates to others (Kamal, friends, family) that Sandra is a person of integrity.

The price of the third option is high, however: she loses Kamal. Had her relationship with Kamal been in its early stages, dissolving it might not be very harmful to both or involve an injustice to Kamal given that the relationship is young. But given that they have been together for ten years, the dissolution is potentially seriously harmful to both because of the emotional, practical, and social toll it would take on them. It might also be unfair to Kamal given the length of their relationship and given that Sandra's veganism was acquired later—it is as if Sandra has changed the terms of the contract midstream.[16] So, whichever option Sandra chooses, she will be morally compromised.

Kyle and Denise

Kyle and Denise have been together for a good ten years. Denise studied philosophy as an undergraduate and took many courses in ethics and applied ethics, her favorite subject, and has come to have an articulate and well-supported view about the wrongness of abortion. Kyle used to be noncommittal about abortion and mostly just agreeing with Denise and going along with what she thinks. Lately, however, he has started immersing himself more in the literature and activism about abortion, and he has started to form his own beliefs about it. Kyle has come to believe that although fetuses are potential human beings, as Denise believes, at early stages they are more accurately described as clumps of human cells, so killing them is permissible. Besides, and having read the famous essay by Judith Jarvis Thomson, he reasons that even if fetuses are persons, so have a right to life, this does not imply that they have a right *to* their mothers' bodies. Unless the mother invites them to the use of her body, no such right exists.

More troublingly, he has started to be less tolerant of people who believe that abortion is wrong, and he has started to believe that they are anti-feminist and anti-women. He now finds himself less able to listen to Denise talk about abortion without thinking to himself that she is terribly mistaken about this issue and that her mistaken beliefs, not to mention her skewed values, are complicit in harm to women. This has put some strain on their relationship, in that they tend to clash whenever the topic comes up (including when other friends and family members are present, some of whom are pro-choice and others of whom are against abortion), so they try to avoid the subject.

They talk it through, however, and Denise is sympathetic to his concerns. She tells him that though she is unlikely to believe that abortion is permissible, she reminds him (1) that she is not politically active when it comes to abortion: she does not protest at abortion clinics, or vote merely on the candidate's views about the issue, for example; (2) that she does not deny the moral permissibility of abortion when the mother's life is in danger; (3) that she believes that pregnant women should receive whatever support they need to go through with the pregnancy so as to assure them, as much as assurances here can be offered, that the child will be given a good home; and (4) that her view is defensible: although she can see describing a fetus as a clump of cells, one can also reasonably describe it as a human embryo that will develop into a human being if given the chance.

Clearly, Kyle feels a conflict. He loves Denise but he also worries about what being with her means for him being pro-choice. The conflict he feels is between his being pro-choice and being with a beloved who is not; it is between being for the rights of women to bodily autonomy and between being with a beloved who believes that these rights are trumped by other rights. He is motivated to act and shape his life by these values, but this acting and shaping are in tension with being motivated to endorse Denise's goodness and adopt her values. His moral reasons and his reasons of love are in conflict; or, if we consider reasons of love to ultimately be moral reasons, then Kyle's conflict is between two sets of moral reasons.

One easy way out is to claim that many couples have to make compromises, so that if Denise's views about abortion are well-supported, then surely Kyle's reasons of love ought to persuade him to compromise on his part and just drop the issue. Again, however, this way out targets the practical aspect of their relationship and does not go into the theoretical issues that create the conflict for Kyle.

Kyle's case, however, is importantly different from Sandra's. First, Denise, unlike Kamal (who eats meat and consumes animal products), is not actively partaking in any practice that indirectly (or directly) causes harm to women (or, for that matter, benefits embryos). Denise's beliefs about abortion remain confined to beliefs. At most, Denise might, through discussions and conversations about this issue, persuade others of her view, and the new converts might, in turn, end up causing harm to women if they decide to act on their newly adopted beliefs. But the probability of all this occurring is so low that it would implausibly morally condemn most of us for doing harm and being responsible for others' actions.

Second, unlike Sandra's inability to defend Kamal's beliefs about the permissibility of humanely killing animals at a young age for the taste of their meat, Kyle can reason in this way: Denise's beliefs about abortion, like some other issues, are not indefensible, which affects what it means for Kyle to maintain his integrity when he is with Denise who holds an opposing view. This aspect of the issue allows Kyle to be able to endorse Denise's moral goodness. Yes, he disagrees with her on an important issue, but he can also see the reasonableness of her view and he knows that moral considerations, such as compassion for would-be babies, motivate her to hold it.

Thus, in this case, not all the four conditions outlined in the introductory paragraph are satisfied: although Kyle's integrity tracks real and worthwhile values, although women's welfare and autonomy are identity-forming values to Kyle, and although Denise has values contrary to those reflected in Kyle's integrity, Denise does not act on her values, and Kyle can justify them: given that human life is important, and that given women are afforded a place in Denise's value-system, Kyle finds Denise's view to be defensible. He disagrees with it, but his disagreement does not block his ability to endorse Denise's goodness, though he cannot adopt those specific values of hers.

Kyle, like Sandra, can do one of three things as far as his values and being with Denise are concerned: force himself to set his qualms aside, revise his values on abortion, or not be with Denise. Kyle's ability to portray Denise's values as defensible allows him to take the first option: he can set aside his qualms that he loves someone whose values are wrong or abhorrent. Kyle, then, need not take the second or third option.

Both these cases hinge on three crucial points: on the incompatibility between some of the lover's values and some of the beloved's regarding an issue, on the centrality of the lover's values to his or her moral identity, and on the lover's ability to depict the beloved's values as morally defensible which allows the lover to set them aside and thus be able to endorse the goodness of the beloved.[17] The first is true of both cases in that some of the values of each partner about a specific issue cannot both be true. The second point is also true of both cases: both Sandra and Kyle view their values about animals and abortion, respectively, as central to their moral identity. The two cases part company on the third: Sandra, for good reason, is unable to render Kamal's values defensible as far as animals are considered, whereas Kyle is able to render Denise's values defensible as far as abortion is concerned.[18]

I will say more in the fifth section about the ability of justifying the beloved's values, but, for now, one might wonder why Kyle has to be able to justify Denise's values if Denise does not act on them. If Denise does not act on them, where is the difficulty? The difficulty stems from the requirement of being able to endorse the beloved's goodness, for someone's goodness does not consist of only their actions, but also of their beliefs and values.[19] For Kyle to be able to endorse Denise as a good person, he needs to be able to justify her values regarding women's limits on bodily autonomy. Note in this regard a twist in the Kamal and Sandra case: assume that Kamal not only is convinced of Sandra's views about animals but that he shares them. It's just that he has a hard time not eating meat because he is often in situations (cultural, traditional) in which he needs to eat meat. Sandra should not have a difficult time endorsing his goodness for she realizes that his actions reflect, not his values, but other factors, such as the necessity for cultural conformity. Sandra can cut Kamal some slack in this respect.[20] So both actions and values matter for the protection of integrity.

MISTAKEN INTEGRITIES AND MISTAKEN DEFENSES

I have been discussing integrity and love from a moral-psychological view, explaining cases of conflict from the point of view of those who experience them, while assuming that their experiences reflect true values and proper reasoning. Consider now a case given by Baltzly and Kennett (2017, 120–122).[21] Jim and Tammy are a married, Christian couple. They believe that a woman's place is in the home, taking care of her husband and children. Now that the children have grown up, however, Tammy has a change of mind about her role and decides to take a part-time job. Jim has a hard time with this, and he feels a conflict between his love for Tammy and his integrity, because his moral commitments prevent him from being able to set aside his qualms about what Tammy wants to do, let alone being able to adopt her new values.

Here, there is a divergence between a subjective and objective conflict between love and integrity—Jim perceives a threat to his integrity where there is none. Let us assume what is obviously true, that Jim is wrong to believe that a woman's place is at home. Then, contrary to what he thinks, his integrity is not in any real danger from his love for Tammy, because he ought to revise his views about women's roles and, therefore, ought to rethink his values and commitments. Of course, *he* thinks that his integrity is threatened, but that is only because he has mistaken values about the role of women. The threat in this case is not *to* Jim's integrity, but *from* his perceived integrity to his love for and relationship with Tammy. Unlike Sandra's and Kyle's cases, Jim's values are not anchored in (or mirrored by) objective moral facts.

The case of Jim illustrates the difference between the actual values of some people and hence how their integrity reflects them, on the one hand, and, on the other, which values they *should* have and hence how their integrity *should* reflect them. Although Jim has values about the role of women, they are incorrect values. He should revise them, which implies a revision in his integrity.

Note that the force of the "should" applies not only to the values one should have but also to the importance that they should have for one. Imagine Rabab who cares about a moral issue but with undue emphasis, such as being passionate about the depiction (or lack thereof) of Arab characters in science fiction. If Rabab refuses to love someone or considers leaving someone who thinks that although it would be good to have more Arab characters in science fiction, really, this is not an issue worth too much moral energy, Rabab seems to have placed undue emphasis on this particular value.

Let's return to Jim and Tammy. Jim is unable to justify Tammy's values regarding the place of women in the workplace, which blocks his ability to endorse her goodness or share her values. Jim's inability indicates the dangers of justifying the beloved's values by the lover: for the lover's views are likely to affect the lover's perception of his ability to pull off this justification. Jim believes that Tammy's values are indefensible, whereas they are. There is a tension between a perceived and a real ability to justify the beloved's values. Even Sandra's and Kyle's abilities can come under scrutiny, because one can argue that Sandra's inability to justify Kamal's values is due to her philosophical blindness to, say, accounts of death that do not see death as a harm,[22] and Kyle's ability to justify Denise's values is due to his not taking what women go through seriously enough. In short, the line between the ability and inability to justify another's values is fuzzy and for various reasons, including the lover's not canvassing all the justifications out there (Sandra) and the lover's not putting sufficient weight on some values (Kyle).[23]

I fully grant the fuzziness. Its existence, however, pervades all our moral reasoning, not just when it comes to integrity—people often rationalize bad things to make them good, fall epistemically short in many ways, are influenced by various biases, and so on. So the best we can hope for is that lovers reason their way through their beloveds' values as well as possible, especially knowing that what is at stake—love and integrity—are crucial values themselves.

PHILOSOPHY AND REALITY

I have argued that given some features of love and integrity, a lover's integrity is endangered by love when her integrity's values are real and worthwhile, when her integrity is crucial to her moral identity, when the beloved has values contrary those reflected by her integrity, when her beloved acts on the beloved's values, and when the lover cannot defend her beloved's values, which blocks her ability to endorse the beloved's moral goodness. How the lover should act in cases of conflict, however, I left an open question, though no matter which option the lover takes, there will likely be a heavy price.

Of the various reasons for why people terminate relationships—a new love, unhappiness, boredom, abuse, betrayal, "irreconcilable differences"—we don't hear much of integrity.[24] And although we do hear of the related concepts of dignity and self-respect, they tend to refer to the lover's unwillingness to continue to be treated badly by the beloved; rarely do they refer to the lover's moral values about things *external* to the relationship. Indeed, we all know of couples who deeply love each other and who have successful relationships, yet who differ on various moral issues, such as animal rights, rights of sexual and gender minorities, nation-building, wars, the role of government in social issues, and so on.

The existence of such cases raises interesting questions for this chapter's argument: Are conflicts between love and integrity simply uncommon? If yes, why? Is it because people tend to have successful relationships only with those who share their values? Is it because the argument that I have pursued in this chapter is too philosophically stuffy—is it, like some philosophical accounts, too highfalutin for reality? Or is it because people's integrity is just not dear enough to them, especially in the face of worthy and powerful potential competitors like love and friendship?

Barring some difficult-to-pull-off empirical work, I can only speculate. But I confess that I often wonder about the realism of some philosophical accounts of love: Does not Helm's idea of *adopting* the beloved's values raise the bar very high for most loves? Why can lovers not adopt *some* of their beloveds' values? Why is adoption even necessary—why is it not enough that they accept or even tolerate them? And must the endorsement of the goodness of the beloved be complete? Or can it be *partial*?[25] I am sympathetic to these rhetorical questions. Although lovers typically view their beloveds as good even when the latter have moral shortcomings, it might be that they are able to do so by endorsing the beloveds' goodness *holistically* or *generally*. That is, they might not be blind to the beloved's moral defects but they might also see that the beloved has other properties that compensate for the defects. And perhaps love is this sight (or vision[26]): the ability to love someone, endorse and vouch for their moral goodness, without being blind to their moral defects, though whether they accept, tolerate, or try to change the defects depends on the case. So the adoption of a beloved's values need not be total, and can be partial; and the endorsement need not be absolute, and can be holistic.

We are on thin ice, however. When is a holistic endorsement of the beloved's goodness compatible or incompatible with the lover's integrity? Surely there are moral defects for which no good moral qualities can compensate, thereby blocking the endorsement. Imagine loving a pedophile, a killer, a rapist, a torturer. Imagine loving someone racist, a supporter of ethnic cleansing, a (cruel?) pimp, a sex trafficker. If the lovers are not, *at the very least*, troubled by their beloveds' moral actions given their (i.e., the lovers') avowed commitments, we would rightly wonder how integrated their values are with each other and with their actions and motives.[27]

Lovers' ability to maintain their integrity depends on their ability to endorse their beloveds as good people *despite* their beloveds having moral defects, in those cases in which such defects morally clash with the lovers' values. The issue is which moral defects—and, assuming that context matters, in which contexts—are minor enough and which are major enough to, respectively, allow and block the endorsement without endangering the lover's integrity. The possibility of making mistakes here is large: if lovers tend to see their beloveds as good to begin with, and if lovers are open to change by their beloveds, then rationalizing away a beloved's serious moral defect is an ever-present danger to the lover's integrity (perhaps Kyle commits this error). On the other hand, lovers have to be careful to not enlarge a beloved's moral defect to the point of not being able to endorse the beloved as good (perhaps Sandra commits this error).

Thinking of love and integrity together raises fascinating issues. In this chapter, I have barely scratched the surface. I have not even canvassed some other types of interesting cases, such as those involving moral lapses (e.g., imagine that both Sandra and Kamal have been vegans, but that Kamal relapses to eating meat). But I hope to have opened the door for future thinking on this topic.[28]

NOTES

1. Soble (1990, ch. 12) and Soble (1997). I have argued that the concern is crucially for the moral well-being of the beloved (Halwani 2018, 138–143).

2. See the essays in Engels Kroeker, and Schaubroeck (2017).

3. Solomon (1991).

4. Abramson and Leite (2011).

5. I use "lover" and "beloved" for ease of discussion. I conceive of their relationship as reciprocal.

6. I assume that each is necessary, though a case can be made that neither (4) nor (5) is.

7. For a review of the literature on integrity, see Cox, La Caze, and Levine (2017), and Scherkoske (2013a) and (2013b).

8. "Typically," because one's values and commitments could be to nonmoral values. I am skeptical about nonmoralized conceptions of integrity, however. For arguments as to why integrity is a moral concept, see Ashford (2000) and Graham (2001). On integrity as a moral virtue, see Halwani (2021).

9. See also Brunning (this volume).

10. They give one example of a Christian couple in which the man is conflicted about his wife wanting to take a job outside the home (2017, 120–122). I discuss this example below.

11. See, for example, Singer (1994, ch. 1), Soble (1997), Helm (2010, 13–20), and Brogaard (2015, 39–40).

12. I am not doing Helm's account justice because I have left out the emotional aspect of it, but what I have explained is what I need for my discussion of integrity.

13. Both these cases are based on real-life couples with whom I have spoken various times about the involved issues (I have changed their names for privacy reasons). Also, my aim is not to issue guidance for the couples—the cases are not how-to manuals—but to show how, given the above features of integrity and love, the two clash.

14. Mary Midgley refers to a "gestalt-shift": "To himself, the meat-eater seems to be eating life. To the vegetarian, he seems to be eating death" (1983, 27).

15. Pismenny (2021) nicely argues how reasons of love (and for love) are not necessarily moral reasons, and can even clash with moral reasons.

16. The question of unfairness to Kamal is unclear, because (a) people do change, and (b) Sandra can break up with him after much thinking and discussion with Kamal.

17. Here, of course, lies one obvious moral danger, which is the temptation to rationalize the beloved's moral values, a process abetted by the willingness of the lover to be changed by the beloved (Baltzly's and Kennett's mutual drawing) and by the tendency of the lover to see the beloved as good (Jones's claim).

18. Kyle's ability to render defensible Denise's views hinges on the difficulty of settling the morality of abortion. This is unlike the ethics of eating meat, whose morality is more straightforward.

19. There is an action-related difficulty, however, that Arina Pismenny has pointed out to me, which is that under some counterfactual conditions (e.g., nationwide permissive abortion laws) Denise would be motivated to act on her values (and if she would not, then her values regarding abortion would be superficial).

20. However, if Kamal shares Sandra's values but eats meat because he does not care enough or because his will is weak, then Sandra would have a difficult time cutting him slack. Thanks to Arina Pismenny for this point.

21. They do not discuss the example in terms of integrity, though they use the example to illustrate the moral danger to Jim. I will use it to argue that the danger to Jim is not to his integrity, but to his love.

22. See Rosenbaum's Epicurean-inspired defense of this claim (1986).

23. For a discussion of moral reasoning in contexts of love, see Brogaard and Pismenny (this volume).

24. At least not in these terms, though it might be included under "irreconcilable differences."

25. Some remarks by Jones seem to imply no room for partial endorsement (2012, 620).

26. To borrow Troy Jollimore's (2011) term (but not necessarily Jollimore's way of unpacking it) for the special insights that love affords the lovers.

27. Cases like Sandra's are similar. The general reaction of non-horror stems from our inability to take animals' lives seriously.

28. I thank Arina Pismenny and Berit Brogaard for comments on an earlier draft. I also thank Helkin Rafael Gonzalez Tovar for discussion.

REFERENCES

Abramson, Kate, and Adam Leite. (2011) "Love as a Reactive Emotion." *The Philosophical Quarterly* 61 (245): 673–699.

Ashford, Elizabeth. (2000). "Utilitarianism, Integrity, and Partiality." *The Journal of Philosophy* 97 (8): 421–439.

Baltzly, Dirk, and Jeanette Kennett. (2017). "Intimate Relations: Friends and Lovers." In *Love, Reason and Morality*, eds. E. Engels Kroeker and K. Schaubroeck, 110–124. London and New York: Routledge.

Brogaard, Berit. (2015). *On Romantic Love: Simple Truths About a Complex Emotion*. New York: Oxford University Press.

Calhoun, Cheshire. (1995). "Standing for Something." *The Journal of Philosophy* 92 (5): 235–260.

Cocking, Dean, and Jeanette Kennett. (2000). "Friendship and Moral Danger." *The Journal of Philosophy* 97 (5): 278–296.

Cox, Damian, Marguerite La Caze, and Michael Levine. (2017) "Integrity." *The Stanford Encyclopedia of Philosophy*, ed. Edward N. Zalta. URL = <https://plato.stanford.edu/archives/spr2017/entries/integrity/>.

Engels Kroeker, Esther, and Katrien Schaubroeck, eds. (2017). *Love, Reason and Morality*. London and New York: Routledge.

Graham, Jody. (2001). "Does Integrity Require Moral Goodness?" *Ratio* 14 (3): 234–251.

Halwani, Raja. (2018) *Philosophy of Love, Sex, and Marriage: An Introduction*, 2nd ed. New York: Routledge.

Halwani, Raja. (2021) "The Virtue of Integrity." *The Saudi Journal of Philosophical Studies 1*(1): 13–25.

Helm, Bennett. (2010) *Love, Friendship, & the Self: Intimacy, Identification, & the Social Nature of Persons*. Oxford and New York: Oxford University Press.

Jollimore, Troy. (2011) *Love's Vision*. Princeton and Oxford: Princeton University Press.

Jones, Ward E. (2012) "A Lover's Shame." *Ethical Theory and Moral Practice* 15 (5): 615–630.

McFall, Lynne. (1987). "Integrity." *Ethics* 98 (1): 5–20.

Midgley, Mary. (1983). *Animals and Why They Matter*. Athens: University of Georgia Press.

Nozick, Robert. (1991). "Love's Bond." In *The Philosophy of (Erotic) Love*, ed. R. Solomon and K. Higgins, 417–432. Lawrence: University Press of Kansas.

Pismenny, Arina. (2021). "The Amorality of Romantic Love." In *Love, Justice, and Autonomy: Philosophical Perspectives*, eds. R. Fedock, M. Kühler, and R. Rosenhagen. New York: Routledge.

Rosenbaum, Stephen. (1986). "How to Be Dead and Not Care: A Defense of Epicurus." *American Philosophical Quarterly* 23 (2): 217–225.

Scherkoske, Greg. (2013a). "Whither Integrity I: Recent Faces of Integrity." *Philosophy Compass* 8 (1): 28–39.

Scherkoske, Greg. (2013b). "Whither Integrity II: Recent Faces of Integrity." *Philosophy Compass* 8 (1): 40–52.

Singer, Irving. (1994). *The Pursuit of Love*. Baltimore: Johns Hopkins University Press.

Soble, Alan. (1990). *The Structure of Love*. New Haven, CT: Yale University Press.

Soble, Alan. (1997) "Union, Autonomy, and Concern." In *Love Analyzed*, ed. R. Lamb, 65–92. Boulder, Colo.: Westview Press.

Solomon, Robert. (1991). "The Virtue of (Erotic) Love." In *The Philosophy of (Erotic) Love*, ed. R. Solomon and K. Higgins, 492–518. Lawrence: University Press of Kansas.

Chapter 11

Vices of Friendship

Arina Pismenny and Berit Brogaard

Friendship, most will agree, is a Good Thing. Few would choose a life without friends, and most of us treasure our friendships as essential to a thriving life. But as Aristotle famously argued, excess of a good thing can be as bad as deficiency: virtue lies in the "mean." In this chapter, we argue that the neo-Aristotelian conception of friendship elaborated in leading contemporary discussions, while highlighting many of friendship's virtues, fails to note some of those virtues' dark sides. It is easy to see that for the sake of a friendship, outsiders are sometimes treated unfairly. If impartiality is essential to morality, friendship seems to motivate some instances of immorality. But we touch only incidentally on the issue of partiality. We will be focusing instead on some more subtle ways in which friendship, on a neo-Aristotelian construal currently widely endorsed, imposes moralistic demands that are in tension with the core values of friendship. We will also be noting that certain intrinsic features of friendship may even undermine the friends' overall well-being.

A central contention of the neo-Aristotelian accounts of friendship is the idea that a "true" friendship has a teleology—the mutual fostering of improvement of character.[1] On this sort of account, true friends are drawn to one another in the first place because of their virtues of character, and it is also an essential function of friendship that it should contribute to the growth and development of the friends' virtuous character. In this chapter, we have two aims. The first is to reject this teleological view of friendship; the second is to survey what might be called vices of friendship—ways in which even a deep and intimate friendship can be bad from a moral point of view. In particular, we will argue that true friendship does not require friends to be each other's moral critics and models. To be sure, friends do influence one another in a variety of ways, including moral ones. However, it is an open question whether this results in their characters' improvement or corruption. The latter outcome is not necessarily incompatible with true friendship.

We begin in the first section by sketching the core features of the neo-Aristotelian account of friendship. In the second section, we put pressure on the robust concern aspect of the neo-Aristotelian accounts by arguing that the requirements of disinterestedness and selflessness on true friendship are unwarranted. The third section argues against the moralistic provision that friends act to improve one another's character. Retracting or refining these requirements leads us to construct a minimal account of "true" friendship in the fourth section. This minimal account outlines the normative space of friendship. Within that space, four affective and motivational features—or "virtues of friendship"—determine the good of true friendships. We call these virtues of friendship *closeness, emotional intimacy, trust,* and *friendship identity.* Armed with that minimal conception of true friendship, in the fifth section we sketch some ways in which a true friendship that possesses the good-making features of true friendship can nonetheless still be bad.

THE NEO-ARISTOTELIAN ACCOUNT OF FRIENDSHIP

Aristotle's account of character friendship has been a strong source of inspiration for prominent contemporary accounts of true friendship. For Aristotle, character friendship is necessary for a fully satisfying life. It helps us to cultivate good character traits and realize our full potential as persons capable of growth and development, both morally and intellectually. On this conception, true friendship involves motivational and affective features such as mutual admiration of character, mutual love, and a life to some extent shared; moreover, friends are expected to serve both as role models and as moral critics for one another.

Before we discuss these features of character friendships, it is important to indicate how virtues fit into the conception of the good life more generally, and how they relate to morality as we now tend to conceive of it. According to Aristotelian virtue ethics, cultivating virtue is necessary for a life of flourishing. But what is virtue? Aristotle's own word for what is commonly rendered as "virtue"—*aretê*—might better be translated as "excellence." This is broader than "morality" as we now commonly understand it. It allows for a distinction between intellectual virtues and virtues of character (*EE* 1221b28–31).[2] The former pertains to theoretical and scientific inquiry: theoretical wisdom (*sophia*), scientific knowledge (*epistêmê*), intuitive understanding (*noûs*), practical wisdom (*phronêsis*), and technical expertise (*technê*) (e.g., *NE* 1112a31–1112b10; *APo.* I.2, 71b9–23; *Met.* 981a5–15). Virtues of character, by contrast, are traits that predispose one to think, feel, and behave in a virtuous way. They include courage, temperance, generosity, honesty, humility, justice, wit, among others. Some of these, such as justice, might be called "moral" virtues as they seem to pertain to the domain of the moral as we construe it today; others, such as wit, seem distinctly nonmoral in nature. Aristotle, however, did not distinguish between moral and nonmoral virtues of character. Instead, all virtues of character for him are excellences that ought to be cultivated in a good life. They include industriousness, humor, confidence, and flexibility. Therefore, when Aristotle said that in a friendship of virtue, friends help each other become better people, he meant it in this broader sense, and not in the narrow moral sense in which some modern thinkers understand virtue (see e.g., Sherman 1993; Badhwar and Jones 2017; Helm 2017a).

Let us now turn to the motivational and affective features that neo-Aristotelians commonly associate with true friendship. These are mutual admiration for character, mutual love, shared life, role modeling, and mutual criticism. We consider each of these in turn.

Mutual admiration of character: True friends admire and respect one another on account of their virtuous character traits (Telfer 1970–71; Whiting 1991; Dawson 2012; Zagzebski 2015; Hoyos-Valdés 2018). The relevant sense of "respect" here is what Stephen Darwall has called "appraisal respect." This contrasts with "recognition respect," which is the kind of unconditional Kantian respect owed to all persons, regarded as autonomous rational agents possessing inherent worth or "dignity" (Darwall 1977).

Appraisal respect is so called because it involves a positive appraisal of a person for her excellence of character; typical examples are courage, honesty, temperance, fairness, kindness, and generosity, among many others; but they can also consist in excellence in what we would regard as nonmoral qualities and skills such as musical talent, teaching, parenting, or cooking. Even when a person excels in a particular pursuit, however, a person's engagement in that pursuit is not worthy of appraisal respect if they do so in a way that manifests a bad character: "If a player constantly heckles his opponent, disputes every close call to throw off his opponent's concentration, or laughs when his opponent misses shots, then even if his skill is such that he would be capable of beating everyone else without such tactics, he is not likely to be respected as a tennis player" (Darwall 1977, 42).

Similarly, on Aristotle's account of character friendship, the respect good friends have for each other is not typically inspired by the intellectual or athletic prowess of a person whose attitudes and behavior are otherwise despicable. The kind of positive appraisal each friend bestows is not typically inspired by their excellence in a narrowly specific pursuit, unless it is accompanied by excellence of character on the whole.

This characteristic of friendship seems to be broadly accepted in the contemporary philosophical literature on friendship. It would seem to imply (though we are not taking a position on this point) that a superior artist, athlete, or scientist who is also dishonest, mean-spirited, and malicious can have only sycophants but not true friends.

Disinterested mutual love. A second mark of true friendship found in neo-Aristotelian accounts is the unselfish, nonutilitarian love that grounds it (Annas 1977, 1988; Annis 1987; Badhwar 1987; Sherman 1987; Thomas 1987, 1989, 1990/1993; Whiting 1991; White 1999). Transactional relationships (e.g., with your hair stylist) are motivated by the expected utility of an agreed-upon exchange of services or goods;[3] freely chosen acquaintanceships are motivated by the joy each person derives from the other's (perhaps fleeting) company or by the other person's utility toward a goal. True character friendship, by contrast, is sustained by mutual love for the other person for their own sake (Aristotle *NE* 1155b31, 1156b9–10).

But what exactly does it mean to love someone for their own sake? As A.W. Price (1990: ch. 4) notes, offering a satisfactory answer to this question is probably one of the most elusive tasks faced by philosophical theory. In a much-discussed article, Michael Stocker (1976) offers some insight into this question. He invites us to imagine a case in which you are in the hospital when your friend, Alma, stops by to visit. You initially think she stopped by because she genuinely cares about you. But when you ask why she came, she replies: "I always try to fulfill my moral duties, and it's my moral duty as a friend to visit you." You are unlikely to be happy with this answer because Alma was motivated to visit you in the hospital by a commitment to fulfilling her moral duties, not by her concern about you for your own sake.

Stocker's overarching aim in his paper is to provide a knockdown objection to ethical theories across the board. Regardless of whether we agree with that conclusion, however, his argument is suggestive for what it tells us about caring about, or loving, another person for their own sake. If you love someone for their own sake, you have a desire to promote their interests. But the desire must not be instrumental, a mere means to some advantage—including the moral credit earned by fulfilling your duty.

Shared lives. The third characteristic concerns the way that character friends get involved in one another's lives. Most contemporary philosophers of friendship agree with Aristotle that true friends have a shared life (Telfer 1970–71; Thomas 1987; Annas 1988; Sherman 1993; Vallor 2012; Elder 2014; Alfano 2016; Hoyos-Valdés 2018). Having a shared life goes beyond simply spending time together. True friendship requires a pattern of interaction that reflects a "capacity to share and co-ordinate activities over an extended period of time" (Sherman 1993, 97). By sharing feelings, thoughts, and arguments with each other, true friends develop a shared conception of what constitutes a good life, which is manifested in a mutual commitment to specific virtuous ends rather than a joint conception of how to realize those ends. Friends who do not arrive at such a shared conception over time fail to become true friends. The convergence of virtuous ends over time is thus a test of true friendship (Aristotle *MM* 1237b17–18).

True friends continue to confirm their shared conception of what constitutes a good life by engaging in joint deliberation and decision making about practical matters. When making joint decisions about what to do, friends are jointly responsible for those decisions. Say you have been the target of workplace bullying and engage in joint deliberation with your best friend about how best to respond to the bully. If you and your friend jointly decide that you should report the person to the Human Resources department, then you and your friend are jointly responsible for this action, even though your friend didn't actually carry out the action (Sherman 1993, 98).

Another way that true friends enjoy a shared life is by taking part in each other's joys and sorrows, accomplishments and failures, as their own, even when they are not acting jointly. Thus, we feel pride when our friends act virtuously and shame when they act viciously, as if their actions were our own (Aristotle *Rh* 2.6 1385a1–3). Say your friend fails to manifest a good temper, for example, by acting with excessive anger in response to a minor slight. In that case, you are disposed to feel as ashamed as you would have been, if you had acted in this way, even though you are not responsible for their fit of anger.

Character improvement. While character friends possess good character traits, they are not perfect. Your friend may fail to pursue ends that are valuable in your eyes. Or she may have valuable ends but give in too frequently to temptation. True friends, however, are motivated by their mutual love for each to encourage each other to change unworthy goals and resist weakness of will. Loving another person for their own sake thus requires having a robust desire to promote their moral flourishing.

A true friend seeks to help her friend overcome weakness of will, remain "steadfast in virtue," and improve their moral disposition. This idea goes back to Plato's *Symposium*, where Phaedrus notes (admittedly in praise of erotic love rather than simple friendship) that a man "is especially ashamed before his lover when he is caught doing something shameful. If only there were a way to start a city or an army made up of lovers and the boys they love! Theirs would be the best possible system of society, for they would hold back from all that is shameful, and seek honor in each other's eyes" (Plato 1997, 178e–179a). True friends can help each other in at least two ways. One is by seeking to set a good example; the other is by serving as a critic (Volbrecht 1990; Sherman 1991, 1993, 1999; Jacquette 2001; Zagzebski 2017).

Emulation. True friends are, as Nancy Sherman puts it, "eminently suited as models to be emulated" (Sherman 1993, 105–6). This is not because true friends are necessarily of equal character. Since true friends need not be perfectly excellent, they are bound to have different strengths and weaknesses. They are models to be emulated only when performing acts that draw on their best character traits. While true friends need not be equal in character to serve as role models for each other, they must not be significantly unequal in power. If they are, the "modeling" risks being grounded in intimidation or constraint.

True friends should furthermore roughly be in agreement about what constitutes a good life. This does not mean that they must be committed to pursuing the same life goals; one can imagine a friendship between a scholar and an athlete, or between a businessman and an artist. But only on the condition that each respects the other's ambitions, even when they do not share them. Many virtues of character cut across vastly different domains of activity. Think of perseverance, for example, sound judgment, or integrity. Or even honor, which can reign, so it is said, even among thieves. Once again, then, the virtues of character that matter most to friendship are of a sort that are not specific to any single activity or pursuit. They can, therefore, provide models for emulation even among friends whose life goals and central preoccupations might remain widely different.

Moral criticism. A second way that true friends can help each other remain "steadfast in virtue" in the face of temptation and improve each other's moral judgment and character is by serving as diligent moral critics, shaming, persuading, or physically preventing each other from giving into weakness of will or pursuing unworthy goals (Whiting 2001; Hoyos-Valdés 2018; Kristjánsson 2000). Thus, contrary to common wisdom, friends should not uncritically accept their friends' flaws or enable their flawed ways the way a person in a codependent relationship enables the other person's shortcomings. As Kristján Kristjánsson puts it:

> The notion of a "critical friend" is paramount here—with the friend being not only a supporter but also a challenger . . . [A]ny constructive dialogue between equal character friends about how to deal with life's exigencies will involve critical engagement with the friend's point of view . . . To accept, unquestioningly, the friend's character flaws, without trying to correct them, is not a sign of true character friendship but rather its opposite: an attitude that in today's academic parlance would probably best be referred to as unhealthy "codependency." (Kristjánsson 2020, 358–359)

True friends are thus expected to encourage each other to act virtuously by means of criticism. Aristotle notes that "it is both a most difficult thing . . . to attain a knowledge of oneself"; hence, just as "when we wish to see our own face, we do so by looking into the mirror, in the same way when we wish to know ourselves we can obtain that knowledge by looking at our friend. For the friend is, as we assert, a second self" (Aristotle *MM* 1213a26). Friends hold a mirror to one another to reveal each other's virtues and vices. This is the way in which they can serve as moral critics for one another, as well as admirers of each other's virtue. It is negative as well as positive feedback that helps facilitate personal growth.

ARISTOTLE'S FRIENDSHIP LOVE IS TOO DISINTERESTED

In this and the subsequent sections, we delve into some problems that arise from two of the neo-Aristotelian marks of friendship we have outlined, viz. the characterization of friendship love and the moralistic demand for character improvement. We begin by voicing our skepticism about the idea of a disinterested form of friendship love—a kind of love whose central aim is to benefit the beloved.

In loving a friend, Aristotle argues, "we say we ought to wish what is good for his sake," rather than for what it can bring to oneself (Aristotle *NE* 1155b31; 1156b9–10). Hence, loving someone may require you to sacrifice your own interests for the sake of the beloved. Corinne Gartner (2017) mentions Aristotle's example of a mother who gives away her child, because doing so is in the child's best interest. By doing so, she is sacrificing her own deep interest in being part of the child's life. But she acts as she does because she is moved by her love of her child, not her own interests.

This conception of love as selfless and disinterested runs thick in the veins of contemporary philosophy (LaFollette 1996; Frankfurt 1999, 2004; White 2001). Also known as the "robust concern view" (Helm 2010, 2017b),[4] the contemporary version of Aristotle's view holds that loving someone requires being sufficiently motivated to promote the other's interests for her own sake (Lafollette 1996; Frankfurt 1999, 2004; Badhwar 2003; Abramson & Leite 2011, 2018; Rorty 2016). As Harry Frankfurt puts it:

> What is essential to the lover's concern for his beloved is not only that it must be free of any self-regarding motive but that it must have no ulterior aim whatsoever. To characterize love as merely selfless, then, is not enough. Although the term "disinterested" is—from the point of view of rhetoric—a bit misleading in its tone and associations, it has the virtue of conveying the irrelevance to love not just of considerations that are self-regarding but of all considerations that are distinct from the interests of the beloved. (Frankfurt, 1999, 167–168)

By construing the goal of love as the promotion of the beloved's interests for her sake, the robust concern view forestalls the objection that the beloved plays a merely instrumental role in the lover's pursuit of their own interest. But the robust concern view is still open to the complaint that it is excessively goal-oriented, and thus distorts the nature of love's concern. David Velleman has been especially forceful in pressing this objection. He has suggested that "love is essentially an attitude toward the beloved himself but not toward any result at all" (Velleman 1999, 354). Indeed, he quips that a lover excessively preoccupied with promoting his beloved's interests "would be an interfering, ingratiating nightmare" (353).

Without going quite so far, we agree that a lover's adoption of the beloved's goals and interests must be limited, lest it gives rise to an "altruists' dilemma": if each friend wants only to benefit the other, they are as likely to hit an impasse as if they are both perfectly selfish (de Sousa 2015, 42). Concern for the friend's intrinsic good is only a consequence of love rather than its defining feature. We can at least agree with Velleman that it is no betrayal of love if "[a]t the thought of a close friend, my heart doesn't fill with an urge to do something for him, though it may indeed fill with love" (Velleman 1999, 353). The first limitation of the "robust concern" view, then, is that it exaggerates the importance of a friend's adoption of their friend's interests and goals.

There is a further objection to the robust concern view that cuts deeper. Unlike parental love of a child (Ferracioli 2014), friendship love tends to elicit desires for reciprocity and emotional intimacy (Wallace 2012; Wonderly 2017; McKeever 2019; Pismenny 2021). In this respect, it is similar to romantic love. As Natasha McKeever observes, "the romantic lover is not usually content to love her beloved from afar; she wants to be loved back and she wants to be near her beloved" (McKeever 2019, 213). This is no less true of friendship love, and it is part of what it means to say that friends have a shared life. While we do not tend to treat our friends as *mere* means to the satisfaction of our own ends, our true friends normally play a role in fulfilling our desire for love. That benefits us, and so in some obvious sense friendship love plays an instrumental role, even though the value of the friend exceeds her instrumental value. In fact, one reason we strive for the kinds of friendships that nurture friendship love is that they help advance our overall flourishing. If so, then friendship love is not, after all, selfless and disinterested in the sense envisioned by some advocates of the robust concern view. That view's insistence that love be disinterested and selfless is an unwarranted constraint on true friendship.

In short, loving a friend for their own sake is a necessary condition for enjoying the goods of the friendship. But this is true whether or not the friends also have instrumental value. There is no need to renounce friendship's instrumental role. In the next section, we explore some of the reasons to reject the neo-Aristotelian teleological and moralistic approach to true friendship.

THE NOTION OF CHARACTER
FRIENDSHIP IS TOO MORALISTIC

A second issue with neo-Aristotelian accounts of true friendship is that they take on board the idea that the goal of friendship is to facilitate the development of virtues and personal growth (Sherman 1987; Badhwar & Jones 2017). As noted earlier, this goal is supposed to be filled by friends' mutual endeavor to be each other's role models and critics. The initial attraction and appreciation of each other's virtues are supposed to lie at the core of this joint project. For although Aristotle's character friends are not perfectly virtuous, the foundation of their friendship and the focus on each friend's positive character traits uniquely situate them to help each other become more virtuous individuals.

This functional view envisages three benefits of Aristotle's character friendships: first, they enrich an individual's life by providing the possibility for deep and meaningful connections (Annis 1987); second, they promote the development of a virtuous character, which is regarded as an integral part of a good life; and third, valuing and pursuing friendship for its own sake manifests the kinds of values that a virtuous person would have (Cooper 1977).

But why should we regard promoting virtuous character development as a necessary feature of true friendship? Aristotle's own answer follows from his teleological conception of friendship as a constituent of a good life, construed as a pursuit of perfect virtue. However, there are good reasons to resist his view. As we will see, true friendship does not require friends to be each other's moral critics or models. No doubt, friends influence one another in a number of ways including moral ones. Yet, as will be clear, this influence can be for the worse as well as for the better. True friendship, we argue, is not necessarily negated by such corruption. Furthermore, although true friends admire one another in some respects, they do not necessarily do so for the reasons that Aristotle had in mind, viz. the truly virtuous character traits. Instead, friends might admire, or even idealize, one another due to the partiality of their relationship.

One problem with the teleological approach is that it paints an overly moralistic picture of true friendship, lacking any grounding in reality. For starters, it is clearly unrealistic to expect that true friendships must begin with mutual admiration of each other's virtuous character. Even if mutual esteem for character were always to characterize true friendships, they could surely arise in less high-minded ways. Friendships often develop between colleagues, or as a gradual elaboration of what begins in what Aristotle calls (somewhat pejoratively) "friendships of pleasure" or "friendships of interest" (Aristotle *NE* 1209b30). But even the deepest of ordinary friendships rarely aim at mutual character improvement, despite making significant contributions to the value of each friend's life.

This point may seem too obvious to mention. But it in fact goes against the grain of much of the philosophical literature on love and friendship, which rarely aim at defining what they are, but rather concentrate on what they ought to be (e.g., Velleman 1999; Kolodny 2003). We deem it more useful to look at the reality of actual true friendships and explore the negative as well as the positive that derive from their nature. But our concern here is not primarily methodological; so we shall not dwell on the moralism of philosophers' attempts to define "friendship." Rather we now want to focus on the moralistic attitude such accounts prescribe for the friends themselves.

One obvious observation that springs to mind is that the attempt one friend makes to improve the other friend's moral character might be resented. This point was noted by Immanuel Kant, according to a discussion of his views on friendship by H.J. Paton. While Kant generally endorses the mutual improvement view of friendship's function, Paton writes, he is also aware of its perils:

> Morally speaking it is the duty of a friend to call attention to the other's faults;
> for this is in his best interests and so is a duty of love. Unfortunately the friend
> thus favoured may take a different view. He may think he is being treated with
> a lack of respect; that this scrutiny and criticism may mean he has already lost
> the esteem of his friend or is about to lose it; or even that to be thus scrutinized
> and admonished is an insult in itself. Kant leaves the problem at that. (Paton
> 1993, 141)

Individuals may differ in how touchy they are when receiving criticism from a friend. The available space where a balance between support and criticism can be sustained will differ from case to case. Moreover, the very capacity to accept and benefit from the friend's criticism may itself be one of the character traits that will help cement a true friendship. Nevertheless, this is a fine line that is easily crossed: When a friend claims to identify some moral defect or impropriety of their friend's behavior, the targeted friend may be equally likely, whether on the basis self-deception or on the contrary of equally sound insight, to blame the critical friend's standards as inappropriate. This could often be plausibly adduced on the basis of the fact that—even on a neo-Aristotelian model of friendship—even the most worthy friends are not perfectly virtuous. A priori, between any two inevitably imperfect friends, either might be in the wrong, and a resulting disagreement could undermine the quality of the very friendship itself.

Once we admit that even the nicest friends are flawed, a graver problem looms for the neo-Aristotelian position. This stems from the fact that if each emulates the other, friends are as likely to lead each other astray as to straighten each other out. Or at the very least, only slightly less likely. For we can admit that in some cases, improvement is more likely than corruption. These would be cases where both friends are of fundamentally good character (which the neo-Aristotelian view we have been surveying seems to assume is in any case a precondition of friendship), *and* where, in addition, both agree comprehensively on both core values and current priorities. Under those conditions, mutual influence may be called upon only to minimize each other's episodes of weakness of will or *akrasia*—cases where we succumb to desires against our better judgment. When in the grip of weakness of will, we often prioritize purely selfish pleasure over promoting other people's interests; and friends who share, or at least know and respect, one another's core values are in a good position to help one another overcome *akrasia*. But cases that satisfy these conditions are unlikely to be the most common.

If we do not assume that friends influence one another only in the direction of moral improvement, we can see how both of the mechanisms that were supposed to be enlisted for such moral growth—emulation and criticism—could work against it. Consider an example from a recent television serial. In an episode of *Ginny and Georgia,* a young girl, eager for acceptance at the school she has just enrolled in is taken shopping by members of the clique she hopes to join. She sees her new friends discreetly pocketing various items, and one of them gestures to her to do the same. When she alone is caught, she explains her action by saying: "I wanted them to like me." In this vignette, both emulation and (all but explicit) potential criticism ("Surely you don't want to be a chicken!") are mechanisms of influence that result in the corruption of a friend.

It may be objected that in this story the girls involved are not yet friends. Ginny wants to be regarded as a friend, so her compliance is instrumental. But as a friendship solidifies, the increasing bond of commitment will increase rather than diminish the strength of the friends' influence on one another. We have agreed that the good of friendship lies, in part, in its capacity to motivate a relatively selfless concern for the other's goals and needs, even while we have rejected the unrealistically moralistic idea that such motivation must inevitably be in a morally commendable direction. But given that amendment, this obviously provides for the possibility that your concern for your friend may move you to do things you would otherwise deem to be wrong. To the extent that friendship fosters a certain selflessness, it affords opportunities for motivating immoral behavior.

To further illustrate this, consider the case from the 1990 film *Death in Brunswick* discussed extensively by Dean Cocking and Jeanette Kennett

(2000). In that movie, Dave helps Carl, who accidentally killed Mustapha, hide the body. "As the joke has it, a friend will help you move house, a good friend will help you move a body" (Cocking & Kennett 2000, 278).

As Cocking and Kennett recognize, this might simply be viewed as a moral dilemma resulting from the plurality of values. Standard, public morality demands that Dave encourage Carl to turn himself in; but friendship's demand is also a moral one: "Dave's helping action may have realized one kind of moral good but failed to realize some other values that might also justifiably have guided his choice" (282). They argue, however, that "a large part of the moral good of friendship need not be expressive of any particular *moral* interest at all" (284).[5]

They stress, in particular, that among the goods of friendship is the special way that friends *direct* and *interpret* one another.[6] In doing so, they do not merely influence the friend's behavior but have a part in the constitution of their identity. That is, at least in part, what it means for a friendship to be a true friendship. As a friend, I will be more inclined to follow your advice, based as it is likely to be on your knowledge of my preferences. On the same basis, I will be more likely to take your interpretations of my behavior seriously. Both of these functions, however, are only contingently related to morality. When they conflict with morality, the fact that my decision may have been determined by my friend's guidance and interpretation does not carry any moral weight of its own. "Indeed, a good friendship might well include a focus on certain vices . . . I am just as likely to be directed by your interest in gambling at the casino as by your interest in ballet" (286).

The central point illustrated by the Carl and Dave story is that some of the features of true friendship that define both what is essential and what is good about it are the very features that threaten morality—in both its broad and narrow senses.

A MINIMAL ACCOUNT OF TRUE FRIENDSHIP

We thus reject the neo-Aristotelian conception of true friendship as a kind of character friendship. As we have seen, this construal of true friendship is too moralistic and involves a notion of robust concern that is unsustainable.

In this section, we propose an alternative minimal account of true friendship as a friendship that satisfies four constraints, or virtues of friendship, which we will call closeness, emotional intimacy, trust, and friendship identity. Let's consider each in turn, starting with closeness.

Closeness. True friendships do seem to involve something like a mutual desire to promote the other's interests. To distinguish this pro-attitude from a robust concern in Frankfurt's disinterested sense, let's call it "closeness" (Brogaard 2020, ch. 2, 2021).

Assuming that we can make sense of an objective notion of interest, we therefore need to understand a friend's concern as pertaining to a person's objective interests and overall prosperity, rather than reflecting their experienced desires. This is not merely because promoting your overall well-being sometimes requires you to endure or perform something unpleasant. It is also because we commonly lack insight into what our own interests are, let alone those of our friends: although objective interests will be closely associated with our well-being, they cannot be assumed to coincide with what we experience subjectively as such.

Since we are operating with an objective notion of interest, we may not know what our own interests are, let alone our friends'. We should therefore understand closeness as requiring one to try and ascertain what one's friends' objective interests are in order to promote whatever these turn out to be. Of course, in the context of true friendship, closeness is reciprocal, so for Tyrone and Cosmo to have a close friendship, they must possess mutual desires to ascertain and promote each other's interests. This provides a preliminary characterization of (one crucial element of) a notion of "closeness" that is compatible with our general ignorance of our friends' interests and even (to some extent) our own.

Despite our reservations about the centrality of "robust concern" in Frankfurt's disinterested sense, we have not followed Velleman in denying that true friends need to care about one another's interests. It is important to acknowledge, however, that caring about each other's interests cannot simply be a matter of being guided by either friend's desires. First, as just noted, the beneficiary may be mistaken about their own interests. Second, very weak desires to promote each other's interests are too easily overridden by stronger desires to do something else. As very weak desires too rarely result in any actual attempts to promote the other's interests, they do not suffice for closeness. Third, we sometimes have desires owing to coercion. For example, you and your enemy could harbor a mutual desire to promote each other's interests as a result of coercion by a third party who is holding a gun to your head. As you do not want to die, you both have a strong desire to promote each other's interests. In the envisaged case, your desires to promote each other's interests are wholly induced by your desires to stay alive. Absent this coercive element, you may well desire to thwart each other's interests. So, your desires clearly don't suffice for closeness.

Our proposal is that the convergence of two people's desires can count as manifesting friendship only if the desires spring from values that determine each person's identity (Brogaard 2021). To account for these kinds of values, we will adopt a valuational account of a person's (real) self, or identity

(Doris 2015). Valuational (or attributional) accounts of agency (as opposed to identity) hold that an action manifests your agency just in case you value that action (Watson 1996).[7] Agency, however, should be kept apart from identity. If you choose sweet potato fries over potato wedges, because you value sweet potato fries more than potato wedges, then your choice expresses your agency. But sweet potato fries presumably are not something you really identify with.

To eliminate trivial values that are unimportant to our identity, we propose to exploit the notion of a core value (for the notion of a core value, see Brogaard 2020, ch. 2). Our core values are those values that matter to who we are. Our core values are partly constitutive of our selves. You assert your self when you perform an action that is an expression of your core values.

John Doris (2015) proposes *irreplaceability* as a criterion for picking out the kinds of values that matter to our selves as opposed to those that matter to our agency but not our selves: "if the object of desiring can be replaced without loss—if life can go on pretty much as it did—then that object is not an object of value" (Doris 2015, 38). Although Doris does not deploy the notion of a core value, the non-fungibility requirement seems well adapted to set such values apart from anything that is merely hard to resist or a convenient way of satisfying some general need. Accordingly, we propose that the desires constitutive of closeness are grounded in matching core values.

Our rendition of closeness allows for the occasional bout of weakness of will (*akrasia*). Weakness of will are cases where we succumb to desires against our better judgment. When in the grip of weakness of will, we often prioritize purely selfish pleasure over promoting other people's interests. The occasional bout of weakness of will does not compromise closeness, because a friendship can be close without being perfectly close. Unlike pregnancies and electoral wins, closeness is not an on-or-off matter. It comes in degrees. This is witnessed by expressions such as "You are closer with Cosmo than Tyrone," "They are my closest friend," "Our friendship is closer now than it ever was." "Close" is thus a gradable adjective, as are "kind," "pretty," "generous," and "trustworthy."

But what exactly does it mean for one friendship to be closer than another? To say that you are closer with Cosmo than Tyrone is not to say that you desire to promote a higher quantity of Cosmo's interests than Tyrone's interests, because even though you are closer with Cosmo than with Tyrone, your closeness with Tyrone entails that you want to promote his interests. Nor does it mean that you desire to promote Cosmo's interests with more fervor than Tyrone's interests, because the felt intensity of desires can vary for reasons that have no bearing on closeness, and standing desires (as opposed to occurrent desires, which may sometimes be mere whims) do not have any felt intensity at all. Rather, to say that you are closer with Cosmo than with

Tyrone is to say that your desire to promote Cosmo's interests ranks higher in your hierarchy of desires than your desire to promote Tyrone's interests.

Emotional intimacy. Another constraint on true friendship is emotional intimacy. It is widely agreed among relationship researchers that emotional intimacy requires sharing sensitive (or "private") information—information of the kind that can make us vulnerable to betrayal, denigration, belligerence, or exploitation by the person we confide in or by people they entrust with the information (Nussbaum 1986: 165–199; Thomas 1987, 1989, 1990/1993, 2013; Flynn 2007; Helm 2017a; Velleman 1999; Brogaard 2020, ch. 2).[8] But it is hard to nail down precisely what counts as the sharing of sensitive information—the kind of information that can make you vulnerable. It is clearly not just about revealing information about your past that you are ashamed of. Nor is it even just verbally conveyed information. It could also be what you look like naked, what you smell like the morning after you went on a crazy booze-filled bender, or what you sound like when singing "I'm a Barbie girl in a Barbie world" in the shower.

To be sure, there are limits to what sorts of information we are willing to share with friends. Empirical data have shown that we sometimes avoid sharing information with friends because we think our friends would consider it "taboo" or start seeing us in a different light (Afifi and Guerrero 1998). We sometimes avoid disclosing private information to close friends because we have a strong need for psychological privacy and autonomy. We also sometimes fear that information disclosed to friends might reach a broader audience. Even when the risk is minuscule, it may not always be one we are willing to take. Nonetheless, Laurence Thomas is surely correct when he observes that a complete unwillingness to share private information is incompatible with true friendship: "The bond of trust between deep friends is cemented by the equal self-disclosure of intimate information" (Thomas 1987, 223).

"Intimate," like "close," is a gradable adjective, which means that some true friendships are more intimate than others, and that one and the same friendship can fluctuate in intimacy. But friendships need not be perfectly intimate to count as intimate as long as they surpass a contextually determined threshold. Gradable concepts of this kind often do not admit of a concrete, specifiable maximum.

Trust. Sharing deeply personal information with each other is the primary means by which true friends convey that they trust each other. But trust of a friend also involves being open to that friend's direction and interpretation. Trust involves both epistemic and emotional aspects: we trust our friends to tell us the truth, and we trust them to do well by us.

There is a sense in which all trust is restricted. This is because trust has a dual focus: one is the trustee's goodwill and truthfulness toward the truster.

The other is the trustee's competence as engaged in the specific pursuit (Brogaard, 2020: ch. 2). You may fail to trust a friend on certain occasions, owing to their lack of competence as engaged in a specific pursuit. For example, you may trust your plumber friend in matters regarding plumbing but not in matters regarding babysitting. But this needn't be because you think your plumber friend doesn't have your and your child's best interests in mind; you may simply distrust your plumber friend as a babysitter because you don't regard her as a competent babysitter.

Like closeness and intimacy, trust is a matter of degree. Trust thus accommodates betrayals of the trustee that are both infrequent and minute. In other words, your trust in a friend's goodwill toward you needn't be unconditional; it only needs to surpass a certain contextually determined threshold.

Friendship identity. When friends share ideas, feelings, and thoughts, including private information, they shape each other's self, or identity. True friendship thus leads to a partially shared, or joint, identity—a special friendship identity (Schoeman 1985; Helm 2008, 2010). That special identity entails changes in each friend, insofar as each of their lives is affected by the friend's specific moral character as well as by the nature of the friends' interaction. But it also results in the constitution of an identity for the friendship itself. One of your friendships might be different from all your other friendships in that you and A are each other's favorite skiing companions; with B, what is special is that you play music together.

True friendships promote collaborative constructions of an identity in each of the friends individually and the friendship that unites them. These identities are especially due to the ways in which friends are expected to guide and interpret one another; in effect, we might call these secularized diversions of the expectation of emulation and criticism, shorn of their moralistic dimension.

However, friendship that results in one friend becoming a mirror of the other is not a true friendship, because it fails to respect each friend's separate identity and autonomous agency. The convergence of two friend's identities to form a unique friendship identity must respect the core values that determine each person's independent identity.

VICES OF FRIENDSHIP

Closeness, emotional intimacy, trust, and friendship identity are paramount to true friendships. They nonetheless each have a dark side. Or so we will argue. What follows does not attempt to pin the faults we find too finely on each of these specific aspects of friendship, though we focus primarily on the perils of trust and closeness.

One of the problems most often noted about trust is that it is exceedingly difficult to determine exactly when it is warranted, and that to trust is to be vulnerable. "Trust is important, but it is also dangerous" (McLeod 2020). The greater your trust, the greater the harm you are likely to suffer if the trust is betrayed. Trust is an essential precondition of friends' ability for sharing intimate information, and as we noted earlier, the hesitation one might feel before trusting a friend with such information reflects the risks involved. But the riskiness of trust and the difficulty of justifying it are not problems that specifically pertain to friendship. What lurks in the very benefit that trust brings to friends is the potential for undermining autonomy.

One version of this problem was already embodied in the story of Carl and Dave: one way in which Dave might be motivated to deceive himself into thinking that there could be nothing wrong with Carl's request is for him to rely on his previous assumption that Carl is a man of good judgment and sound principles, someone who could not be asking him to do something seriously immoral. A more trivial story is told of one spouse upgrading another when crossing the street: "You never look before crossing the street! What happens when I'm not there to look out for you?" And the answer comes: "When you're not there, I look." Fair enough when it is about crossing the street. But one can well imagine cases where the trust accorded to a friend amounts to a sort of permanent delegation of authority over a more complex domain of deliberation resulting in a certain dereliction of responsible agency. One notorious example that might be cited is a relationship between Bertrand Russell and Ralph Schoenman. In that relationship one seems to see that the trust Russell had in Schoenman gradually led to a certain uncertainty in Russell's own mind about where his own positions lay; although in that case the discrepancy in their ages clearly contributed to the widening rift that Russell appears to have taken far too long to notice.

Conflicts may also arise between closeness and the autonomy constraint on friendship identity. Recall that the convergence of two people's values can count as manifesting a friendship identity only if those values are tied to the core values that determine each person's identity. This is so even when those core values are stripped of the requirement that they count only if they are morally sound. Yet, closeness requires being motivated to act in the friend's best interest. So, a true friendship can commit a friend to be motivated to act in ways that run counter to their own core values. It might well be (though we will not undertake to defend this point here) that it is in Carl's best interest that Dave helps him get rid of the body. In that case, the closeness of their friendship obligates Dave to help Carl get rid of Mustapha's body, even if Dave thinks doing so is morally unjustified, because of the harm inflicted on Mustapha's wife and son. Closeness can thus compel us to jettison our true selves, which runs counter to the demands of the identity constraint.

Further issues arise with regard to the core values that ground the closeness constraint. Owing to self-ignorance, we are not always aware of our own core values. But if we do not know whether it is a core value of ours to promote another person's interests, then we lack knowledge of whether our true friendship with them demands that we act on our desire to promote their interests. Doris argues that collaborative deliberation may help us better identify our values (Doris 2015). But collaborative deliberation involves moral dangers of its own. Suppose Dave and Carl embark on collaborative deliberation about whether Dave's desire to help Carl move the body is grounded in Dave's core values. Given how much hinges on Dave helping Carl, they may well reason that because Carl is Dave's close friend, Dave's desire to help Carl must be anchored in Dave's core values. Reflecting on *Death in Brunswick*, Daniel Koltonski (2016) goes as far as to argue that if, after collaboratively deliberating on what to do, Dave and Carl reach an impasse, respect for Carl's autonomous agency requires Dave to defer to Carl's judgment. Rather than unearthing our most important values, collaborative deliberation can thus result in our valuing, and identifying with, actions we originally rejected as immoral.

Additionally, the very assumption that there are such things as core values could be problematic because given the criterion of non-fungibility, it might inhibit a significant, positive change that people might otherwise be capable of making in their own lives. One indication of this might be the finding that people who lose the love of their life are surprisingly resilient; widows (but not so much widowers, for reasons that are interesting but beyond the scope of this chapter) often recover from their initial grief to the point that they report feeling that they are getting a new lease on life (Moller 2007). A widow may have a desire to find a new life partner. But she may suppress this desire because she believes—however irrationally—that doing so would show that her deceased life partner was replaceable by a new life partner and hence that her closeness to her late partner was not a core value after all. So, the widow's belief that her core values concern her deceased partner and not a potential new love could end up inhibiting her overall flourishing. On the broad Aristotelian notion of morality, suppressing her desire to find a new life partner and find happiness again would not be a moral or virtuous thing to do.

There are other moral dangers as well. When two people are close, they can attain an understanding of their identity only in the context of a kind of collaborative mutual discovery. But this presents a further danger, as there is no guarantee that this discovery will not be something more like a *folie à deux*, "enabling," or codependency. Many ordinary romantic relationships and friendships are plagued by codependency. But as an extreme example, consider Charles Manson and his California quasi-commune, formed in 1967. Regardless of the precise details of the real case, we can grant, for argument's

sake, that Manson's friendships and love relationships with his follow-
ers were characterized by mutual closeness, emotional intimacy, trust, and
friendship identity; yet, Manson's mesmerizing, almost hypnotic, personality
and the codependency of the friendships he maintained with the people in his
quasi-commune undermined, rather than clarified, each friend's attempt to
elaborate and understand their own identity.

More generally, the closeness, intimacy, trust, and identity constraints on
true friendship must necessarily contrast with the distance that separates the
cluster of true friends from those that are outside it. And that may lead to
the cluster becoming a clique and undermining each true friend's capacity to
evaluate the qualities and opinions of those who are less close—but might be
no less wise. Thus, the very benefit of true friendship that consists in closeness, intimacy, trust, and identity may insulate us from certain experiences
that might enlarge our core values and enrich our experience of life. Therein
lie the vices of true friendship.

CONCLUSION

We have explored in this chapter some important ways in which the neo-
Aristotelian conception of "friendships of character" might be misrepre-
senting the essential nature of true friendship. We first expounded some
reasons to qualify the widely held requirement that friendship entail love of
the friend "for their own sake." We then showed that the effort to represent
friendship as an inherently moral good, while uncontroversial in itself, has
led many thinkers wrongly to suppose that "true" friendship must inevitably
strive for moral improvement, through both mutual emulation and mutual
admonition. We have argued that on the contrary, there are some inherent
potential conflicts between the requirements of morality as generally understood and the duties and expectations of friendship. These conflicts, we
suggested—following Cocking and Kennett (2000)—cannot be mitigated by
pretending that we can harmonize the demands of friendship with morality
overall. In addition, we have suggested that in some other, more subtle ways,
the very good of friendship relies on certain characteristics which have their
own dark side. The trust, closeness, identity, and emotional intimacy that are
constitutive of true friendship sometimes tend to undermine not only morality in general but even the very benefits for which true friendship itself is
rightly prized.

Acknowledgements: We are grateful to Marriah Alcantara, Ronald de
Sousa, Janelle Gormley, and Alan Soble for their extremely helpful comments and suggestions on an earlier version of this chapter.

NOTES

1. We use "true" as a modifier, not to indicate that friends must be morally good, but rather as a tool for disambiguating "friend" and "friendship," therefore, leaving out the shallower senses of "friend" and "friendship" (e.g., "Facebook friend"). We take modifiers like "good," "genuine," and "real" to serve the same end. Thanks to Alan Soble for pressing us on this.

2. *EE = Eudemian Ethics*; *NE = Nicomachean Ethics*; *Met. = Metaphysics*; *APo. = Posterior Analytics*; *MM = Magna Moralia*; *Rh = Rhetoric*. All Aristotle references are based on the English translation of his complete works in Barnes (1984).

3. *Philia* and its verb form *philein* refer to love in a generic sense that includes not only friendship love but also familial and parental love. Aristotle uses *philia* even more broadly, to refer to kinds of human relationships for which we would not now use the word "friendship," such as that between a carpenter and a customer or that between a father and his newborn baby.

4. We have adopted this handy term which Helm seems to have coined to refer to views of a number of authors, none of which actually use it. Thanks to Alan Soble for pointing this out.

5. Cocking and Kennett (2000) thus deny that all special relationship duties and values are *moral* duties and values as opposed to, say, *sui generis* duties grounded in the relationship itself (cf., Wallace 2012; Pismenny 2021; Brogaard 2021).

6. See also Brunning (this volume) on what he calls "fashioning."

7. A distinction should here be drawn between causal agency and valuational agency. An agent S exercises causal agency with respect to E just in case S forms a belief/desire pair, or an intention, that is the non-deviant cause of E. Here, "agency" refers to valuational agency.

8. Velleman (1999) argues for the key role of emotional intimacy in love rather than friendship per se.

REFERENCES

Abramson, K., & Leite, A. (2011). Love as a reactive emotion. *Philosophical Quarterly*, 61(245): 673–699.

Abramson, K., & Leite, A. (2018). Love, value, and reasons. In Grau, C. & Smuts, A. (eds.), *The Oxford handbook of philosophy of love*. Oxford University Press.

Afifi, W. A., & Guerrero, L. K. (1998). Some things are better left unsaid II: Topic avoidance in friendships. *Communication Quarterly*, 46(3): 231–249.

Alfano, M. (2016). Friendship and the structure of trust. In A. Masala & J. Webber (eds.), *From Personality to Virtue*. Oxford University Press, pp. 186–206.

Annas, J. (1977). Plato and Aristotle on friendship and altruism. *Mind*, 86(344): 532–54.

Annas, J. (1988). Self-love in Aristotle. *Southern Journal of Philosophy*, 7(1), 1–18.

Annis, D. (1987). The meaning, value, and duties of friendship. *Philosophy and Philosophical Research*, 24(4), 349–356.

Badhwar, N. K. (1987). Friends as ends in themselves. *Philosophy & Phenomenological Research*, 48(1), 1–23.

Badhwar, N. K. (1991). Why it's wrong to be always guided by the best: Friendship and consequentialism. *Ethics*, 101(3), 483–504.

Badhwar, N. K. (Ed.). (1993). *Friendship: A philosophical reader*. Ithaca, NY: Cornell University Press.

Badhwar, N. K. (2003). Love. In LaFollette, H. (ed.), *The Oxford Handbook of Practical Ethics*. Oxford: Oxford University Press, pp. 42–69.

Badhwar, N. K., & Jones, R. (2017). Aristotle on the love of friends. In C. Grau & A. Smuts (eds), *The Oxford Handbook of Philosophy of Love*. New York: Oxford University Press. doi: DOI: 10.1093/oxfordhb/9780199395729.013

Baier, A. C. (1995). Trust and anti-trust. In A. C. Baier (ed.), *Moral prejudices: Essays on ethics* (pp. 125–130). Cambridge: Harvard University Press.

Barnes, J. (Ed.). (1984). *The complete works of Aristotle* [Revised Oxford translation] (Vol. 2). Bollingen Series, vol. 72. Princeton: Princeton University Press.

Brogaard, B. (2020). *Hatred: Understanding our most dangerous emotion*. New York: Oxford University Press.

Brogaard, B. (2021). Practical identity and duties of love. Disputatio Lectures 2018. *Disputatio*, May 2021, 60.

Cocking, D., & Kennett, J. (2000). Friendship and moral danger. *Journal of Philosophy*, 97(5), 278–296.

Cooper, J. (1977). Aristotle and the forms of friendship. *The Review of Metaphysics*, 30(4), 619–648.

Darwall, S. L. (1977). Two kinds of respect. *Journal of Philosophy*, 88(1), 36–49.

Dawson, R. (2012). Is Aristotle right about friendship? *Praxis*, 3(2):1–16.

de Sousa, R. (2015). *Love: A very short introduction*. Oxford: Oxford University Press.

Doris, J. (2015). *Talking to our selves: Reflection, ignorance, and agency*. Oxford: Oxford University Press.

Elder, A. (2014). Excellent online friendships: An Aristotelian defense of social media. *Ethics and Information Technology*, 16(4), 287–297.

Ferracioli, L. (2014). The state's duty to ensure children are loved. *Journal of Ethics and Social Philosophy*, 8(2), 1–19.

Flynn, P. C. (2007). Honesty and intimacy in Kant's duty of friendship. *International Philosophical Quarterly*, 47(4). 417–424.

Frankfurt, H. G. (1999). On caring. In *necessity, volition, and love* (pp. 155–180). Cambridge, New York: Cambridge University Press.

Frankfurt, H. G. (2004). *The reasons of love*. Princeton: Princeton University Press.

Gartner, C. (2017). Aristotle on love and friendship. In C. Bobonich (ed.), *The Cambridge companion to ancient ethics*. Cambridge, UK: Cambridge University Press, pp. 143–163.

Gomez-Lavin, J., Prinz, J., Strohminger, N., & Nichols, S. (2020). Expansive interdisciplinarity and the moral self. In N. E. Snow & D. Narvaez (eds.), *Self, motivation, and virtue: Innovative interdisciplinary research* (pp. 25–41). Routledge.

Helm, B. (2008). Plural agents. *Noûs*, 42, 17–49.

Helm, B. (2010). *Love, friendship and the self: Intimacy, identification and the social nature of persons.* Oxford: Oxford University Press.

Helm, B. (2017a). Friendship. *The Stanford Encyclopedia of Philosophy* (Fall 2017 Edition), Edward N. Zalta (ed.), Retrieved from URL <https://plato.stanford.edu/archives/fall2017/entries/friendship/>.

Helm, B. (2017b). Love. In Edward N. Zalta (ed.), *The Stanford Encyclopedia of Philosophy*, Fall 2017 edition. Retrieved from <https://plato.stanford.edu/archives/fall2017/entries/love/>

Hoyos-Valdés, D. (2018). The notion of character friendship and the cultivation of virtue. *Journal for the Theory of Social Behaviour*, 48(1), 66–82.

Jacquette, D. (2001). Aristotle on the value of friendship as a motivation for morality. *The Journal of Value Inquiry*, 35, 371–389.

Jones, K. (1996). Trust as an affective attitude. *Ethics*, 107(1), 4–25.

Kolodny, N. (2003). Love as valuing a relationship. *Philosophical Review*, 112(2): 135–89.

Koltonski, D. (2016). A good friend will help you move a body: Friendship and the problem of moral disagreement. *Philosophical Review*, 125(4): 473–507.

Kristjánsson, K. (2020). Aristotelian character friendship as a "method" of moral education. *Studies in Philosophy and Education*, 39, 349–364.

LaFollette, H. (1996). *Personal relationships: Love, identity, and morality*, Cambridge, MA: Blackwell Press

McKeever, N. (2019). What can we learn about romantic love from Harry Frankfurt's account of love? *Journal of Ethics & Social Philosophy*, 14(3), 204–226.

McLeod, C. 2020. Trust, *The Stanford Encyclopedia of Philosophy* (Fall 2020 Edition), Edward N. Zalta (ed.), URL = <https://plato.stanford.edu/archives/fall2020/entries/trust/>.

Moller, D. (2007, June). Love and death. *Journal of Philosophy*, 104(6), 301–316.

Monk, R. (2001). *Bertrand Russell [Vol. 2:] 1921-70: The Ghost of Madness*. New York: Free Press.

Nisbett, R. E., & Wilson, T. (1977). Telling more than we can know: Verbal reports on mental states. *Psychological Review*, 84(3), 231–259.

Nussbaum, M. C. (1986). *The fragility of goodness*. Cambridge: Cambridge University Press.

Paton, H. (1993). Kant on friendship. In N. K. Badhwar (Ed.), *Friendship: A philosophical reader* (pp. 133–154). Ithaca: Cornell University Press.

Pismenny, A. (2021). The amorality of romantic love. In R. Fedock, M. Kühler, & R. Rosenhagen (eds.), *Love, justice, and autonomy: Philosophical perspectives* (pp. 23–42). London: Routledge.

Plato. (1997). *Complete works* (J. Cooper & D. Hutchinson, eds). Indianapolis: Hackett.

Price, A. W. (1990). *Love and friendship in Plato and Aristotle*. Oxford: Clarendon Press.

Rorty, A. (2016). The burdens of love. *Journal of Ethics*, 20(4), 341–354.

Schoeman, F. (1985). Aristotle on the good of friendship. *Australasian Journal of Philosophy*, 63(3), 269–282.

Sherman, N. (1987). Aristotle on friendship and the shared life. *Philosophy and Philosophical Research*, 47(4), 589–613.

Sherman, N. (1991). *The fabric of character: Aristotle's theory of virtue.* Oxford University Press.

Sherman, N. (1993). Aristotle on the shared life. In N. K. Badhwar (ed.), *Friendship: A philosophical reader* (pp. 91–107). Ithaca: Cornell University Press.

Sherman, N. (1999). Character development and Aristotelian virtue. In D. Carr & J. Steutel (eds.), *Virtue theory and moral education.* London: Routledge.

Soble, A. (1997). Union, autonomy, and concern. In R. E. Lamb (ed.), *Love analyzed* (pp. 65–92). Boulder, CO: Westview.

Stocker, M. (1976). The schizophrenia of modern ethical theories. *Journal of Philosophy*, 73(13), 453–466.

Strohminger, N., & Nichols, S. (2014). The essential moral self. *Cognition*, 131(1), 159–171. https://doi.org/10.1016/j.cognition.2013.12.005.

Strohminger, N., & Nichols, S. (2015). Neurodegeneration and identity. *Psychological Science*, 26(9), 1469–1479. https://doi.org/10.1177/0956797615592381.

Telfer, E., (1970–71). Friendship. *Proceedings of the Aristotelian Society*, 71. 223–241.

Thomas, L. (1987). Friendship. *Synthese*, 72. 217–236.

Thomas, L. (1989). Friends and lovers. In G. Graham & H. LaFollette (eds.), *Person to Person* (pp. 182–198). Philadelphia, PA: Temple University Press.

Thomas, L. (1990/1993). Friendship and other loves. Reprinted in N. Badhwar (ed.), *Friendship: A philosophical reader* (pp. 48–64). Cornell University Press.

Thomas, L. (2013). The character of friendship. In D. Caluori (ed.), *Thinking about friendship: Historical and contemporary perspectives* (pp. 30–46). New York: Palgrave Macmillan.

Vallor, S (2012). Flourishing on facebook: virtue friendship & new social media. *Ethics and Information Technology*, 14(3), 185-199.

Velleman, D. (1999). Love as a moral emotion. *Ethics*, 109, 338–374.

Volbrecht, R. M. (1990) Friendship: Mutual apprenticeship in moral development. *Journal of Value Inquiry*, 24(4), 301–314.

Wallace, R. J. (2012). Duties of love. *Proceedings of the Aristotelian Society*, 86, 175–198.

Watson, G. (1996). Two faces of responsibility. *Philosophical Topics*, 24, 227–224.

White, R. J. (1999). Friendship: Ancient and modern. *International Philosophical Quarterly*, 39, 19–34.

White, R. J. (2001). *Love's philosophy.* London: Rowman & Littlefield.

Whiting, J. E. (1991). Impersonal friends. *The Monist*, 74, 3–29.

Wilson, T. D. (2002). *Strangers to ourselves: Discovering the adaptive unconscious.* Cambridge, MA; London: Harvard University Press, Belnap.

Wonderly, M. (2017). Love and attachment. *American Philosophical Quarterly*, 54(3): 232–250.

Zagzebski, L. (2015). Admiration and the admirable. *Proceedings of the Aristotelian Society*, 89(1): 205–221.

Zagzebski, L. (2017). *Exemplarist moral theory.* Oxford: Oxford University Press.

Chapter 12

Internal Bleeding

How Covert Misogyny within Loving Relationships Tears Us Apart

Caroline R. Lundquist

INTRODUCTION:

The countertops in my grandmother's kitchen were a 1970s orange, and she was forever wiping them down. Every time I sat at the breakfast bar with my siblings or cousins, grandma was there. She always seemed to be in that kitchen, her presence as indelible as the orange of the countertops.

At family meals she barely sat down. By the time she had finished cooking and table-setting and serving, she was back in the kitchen washing and drying and putting away. The other women would soon join her. We all understood; this was the labor of love.

From one perspective, my grandmother was a model of feminine virtue, beyond moral reproach. She gave her time—her life—to caring for her family, asking nothing in return, save their health and happiness, and this generosity verging on radical altruism was the commendable meaning of her life. From another perspective, my grandmother was the victim of structures that devalued her time and seduced her into thinking that her dreams and ambitions held no value and must be cast aside in service to her husband and children. She was robbed of the opportunity to live the kind of life she wanted to, to become the person she wanted to be, bound as she was since girlhood to the kitchen, the laundry room, and the bedside. Although she died some years ago, I think about her life almost every day. For me, so much is at stake in the judgment of which perspective is more correct, since this judgment has profound implications for the meaning of my own life, and especially for the meaning of the loving relationships that to a great extent constitute it. A judgment feels necessary, but when I think about her life, I find it impossible to settle comfortably into either perspective; both feel equally compelling.

I am beginning to understand why this existential back and forth is as inevitable as it is unsettling. In a word, it's an instance of *zozobra*. The Spanish word zozobra can be translated as "worry," "anxiety," or "inquietude," but in the context of sailing it means "keel over" or "capsize." As an existential mood, zozobra is a state of dizziness and confusion brought about by the destabilization of our reality; a state in which we toggle endlessly between competing perspectives. As Francisco Gallegos and Carlos Alberto Sánchez write, zozobra is "the peculiar form of anxiety that comes from being unable to settle into a single point of view" (Gallagos and Sánchez 2020). The concept emerged in the early nineteenth century as Mexican philosophers sought to make sense of the feeling of "having no stable ground and feeling out of place in the world" brought about by "wave after wave of profound social and spiritual disruption," the legacy of colonization (Gallagos and Sánchez 2020). In the aftermath of colonization, zozobra is an idea we need. In this historical moment, in which the legacy of structural misogyny continues to colonize our collective consciousness even as feminist discourses grow ever more insistent, it is also essential to understanding the anxiety and discontent women often feel within our hetero relationships.[1]

Like the ceaseless listing of a storm-tossed ship, zozobra's merciless toggling between competing perspectives is devastating to the person who experiences it. As the philosopher Emilio Uranga puts it: "In this to and fro the soul suffers, it feels torn and wounded" (Uranga 1952). In loving hetero relationships, an existential mood of internal bleeding is the inevitable result of a persistent zozobra that shifts between covertly misogynistic norms and the often inarticulable feelings we have that *something is not right*, feelings that the burgeoning vocabulary of feminist discourse helps us to articulate. Under covert misogyny, this often-inarticulable to and fro and the even more inarticulable feeling it produces in us are not just elements of, but are indeed central to hetero loving relationships. If we are to have any hope of stemming the internal bleeding we experience when we love someone whose love is a vehicle of misogyny, we need to understand how and why zozobra belongs to the very fabric of hetero relations in this, the age of covert misogyny.

Within loving hetero relationships, zozobra produces existential injury, injury that is not always visible nor easy to locate, but is deeply felt and potentially shattering. Persistent zozobra saps us of our vitality; over time it urges us to settle into the perspective that requires the least resistance, which is usually the perspective that tells us that the devaluation of our time and preferences is normal and natural or the best we can hope for in an imperfect world. Evading zozobra in this way makes us complicit in a system that steals our time, and in so doing, gradually robs of our very lives. It persuades us to settle for romantic relationships that foreclose authentic self-actualization and deep satisfaction, and professional relationships that limit our practical and existential freedom. Perhaps worse, it makes us complicit in a system that does the same to other women. Yet the alternatives of, on the one hand, remaining in a zozobra state, and, on the other hand, settling into a resistant perspective, hardly feel preferable; one slowly exhausts us psychically, and the other may leave us convinced that loving, fulfilling, and empowering hetero relationships are unattainable.

If only it was possible to steady the ship without losing ourselves in the process. If only we could bring the competing horizons closer together, or find a new horizon marking a stable world where we could dwell comfortably. Reconciling our cultural norms and deepest feelings may require nothing short of a revolution in thinking about what it means to be a woman or man, what hetero relations look like, and what love requires of us morally. But perhaps that work can begin with an articulation of how and why misogyny within hetero relationships tears us apart inside and destabilizes our relationships, and of the deep reasons why we so seldom *understand* why we feel torn apart and why our relationships are suffering. In this chapter, I illustrate the psychic and moral cost of hetero love under covert misogyny by exploring the nature of and reasons for women's sense of zozobra within our hetero relationships. My hope is that simply giving language to these experiences will help readers to feel more at home in their own psyches, more resistant to the existential nausea of a world in which we are perhaps doomed to a degree of zozobra, and more hopeful about the prospect of a future in which loving men need not tear us apart inside.[2]

"EVERYONE KNOWS THAT": HOW DISCOURSES ABOUT GENDER SHAPE OUR REALITY

She was not the first student to share her rape experience with me. "Rape experience" is the name I ascribe to it; she would not use the word "rape," but instead referred to her experience as a "bad date" or "breakup." I had heard young women minimize their rape experiences before, and try to rationalize away their ensuing feelings. I understood that these responses were all-too typical. But there was something about the absolute conviction with which she framed her rape experience and its emotional aftermath that unsettled me deeply, and still does.

I insistently used "he" statements during our conversation, to place the blame where it belonged. She could not. I lost track of the number of times she said, with tears streaming down her face, "I never should have hugged him," and "I sent the wrong signals." It had been nine months, and she didn't know why she wasn't over "the breakup." She felt she should be over it; after all, it was her fault because she hugged him, and "You. Can't. Send . . ." (she punctuated each word) "The. Wrong. Signals. Everyone *knows that." What hope is there for an argument leveled against what everyone 'just kind of knows'?*

There is at present a debate among feminist theorists regarding the ontological status of and relationship between *sexual difference* and *gender* between, roughly, as Bonnie Mann describes them, "those feminists who wish to claim sexual difference as an ontological difference that is a positive resource for feminism, and those feminists who wish to deconstruct sexual difference all the way down."[3] I will mostly leave aside this debate and instead echo Mann's conviction that, regardless of which view we favor, "gender has *ontological* weight," such that "it anchors one's existence, it anchors one's sense of belonging to a community and to a world," hence "one is unmoored if it is undone" (1). Gender is, theoretical debates notwithstanding, a fundamental element of our lived experience.

As Mann is wise to point out, acknowledging that gender has ontological weight does not amount to claiming that gender is "a fixed biological thing," nor even that "it is a fixed social thing that can be empirically pinned down once and for all" (Mann 2013, 1). As a social phenomenon, gender *is* difficult or impossible to pin down, and this is, in my view, an important reason for the epistemological dizziness of zozobra. What we think it means to be a man or a woman often directly contradicts what we (also) think it means to be a man or a woman.[4] We are of different minds on the matter, perhaps unable to feel at home in either (or any), as each set of beliefs implies a different yet equally plausible world.

Gender has both ontological and *epistemological* ramifications, and these are reciprocal.[5] Our "knowledge" about gender profoundly shapes our reality, as we work to make our lived experiences fit with what we 'know.' Our daily experiences of the world—read through our sense of what is true—in turn reinforce our understanding of how the world is. And in the end, "everyone just kind of knows" all kinds of things about gender. When it comes to gender, we are caught in an epistemological-ontological circle of reification. The problem here is not just that the sets of truths about gender that are reified as "how things are" are often contradictory, which lays the ground for existential zozobra, but also that they may never have been true to begin with.

Feminist theorists have contributed to our understanding of how discourses about gender, sex, and love impact our perceptions of our experiences, ourselves, each other, and the world we share. What we "just kind of know" has *everything* to do with the discourses we are immersed in. If we want to understand the zozobra state of love under covert misogyny, we must understand the nature and constructive power of discourse.

As social psychologist Lynn Phillips explains:

Discourses reflect dominant ideas and practices that tell us what is normal, natural, or simply "the way things are" or "the way they should be." Like the clear surrounding fluid in the lava lamp, discourses help share our thinking, often without our awareness that they are even there; they also provide the raw materials from which we form our perceptions and interpret our experiences. (Phillips 2000, 37)

In *Flirting with Danger: Young Women's Reflections on Sexuality and Domination*, Phillips explores how young women process and internalize the myriad and often-conflicting messages they receive about gender, sex, and love as they are growing up. Phillips organizes their insights, which are drawn from numerous interviews with a racially and culturally diverse array of college-aged women, into discursive constellations or identifiable discourses that reflect deeply entrenched cultural norms. Unfortunately, as Phillips finds, rather than settling into singular, navigable discourses, "these women's narratives gave voice to four pairs of *conflicting* discourses" that "did not sit neatly in isolation" (38, *emphasis mine*). Not only did young women find themselves navigating, for example, conflicting discourses about what it means to be a "good woman," but they simultaneously found themselves navigating intersecting sets of conflicting discourses. As Phillips writes, "the contradictions and 'booby traps' were dizzying" (36). In trying to make sense of their own experiences within this tangled web of (generally faulty) discourses, women found themselves either at a loss, or worse, compelled to accept sometimes devastatingly self-destructive conclusions. This was perhaps most clearly the case in instances of rape.

To understand how intertwining sets of conflicting discourses lay booby traps for women as we work to make sense of our experiences, I want to introduce two pairs of discourses Phillips identifies, and illustrate how they intertwine for women who are processing an experience of sexual assault. The first set of discourses—the *pleasing woman discourse* and the *together woman discourse*—is about "good womanhood," and the second—the *normal/danger discourse* and the *male sex drive discourse*—is about "normal" male sexuality.

Phillips's interviews revealed two stories about what "good womanhood" can be, which she terms the *pleasing woman discourse* and the *together woman discourse*. Both discourses capture "women's agency, desires, entitlement, and 'proper' roles" (38). The *pleasing woman discourse*, which is the more traditional of the two, holds that "integral to women's proper gender roles is the desire and ability to be pleasant, feminine, and subordinate to men" (39). This role stresses sexual "purity" as well as "service to men and children" (39). As Phillips notes, the *pleasing woman discourse* carries on the mainstream Western cultural associations between femininity and "passivity, softness, and martyrdom" (38).[67] As evinced by portrayals of the "good woman" in film and on television, the *pleasing woman discourse* "emphasizes selflessness and deference to men as essential elements of good womanhood" (42). The ideal woman under the *pleasing woman discourse* seems to lack meaningful agency; she is both actively passive (in the sense of ignoring her own desires and tailoring her appearance and behavior so as to please men) and passively or selflessly active (ready to "satisfy the wants and needs of men"). She is active, then, primarily or exclusively in the sense of being *prêt à servir*.[8]

Competing with the *pleasing woman discourse*, the "more contemporary, but still problematic" *together woman discourse* borrows heavily from liberal individualistic notions of the self. This discourse "promotes the notion that a 'together' woman is free, sexually sophisticated, and entitled to accept nothing less than full equality and satisfaction in her sexual encounters and romantic relationships" (47). The *together woman discourse* embraces the "liberal, androcentric 'ideals' of total autonomy, self-direction, and entitlement to sex and relationships without personal responsibility" (47). The *together woman discourse* holds that a woman can "have it all," and unapologetically pursue her own "pleasure and fulfillment" (47). Whereas adhering to the *pleasing woman discourse* may leave women feeling disempowered, the *together woman discourse* "promises a sense of freedom, excitement, and a certain power over men" (47).

Both discourses harbor potential threats to women's health and autonomy, and both contain internal contradictions.[9] What's worse, Phillips finds that young women "cannot simply choose one" of these discourses, but instead "feel compelled to accommodate themselves to expectations of both, despite their apparent mutual exclusivity" (38–39). When aspects of the two discourses are combined—as they may be when women attempt to make sense of their rape experiences—the results can be devastating. Compounding the problem are the conflicting messages women receive about "normal" male sexuality, which intersect in potentially destructive ways with the *pleasing woman* and *together woman* dyad of discourses.

As Phillips points out, discourses about good womanhood are entangled with discourses about "normal" male heterosexual behavior. Here again "two competing discourses vie for women's attention" (52). The first, *the normal/ danger discourse*, "suggests that healthy and abusive relationships are mutually exclusive," while the second, the *male sexual drive discourse*, holds that aggression is a "normal and inevitable" part of men's sexual behavior (52). The *normal/danger discourse* brings to mind archetypal villains and heroes— predatory wolves and noble woodsmen, and is ubiquitous in popular media:

"From movies to soap operas to romance novels, we can see images of the strong and heroic man rescuing the helpless woman from the ruthless villain" (53). Under this discourse, there are good men and bad men, safe men and dangerous men, nice guys and creeps, gentle men and abusive men, and it is easy to tell the difference between them.

Although it involves a decidedly different vision of male sexuality, the *male sexual drive discourse* exists alongside the *normal/danger dichotomy discourse*. Under the former, "boys will be boys," and boys will be sexually aggressive. As Phillips writes, "This discourse tells us that men possess a natural sex drive that is inherently compelling and aggressive" (58). Here male sexual aggression is not merely normalized (justified, often, via appeals to biology), but erotically idealized.[10]

Already a dangerous notion, the *male sexual drive discourse* becomes most noxious when woven into the web of discourses that tell women to be simultaneously passive *and* active, ready to please men via self-objectification *and* sexually in control, trusting of "safe men" *and* ready to be rescued from "creeps." When young women try to make sense of their experiences in the light of these competing and contradictory discourses, they are led to irrational yet compellingly convincing conclusions. My student was no less certain that her "friend" was a "nice guy" (courtesy of the *normal/danger dichotomy*) than she was that she deserved to be raped because she "sent the wrong signals" (*pleasing women* must be sexually demure) to a man (and we all know how *sexually aggressive men* are) when she didn't mean to (and *together women* are always in control). Nine months later and she was still "so broken inside," and it just didn't make sense. How can anything make sense when one's epistemic reality has been constructed in overtly irrational ways? How can one possibly shake the feeling that the ship is about to capsize, especially when things go wrong?

My student's sense of existential confusion didn't necessarily stem from an inability to settle into one of two conflicting worldviews. For her, the conflict seemed to be between the certainty she felt that she was making sense of her experience as she should, using what she knew to be true, and the deeply felt sense that *something was still wrong*. The conflict could not be resolved, because she could not articulate what happened to her in a way that aligned with the feelings she was having. Escaping this state would have required that she had new discourses to draw from; new ways of making sense of what her rapist did to her and why she felt the way she did. I will argue below that one potential remedy for zozobra consciousness is the introduction of *ideas we need*, a remedy which is rendered all the more potent by *epistemic echoing*. But even where alternative discourses exist, we may feel pulled in two or more directions at once, especially under a system of covert misogyny that presses us to discount our intuitions. I will return to this problem below. But first, I want to examine how misconceptions about abuse may leave us at a loss when we try to make sense of the *something is wrong* feelings we too often experience within our loving relationships.

"HE'S NOT ABUSIVE": REAL LOVE, ABUSIVE LOVE, AND WHY WE CAN'T TELL THE DIFFERENCE

My mother is knocking on the bathroom door. I am crying so hard that I can't catch my breath and nearly vomit. I say I'm fine, that I'll be out in a minute.

An hour earlier I am in the car with my fiancé. We're on our way to visit family for a wedding. Lately he's been staying out late with a female friend while I'm home with our infant daughter. I work up the courage to say that I think we need to establish some rules about spending time with friends of the opposite sex before we get married.

He flies into a rage. He yells and pounds the steering wheel so loud the car windows vibrate. Our daughter is screaming. I am terrified, and beg him to pull over. I grab our daughter and run. We hide behind a building. I've never seen anger like this in anyone. I feel like he may hurt me, or us. But we've been together for years, and he's never hit me, or her. He throws things. He yells and curses and sometimes hits things. But he's not abusive. He's not abusive.

. . . I am in the bathroom the night before my wedding trying to breathe and trying not to vomit. He's not abusive. He's never *been abusive.*

It's a cliché, and we should know better, but the thought persists: "Why did she stay with him? *I* would never let a man do that to me." But perhaps we are not to blame. The discourse surrounding abusive relationships is so rife with misconceptions that it seems to mostly consist *of* misconceptions. Here again, what we "just kind of know," may simply be wrong. Misconceptions about abusers, abuse, and abuse victims are problematic not only because they inhibit the compassion we should feel for victims of abuse, but also and especially because they blind us to a possibility that we, too, might become or *already be* victims of abuse.

Perhaps the most dangerous misconception about abusers is that they are obviously different from other people; that something about their appearance or public demeanor betrays what they are capable of in those intimate moments when the only witnesses are those closest to them. This belief is supported by the *normal/danger* dichotomy described by Phillips, according to which "Essentially, there are 'good guys' and 'bad guys,' and the two categories do not overlap," and under which "'normal' hetero-sexual encounters, relationships and men are distinct from those that are 'dangerous' or 'exploitative'" (52). The normal/danger dichotomy evokes popular cultural stereotypes of heroes and villains, or shady "perverts" lurking the shadows and shining "rescuers" waiting to intervene on a victim's behalf. These stereotypes tend to be racist and classist, implanting the vague but persistent sense that abusers are poor, uneducated and non-white.[11] In reality, as criminologist Susan R. Paisner writes, "domestic abuse is what might be called an ecumenical crime, with no regard for age, ethnicity, financial status or educational background" (Paisner 2018).

The normal/danger dichotomy also encourages us to ignore the fact that a partner may not become overtly abusive until months or years into the relationship. Men who eventually abuse tend to fit the "good guy" mold all too well, especially during the early stages of relationships. They may be especially charming, finessing their way into the hearts of their partners' family members and friends. They may be more inclined than average to wax heroic, cementing their partners' impressions of their "good guy" status. As Amanda Kippert of DomesticShelters.org writes, "Some abusers are literal Prince Charmings—in fact, survivors [. . .] have used that exact phrase to describe the person they first met" (Kippert 2019).[12] For women steeped in the *normal/danger* dichotomy discourse, it is only natural that a degree of cognitive dissonance might accompany early instances of abusive behavior that would otherwise represent red flags. Subtly controlling or cruel gestures are dismissed easily enough when someone "just kind of knows" that "good guys don't hurt women," and when their "good guy" is better than most, or a real Prince Charming.

The "it's easy to spot an abuser" myth nudges culpability to the side of the abuse victim, who "should have known better," and it is not the only misconception to do so. One of the most popular misconceptions about abuse is that intelligent and/or educated women cannot experience it. In 2016, Bud Pierce, Republican candidate for Oregon governor, echoed this view, stating that "A woman that has great education and training and a great job is not susceptible to this kind of abuse" (Friedman 2016).[13] As Paisner writes, in March 2017, "a British judge gave a suspended sentence to a man who admitted beating his wife with a cricket bat and forcing her to drink bleach, because, the judge said, the victim was 'plainly an intelligent woman' " (Paisner 2018). Katie Ray-Jones, president of the National Domestic Violence Hotline (NDVH), encounters this misconception on a regular basis. In a recent interview, she recounted a conversation with a highly educated victim:

> One day we were having high call volume and I hopped on the line and there was a doctoral student calling me, and all she kept saying was, "How could I be so dumb? I'm working on a Ph.D." Domestic violence doesn't say, "OK, you have a Ph.D, I'm not going to touch you." (Filipovik 2018)

Drawing from her experiences working for the Hotline, Ray-Jones drives home the point that "Domestic violence does not discriminate":

> [W]e receive over 22,000 calls a month. We hear from every socioeconomic class, every race, every education level, every geographic region. We've had doctors who have called us, women who call us and say they live in mansions and their husbands work on Wall Street and they don't know how to get out. (Filipovik 2018)

Another popular misconception that keeps women accountable for their own victimization is the belief that "it's obvious a woman should leave" an abusive relationship. This view is the lifeblood of the "Why did she stay with him?" trope. Domestic violence prosecutor Michelle Kaminsky points out how "We talk about it as if it's a very simple solution: If someone is very abusive to you, you just walk away." But as Kaminsky explains, "it's a very complex situation. If you are economically dependent on someone and you depend on them to pay the bills [. . .] or if you're the one working and you can't afford child care, that makes it harder to leave" (Filipovik 2018). Victims of abuse who contemplate leaving must also face existential repercussions, including, in so many cases, threats to their very lives or the lives of their children. In too many situations, staying within an abusive relationship may feel like or objectively *be* the most rational decision a woman can make.

Kaminsky also points out a fact about abusive intimate relationships we seldom stop to think about: an abusive partner "is probably not abusive at every moment of the day," so for people in abusive relationships, "the abuse is not necessarily what defines the relationship" (Filipovik 2018). Indeed, labeling "abusive relationships" as such runs the risk of covering over the fact that they *are* relationships. As we know, and as Kaminsky reiterates, relationships are complex. This observation relates to a further misconception that is so entrenched we hardly seem capable of questioning it, namely, the belief that "real love" and "abusive love" are mutually exclusive, such that victims of abuse cannot *really* love the partners who abuse them.[14] What makes the phenomenon of relationship abuse especially tragic is that victims often genuinely love and care for their abusers. This insight is essential not only to understanding why abusive relationships often persist for years or decades in situations where victims are at liberty to leave, but also to appreciating the existential suffering women experience within overtly and covertly abusive relationships: as victims of covert misogyny, we often love and care deeply for the men who abuse us in subtle ways, and it is precisely *because* we care for them that the abuse rips us apart inside.

There is so little empathy within our collective consciousness for women who experience abuse within loving relationships. We are far too inclined to otherize. Perhaps the matter would feel different if we began by asking, "What does it feel like to love someone who hurts you?" Here is an experience we can no doubt relate to. It is difficult to imagine a loving relationship in which partners do not at least occasionally hurt each other, and we know what it feels like to love someone who we are angry at or disappointed in; the deep feelings of care and affection do not simply vanish because the person we love has behaved thoughtlessly or said something unkind. Nor do they simply vanish in more extreme cases, as any child of a controlling or passive-aggressive parent understands. Abusive love can be "real" love, enlivened as it is by so many of the pro-social tendencies (including empathy, care, and altruism) that we expect in "healthy" relationships. And this is a truth we must confess, if we are to have any hope of making sense of the zozobra state we so often embody within covertly abusive loving relationships.

To say that "real love" and abusive love are not, at least as they are experienced, mutually exclusive, is in no way to dismiss the moral wrongness of abuse. It is important here to distinguish between the descriptive or experiential and the normative; women can love men who abuse them, but abuse *should not* be a part of a loving relationship. Any abuse, whether physical, emotional, or of any other kind, within any loving relationship is a very real moral wrong. But unless we can replace our misconceptions about abusive love—including the misconception that "real love" and "abusive love" cannot coexist—with accurate conceptions, we run the risk of continuing to dismiss victims, and of blinding ourselves to the abuse we may *already be experiencing* within our loving relationships: the abuse that throws us into a zozobra state as we try to square our deep feeling that "something is wrong" with our rational conviction that nothing *can* be wrong, since we are in a loving relationship with "a good guy."

One of the misconceptions most in need of correction is the view that, under structural or systemic misogyny, overtly abusive relationships are fundamentally *different* from covertly abusive ones. In reality, the patterns of thinking, feeling, and acting that typify overtly abusive relationships, and the assumptions that encourage witnesses, victims, and perpetrators to brush them off as normal and acceptable, are present in "normal," yet covertly abusive loving relationships under a system of covert misogyny. Covert misogyny loves to hide, and it loves to hide abuse.

"IS THIS NORMAL?": UNDERSTANDING COVERT MISOGYNY

I am at my first academic philosophy conference, waiting for the session on Heidegger's metaphysics to begin. There are about twenty people in the room; I am one of the two women. The other sits several seats away to my right. She looks the picture of professionalism; I admire her confident posture. The first paper is read; to my novice ears it sounds like pretentious word salad. The other woman raises her hand to ask a question. She phrases it eloquently, her words like a knife to the bone of the author's argument. I suddenly understand what the paper was about, and like her, I see a fundamental flaw in the reasoning.

There is a kind of dismissive grumbling; her question receives no response. The moderator thanks her and asks if there are other questions. A man sitting two places to her left raises his hand. He asks the same question she just asked, although with less precision and more bravado. Suddenly the men sit at attention. One after another they comment on the intriguing question that has been put forth. After an extensive discussion, the moderator thanks the (male) scholar for raising such a productive concern.

My jaw is on the floor. This must be some kind of joke. I look over at her and she sees me. I don't think there is a name for her expression; clearly this is not her first rodeo. I suddenly wonder why I am in this space, and if I can have any kind of future in this profession. And I suspect that these men are full of shit.

Consciousness of male privilege is on the rise in public discourse, and this represents meaningful progress in the ongoing struggle for gender equity. But masculine entitlement continues to run rampant, whether in the private sphere of the home or in the more public sphere of the workplace, and no wonder; 10,000 years of male chauvinism cast a long shadow indeed, and one that tends to impede our vision. The misogyny that was once unapologetic and overt, stemming from popular cultural and religious assumptions of male superiority, has begun to retreat on a global scale (though certainly it remains robust in many nations, subcultures, and homes). Where it has for the most part retreated, it has left in its wake more subtle forms of misogyny. As is so often the case with cruelty of any kind, the subtlest forms are often the most devastating in part because they are so difficult to call out and condemn. As I will argue, covert misogyny has much in common with the overt misogyny that underlies overly abusive relationships, and can and should be understood as a form of institutional cruelty. Covert misogyny tends to induce zozobra consciousness as victims struggle to reconcile their deep feelings that "something is wrong" with the messages they receive that "this is normal." Over time, it produces existential internal bleeding as women feel torn apart inside; alienated within too many of their relationships.

If there is a boundary marking the division between overt and covert misogyny, it is unclear where it should be placed. But it is useful to distinguish between more and less obvious forms or expressions of misogyny, if only in order to notice how the former can be transmuted into the latter under the gaze of a culture that insists that women are equal in dignity to men. Overt misogyny includes the conscious conviction that men are superior to women and are entitled to behave and be treated in ways that convey that view. Under a system of overt misogyny, it would be appropriate that men's and women's work be clearly distinguished, and men's work economically rewarded and culturally valued above women's. Under such a system, women's time and preferences, including existential preferences regarding the patterns of a day and the projects of a life, would be of less concern than men's. Women's bodily autonomy would be unrecognized, and women's bodies would be instrumentalized to serve men's needs and desires. As such, men would be entitled to hit and hurt women's bodies, and to use women's bodies as a means for their sexual gratification with no regard for women's consent or pleasure. Women's bodily capacities, including reproductive capacities, would be reduced to mere means for men's fulfillment and aggrandizement. Women's labor would similarly become a means to ends designated by men. Under a system of overt misogyny, women would be second-class citizens, institutionally as well as within the home.

On the face of it, a system of overt misogyny looks very different from and more harmful than a system of subtle or covert misogyny. But here appearances may be deceiving. In just the way that an external wound "presents" differently from an internal, hidden wound, covert misogyny is dangerous precisely because it escapes diagnosis. It may even be dismissed, by the patient in particular, as merely imaginary. A hidden wound is harder to identify, understand and heal than a visible one, but can be felt deeply, and is at least as devastating to the individual suffering. In part, for this reason, I prefer the term *covert misogyny* to two other terms that have appeared in the literature and discourse on misogyny: *soft misogyny* and *misogyny without misogynists*. By way of illustrating what a system of covert misogyny entails, I will briefly explore what conceptually distinguishes these terms.

Justine Dunlap employs the term *soft misogyny* to capture "the bias, often implicit, that operates in people who are not, at core, misogynists, but who nonetheless attribute substantial culpability to the domestic violence victim" (Dunlap 2016, 778). Soft misogyny consists of "behaviors and beliefs dismissive of and harmful to women that occur without the conscious knowledge of the belief-holder" (778). Soft misogyny is, on Dunlap's view, what *New York Times* writer Nicolas Kristof previously referred to as "misogyny without misogynists."

Borrowing from Eduardo Bonilla-Silva's phrase *racism without racists*, Kristof employs the term *misogyny without misogynists* to capture the implicit bias of white men against women; he writes, "It's not that we white men are intentionally doing anything wrong, but we do have a penchant for obliviousness about the way we are beneficiaries of systematic unfairness" (Kristof 2015).[15]

Kristof argues that "there are die-hard racists and misogynists out there, but the bigger problem seems to be well-meaning people who believe in equal rights yet make decisions that inadvertently transmit both racism and sexism" (Kristof).

While I agree with Dunlap and Kristof that a subtle and often nameless form of misogyny runs rampant within our culture, gradually replacing more overt forms of misogyny (even as it buttresses them), I take issue with the idea that the agents of this misogyny are not themselves misogynists, and that their misogynistic behavior is in no meaningful sense conscious. In any instance of cruelty or abuse, it is the victim's perspective, not the perpetrator's, that *matters*. What matters most here is that the perpetrators of covert misogyny *embody* and *enact* misogyny, regardless of their degree of self-consciousness. And they may be more conscious of the meaning of their behaviors than Dunlap and Kristof seem to assume. The feelings of entitlement that prop up everyday misogyny betray deep if not *wholly* conscious convictions about the rightness of men's superior standing in the world, convictions that men can and should be held accountable for, and must learn to recognize in themselves by analyzing their patterns of thinking, feeling, and acting.[16]

To label the somewhat subtler misogyny of this moment as "soft" risks underestimating the profound impact it can have on women's lives; to label it "misogyny without misogynists" is to fail to hold its perpetrators account-able, which implies failing to respect their conscious agency and capacity for reform. The term "covert misogyny" is far more suitable, not only because it invites us to call out individual perpetrators (covert operators), but also because it highlights the institutionally enabled, often-deliberate *hiddenness* of the behaviors involved. As is the case with covert racism, the plausible deniability of covert misogyny "benefits perpetrators by allowing them to deny responsibility and culpability while simultaneously undermining its victim's ability to claim damage(s)" (Coates and Morrison 2011, 2). Covert misogyny, like overt domestic abuse, involves tactics like coercion and gas-lighting that aim to compel victims to question or dismiss their felt sense that wrongdoing has occurred, and that throw victims into a zozobra state as they try to reconcile their felt sense that "something is wrong" with (often-internalized) misogynistic beliefs that insist "everything is okay."[17] Covert misogyny is an idea we need, and an idea we need to collaboratively flesh out.

"DID I DESERVE THAT?": COVERT MISOGYNY
AS INSTITUTIONAL CRUELTY

We have a very special guest at tonight's meeting of our undergraduate eth-ics club. Our guest is a geographer and humanitarian working at the U.S.-Mexico border; he specializes in the concept of borders.

After his talk, I pose a question about the nature and meaning of borders to our students. Several hands shoot up. Before I can call on anyone, a male colleague interjects loudly, "You really need to take a [his academic discipline] class. We know all about that." Having wholly dismissed the question and ignoring the students waiting to speak, he redirects the conversation to his area of expertise. I sit, stunned, embarrassed, and insulted, wondering how to respond.

Perhaps fifteen minutes later, one of our most gifted students asks a fascinating question. Again, my colleague lays siege to the conversation in order to reference his own expertise, insulting the (female) student's intelligence in the process. I can't believe I'm not calling him out, if not for my sake, then for hers. But I don't want to take more attention away from our guest. And really, the students and I are quite used to this kind of behavior. By the next day, my colleague will have become not only charming but also genuinely kind, once again.

If my colleague always behaved this rudely, and/or if I were in a position to keep my job without continuing to work with him or men who behave in similar ways, then there would be no justification for failing to confront his behavior. But as is the case with so many instances of more overt abuse, here the perpetrator is often "a really nice guy," and genuinely likeable, and I, like so many women in male-dominated professions, have no choice but to work with people who, like him, are expert and perhaps inadvertent practitioners of covert misogyny. A similar dynamic can happen in the domestic sphere, where women genuinely love and do not have the means to separate from the men who, with a casual cruelty, exploit our labor and damage our self-esteem. What makes both experiences of covert misogyny so devastating is precisely the positive regard and genuine love we feel for the men who are tearing us apart inside; what makes both so tragic is that they may feel like, and in fact *be*, the best we can hope for.

The dynamics of covert misogyny, like those of overt abuse, are complex, and covert misogyny can find expression in all kinds of behaviors in the home, workplace and beyond. Although I cannot fully explore these dynamics of covert misogyny nor catalog their expressions here, I want to put forth two claims, by means of paving the way for future analysis. First, *covert misogyny can and should be seen as a form of institutionalized cruelty*, and second, *covert misogyny importantly involves the theft of time, which is a grave moral wrong.*

I draw the term "institutionalized cruelty" from ethicist Philip Hallie. Hallie understood that, despite its etymology, cruelty need not involve the shedding of blood, nor bodily harm more generally.[18] Real or substantial cruelty instead involves and is fundamentally *about* "the maiming of a person's dignity, the crushing of a person's self-respect" (Hallie 1981, 23). Hallie points out that when cruelty persists over time, as it does under institutionalized cruelty, it becomes dangerously subtle.[19] This happens because "in a persistent pattern of humiliation . . . both the victim and the victimizer find ways of obscuring what has been done" (24). Both victimizers and victims internalize the power differential at the heart of institutionalized cruelty such that victims feel "the way they are being treated is justified by their 'actual' inferiority, by the inferiority they themselves feel," and victimizers "feel that since they are superior, even esthetically [. . .] they deserve to do what they wish, deserve to have these lower creatures under their control" (24).

Covert misogyny is an instance of institutionalized cruelty. It involves a real and/or imagined disparity in power between men and women grounded in the assumption that men are superior to and more important than women. It involves the persistent humiliation of women and the persistent maiming of women's dignity. The power difference that grounds it is reinforced by aesthetic and linguistic norms, including a palpable absence of language that calls it out and/or designates it as wrong.[20] The norms and convictions that perpetuate it colonize the minds of both victims and perpetrators, leading the latter to dismiss or rationalize away their suffering and the former to justify and indeed take pride in their ongoing cruelty.[21] It is a system of unequivocal and deeply serious moral wrongdoing that must be called out and redressed.

For Hallie, liberation from cruelty requires either the dissolution of the power differential that is its lifeblood, or total liberation from the cruel relationship. Hence, he argues that "Either the victim should get stronger and stand up to the victimizer, and thereby bring about a balance of their power, or the victim should free himself from the whole relationship by flight" (Hallie 1981, 25). If dissolution of the differential is the more plausible solution of the two, it is not clear why this cannot also stem from the victimizer's conscious choice to share power. Such a choice would require (and might indeed be motivated by) the victimizer's acute recognition of a fundamentally unjust power dynamic. We can certainly imagine ways to render institutionalized cruelty, including covert misogyny, visible; to raise the consciousness of both victims and perpetrators, and to appeal to a shared sense of fairness or justice. We might begin, for example, by noticing how men's time and women's time are valued differently under a system of covert misogyny; a difference that underlies countless and varied expressions of misogyny, and that can easily be seen (by anyone with a minimal sense of fairness and the intuition that time *matters*) as morally wrong.

"THERE ARE SO MANY OTHER THINGS I COULD BE DOING RIGHT NOW": THE BLEEDING TO DEATH OF TIME UNDER COVERT MISOGYNY[22]

I run the number sometimes. I estimate the number of hours my grandmother spent in the kitchen each day, multiply that by the number of days in a year, then multiply that by the number of years she spent doing unpaid labor (in addition to the paid labor she did for most of her adult life). My conservative number is 47,450 hours, which works out to 5.42 years' worth of 24-hour days. And that's just the time spent in the kitchen.

How could her life have been different if she had spent just half of those hours doing things she might have preferred to do? What books could she have read? Which friendships could she have fostered? How many moments of peace could she have enjoyed? And how many have I been deprived of, in my life that is so unsettlingly similar to hers?

Recognizing that covert misogyny is an instance of institutionalized cruelty should be enough to convince a skeptic that it is morally wrong. But it is also wrong for another, far simpler reason: it involves the theft of time. Time is the very *substance* of a human life; the most irrecuperable of all things someone can lose. When a person is murdered, their death is always tragic. But we feel it is more tragic when that person is young, or very young. And this is reasonable, because the time they were deprived of is greater than it would have been, had they been older. We rightly lament the loss of years because we know they are years the person might have spent experiencing the world, and other people, and finding meaning and purpose in their life. We understand, then, if only intuitively, that time theft is a moral wrong, but it is one we have mostly become inured to under systemic misogyny.

Women's time is devalued under overt misogyny in obvious ways when, for example, women are paid less for doing the same work as men, or when women are unable to refuse sex, or forced to bear and raise children. The problem is more insidious under a system of covert misogyny, because it happens in so many ways, because the patterns of behavior involved are so "normal," and because we often lack the language that would enable us to recognize that time theft is taking place. But perhaps when time theft is occurring, we often at least *sense* that something is wrong.

The "something is wrong" feeling can arise during moments when a woman is doing unpaid labor, when her colleague is talking over her, when her lover is guilt-tripping her into having sex when she doesn't want to, or when a passing microaggression changes the meaning of the space she inhabits. Zozobra consciousness may soon follow, as she tries to reconcile her felt sense "that something is wrong" with the fact that nothing unusual has happened. But, of course, "nothing unusual" in no way implies "nothing morally wrong." Instances of time theft under covert misogyny may be wrong for subtly different reasons; it is important to learn to recognize and name them, and to find ways to explain why they are wrong.

Consider, for example, the disproportionate division of unpaid labor within heterosexual couples' homes, a state of affairs that appears to be quite "normal" in contemporary America, and that has been magnified and compounded during the Covid-19 pandemic.[23] When a woman does a disproportionate amount of unpaid labor, she is disproportionately giving over or being deprived of time that she could have used to meet her physical and mental health needs, maintain or further her career, foster her relationships, or otherwise enrich her life. The economic consequences of this loss of time matter. So do the existential ones. There is a qualitative difference between a life with little "disposable" time and a life with more. Being constantly overwhelmed by (disproportionately distributed) household and family responsibilities can be physically exhausting and emotionally devastating, as is evinced by working women's reflections on their attempts to cope with the additional burdens of homeschooling and caring for children full-time during the Covid-19 pandemic.[24]

Time theft happens in the workplace as well, and in numerous ways. When traditionally "feminine" or "domestic" tasks are foisted upon women; when we are asked to take notes in a meeting with male colleagues, to bring coffee or food, or when it is left to us to clean up colleagues' messes, time theft is taking place. But time theft also happens when male colleagues dominate conversations, assuming more "air time" than is fair or reasonable, interrupting women speakers, ignoring comments made by female colleagues, or "delegating expertise" to women only on those topics they wish to hear women speak about. The latter is especially likely to go undetected because it may appear to be or even feel like a gesture of "inclusiveness." But, like time theft more generally, it is a covert means of exercising power over women.

Time theft may go hand-in-hand with the theft of space. When a man sits or stands uncomfortably close to a woman, he not only invades her personal space but also changes the felt meaning of the space. This is especially palpable in instances of "creeping" or sexual harassment, as Bonnie Mann explains: "one knows one has encountered a creeper when one experiences the sexualized theft of time" (Mann 2012, 26). For the woman reading a book on the subway, the approach of a "creeper" changes the meaning of the space; the meaning of the situation. He steals her time by changing its meaning. And this is another reason why misogynistic time theft is wrong: it detracts from a woman's ability to determine the meaning of a moment, a day, and over time, a life. The theft of time is the partial theft of a life; maybe that is why it makes us feel like we are dying inside, if only a little.

"WHY DO WE THINK IT'S JUST US?" EPISTEMIC ECHOING AND OTHER SOLUTIONS

"Why do we say these things to ourselves!? Why do we tell ourselves it's just us, or we're being too sensitive!?" For the first time since this problem

began, I feel validated. For the first time in months, I feel like there might be some hope.

I am sitting at a small café table with a female colleague, processing experiences of working with our misogynist colleague. From his perspective, she quit because she "had family matters to attend to." She, of course, tells a different story. Like me, she "tried everything." Like me, she felt perpetually humiliated and found it easiest to slip into a submissive role rather than having to fight enervating daily battles. Like me, the years of misogyny had damaged her confidence, and filled her with anger and anxiety that bled into her home life and impacted her mental health. Like me, she felt vindicated—transformed—by the conversation we were at last having.

There is no "outside" of a system of covert misogyny, and that is why zozobra consciousness feels so inescapable. Too many of the men we love, who love us—partners, friends, colleagues, family members—embody and enact misogyny, and we are hard-pressed to reconcile the loving feelings we have for them with our felt sense that something is wrong, and that we deserve better. We can try to die on every hill—constantly disrupting misogynistic behaviors—which is *exhausting* and potentially detrimental to our relationships and careers, or we can settle into the *pleasing woman* complacency that keeps the peace but enables abuse. The pro-social tendencies that belong properly to love might encourage the latter. Or, discontent with either response, we can live in a zozobra state, torn apart inside. There *has* to be a better way. Covert misogyny loves to hide, and it hides from its perpetrators most of all, who may assume that because they are not overtly abusive, they are good to women (another instance of the *normal/danger* dichotomy); who rarely sense their own entitlement even as they are enacting it. It is for this reason that we need to rethink the view that covert misogyny is a women's problem; it is, first and foremost, a *men's* problem, though one that we all need to raise our consciousness of.

For women, consciousness-raising requires the sharing of experiences. The magic of consciousness-raising lies in its simplicity: when we share our experiences, we notice patterns, and these patterns illuminate systems that were previously obscured or invisible. We then become more resistant to the mechanisms of covert misogyny, and especially to the kind of gaslighting that pushes us to assume we're just imagining things; that everything is alright, even though it doesn't feel that way (or worse, that there is something wrong with *us*). We also learn to *name* the things we are experiencing, which is both a product of and a boon to consciousness-raising efforts. Having names for our experiences enables the epistemic echoing which not only validates our experiences, but also places us within a community of others who feel as we do. As one of my students recently put it, "Having a name for something makes you feel less alone."[25] The advent of the term "mansplaining" was cathartic for many women; speaking into visibility an elusive but deeply felt phenomenon. "Mansplaining" is an idea we need, and there are many, many more such ideas waiting to be named as we work to pull covert misogyny out of its hiding places within our society and within ourselves.

I find it difficult to accept the view that the burden of liberation should fall primarily on the shoulders of those who are oppressed. It may happen that it often does, but the oppression is a wrong, and victims should not be primarily responsible for ameliorating a situation in which wrongdoing is taking place. The role of the victim should be, at most, to make the wrongdoing visible to the perpetrator, who bears primary responsibility. In the case of covert misogyny, women are doing the difficult work of consciousness-raising, but the larger task of ameliorating the situation is and should be primarily the task of men. The problems of toxic masculinity—which is as toxic to men as it is to women—and covert misogyny are not separate problems. They have a shared history. Hyperbolic, toxic masculinity arose as women gained meaningful personal and political freedoms, gaining access to the spaces once reserved for men. As shifting gender roles called the meaning of masculinity into question, men sought refuge in bloated notions of masculinity that would render it more distinguishable from femininity. This history matters, because it helps us to understand that the norms we have inherited were created, and what has been created can be improved or cast aside. This recreation is daunting work, but it is the work we all must do if we are to pave the way for loving relationships that don't tear so many of us apart inside.

"FINALLY"

My husband puts some of the clean dishes away, putting others on the counter, and goes off to do something else. As I put the remainder in the cupboard, he comes back into the room and says, slightly offended, but smiling, "I was going to do that." I am tempted to quip, "Oh, what stopped you?" He asks, with only a hint of irony, "Is this stealing your time?" It gives us both something to think about.

There's something about the idea of time theft that moves him. There's something about the idea that taking time is partial killing that unsettles his routines. So much has changed in our nearly two decades together. After years of work and counseling, he doesn't lose his temper like he used to. He understands where it came from, and understands the damage done. So much has changed during the pandemic. He values my time more now. I haven't done his laundry in months, and do less of the childrens'. He rarely interrupts me when I am speaking. He takes our daughter to her music lesson without my asking "for a favor." I find I have more time; more time to write this. I feel a renewed sense of my own dignity; a dignity I didn't even know had been so greatly diminished.

The changes don't come easily, and demand a lot from us both. But with each passing day, I feel like there is more hope. I feel like the ship is slowly, very slowly, beginning to steady, and in the distance, I sense the horizon of a world we can both—we can all—comfortably dwell within.

NOTES

1. For some recent philosophical accounts of structural misogyny, see Manne (2017) and Brogaard (2020, ch. 6).

2. I employ the ambiguous phrase "loving men," which can be heard as both "loving people who are men," and "men who are loving," because it can and should be heard in both ways.

3. And must continue, since, as Mann writes, "[W]e (contemporary feminist thinkers) find ourselves negotiating a divide over whether 'sexual difference' and 'gender difference' are simply ways of talking about the long-term effects of being socially constituted as women and men, or whether these terms (or the first of them at least) name a site from which meaning is or can be generated that escapes the drag of an enormous historical weight [. . .] The need to provide an alibi for egregious social hierarchies that organize the parasitic appropriation of women's labor, both reproductive and productive, by men, has been so entangled with efforts to describe what natural sexual difference is, that any attempt to address these differences is inescapably burdened by that history" (Mann 2014, 30–31).

4. Sometimes the conflict is between what we think it means to be a man or a woman and how we feel, as in cases where it is difficult or impossible to make sense of our experiences via the language and norms available to us.

5. And what it means to be a man or a woman often contradicts what it feels like to be a man or a woman, leading to the kind of inner distress that is the focus of this chapter.

6. Which, as Phillips points out, has long been noted by feminist theorists, including Bordo (1989), Brownmiller (1984), Miller (1986) and Steiner-Adair (1990).

7. Phillips also notes that the pleasing woman is "typically portrayed as white," and "middle- or upper-class," (39) and that the pleasing woman discourse promotes "very narrow, often unhealthy, and classist and racists standards of beauty" (42).

8. Here I have in mind both senses of this term: *ready to be of service* and *ready to be served up.*

9. Under the pleasing woman discourse, for example, women are encouraged to express sexual independence in order to please and attract men: "Men," as women's magazines suggested, "are mesmerized by a woman who knows her own mind and body, and is not afraid to take control" (Phillips 200, 48).

10. As is evident in Jackson Katz's analysis of the link between masculinity and sexual domination of women. See Katz, Jackson, Jeremy Earp, and David Rabinovitz. 2013. *Tough Guise 2: Violence, Manhood & American Culture.* Northampton, MA: Media Education Foundation, 2013.

11. See, for example, Angela Davis, "Rape, Racism and the Myth of the Black Rapist," in *Women, Race and Class,* New York: Vintage Books, 1983.

12. The Prince Charming guise often serve an insidious purpose, as Kippert explains: "Unfortunately, what survivors come to learn is that it's all an act used to deflect attention from what they may someday disclose to friends—that Prince Charming yells, threatens, shoves, hits" (Kippert 2019).

13. A statement for which he later apologized, saying: "I know that any woman, regardless of economic status, can be subject to domestic violence and sexual abuse" (Friedman 2016).

14. And that abusive partners cannot *really* love the person they are abusing, which is an equally problematic assumption.

15. See Eduardo Bonilla-Silva, *Racism Without Racists: Color-Blind Racism and the Persistence of Racial Inequality in America*, Rowman & Littlefield Publishers; Fifth edition (June 9, 2017).

16. A claim that Kristoff would no doubt agree with, given the call to action issued in his article.

17. Although my use of the term "covert misogyny" was not initially inspired by the term "covert racism," there are important parallels between the two concepts. Like covert racism, covert misogyny is "hidden; secret; private; covered; disguised; insidious; or concealed [. . .] it serves to subvert, distort, restrict, and deny rewards, privileges, access, and benefits" (Coates and Morrison 2011, 1–2).

18. As Hallie writes, "The Latin *crudus* is related to still older words standing for bloodshed, or raw flesh. According to the etymology of the word, cruelty involves the spilling of blood" (Hallie 1981, 23).

19. Hallie writes, "Institutionalized cruelty [. . .] is the subtlest kind of cruelty" (24).

20. As Phillips argues when she points out that many discourses about gender, "are absent or seem to be denied" (Phillips 2000, 77).

21. Under systemic misogyny, whether overt or covert, playing the role of oppressor reinforces men's pride in part because it reinforces their perceived masculinity. See, for example, Jackson Katz's film *Tough Guise 2: Violence, Manhood & American Culture.*

22. I borrow the phrase "the bleeding to death of time" from the poem "Counting the Beats" by Robert Graves.

23. See, for example, Amanda Taub's "Pandemic Will 'Take Our Women 10 Years Back in the Workplace," *New York Times*, September 6, 2020.

24. My favorite example of this is Caroline Faria's satirical letter, "Call for Papers" (2020. *ACME: An International Journal for Critical Geographies.* 19, no. 2: 413–23).

25. For a rich exploration of the relationship between epistemic echoing and epistemic resistance, see: Pohlhaus, G. (2020). Gaslighting and Echoing, or Why Collective Epistemic Resistance is not a "Witch Hunt". Hypatia, 35(4), 674-686. doi:10.1017/hyp.2020.29.

REFERENCES

Bonilla-Silva, Eduardo. 2017. *Racism Without Racists: Color-Blind Racism and the Persistence of Racial Inequality in America.* Rowman & Littlefield Publishers, Fifth edition.

Brogaard, Berit. 2020. *Hatred: Understanding our Most Dangerous Emotion.* New York: Oxford University Press.

Coates, Rodney D. and Janet Morrison. 2011. *Covert Racism: Theories, Institutions, and Experiences.* Brill, June 9, 2011.

Davis, Angela. 1983. "Rape, Racism and the Myth of the Black Rapist," in *Women, Race and Class,* New York: Vintage Books.

Dunlap, Justine A. 2016. "Soft Misogyny: The Subtle Perversion of Domestic Violence Reform," *Seton Hall Law Review* 46, no. 3 (2016): 775–812.

Faria, Caroline. 2020. "Call For Papers," *ACME: An International Journal for Critical Geographies* 19, no. 2: 413–423.

Filipovok, Jill. 2018. "14 Misconceptions About Domestic Violence," DomesticShelters .or, January 29, 2018. https://www.domesticshelters.org/articles/domestic-violence -op-ed-column/14-misconceptions-about-domestic-violence

Friedman, Gordon. 2016. "Bud Pierce Apologizes Again for Comments About Women," Statesman Journal, October 5, 2016. https://www.statesmanjournal.com /story/news/politics/2016/10/05/gop-oregon-governor-candidate-apologizes-again -comments-women/91624316/

Gallagos, Francisco and Alberto Sánchez. 2020. "That anxiety brought on by the election, pandemic, economy, all of 2020? It's called 'zozobra'." *Chicago Tribune*, November 2, 2020.

Hallie, Philip. 1981. "From Cruelty to Goodness." *The Hastings Center Report*, 11, no. 3: 23–28.

Katz, Jackson, Jeremy Earp, and David Rabinovitz. 2013. *Tough Guise 2: Violence, Manhood & American Culture.* Northampton, MA: Media Education Foundation.

Kippert, Amanda. 2019. "When Abusers Turn on the Charm," DomesticShelters.or g, April 1, 2019. https://www.domesticshelters.org/articles/identifying-abuse/when -abusers-turn-on-the-charm?color=c0249a&widget_name=article_library&width =300px

Kristof, Nicholas. 2015. "Straight Talk for White Men," *New York Times*, February 21th, 2015.

Mann, Bonnie. 2014. *Sovereign Masculinity: Gender Lessons from the War on Terror.* New York: Oxford University Press, 2014.

Mann, Bonnie. "Creepers, Flirts, Heroes, and Allies: Four Theses on Men and Sexual Harassment." *APA Newsletters: A Newsletter on Feminism and Philosophy* 22, no. 2 (2012): 24–31.

Manne, Kate. 2017. *Down Girl: The Logic of Misogyny.* New York: Oxford University Press.

Paisner, Susan R. 2018. "Five Myths About Domestic Violence," *Washington Post*, February 22, 2018. https://www.washingtonpost.com/outlook/five-myths

/five-myths-about-domestic-violence/2018/02/23/78969748-1819-11e8-b681
-2d4d462a1921_story.html

Phillips, Lynn. 2000. *Flirting with Danger: Young Women's Reflections on Sexuality and Domination*. New York: New York University Press, 2000.

Taub, Amanda. 2020. "Pandemic Will 'Take Our Women 10 Years Back in the Workplace," *New York Times*, September 6th, 2020.

Chapter 13

Interrogating the Immorality of Infidelity

Jennifer L. Piemonte, Staci Gusakova,
Jennifer D. Rubin, and Terri D. Conley

INTRODUCTION

Infidelity is strongly condemned from a moral standpoint; cheating is among one of the worst transgressions one can make against another individual and is often considered a wholly sinful act (Allen 2018; Conley et al. 2012; McAnulty & Brineman 2007). Eighty-nine percent of Americans agree that cheating is morally wrong (Gallup, 2020). Most people's biggest fear in romantic and/or sexual relationships is that they will be the victim of infidelity (Leeker & Carlozzi 2014; Treas & Giesen 2000). By and large, people who cheat are shamed, stigmatized, and ostracized, and in some cases punished by law (Siegel 1992; Sharp, Walters, & Goren 2013; Tsapelas, Fisher, & Aron 2010).

Both the popular media and the academic research on extradyadic relations reflect this stern perspective (Abrahamson et al. 2012). That means that research questions and proposals often begin from the premise that infidelity is immoral and negative (see Blow & Hartnett 2005 or Kulibert & Thompson 2019 for reviews). Studies therefore risk deterring respondents from honestly reporting about their experiences. For example, researchers must often anticipate social desirability effects—a form of response bias that occurs when study participants provide answers that are likely to be viewed favorably (by either the researchers or the participants themselves; Krumpal 2013). This effect may be exacerbated by any implicit stigma incorporated into the study design, such as survey questions worded in ways that clearly condemn the behavior in question.

Of course, researchers often aim to be neutral and judgment-free. This is in part why research on infidelity varies widely in defining cheating, how cheating is measured, and the time period during which cheating is assessed. This leads to inconsistent answers to the practical questions about cheating's commonality and of an individual's likelihood of being cheated on. How can the scholarly community advance its approach to researching relationships? Moreover, how can members of the general public make more precise and nuanced 's judgments when assessing the morality of someone's actions or behaviors?

We suggest that the actions of someone who intentionally (and/or habitually) pursues extradyadic sex constitute a different moral judgment than those of someone who has extradyadic sex after succumbing to a tempting prospect offered to them. This is based on the psychological perspective that approach and avoidance behaviors are part of distinct cognitive systems facilitating motivation (Elliot 2006). Someone motivated to seek out an opportunity to break the agreement with their relationship partner is undergoing different decision-making processes than someone who has never intended to break their agreement, but in fact does so when they find themselves in circumstances that facilitate the liaison. Because people tend to make moral judgments about others based on their perceived intention, most would judge the former type of infidelity as less immoral than the latter type (Cushman 2008).

In this chapter, we further consider the latter type of infidelity, or when someone cheats after having been approached, rather than when someone cheats as a result of seeking out an available partner. Therefore, we discuss the frequency of infidelity among those who were presented with the opportunity. Focusing on cheating under these conditions is important for a more comprehensive understanding of the likelihood of infidelity. The psychological characteristics of someone who initiates cheating likely differs from someone who is passively approached and accepts an invitation (Elliot & Thrash 2002). Furthermore, the psychological processes related to these behaviors also differ and are likely impacted by situational factors (Simpson & Winterheld 2012).

As we will discuss, there is more consistency among reported rates of infidelity when specifically looking at those in relationships who were given the opportunity to cheat, and not collapsing rates of infidelity across all persons who belong to committed relationships. In other words, the number of people in relationships who have not been propositioned for an extradyadic encounter obscures the frequency with which people in committed relationships report accepting such offers. In the present research, we find a relatively high rate— with an average across studies near 40 percent—among those who were offered the opportunity to cheat. Our findings indicate that for most partnered people, the risk of being cheated on is based less on their partner's moral character and more on whether their partner might be presented with the opportunity.

The relative commonality of cheating if given the opportunity implicates society's incessant moralizing of infidelity. We suggest that moving forward, researchers, practitioners, and journalists consider infidelity not as a sin, but as a common behavior. This would hopefully decrease the stigma associated with cheating, given that shame and stigma rarely lead to desired behaviors or positive outcomes (Aronson, Fried, & Stone 1991; Williamson et al. 2014). We also suggest that scholars and professionals account for different contexts and forms of cheating—especially approachers versus recipients. Doing so should lead to more consistent and nuanced statistics on extradyadic behaviors in relationship and psychological literature.

INCONSISTENCIES IN INFIDELITY RESEARCH

Infidelity is typically defined as having sexual contact with someone outside of a monogamous relationship (Mark, Janssen, & Milhausen 2011). Infidelity has negative ramifications for people who are cheated on, as well as for the relationships in which cheating occurs (e.g., Blow & Hartnett 2005; Cano & O'Leary 2000; Charny & Parnass 1995; Previti & Amato 2004). It is, therefore, reasonable that cheating statistics have been of interest to researchers and the public.

Typically, infidelity research has focused on whether a participant has ever cheated on a relationship partner. Depending on sample and question phrasing, anywhere from 11 percent to 72 percent of men and 4.6 percent to 70 percent of women have cheated on their partners (e.g., Brand et al. 2007; Cox 2008; Davis & Smith 1991; Goldberg et al. 2008; Greeley 1994; Hite 1991; Mark, Janssen, & Millhausen 2011; Martins et al. 2016; Munsch 2015). Based on these statistics, we can conclude that large numbers of people cheat on partners in their lifetime.

Other studies show that there is reason to be optimistic about relationship loyalty. In one representative study, only 3 percent of the U.S. population cheated on a spouse in the last year (Laumann et al. 1994). Another representative study demonstrated that 1 percent of individuals surveyed in person and 6 percent of individuals surveyed online reported infidelity in the last year (Whisman & Snyder 2007). Thus, although the percentage of people ever cheating on a partner is still high, rates of recent cheating may be much lower.

In general, cheating statistics tend to highlight whether a person has cheated at all, without considering the circumstances under which the cheating occurred. In fact, whether infidelity occurred is often treated as an indicator of the health or success of an entire interpersonal relationship (Hall & Fincham 2006). Media headlines and self-help guides often insist that infidelity indicates that a romantic relationship is "doomed" (Wynne 2019). As the counterpart to this heuristic, researchers and laypeople alike take the absence of infidelity as evidence for a person's commitment to and/

or love for their partner (Conley et al. 2017; Perel 2007). These are implicit assumptions that are built into not only research questions and study designs but also clinical practice and therapeutic guidelines. In both settings, comprehensive understandings of interpersonal relationships are of the utmost importance. How can the scholarly community improve infidelity research, including more refined process-based theories and more accurate outcome measures?

One way to collect and analyze more nuanced data is for researchers to identify specific parameters for the type of infidelity under investigation. For example, is the study focused on emotional affairs or one-night-stands? Each represents an experience of disloyalty to an intimate relationship (Fish et al. 2012; Solomon & Teagno 2010). Each also connotes distinct intra- and interpersonal processes (Girard, Connor, & Woolley 2018). From a psychological perspective, behaviors that are planned activate different sets of cognitive systems than behaviors that are reactive (Fishbein & Ajzen 1975). Therefore, one way to categorize types of cheating is in terms of whether or not it was planned. Distinguishing by intention aligns with the culpable control model (discussed in more detail below; Alicke 2000), which highlights the importance of perceived intention when making moral judgments.

PLANNED VERSUS UNPLANNED CHEATING

A person with the conscious and explicit intention of cheating has many available courses of action. Planned infidelity takes a variety of forms, and this number has grown in the age of digital media. Internet forums, social media, and online dating (especially given the nearly ubiquitous web-cameras on personal computers and cell phones) allow for increased access to both familiars and strangers (Buunk, Dskstra, & Massar 2018). For those intending to go behind their partner's back, there are inordinate opportunities to seek out possible partners or reconnect with former flames. Taking steps to facilitate inconspicuous interactions takes forethought and planning; this type of cheater is highly motivated to engage in liaisons that are forbidden by their partnership agreement.

The psychology behind this type of infidelity tends to lean more toward pathological cheating, or someone who is a serial adulterer (Knopp et al. 2017). The implications for the primary relationship, and each individual's commitment to it, are often serious. Research by clinicians indicates that serial or habitual adulterers can be understood from psychiatric or other behavioral health perspectives, such as using frameworks of addiction, personality disorders, or dysfunctional risk/reward cognitive processes (Warach, Josephs, & Gorman 2018). This clearly represents a form of infidelity distinct from opportunistic infidelity, where someone has no plan to cheat but ultimately does cheat when they succumb to their desires.

Does someone who engages in an opportunistic liaison exhibit the same (im)morality as a habitual cheater? Based on a critical review of psychological literature on people's moral judgments, we argue that this is not so. From a psychological perspective, morality is grounded in theory of mind, that is, the ability to attribute mental states (such as beliefs, thoughts, and feelings) to others (Wimmer & Permer 1983). In other words, mindreading is the process of "putting oneself in another's shoes" and imagining their experience. Mindreading allows people to imagine how much actors desired to act, intended to act, and contributed to harm incurred from said act (Gray, Young, & Waytz 2012). Below, we will review how people make moral judgements based on the perceived harm committed, even without confirmed knowledge of the perceived agent's desire or intention.

THE PERCEIVED SELF-CONTROL OF MORAL ACTORS

People identify immorality by (1) norm violations (an indicator of an unusual event), (2) negative affect (bad feelings about the unusual event), and (3) perceived harm (observed consequences of the unusual event) (Nichols 2002; Schein & Gray 2017). Norms—specifically injunctive norms (Reno, Cialdini, & Kallgren 1993)—indicate how people *should* behave. Thus, a norm violation occurs when an actor fails to behave in accordance with how others expect and would like them to behave. The violation of an expectation does not denote immorality on its own, however. People's affective responses to observing norm violations help differentiate lesser from more severe transgressions. On the one hand, a mild or positive response is more likely to indicate that someone has violated a conventional. Take, for example, feeling excited when, while walking in a public park, noticing, a crowd congregating in preparation for a "flash mob." People lining up for a choreographed dance is certainly out of the norm for a typical afternoon in the park, but likely an innocuous or harmless norm violation. On the other hand, strong negative affect is more likely to point toward a *moral* norm violation, one that poses a risk of harm to the actor or others. Consider feeling angry or fearful when noticing a group of people congregating in the park, but this time aggressively advancing around a helpless animal. Finally, perceived harm is a critical component in identifying immorality. People are motivated at a basic, fundamental level to avoid harm, and our automatic psychological processes serve this function when traversing social situations (Schein & Gray 2017). The presence of suffering victims, for example, serves as the visible norm violation and induces negative affect in observers who are then motivated to identify the suffering's cause.

We make moral judgments largely automatically in response to such observations. Functionally, moral judgments allow us to navigate our environments safely and securely because it is important to identify transgressors, who may pose a threat to a successful social group (Ames & Fiske 2015). In-group cohesion motivates humans to evaluate other actors and actions and to prefer just or fair outcomes over unjust or unfair outcomes. The cognitive and affective processes involved in making moral judgments are both conscious and unconscious, indicating that although we make judgments automatically, there is flexibility in amending our initial attitudes (Guglielmo, Monroe, & Malle 2009; Monroe & Malle 2019).

For as long as scholars across fields have investigated morality, they have highlighted the importance of personal control (Kant 1785/1996; Piaget 1932; Heider 1958; Shaver 1985; Cushman 2008; Cornwell & Higgens 2019). Across psychological theories of morality there is a constant emphasis on the process of attributing the immoral action to a combination of the actor and the environment (akin to the "person-situation debate" among social and personality psychologists, e.g., Ross & Nisbett 1991). While children tend to use perceived harm and observed consequences to determine whether someone has behaved immorally, adults rely more heavily on the actor's intention, sometimes even if no consequences occur (Cushman 2008). Establishing whether immorality occurred due to an individual or due to the situation is important for subsequent processes, such as identifying potential threats or transgressors, allocating blame and punishments, or pursuing justice and group cohesion (Heider 1958). As such, it becomes critical to know the extent to which an actor has control over an immoral occurrence.

The culpable control model (Alicke 2000) synthesizes findings across literature and highlights personal control as an overarching construct that people use when making moral judgments. This model organizes the three factors that people use as criteria when determining how much personal control informed an actor's behavior. First, *intention*, which refers to the internal state of an actor and comprises the actor's beliefs and desires. Second, *causation*, or the observable behavior and events that are regarded as the likely source of the intended outcome. Third, *foresight*, which assesses the extent to which the actor had, or should have had, knowledge of future consequences and whether they could, or should have mitigated or prevented them. Each construct provides information about the actor and their impact on a given outcome, which is central to assigning blame. Attributing responsibility to someone in causing an immoral outcome is important information for safely and successfully traversing social life, especially for protecting oneself from similar or future transgressions.

Copious empirical studies find support for the culpable control model, evidencing in various ways that people attend to an individual's planned intention when making a moral judgment about them or their behavior (see Cornwell & Higgens 2019 for a more thorough review). Intention is so important that people prioritize the mental state of the actor over the coerciveness of the circumstances in assessing the actor's moral responsibility (Cushman 2008). When people observe a norm violation and perceive harm, they have cues that an immoral act has occurred and thus begin to evaluate the causes behind the transgression and preventability of the consequences. In fact, when the perceived combination of character and context indicates more influence from the actor's character than from the context, people make more severe moral judgments and condemn the actor more strongly (Alicke 2000; Monroe & Malle 2019; Reeder et al. 2002).

Demonstrating this process, research participants who read about an individual committing an immoral behavior (i.e., killing someone) perceived the individual differently when the individual's actions directly versus indirectly caused the behavior (Pizarro, Ulhmann, & Bloom 2003). Across all conditions, the story made clear that the individual internally desired and planned to engage in the immoral behavior. This internal motivation provides information about the morality of the actor's character, but participants attenuated their judgments of the actor based on whether their actions directly or indirectly caused the death. Specifically, those who read the story in which the actor indirectly caused the death judged the actor to be less morally responsible than those who read that the actor directly caused it, even though in both cases the actor wanted and planned to kill an innocent person—indicating equivalently immoral characters. Researchers have tested many different stories and consistently found that when things do not go as planned for a perceived actor, even if the exact same harmful or negative outcome occurs, people assign less blame to the actor (Pizarro, Uhlmann, & Bloom 2003; Reeder et al. 2002).

When it comes to relationship infidelity, there is certainly a range of ways in which an individual's character interacts with a given situation's circumstances that result in cheating. For example, a person may desire (i.e., exhibit intention, or the first component of the culpable control model) to have sex with people outside of their monogamous partner. Imagine that this person subsequently takes behavioral steps to locate circumstances that facilitate sex with no strings attached, such as frequenting a popular nightclub or signing up for a meetup app. Taking such steps demonstrates the person's foresight (i.e., the third component of the culpable control model) into their likelihood of transgressing. As a comparison, consider another individual who also desires extradyadic sex, but who still intends to be faithful to their monogamous relationship. What do we make of their moral character if, despite not deliberately seeking an extradyadic partner, they do indeed engage in a sexual tryst or affair? The psychological literature reviewed here suggests that the difference in intention should attenuate the blame assigned to the latter person as compared to the former.

SITUATIONAL INFLUENCES ON
IMMORAL BEHAVIOR

Despite the wide variety of situations that constitute relationship infidelity (e.g., serial cheating, a long-term love affair, no-strings-attached extradyadic sex), discussions of cheating largely assume that the consequences of these different types of situations do not differ (Knopp et al. 2017). Researchers have delineated different motivations for cheating as well as catalogued unfortunate negative outcomes both for implicated individuals and the relationships between them (Fincham & May 2017). Scholars and clinicians are far less likely to acknowledge a spectrum of assignments or degrees of moral responsibility or blame when it comes to relationship infidelity. While a few studies have investigated what people think and feel about infidelity, they tend to concentrate on analyzing which behaviors people consider cheating, such as whether physical activity is required, or the extent to which online interactions constitute disloyalty (Gibson, Thompson, & O'Sullivan 2016). There is less research on how we think and feel about people who engage in infidelity, as well as how likely we are to engage in infidelity ourselves.

The cognitive and emotional processes that occur in enticing situations generalize across areas of temptation (Gino et al. 2011). Francesca Gino (2015) highlights countless examples of people behaving immorally or unethically when presented with the opportunity, from the economic sphere (e.g., finding creative ways to evade paying full taxes) to the workplace (e.g., overrepresenting contributions to teamwork), to relationships (e.g., lying to people to avoid hurting others' feelings). People lie fairly easily when the situation seems to call for it, and are motivated easily—essentially automatically—by extrinsic rewards such as money, or by intrinsic psychological rewards, such as pleasure or a boost to self-image (Abramson & Pinkerton 2002; Mazar, Amir, & Ariely 2008).

Research on intentional versus unintentional unethical behavior highlights the role of situational factors in compelling people's behavior, ranging from the innocuous, such as social norms, emotional contagion, or role adoption, to the coercive, such as threats to well-being or appeals from authority (Moore & Gino, 2013; Wiltermuth 2011). Each of these factors may appear in the context of opportunity-based sexual infidelity. For example, a partnered individual who happens to patronize a bar on what the individual did not know was "singles night" would likely find themselves in interactions wherein social norms include conveying attraction and looking for available, interested parties. In this case, an available (i.e., single) person who approaches someone is initiating an encounter that includes a sequence of expectations. The social norms determining those expectations of course depend heavily on the cultural and local contexts (Gino 2015). But in general, it can be difficult to resist going along with what we perceive others to expect from us.

In this way, role adoption is a particularly influential factor. Cultural scripts have an incredibly strong, *implicit* power over people's behavior (Bargh & Williams 2006; Doris 2015; Goddard & Wierzbicka 2004). In fact, reminding people of a certain role will induce them to report attitudes more in line with that role (Gino 2015). As an example, priming people with the role of parenthood causes them to make stronger moral judgments than those who were not primed (regardless of whether they were parents themselves or not; Eibach, Libby, & Ehlrlinger 2009). Gender-priming is another example. Sex-based gender roles are strong and salient in the United States, referring to the complementary roles involved in courtship, romantic, or sexual relations, are strong and salient in the United States (Sanchez, Fetterolf, & Rudman 2012). These roles are very easily activated, as Hundhammer and Mussweiler (2012) demonstrated in a series of experiments. In these studies, people who were primed with cues related to sexual activity (both visual and verbal) (1) more quickly self-categorized as a woman or man; (2) identified more strongly with their gender; (3) increased self-stereotyping; and (4) engaged in more concordant gender-role behaviors (all compared to those in the control conditions) (Hundhammer & Mussweiler 2012). Once these roles are primed, it can be difficult to resist what the setting compels one to do. The power of what we believe others expect of us is immense—people often behave in ways simply because it is easier to go along with what the situation appears to compel and what the other people in the situation appear to want or expect (Cooper & Withey 2009). Of course, this challenge is exacerbated if the individual's internal desire aligns with the unfolding situation.

Finally, the situation is an important factor in people's cheating behavior because of the power that psychological closeness (defined as "feelings of attachment and perceived connection towards another person"; Gino & Galinsky 2012, 16) plays in distancing people from their moral compasses (Gino & Galinsky 2012). People's own self-concept can expand to include others, depending on the nature of the relationship between them, their shared emotions, and stakes of the local environment (Aron & Aron 1986; Aron, Aron, & Smollan 1992). As people become psychologically closer, the boundaries between them blur and can lead them to think, feel, and/or act more consistently with each other's internal states. This imitation or cohesion is maintained even if the others we feel close to are behaving immorally (Gino, Ayal, & Ariely 2009). For example, Francesca Gino and Adam Galinsky (2012) asked participants to judge a target actor's unethical behavior. Those who were first asked to take the actor's perspective rated them as less immoral. In a second study, participants who were told they shared a birth month with the immorally behaved target actor were more likely to cheat in a subsequent math question task than participants who were not told they shared this characteristic (Gino & Galinsky 2012). Merely sharing a birth month with a cheater seems to potentially convey a sense of permission for others to also cheat. As summarized by the authors, "feelings of psychological closeness create vicarious possibilities, even when subtly induced" (Gino & Galinsky 2012, p. 16).

Opportunities for extradyadic liaisons are often, in comparison, *not* so subtle. At one end of the spectrum lies deliberately targeted ads, such as the infamous "Life is short. Have an affair" of the *Ashley Madison* meetup service, or such as the spam advertisements that populate poorly secured websites, promising sexy, interested people on the other end of the phone line. Of course, being face-to-face with others also encourages closeness; psychological feelings of distance often scale to match physical proximity (Mallen, Day, & Green 2003; Sundstrom & Altman 1976). If a monogamously partnered individual is directly propositioned, they will likely feel desired. While feeling wanted is enjoyable on its own, if the individual returns the desire, feelings of closeness to the propositioner may be activated.

As reviewed above, feeling close to others—such as a sense of shared desires or emotions—leads us to behave more in alignment with the others' internal state. Therefore, for many cases of infidelity, the inherent, dispositional morality of the cheater's character may be less responsible than the dovetailing of multiple psychological processes, at the social-contextual, interpersonal, and cognitive levels, that are associated with being offered the opportunity to cheat. In the current studies, we provide an initial look at just how common it is for people to engage in immoral behavior that may be unaligned with their goals or identity by capturing the rates of cheating, given the conditional probability of being propositioned.

SUCCUMBING TO TEMPTATION

What psychological processes occur in the presence of desirable opportunities? Self-control research indicates that the salience and frequency of meeting tempting stimuli influences capitulation (Fujita 2011; Kroese et al. 2011; Hofmann et al. 2012). For example, Marina Milyavskaya and colleagues (2015) found that participants who made the most progress toward their personal goals were those who reported encountering the fewest temptations. Similarly, in research on addiction, interviews with people in addiction recovery show that their success and goal attainment is dependent on developing strategies to preserve willpower by modifying their environments

(Snoek, Levy, & Kennett 2016). This pattern of results has also been found in research assessing the relationship between environment and food intake: in an experiment where participants kept a week-long food diary, those in the condition with a greater physical distance from their meals reported healthier food choices (Cole, Dominick, & Balcetis 2020). Taken together, these findings indicate the importance of controlling the environment to circumvent temptation.

The Process Model of Self Control supports for the efficacy of situation-based strategies in resisting temptation, with evidence documented in cases of substance use, health behaviors (i.e., eating and exercise), and retirement savings (Duckworth, Gendler, & Gross 2016). This approach is successful because it capitalizes on automatic processing and reduces the need for self-regulation resources, which is widely understood to be effortful and subject to depletion (Baumeister et al. 1998; Inzlicht & Schmeichel 2012). This automatic processing could be easily swayed toward indulgent behaviors if relevant reminders, or stimuli, are present (Forman & Butryn 2015). For example, the smell of tasty food, the sound of exciting television, or the sight of flowing alcohol are all likely to engage implicit processes, against which self-control efforts will struggle to win.

Our perspective is that for most partnered people, the risk of being cheated on is based less on their partner's moral character and more on whether their partner might be presented with the opportunity. In other words, we propose that a more relevant question for most partnered people is whether their partner would cheat *if given the chance*. We wondered if, when considering this conditional probability, a very different (and less comforting) picture of cheating might emerge because across domains, humans have great difficulty resisting temptation.

CURRENT RESEARCH

Based on research from a wide variety of contexts, one strategy for promoting self-control is to avoid temptation within the proximal environment. We find no plausible reason why avoidance of sexual temptation should have a different mechanism than other forms of temptation. That is, when people are presented with a desirable sexual offer, we hypothesize that large numbers will accept it.

The current descriptive research addresses a simple question: how likely are people to cheat when presented with the opportunity? Based on reviews of both cheating and self-control literatures, we hypothesize that cheating rates will be substantially higher among those who were given the opportunity to cheat in the past year. Distinguishing between instances of planned and unplanned cheating allows for nuance in answering the practical question of the risk of being subject to infidelity.

METHOD

Participants, Procedure, and Methods

Participants were recruited for online surveys via social networking pages (e.g., Facebook and Twitter) of approximately 100 student researchers (Sample 1) and the Craigslist volunteer section (Samples 2, 3, and 4). Demographic information is presented in table 13.1.

Participants answered questions to ascertain whether they had committed infidelity. First, we asked, "Right now, do you consider yourself to be SINGLE or do you consider yourself IN A RELATIONSHIP?" If they considered themselves to be in a relationship, we asked, "Are you currently in a monogamous relationship?"

We asked participants in monogamous relationships, "Within the last year, has anyone OTHER THAN YOUR RELATIONSHIP PARTNER invited you to have a sexual encounter with her/him? (Please answer whether this HAPPENED, regardless of whether you agreed to the offer)." This question established the percentage of people who had been invited to cheat in the past year.

Finally, we asked, "Did you have a sexual encounter with this person/any of these people?" In each sample, we excluded participants who were single or in nonmonogamous relationships.

Table 13.1 Demographics

	Study 1	*Study 2*	*Study3*	*Study 4*
Participants *N*	102	444	269	322
Age *M* (*SD*)	34.48	28.47	25.55	21.93
	(13.587)	(10.107)	(8.72)	(10.584)
Gender (%)				
Female	52.9	52.0	100	75.1
Male	43.1	45.9		18.6
Ethnicity (%)				
African American/Black	5.9	2.0	10.0	12.4
Asian American	3.9	3.6	6.3	4.7
European American/White	73.5	79.1	75.8	57.1
Hispanic/Latino/Latina	6.9	4.3	2.2	12.7
Other	9.9	11.0	5.7	13.1
Undergraduate Student (%)				
No	80.4	67.6	26.4	
Yes	19.6	32.4	73.2	

Note: Not all percentages will total 100

RESULTS

In each sample, we selected individuals who identified as being in a monogamous relationship from the larger pool of participants. Sample sizes were 102 (Sample 1), 363 (Sample 2), 443 (Sample 3), and 331 (Sample 4).

Sample 1

Forty-five monogamous participants (44%) from Sample 1 had been propositioned for sex in the past year. Of those who had received an offer, twenty-three (42%) accepted the offer.

Sample 2

One-hundred fifty-seven monogamous participants (43%) in this sample reported sexual propositions in the last year. Sixty-five of those who were propositioned (42%) accepted.

Sample 3

Of the 191 participants (43%) monogamous participants who reported a sexual proposition within the year, 61 (33%) accepted it.

In this sample, we also asked a question about the desirability of the proposer. Among those who received an offer, 133 (70%) of them found the proposer sexually desirable. Of those who found the proposer sexually desirable, fifty-six (42%) accepted the offer.

Sample 4

Of the monogamous participants in this sample, 150 (45%) reported having been sexually propositioned in the last year; forty-two (28%) accepted the offer.

DISCUSSION

We were unable to collect samples that are nationally representative—a major feat even when the research is not on sensitive topics such as infidelity and sexual behavior; however, consideration of whether participants had been invited to cheat can help us interpret prior statistics about infidelity. Across our four studies, we find that about 14–23 percent of monogamous participants reported any kind of cheating in the last year. We also consistently found that about 30–40 percent of people who had been propositioned for extradyadic sex within the past year accepted the offer.

These findings could be read as either optimistic or pessimistic. Based on representative studies of cheating in the last year, rates of cheating are quite high (and perhaps uncomfortably high for partnered monogamous individuals). However, the high levels of people who passed opportunities to cheat on their partner when given the possibility (and, based on findings in our third sample, when given an attractive possibility) is quite remarkable. These data suggest that the avoidance of infidelity is important to participants in our studies, given that many people resisted offers to cheat.

However, the commonality of accepting these tempting invitations implicates the egregious moral condemnation of people who engage in unplanned cheating. Someone who explicitly seeks to break an agreement they have with a loved one should be assigned a higher degree of moral blame than someone who accepts a proposition or succumbs to inviting circumstances. It is important to use a wide spectrum of moral blame, rather than polarizing to "wholly right" or "wholly wrong." And the consistency in opportunistic cheating frequency rates across samples supports existing literature on the relatively poorer job people do at resisting what they desire as their proximity to it increases.

Yet, people who fail to resist their off-limit food cravings or who give in to unethical financial decisions do not seem to receive the same, harsh judgments of immoral character as do people who fail to resist a sexual temptation. Certainly, the harm directly inflicted upon the victim of infidelity is more immoral than cheating on one's own diet. To the extent that moral judgments function to support the safety and success of social groups, a transgression that disrupts interpersonal relationships are worse than those that disrupt one's relationship with oneself (Ames & Fiske 2015). Still, this does not mean we should uncritically or indiscriminately assign moral blame across types of infidelity. Our findings indicate the relative commonality of succumbing to sexual temptation or accepting a desirable sexual offer. This indicates the need to consider situational factors when assigning moral blame, such as the interpersonal dynamics and the environmental norms of a given setting, or the amount of foresight had by the cheating individual.

The rigidity of moral norms, especially in tandem with monogamy's valuation, may pose a challenge for exhibiting more nuanced reactions to instances of cheating. One strategy may be to encourage, among scholars and laypeople alike, differentiating between judgments of an individual's moral behavior from judgments of their moral character. This distinction is rooted in the way that guilt and shame are associated with separate motivational processes—either activating or inhibiting behavior (Clore, Schwarz, & Conway 1994). Guilt is more often felt about one's actions or behaviors, whereas shame is more often felt about the self or one's identity (Tangney 1991). Guilt, then, motivates approach behaviors and is associated with taking corrective steps (Tangney et al. 1996). Shame, on the other hand, is inhibiting because it motivates avoidance behaviors, but rather than avoiding the stigmatized behavior, people tend to avoid prevention or correction of the wrongs (Wicker, Payne, & Morgan 1983).

Experiencing stigma, as it turns out, incurs shame (Corrigan & Watson 2002; Major, Mendes, & Dovidio 2013). Is weakness of the will (akrasia) that results in interpersonal harm so deserving of moral condemnation that we want to induce paralyzing shame? Maybe from the perspective that assumes perfect rationality, but not from a perspective informed by scientific, psychological processes experienced by the average person on a day-to-day basis. The misperception and incongruence that characterizes human construal and attribution indicate that we should expect far fewer successful displays of resisting temptations than perhaps our polite society demands (Doris 2015).

IMPLICATIONS FOR MONOGAMY MAINTENANCE

We also consider the meaning of these statistics for our cultural relationship with infidelity. Our findings suggest that cheating may be substantially higher if people are provided the opportunity to cheat. This raises the question: what is the best way to navigate infidelity and monogamy?

First, we suggest that the much-maligned strategy utilized by former vice president Pence—that is, never being alone with a person of the gender to which you are attracted (Parker 2017)—is actually reasonable from a self-control perspective (its implications for discrimination against women and Pence's self-view are more problematic, of course). That is, one of the best ways to avoid infidelity is to avoid being sexually propositioned. This is analogous to successfully developing healthy eating habits by making sure that unhealthy food does not enter one's home (Campbell et al., 2007). Preventing opportunities to be sexually propositioned may look like avoiding social situations in which dating or sexual interest is the norm, or avoiding physical or psychological conditions that invite akrasia, such as intoxication from drugs and/or alcohol.

Second, we question whether the negative reputation of cheaters is deserved. If someone with a sweet tooth indulges in a dessert only once a week, for thirty years, we would likely believe that person to be highly committed to avoiding sweets. However, the stigma against infidelity is so strong that if a person engages in extradyadic sex once over thirty years, public assessment would likely condemn this person as a failure (hence the old adage "once a cheater, always a cheater"; Knopp et al. 2017). The data presented here give new reason to question whether this assessment is fair.

Given widespread inability to resist temptation, why do we judge those who respond accordingly after receiving a tempting offer?

Perhaps people judge cheating so harshly because we do not have accurate estimations of the rate at which it occurs (like many social and psychological phenomena; Doris 2015), so it is especially easy for people to underestimate the likelihood of accepting a tempting offer to cheat. This misperception may lead to a form of pluralistic ignorance—the perception that many more people engage in a given behavior than in actuality. Regarding infidelity, people may thus overestimate the frequency with which individuals resist or reject a tempting offer from desirable others. With this framing, it follows that people make potentially misplaced attributions about the moral character of someone who fails at resisting.

We also suggest that the especially strong moral outrage expressed in response to relationship infidelity is a product of the moral position that monogamous marriages and relationships have historically occupied (and continue to occupy) in U.S. society (Conley & Piemonte 2020). Our cultural norms and values include assumptions about the perfection of monogamy as a relationship arrangement or family structure. The United States also appears to have especially stringent norms about infidelity. A full 94 percent of American respondents reported that infidelity is always or usually wrong, a number that is substantially higher than that of other countries surveyed (Widmer, Treas & Newcomb 1998). That normative attitudes towards infidelity vary across cultures (and historical time periods) suggests that such attitudes condemning cheating derive from how a culture understands, values, and treats monogamy and other dyadic relationships (as opposed to deriving from either an immutable component of relationship integrity or inherently "true" moral judgments.

ACCURACY OF CHEATING STATISTICS

In his report on trends in sexuality in the United States, Tom Smith (2006) commented that "representative, scientific surveys . . . indicate that extramarital relations are less prevalent than pop and pseudo-scientific accounts contend" (p. 8). Smith suggests the rate of infidelity in the last year is 3 percent. Smith's confidence is based on the idea that the survey data collected via representative samples is the most accurate estimate of cheating. But like all self-report data, these surveys risk a socially desirable response bias. These concerns are likely compounded in the context of sensitive topics, and is an activity that is severely stigmatized in the United States—for example, it is perceived as less acceptable than suicide (Newport & Himelfarb 2013).

Given the stigma surrounding cheating, participants may be especially motivated to portray themselves as faithful and incidents of cheating could be reframed as something else if they depart from an individual's idiosyncratic definition of infidelity or sex (Anderson 2010; Conley et al. 2013). For example, someone could posit that only intercourse between a man and a woman qualifies as cheating and neither does oral sex nor sex between people of the same gender. With such flexible definitions of sex and monogamy, people who are objectively having sexual contact outside a monogamous relationship could plausibly identify themselves as faithful partners.

We would like to see nationally representative replications of our findings that utilize methods to address social desirability effects. We hope that these findings will inspire authors to consider the conditional probability of being approached for an extradyadic encounter when they address infidelity.

CONCLUSION

Columnist Dan Savage popularized the term "monogamish"—referring to a relationship agreement in which infidelity is allowed occasionally (Savage 2011). He suggests that lifting extreme prohibitions on infidelity might actually save otherwise healthy marriages. We follow his line of reasoning in the context of these data and suggest that departures from monogamy be viewed with greater understanding.

In this chapter, we articulate a perspective on relationship infidelity rooted in understanding the combination of individual and situational influences. Despite the ferocity with which cheating and cheaters are condemned, we find that engaging in infidelity is not all that rare, when examined under a conditional probability. The condition we investigate is having been approached and offered the opportunity to cheat on a monogamous partner. This condition results in a much more consistent rate (and perhaps an uncomfortably high rate) of reported instances of infidelity when considered in comparison to infidelity engaged in by those approachers who purposefully plan and seek out an extradyadic liaison. It is important to distinguish between types, or circumstances of, infidelity because the cognitive processes associated with acquiescing to such a request— especially one that is mutually desired—are distinct from those associated with planning and pursuing an immoral behavior. It is much easier, or common, than polite society might expect, to succumb to romantic or sexual temptation in the face of desirable and encouraging situational factors.

We find that between 30 and 40 percent of partnered individuals who are propositioned for a sexual liaison report accepting the invitation. This rate is much higher than many (especially those in monogamous relationships) find comfortable. A more accurate understanding of the situational influences on behavior may allow people to make different moral judgments about the someone who cheats after signing up for Match.com and, someone who cheats after being approached at a public venue. Because self-control is such an important factor in assigning moral blame, information about the circumstances within which an actor behaves would help attenuate the moral judgments made about their character.

REFERENCES

Abrahamson, I., Hussain, R., Khan, A., & Schofield, M. J. (2012). What helps couples rebuild their relationship after infidelity? *Journal of Family Issues, 33*(11), 1494–1519.

Abramson, P. R., & Pinkerton, S. D. (2002). *With pleasure: Thoughts on the nature of human sexuality.* Oxford University Press.

Alicke, M. D. (2000). Culpable control and the psychology of blame. *Psychology Bulletin, 126,* 556–574. doi: 10.1037/0033-2909.126.4.556.

Allen, T. C. (2018). In covenant: A grounded theory exploration of what helps evangelical marriages recover after sexual infidelity by the husband. *Doctoral Dissertations and Projects*, 1766. https://digitalcommons.liberty.edu/doctoral/1766.

Ames, D. L., & Fiske, S. (2015). Perceived intent motivates people to magnify perceived harms. *PNAS, Early edition.* doi: 10.1073/pnas.1501592112.

Anderson, E. (2010). "At least with cheating there is an attempt at monogamy": Cheating and monogamism among undergraduate heterosexual men. *Journal of Social and Personal Relationships, 27,* 851–872.

Aron, A., & Aron, E. N. (1986). *Love and the expansion of self: Understanding attraction and satisfaction.* New York: Hemisphere Publishing Corp/Harper & Row Publishers.

Aron, A., Aron, E. N., & Smollan, D. (1992). Inclusion of other in the self scale and the structure of interpersonal closeness. *Journal of Personality and Social Psychology, 63,* 596–612.

Aronson, E., Fried, C., & Stone, J. (1991). Overcoming denial and increasing the intention to use condoms through the induction of hypocrisy. *American Journal of Public Health, 81,* 1636–1638.

Bargh, J. A., & Williams, E. L. (2006). The automaticity of social life. *Current Directions in Psychological Science, 15,* 1–4.

Baumeister, Bratslavsky, Muraven, & Tice, (1998). Ego depletion: Is the active self a limited resource? *Journal of Personality and Social Psychology, 74,* 1252–1265.

Blow, A. J., & Hartnett, K. (2005). Infidelity in committed relationships I: A methodological review. *Journal of Marital and Family Therapy, 31,* 183–216.

Brand, R. J., Markey, C. M., Mills, A., & Hodges, S. D. (2007). Sex differences in self-reported infidelity and its correlates. *Sex Roles, 57,* 101–109.

Buunk, A. P., Dskstra, P., & Massar, K. (2018). *The universal threat and temptation of extradyadic affairs.* In A. L. Vangelisti & D. Perlman (Eds.), *The Cambridge handbook of personal relationships* (pp. 353–364). Cambridge University Press. https://doi.org/10.1017/9781316417867.028.

Campbell, K. J., Crawford, D. A., Salmon, J., Carver, A., Garnett, S. P., & Baur, L. A. (2007). Associations between the home food environment and obesity-promoting eating behaviors in adolescence. *Obesity, 15,* 719–730.

Cano, A., & O'Leary, K. D. (2000). Infidelity and separations precipitate major depressive episodes and symptoms of nonspecific depression and anxiety. *Journal of Consulting and Clinical Psychology, 68,* 774–781.

Charny, L. W., & Parnass, S. (1995). The impact of extramarital relationships on the continuation of marriages. *Journal of Sex and Marital Therapy, 21,* 100–115.

Clore, G. L., Schwarz, N., & Conway, M. (1994). Affective causes and consequences of social information processing. In R. S. Wyer, Jr. & T. K. Srull (Eds.), *Handbook of social cognition: Basic processes; applications* (pp. 323–417). Lawrence Erlbaum Associates, Inc.

Cole, S., Dominick, J. K., & Balcetis, E. (2020). Out of reach and under control: Distancing as a self-control strategy. *Personality and Social Psychology Bulletin.* doi: 10.1177/0146167220949813.

Conley, T. D., Matsick, J. L., Moors, A. C., & Ziegler, A. (2017). Investigation of consensually nonmonogamous relationships: Theories, methods, and new directions. *Perspectives on Psychological Science, 12,* 205–232. doi: 10.1177/1745691616667925.

Conley, T. D., Moors, A. C., Matsick, J. L., & Ziegler, A. (2013). The fewer the merrier?: Assessing stigma surrounding consensually non-monogamous romantic relationships. *Analyses of Social Issues & Public Policy, 13,* 1–30.

Conley, T. D. & Piemonte, J. L. (2020). Monogamy as public policy for STD prevention: In theory and in practice. *Policy Insights from the Behavioral and Brain Sciences* [Special Issue – Social Psychology and Social Issues], 7, 181–189. doi. org/10.1177/2372732220943228.

Conley, T. D., Ziegler, A., Moors, A. C., Matsick, J. L., & Valentine, B. (2012). A Critical Examination of Popular Assumptions About the Benefits and Outcomes of Monogamous Relationships. *Personality and Social Psychology Review, 17*(2), 124–141.

Cooper, W. H., & Withey, M. J. (2009). The strong situation hypothesis. *PSPR, 13,* 62–72. https://doi.org/10.1177/1088868308329378.

Cornwell, J. F. M., & Higgens, E. T. (2019). Sense of personal control intensifies moral judgments of others' actions. *Frontiers of Psychology, 10,* 2261. doi: 10.3389/fpsyg.2019.02261.

Corrigan, P. W., & Watson, A. C. (2002). The paradox of self-stigma and mental illness. *Clinical Psychology: Science and Practice, 9,* 35–53. https://doi.org/10.1093/clipsy.9.1.35.

Cox, A. (2008). Sex differences in feelings of guilt arising from infidelity. *Evolutionary Psychology, 6,* 436–446.

Cushman. (2008). Crime and punishment: distinguishing the roles of causal and intentional analyses in moral judgment. *Cognition, 108,* 353–380. doi: 10.1016/j.cognition.2008.03.006.

Davis, J. A., & Smith, T. W. (1991). General social surveys, 1972-1991: Cumulative codebook (No. 12). National Opinion Research Center (NORC).

Doris, J. M. (2015). *Talking to our selves: Reflection, ignorance, and agency.* Oxford University Press.

Druckerman, P. (2008). *Lust in translation: Infidelity from Tokyo to Tennessee.* Penguin Publishing House.

Duckworth, A. L., Gendler, T. S., & Gross, J. J. (2016). Situational strategies for self-control. *Perspectives on Psychological Science, 11,* 35–55.

Eagly, A. (1987). *Sex differences in social behavior: A social-role interpretation.* Hillsdale, NJ: Lawrence Erlbaum Associates, Inc., Publishers.

Eibach, R. P., Libby, L. K., & Ehrlinger, J. (2009). Priming family values: How being a parent affects moral evaluations of harmless but offensive acts. *Journal of Experimental Social Psychology, 45,* 1160–1163. doi: 10.1016/j. jesp.2009.06.017.

Elliot, A. J. (2006). The hierarchical model of approach-avoidance motivation. *Motivation and Emotion, 30,* 111–116.

Elliot, A. J., & Thrash, T. M. (2002). Approach-avoidance motivation in personality: Approach and avoidance temperaments and goals. *Journal of Personality and Social Psychology, 82,* 804–818.

Fincham, F. D., & May, R. W. (2017). Infidelity in romantic relationships. *Current Opinion in Psychology, 13,* 70–74.

Fish, J. N., Pavkov, T. W., Wetchler, J. L., Bercik, J. (2012). Characteristics of Those Who Participate in Infidelity: The Role of Adult Attachment and Differentiation in Extradyadic Experiences, *The American Journal of Family Therapy, 40,* 214–229. doi: 10.1080/01926187.2011.601192.

Fishbein, M. A., & Ajzen, I. (1975). *Belief, attitude, intention, and behaviour: An introduction to theory and research.* Reading, MA: Addison-Wesley.

Forman, E. M., & Butryn, M. L. (2015). A new look at the science of weight control: How acceptance and commitment strategies can address the challenge of self-regulation. *Appetite, 84,* 171–180.

Fujita, K. (2011). On conceptualizing self-control as more than the effortful inhibition of impulses. *Personality and Social Psychology Review, 15,* 352–366.

Gallup. (2020). Gallup poll: Moral issues. Retrieved from http://www.gallup.com/poll/1681/Moral-Issues.aspx.

Gibson, K. A. V., Thompson, A. E., & O'Sullivan, L. F. (2016). Love thy neighbour: Personality traits, relationship quality, and attraction to others as predictors of infidelity among young adults. *The Canadian Journal of Human Sexuality, 25,* 186–198.

Gino, F. (2015). Understanding ordinary unethical behavior: Why people who value morality act immorally. *Current Opinion in Behavioral Sciences, 3,* 107–111.

Gino, F., Ayal, S., & Ariely, D. (2009). Contagion and differentiation in unethical behavior: The effect of one bad apple on the barrel. *Psychological Science, 20,* 393–398.

Gino, F., & Galinsky, A. D. (2012). Vicarious dishonesty: When psychological closeness creates distance from one's moral compass. *Organizational Behavior and Human Decision Processes, 119,* 15–26.

Gino, F., Schweitzer, M. E., Mead, N. L., & Ariely, D. (2011). Unable to resist temptation: How self-control depletion promotes unethical behavior. *Organization Behavior and Human Decision Processes, 115,* 191–203.

Girard, A., Connor, J. J., & Woolley, S. R. (2018). An exploratory study of the role of infidelity typologies in predicting attachment anxiety and avoidance. *JMFT, 46,* 124–134. https://doi-org.proxy.lib.umich.edu/10.1111/jmft.12371.

Goldberg, P. D., Peterson, B. D., Rosen, K. H., & Sara, M. L. (2008). Cybersex: The impact of a contemporary problem on the practices of marriage and family therapists. *Journal of Marital and Family Therapy, 34,* 469–480.

Gray, K., Young, L., & Waytz, A. (2012). Mind perception is the essence of morality. *Psychological Inquiry, 23*(2), 101–124. doi: 10.1080/1047840X.2012.651387.

Greeley, A. (1994). Marital infidelity. *Society, 31,* 9–13.

Guglielmo, S., Monroe, A. E., & Malle, B. F. (2009). At the heart of morality lies folk psychology. *Inquiry, 52,* 449–466. doi: 10.1080/00201740903302600.

Hall, J. H., & Fincham, F. D. (2006). Relationship dissolution following infidelity: The roles of attributions and forgiveness. *Journal of Social and Clinical Psychology, 25,* 508–522. doi: 10.1521/jscp.2006.25.5.508.

Heider, F. (1958). *The psychology of interpersonal relations.* John Wiley & Sons Inc.

Hite, S. (1991). *The hite report on love, passion and emotional violence.* Optima.

Hofmann, W., Baumeister, R. F., Förster, G., & Vohs, K. D. (2012). Everyday temptations: An experience sampling study of desire, conflict, and self-control. *Journal of Personality and Social Psychology, 102,* 1318–1335.

Hundhammer, T., & Mussweiler, T. (2012). How sex puts you in gendered shoes: Sexuality-priming leads to gender-based self-perception and behavior. *JPSP, 103,* 176–193.

Inzlicht, M., & Schmeichel, B. J. (2012). What is ego depletion? Toward a mechanistic revision of the resource model of self-control. *Perspectives on Psychological Science, 7,* 450–463. doi: 10.1177/1745691612454134.

Kant, I. (1785/1996). *The metaphysics of morals (Cambridge Texts in the History of Philosophy)* 2nd edition. Edited by Mary J. Gregor.

Knopp, K., Scott, S., Ritchie, L., Rhoades, G. K., Markman, H. J., & Stanley, S. M. (2017). Once a cheater, always a cheater? Serial infidelity across subsequent relationships. *Archives of Sexual Behaviour* 46, 2301–2311. doi: 10.1007/s10508-017-1018-1.

Kroese, F. M., Adriannse, M. A., Evers, C., & De Ridder, T. D. (2011). Instant success. *Personality and Social Psychology Bulletin, 37,* 1389–1397.

Krumpal, I. (2013). Determinants of social desirability bias in sensitive surveys: A literature review. *Quality & Quantity, 47,* 2025–2047.

Kulibert, D., & Thompson, A. E. (2019). Stepping into their shoes: Reducing the actor-observer discrepancy in judgments of infidelity through the experimental manipulation of perspective-taking, *The Journal of Social Psychology, 159,* 692–708, doi: 10.1080/00224545.2018.1556575.

Laumann, E. O., Gagnon, J. H., Michael, R. T., & Michaels, S. (1994). *The Social organization of sexuality: Sexual practices in the United States.* University of Chicago Press.

Leeker, O., & Carlozzi, A. (2014). Effects of sex, sexual orientation, infidelity expectations, and love on distress related to emotional and sexual infidelity. *Journal of Marital and Family Therapy, 40*, 68–91.

Major, B., Mendes, W. B., & Dovidio, J. F. (2013). Intergroup relations and health disparities: A social psychological perspective. *Health Psychology, 32,* 514–524.

Mallen, M. J., Day, S. X., & Green, M. A. (2003). Online versus face-to-face conversation: An examination of relational and discourse variables. *Psychotherapy: Theory, Research, Practice, Training, 40*, 155–163.

Mark, K. P., Janssen, E., & Milhausen, R. R. (2011). Infidelity in heterosexual couples: Demographic, interpersonal, and personality-related predictors of extradyadic sex. *Archives of Sexual Behavior, 40*, 971–982.

Martins, A., Pereira, M., Andrade, R., Dattilio, F. M., Narciso, I., & Canavarro, M. C. (2016). Infidelity in dating relationships: Gender-specific correlates of face-to-face and online extradyadic involvement. *Archives of Sexual Behavior, 45*, 193–205.

Mazar, N., Amir, O., & Ariely, D. (2008). The dishonesty of honest people: A theory of self-concept maintenance. *Journal of Marketing Research, 45,* 633–644.

McAnulty, R. D., & Brineman, J. M. (2007). Infidelity in Dating Relationships, *Annual Review of Sex Research, 18,* 94–114.

Milyavskaya, M., Inzlicht, M., Hope, N., & Koestner, R. (2015). Saying 'no' to temptation: Want-to motivation improves self-regulation by reducing temptation rather than by increasing self-control. *Journal of Personality and Social Psychology, 109*, 677–693.

Monroe, A. E., & Malle, B. F. (2019). People systematically update moral judgments of blame. *Journal of personality and social psychology, 116*(2), 215–236.

Moore, C., & Gino, F. (2013). Ethically adrift: How others pull our moral compass from true North, and how we can fix it. *Research in Organizational Behavior, 33,* 53–77.

Munsch, C. L. (2015). Her support, his support: Money, masculinity, and marital infidelity. *American Sociological Review, 80*, 469–495.

Newport, F., & Himelfarb, I. (2013). "In U.S., Record-High Say Gay, Lesbian Relations Morally OK", May 2–7, in *Gallup News*. Retrieved from http://www.gallup.com/poll/162689/record-high-say-gay-lesbian-relations-morally.aspx.

Nichols, S. (2002). Norms with feeling: Towards a psychological account of moral judgment. *Cognition, 84*, 221–236.

Parker, A. (2017). Karen Pence is the vice president's 'prayer warrior,' gut check and shield. *The Washington Post*. Retrieved Sep 2018 from https://www.washingtonpost.com/politics/karen-pence-is-the-vice-presidents-prayer-warrior-gut-check-and-shield/2017/03/28/3d7a26ce-0a01-11e7-8884-96e6a6713f4b_story.html?tid=a_inl&utm_term=.44522ad09a9f.

Perel, E. (2007). *Mating in captivity: Unlocking erotic intelligence*. Harper.

Piaget, J. (1932). *The Moral Judgment of the Child*, trans. M. Gabain. Free Press.

Pizarro, D. A., Uhlmann, E., & Bloom, P. (2003). Causal deviance and the attribution of moral responsibility. *Journal of Experimental Social Psychology, 39,* 653–660. doi: 10.1016/S0022-1031(03)00041-6.

Previti, D., & Amato, P. R. (2004). Is infidelity a cause or a consequence of poor marital quality? *Journal of Social and Personal Relationships, 21,* 217–230.

Reeder, G. D., Kumar, S., Hesson-McInnis, M. S., & Trafimow, D. (2002). Inferences about the morality of an aggressor: the role of perceived motive. *Journal of Personality and Social Psychology, 83,* 789–803. doi: 10.1037/0022-3514.83.4.789.

Reno, R. R., Cialdini, R. B., & Kallgren, C. A. (1993). The transsituational influence of social norms. *Journal of Personality and Social Psychology, 64,* 104–112.

Ross, L., & Nisbett, R. E. (1991). *The person and the situation: Perspectives of social psychology.* Mcgraw-Hill Book Company.

Sanchez, D. T., Fetterolf, J. C., & Rudman, L. A. (2012). Eroticizing inequality in the United States: The consequences and determinants of traditional gender role adherence in intimate relationships. *Journal of Sex Research, 49,* 168–183.

Savage, D. (2011). *Savage love.* Retrieved December 04, 2017, from https://www.thestranger.com/seattle/SavageLove?oid=9125045.

Schein, C., & Gray, K. (2017). The theory of dyadic morality: Reinventing moral judgment by redefining harm. *Personality and Social Psychology Review, 22,* 32–70. https://doi.org/10.1177/1088868317698288.

Sharp, D. I., Walters, A. S., & Goren, M. J. (2013). Effect of cheating experience of attitudes toward infidelity. *Sexuality and Culture, 17,* 643–658.

Shaver, K. G. (1985). *The attribution of blame: Causality, responsibility, and blameworthiness.* Springer.

Siegel, M. J. (1992). For better or worse: Adultery, crime, and the constitution. *Journal of Family Law, 30,* 45–95.

Simpson, J. A., & Winterheld, H. A. (2012). Person-by-situation perspectives on close relationships. In K. Deaux & M. Snyder (Eds.), *Oxford library of psychology: The Oxford handbook of personality and social psychology* (pp. 493–516). Oxford University Press.

Smith, T. W. (2006). *American sexual behavior: Trends, socio-demographic differences, and risk behavior* (General Social Survey Topical Report No. 25). Retrieved from National Opinion Research Center website: www.norc.org/PDFs/Publications/AmericanSexualBehavior2006.pdf.

Snoek, A., Levy, N., & Kennett, J. (2016). Strong-willed but not successful: The importance of strategies in recovery from addiction. *Addictive Behaviors Reports, 4,* 102–107.

Solomon, S. D., & Teagno, L. J. (2010). Recovering from sexual and other types of infidelity, part I: A typology of infidelities. In J. Carlson & L. Sperry (Eds.), *Recovering intimacy in love relationships: A clinician's guide* (pp. 15–38). Routledge.

Sundstrom, E., & Altman, I. (1976). Interpersonal Relationships and Personal Space: Research Review and Theoretical Model. *Human Ecology, 4,* 47–67.

Tangney, J. P. (1991). Moral affect: The good, the bad, and the ugly. *Journal of Personality and Social Psychology, 61,* 598–607.

Tangney, J. P., Miller, R. S., Flicker, L., & Barlow, D. H. (1996). Are shame, guilt, and embarrassment distinct emotions? *Journal of Personality and Social Psychology, 70,* 1256–1269.

Treas, J., & Giesen, D. (2000). Sexual infidelity among married and cohabiting Americans. *Journal of Marriage and Family, 62,* 48–60.

Tsapelas, I., Fisher, H. E., & Aron, A. (2010). Infidelity: When, Where, Why. In W. R. Cupach & B. H. Spitzberg (Eds.), *The dark side of close relationships*, 1st edition. Taylor & Francis Group.

Warach, B., Josephs, L., & Gorman B. S. (2018). Pathways to infidelity: The roles of self-serving bias and betrayal trauma. *Journal of Sex & Marital Therapy, 44*, 497–512. doi: 10.1080/0092623X.2017.1416434.

Whisman, M. A., & Snyder, D. K. (2007). Sexual infidelity in a national survey of American women: differences in prevalence and correlates as a function of method of assessment. *Journal of Family Psychology, 21*, 147–154.

Wicker, F. W., Payne, G. C., & Morgan, R. D. (1983). Participant descriptions of guilt and shame. *Motivation and Emotion, 7*, 25–39.

Widmer, E. D., Treas, J., & Newcomb, R. (1998). Attitudes toward nonmarital sex in 24 countries. *Journal of Sex Research, 35*, 349–358.

Williamson, L., Thom, B., Stimson, G. V., & Uhl, A. (2014). Stigma as a public health tool: Implications for health promotion and citizen involvement. *International Journal of Drug Policy, 25*, 333–335.

Wiltermuth, S. S. (2011). Cheating more when the spoils are split. *Organizational Behavior and Human Decision Processes, 115*, 157–168.

Wimmer, H., & Permer, J. (1983). Beliefs about beliefs: Representation and constraining function of wrong beliefs in young children's understanding of deception. *Cognition, 13*, 103–128. doi: 10.1016/0010-0277(83)90004-5.

Wynne, G. (2019). "If you both cheated, is your relationship doomed? An expert weighs in." EliteDaily, Retrieved February, 2021 from https://www.elitedaily.com/p/if-you-both-cheated-is-your-relationship-doomed-experts-weighs-in-16795324.

Index

About the Authors

Bianca P. Acevedo is a research scientist at the University of California, Santa Barbara. She has done extensive research and received global recognition for her work on the science of love, highly sensitive persons, and mind–body practices. She has taught courses on close relationships and positive psychology, and was the recipient of the 2012 International Women in Science Award. She is the developer of the LoveSmart App and her most recent book *The Highly Sensitive Brain* discusses the science, assessment, and impact of high sensitivity. She was also the editor of the 2020 Special Edition of Frontiers in Psychology on "The Science of Pair-bonding." For more information, please visit www.biancaacevedo.com.

Katherine Aumer, assistant professor of psychology at the University of Hawai'i–West O'ahu, received a BA in psychology and a BA in theater from the University of Iowa and her PhD in social/personality psychology from the University of Texas at Austin. Dr. Aumer is the head of the Emotions and Relationships Research Lab, which is dedicated to understanding the social and cultural factors that contribute to interpersonal hate, relationship satisfaction, and experiences of discrimination and prejudice. She has published two edited volumes: The Psychology of Love and Hate in Intimate Relationships (2016) and the Psychology of Extremism (2021). Her work has been published in *Social Justice Research, Personality and Social Psychology Bulletin, Journal of Relationships Research, The Proceedings of the American Society for Information Science and Technology, Ethnic and Racial Studies, Sexual and Relationship Therapy, Journal of Relationships Research, Interpersona, International Society for Research on Emotion,* and *Proceedings of the Human Factors and Ergonomics Society Annual Meeting.*

Aaron Ben-Ze'ev is a professor of philosophy at the University of Haifa. He received his PhD from the University of Chicago (1981). Major books: *The Subtlety of Emotions* (MIT, 2000), *Love Online* (Cambridge UP, 2004), *In the Name of Love* (with Goussinsky, Oxford UP, 2008); *The Arc of Love* (University of Chicago Press, 2019). At the University of Haifa, he was the president (2004–2012), rector (2000–2004), dean of research (1995–2000), and chairperson of the Philosophy Department (1986–1988). He is the founding and former president of the European Philosophical Society for the Study of Emotions.

Berit "Brit" Brogaard is a professor of philosophy and Cooper Fellow at the University of Miami. Their areas of research include philosophy of perception, philosophy of emotions, and philosophy of language. They are the author of *Transient Truths* (2012), *On Romantic Love* (2015), *The Superhuman Mind* (2015), *Seeing & Saying* (2018), and *Hatred: Understanding Our Most Dangerous Emotion* (2020).

Luke Brunning is a lecturer in ethics at the University of Birmingham, UK. Before that he was a British Academy postdoctoral research fellow at the University of Oxford. His research focuses on romantic life and ethics construed broadly. His recent publications include "Asexuality" in the *Journal of Applied Philosophy* (with Natasha McKeever'), "Compersion: An Alternative to Jealousy?" in the *Journal of the American Philosophical Association*, and the book *Does Monogamy Work?*

Terri D. Conley is a professor of psychology at the University of Michigan, Ann Arbor. She has been trained in social psychology at the University of Wisconsin-Madison and UCLA. She primarily studies antecedents and consequences of nescience, irrationalities in risk perception, and gender differences in sexuality.

Ronald de Sousa is a professor emeritus of philosophy at the University of Toronto. His current research bears on emotions, sex and love, and the role of the dual mental processing hypothesis on emotional rationality. His books include *The Rationality of Emotion* (1987), *Why Think? Evolution and the Rational Mind* (2007), *Emotional Truth* (2011) and *Love, a Very Short Introduction* (2015). Many of his papers can be accessed at http://www.chass .utoronto.ca/~sousa

Gen Eickers is a postdoc at the University of Education Ludwigsburg, Germany, where they work on a project on digital discrimination of LGBTQ+ people. Gen's work is located at the intersections of philosophy of mind, social psychology, and social epistemology, specifically addressing questions around social interaction, emotion, and gender. They have published on emotion, social interaction, and trans issues.

Michael A. Erickson is an associate professor of psychology at University of California, Riverside, received a BS in cognitive science from the University of California, San Diego, and a PhD in psychology and in cognitive science from Indiana University, Bloomington. Along with his other areas of interest, Dr. Erickson investigates people's use of concepts and categories. His work has been published in the *Journal of Experimental Psychology: General*; *Psychonomic Bulletin and Review*; *Memory and Cognition*; the *Journal of Experimental Psychology: Learning, Memory, and Cognition*; and *Nursing Education*.

Staci Gusakova is a PhD candidate in the Psychology and Women's & Gender Studies programs at the University of Michigan, Ann Arbor. Her doctoral work highlights how social inequities affect people's sexual and romantic lives. Her dissertation looks at how experiences of prejudice-related stress (e.g., discrimination) effect the well-being of interracial and same-race male couples.

Raja Halwani is a professor of philosophy at the School of the Art Institute of Chicago. His major research interests are in philosophy of sex and love, queer philosophy, moral and political philosophy, animal ethics, and philosophy of art. In addition to authoring numerous essays, he is the author or editor of *Virtuous Liaisons: Care, Love, Sex, and Virtue Ethics* (2003), *Sex and Ethics: Essays on Sexuality, Virtue, and the Good Life* (2007), *The Israeli-Palestinian Conflict: Philosophical Essays on Self-Determination, Terrorism, and the One-State Solution* (2008, coauthored with Tomis Kapitan), *Love, Sex, and Marriage: A Philosophical Introduction* (2010; 2018 [2nd ed.]), *Queer Philosophy: Presentations of the Society for Lesbian and Gay Philosophy*, 1998–2008 (2012), and *The Philosophy of Sex: Contemporary Readings* (6th ed. [2013]; 7th ed. [2017]; and the forthcoming 8th edition).

Caroline R. Lundquist is a philosopher and an educator. After receiving her PhD in philosophy from the University of Oregon, she decided to stay in the Eugene community—her childhood home. She teaches ethics courses for the Clark Honors College, the Department of Philosophy and the Prison Education Program at the University of Oregon, and teaches philosophy courses at Lane Community College. She is the co-director of Carnegie Global Oregon, and ethics-based student community at the University of Oregon, and the co-managing editor of Hypatia. At Lane Community College, Caroline has served on numerous committees and headed several projects related to critical thinking and innovations in discussion-based education. With her friend and colleague Paul Bodin, she regularly leads public philosophical discussions and philosophy discussions for children. Caroline loves to write, and most of her academic writing focuses on kindness and entitlement. Caroline lives with her husband, who teaches high school science, and her two highly philosophical children. When she isn't teaching or writing, she loves to read, write, cook, sew, and (most of all) work in her garden.

Donatella Marazziti, MD, is a professor of psychiatry at the Department of Clinical and Experimental Medicine, University of Pisa, and professor of clinical psychology at Saint Camillus International University of Health and Medical Sciences – UniCamillus, Rome, Italy. She is editor-in-chief of Clinical Neuropsychiatry, field editor of CNS Spectrums and of Current Medicinal Chemistry while being also in the editorial board of several other international journals. She graduated in Medicine and Surgery in Pisa (1981) where she later obtained her Specialty in Psychiatry (1985) and in Biochemistry (1990). Her research interests are focused on biological markers in psychiatric and normal conditions, emotions, attachment, psychopharmacology and clinical psychiatry and psychology. She was awarded different international and national prizes. She is a member of several international and national scientific societies and committees. She has participated actively in hundreds of conferences, seminars, and teaching activities. She has authored more than 600 papers, mainly in international journals (378 in the *Pubmed*, H-index: 55), chapters in books, 8 books, 2 essays, and 1 novel.

Jennifer L. Piemonte is a PhD candidate in the Psychology and Women's & Gender Studies programs at the University of Michigan, Ann Arbor. Her primary research program focuses on attitudes and behaviors related to gender and sexuality. As an interdisciplinary scholar, Jennifer's broader research interests include the effects of stigma on policy and practices.

Arina Pismenny is lecturer in philosophy at the University of Florida. Their primary areas of research are moral psychology, philosophy of emotions, and philosophy of love, sex, and gender. Their current projects include elucidating the relationship between romantic love and morality, analyzing the rational structures of affective states and complexes such as emotions, sentiments, and syndromes, and investigating the connections between emotions and social justice.

Jennifer D. Rubin earned a dual PhD in psychology and gender and women studies from the University of Michigan, Ann Arbor. She has examined a variety of social issues ranging from gender harassment on Twitter to prejudice experienced by LGBTQ+ people. She is currently a senior research scientist in the Seattle area focused on understanding the components that create inclusive learning environments in the classroom and beyond.

Lotte Spreeuwenberg is a PhD candidate at the University of Antwerp. She is researching love, ethics, and moral psychology at the University of Antwerp, with research stays at the University of Liverpool and CUNY. She is writing her doctoral dissertation "Against the fat relentless ego: Love at the centre of morality," focusing on Iris Murdoch as an overarching author. She has published on love in both academic and public philosophy, mostly focusing on feminist debates. Together with Martha Claeys she produces and hosts philosophy podcast Kluwen, which aims at showing that philosophy deserves life beyond academia.

Robert J. Sternberg is a professor of human development at Cornell University and an honorary professor of psychology at Heidelberg University, Germany. His BA is from Yale, his PhD from Stanford, and he holds thirteen honorary doctorates. Sternberg is past president of the American Psychological Association and the Federation of Associations in Brain and Behavioral Sciences. His main areas of interest are intelligence, creativity, and wisdom. His latest book *Adaptive Intelligence* was published by Cambridge University Press in 2021. According to Google Scholar, he has been cited over 205,000 times in the scholarly literature with an H-index of 218.

Alessandra Della Vecchia is a medical doctor and resident at the Specialty School of Psychiatry at Pisa University, Department of Clinical and Experimental Medicine. She contributed to the review process of scientific articles at the Clinical Neuropsychiatry—*Journal of Treatment Evaluation* (Giovanni Fioriti), as well as at the Environment International (Elsevier). She graduated in medicine and surgery in Pisa (2017). Her research interests are focused on biological markers in psychiatric and neurodegenerative conditions, psychopharmacology, and clinical psychiatry and psychology.